INSIGHT GUIDE

american SOUTHWEST

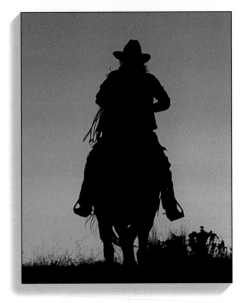

D1111513

Discovery CHANNEL

APA PUBLICATIONS   L

Part of the Langenscheidt Publishing Group

INSIGHT GUIDE
american SOUTHWEST

ABOUT THIS BOOK

Editorial

Editor
Scott Rutherford
Editorial Director
Brian Bell

Distribution

UK & Ireland
GeoCenter International Ltd
The Viables Centre , Harrow Way
Basingstoke, Hants RG22 4BJ
Fax: (44) 1256-817988

United States
Langenscheidt Publishers, Inc.
46–35 54th Road, Maspeth, NY 11378
Fax: (718) 784-0640

Canada
Prologue Inc.
1650 Lionel Bertrand Blvd., Boisbriand
Québec, Canada J7H 1N7
Tel: (450) 434-0306. Fax: (450) 434-2627

Australia & New Zealand
Hema Maps Pty. Ltd.
24 Allgas Street, Slacks Creek 4127
Brisbane, Australia
Tel: (61) 7 3290 0322. Fax: (61) 7 3290 0478

Worldwide
**Apa Publications GmbH & Co.
Verlag KG (Singapore branch)**
38 Joo Koon Road, Singapore 628990
Tel: (65) 865-1600. Fax: (65) 861-6438

Printing

Insight Print Services (Pte) Ltd
38 Joo Koon Road, Singapore 628990
Tel: (65) 865-1600. Fax: (65) 861-6438

©2000 Apa Publications GmbH & Co.
Verlag KG (Singapore branch)
All Rights Reserved
First Edition 1984
Fifth Edition 2000

CONTACTING THE EDITORS
Although every effort is made to
provide accurate information, we
live in a fast-changing world and
would appreciate it if readers
would call our attention to any
errors or outdated information
that may occur by writing to:
**Insight Guides, P.O. Box 7910,
London SE1 1WE, England.
Fax: (44 20) 7403-0290.
e-mail:
insight@apaguide.demon.co.uk**

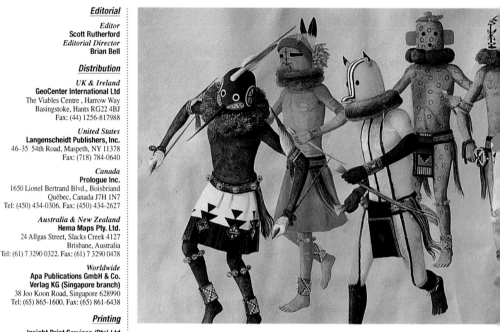

This guidebook combines the interests and enthusiasms of two of the world's best known information providers: Insight Guides, whose titles have set the standard for visual travel guides since 1970, and Discovery Channel, the world's premier source of nonfiction television programming.

The editors of Insight Guides provide both practical advice and general understanding about a destination's history, culture, institutions and people. Discovery Channel and its Web site, www.discovery.com, help millions of viewers explore their world from the comfort of their own home and also encourage them to explore it first hand.

This fully updated edition of *Insight: American Southwest* is carefully structured to convey an understanding of the region and its culture as well as to guide readers through its sights and activities:

◆ The **Features** section, indicated by a yellow bar at the top of each page, covers the history and culture of the country in a series of informative essays.

◆ The main **Places** section, which is indicated by a blue bar, is a complete guide to all the sights and areas worth visiting. Places of special interest are coordinated by number with the maps.

◆ The **Travel Tips** listings section, with an orange bar, provides a handy point of reference for infor-

Map Legend

——··—	International Boundary
————	State Boundary
⊖	Border Crossing
—·—·—	National Park/Reserve
————	Ferry Route
✈ ✈	Airport: International/Regional
🚌	Bus Station
■	Parking
●	Tourist Information
✉	Post Office
✝ ✝	Church/Ruins
✝	Monastery
☾	Mosque
✡	Synagogue
⌂ ⌂	Castle/Ruins
∴	Archeological Site
∩	Cave
1	Statue/Monument
★	Place of Interest

The main places of interest in the Places section are coordinated by number with a full-colour map (e.g. ❶), and a symbol at the top of every right-hand page tells you where to find the map.

mation on travel, hotels, shops, restaurants and more. You can locate information quickly by using the index printed on the cover flaps, which are also designed to serve as useful bookmarks.

◆ The **photographs** are chosen not only to illustrate geography and attractions but also to convey the many moods of the region.

The contributors

This edition of *Insight: American Southwest* was revised by **Scott Rutherford**, an experienced Insight editor. Building on the original edition produced by **Virginia Hopkins**, the book has been completely updated by experts in the region. In the Places section, the Phoenix, Albuquerque, Santa Fe and Taos chapters were all updated by Rutherford himself, while **Nicky Leach**, a frequent contributor

to Insight Guides, revamped the Southern Utah, Northern Arizona and Southern New Mexico chapters and wrote the essay on flora and fauna. **Larry Cheek**, another Insight regular, wrote the regional arts and literature chapters.

David Williams, who is based in Seattle but originally from the Tucson area, wrote the detailed and informative geology and geography chapter and researched the chapters on Tucson and Southern Arizona. **Manya Winsted** wrote the article on the distinctive cuisine of the Southwest, while **Michael Singer** contributed the box on Indian food and updated the Southwest in Film chapter.

Sandra Scott provided information for the book's picture stories, and contributed additional material to numerous other chapters. Editorial assistance was provided by US-based **Barbara Balletto** and by **Teresa Machan**, based in Insight's London office. Indexing was completed by **Peter Gunn**.

Many of the new images in this edition were supplied by **Catherine Karnow** and **Blaine Harrington**, two of Insight's top photographers.

Contributors to previous editions of *Insight Guide: American Southwest* whose work is still evident in this edition include Insight editor **John Gattuso**, best-selling author **Tony Hillerman**, **Bruce Berger**, writer and photographer **Buddy Mays**, **Stan Steiner**, writer and photographer **Richard Erdoes**, the Pueblo Indian writer **Leslie Marmon Silko**, **Rudolfo Anaya**, **Randy Udall**, **Ruth Armstrong**, **Suzi Barnes**, **Tom Miller**, **Barbara Chulick**, **Alison Sekaquaptewa**, **Ned Anderson**, **Ofelia Zepeda** and **Matthew Jaffe**.

INSIGHT GUIDE
american SOUTHWEST

CONTENTS

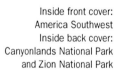

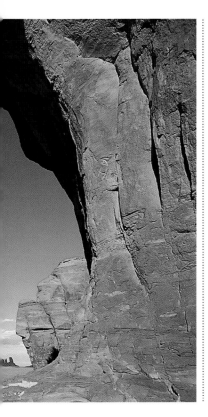

Arches
National
Park

Travel Tips

Insight on ...

Information panels

Places

AMERICAN SOUTHWEST

The culture of the Pueblo Indians mingles with the legacy of the Spanish Colonials to create an alluring experience

Makers of maps like to keep things orderly and will define the American Southwest in terms of state boundaries. But those who live there know that another boundary must be applied. The Southwest begins where the land rises out of that vast ocean of humid air which covers midland America and makes it the fertile breadbasket of half the world. And it ends along that vague line where winter cold wins out over sun and even the valleys are buried under snow. There is one ever more essential requirement. Wherever you stand in the Southwest there must be, on one horizon or another, the spirit-healing blue shape of mountains. Thus you have Arizona and New Mexico, a slice of southern Colorado, much of southern Utah, and part of Nevada.

The Southwest is high – an immense tableland broken by the high ridges of the southern Rocky Mountains – and dry, with annual precipitation varying drastically with altitude. This highness and dryness affects the air, making it oddly transparent and adding a clarity to everything one sees. The few minutes required to travel from the Rio Grande in downtown Albuquerque to the top of the Sandia Ski Basin takes one through five of North America's biological life zones – from the Upper Sonoran Desert to the cool spruce forests of the Arctic-Alpine zone.

But what attracted scores of artists to Taos was not beauty, but culture. The Southwest was Spanish Colonial country and it is also the heartland of America's Indian country. The complex culture of the Pueblo Indians has survived in centuries-old adobe villages scattered up and down the Rio Grande. And so has America's largest tribe, the Navajo. Some 200,000 strong, they occupy a vast reservation which sprawls across the heart of the Southwest in Arizona, New Mexico and Utah. These original Americans give the Southwest a Holy Land, a territory of shrines and sacred mountains.

A man tries to explain why he has returned to this empty land from a lonely, crowded California city. He looks down into the immense sink which spreads below the southwest slope of the Chuska Mountains and purveys a wilderness of sun-baked stone stretching into the distance. Gray caliche, wind-cut clay as red as barn paint, great bluish outcrops of shale and cracked salt flats where mud formed by the "male rains" of summer tastes as bitter as alum. Everything is worn, eroded and tortured. The desert teems with life, but there is no life here. Not even cactus or lizard survives, nor an insect for it to feed upon. Map-makers would call it Desolation Sink. "The Navajo name for this," he says, "is Beautiful Valley." ❏

PRECEDING PAGES: Taos Pueblo draped with winter; bleached cattle skull; Mesa Arch in Canyonlands National Park; White Sands National Monument.
LEFT: sunrise touches the clouds above Monument Valley.

A REVEALING LAND

Don't discount the desert as an empty, boring place. The geology of the American Southwest is highly complex, both mesmerizing and enriching in what it reveals

Few places in the world can rival the desert of the American Southwest for its striking geological structures. It is a geologist's paradise, but it is also a fine place for non-geologists to make a foray into the subject. The rocks are beautiful and the stories they tell are easy to learn. In addition, one doesn't need to contend with those intrusive green things called trees, which so often prevent an observer from seeing rocks.

As the great explorer of the Grand Canyon, John Wesley Powell, wrote more than a century ago, "Wherever we look there is but a wilderness of rocks, deep gorges where the rivers are lost below cliffs and towers and pinnacles and ten thousand strangely carved forms in every direction, and beyond them mountains blending with the clouds."

John Wesley Powell also was the first person to compare the geology of the Southwest to a vast book waiting to be read. Like all good stories, this one is best told from the beginning.

Beginnings

The oldest rocks in the Southwest, and some of the oldest rocks on the planet, rest in the depths of the Grand Canyon. The 2-billion-year-old rocks are known as the Vishnu Schist and consist of sediments originally deposited into a sea that washed onto a shore at the edge of a continent. These rocks were then uplifted and folded into a mountain chain, injected with veins of molten rock and then uplifted and folded again. And possibly yet again. This created a rock that today is banded and contorted in some places, and platy and shiny in others.

The next oldest rocks in the Grand Canyon, which rest directly on top of the Vishnu Schist, are only 545 million years old. Did no deposition occur in the intervening 1.2 billion years? Or were rocks deposited and then beveled away by erosion? No one knows. Geologists call a

feature like this, where two rocks of vastly different ages are in contact, an unconformity. Unconformities are more the norm in geology than the exception to the rule. No matter where one looks in the rock record, more pieces are missing than are present. Erosion sometimes complicates the matter.

LEFT: Monument Valley, on the border of southern Utah and northern Arizona, is sacred land for the Navajo people. **RIGHT:** Southern Utah.

A BRIEF HISTORY OF EARTH

Years Ago	Event of Some Significance
4.6 billion:	Formation of the earth
4.3 billion:	The crust, ocean and atmosphere form
3.96 billion:	The oldest known rocks (Yukon, Canada)
3.9 billion:	End of the major meteorite impacts
3.5 billion:	The oldest known fossils (of bacteria)
2.4 billion:	Large continents develop
2.0 billion:	The atmosphere becomes oxygen-rich
1.45 billion:	Single-cell organisms develop
680 million:	Multi-celled animals develop
290 million:	Dinosaurs begin their dominance
100 million:	Flowering plants take root

The 500-million-year-old sandstones of the Grand Canyon were deposited at the edge of another sea that left behind sediments from Arizona to Canada. It remained in the region for many millions of years, depositing additional sediments. Geologists find fine examples of fossil trilobites – intriguing because they were one of the first organisms on the planet to contain a skeleton. The Grand Canyon trilobite fossils range in size from a quarter of an inch to around 3 inches (7.5 cm) in length.

TRILOBITES

Trilobites, an extinct order of woodlouse-like animals, were one of the first animals to form a protective casing. Nowadays, fossils of trilobites are common.

Period (408–360 million years ago), is often called the Age of Fish. In the next period, the Mississippian (360–320 million years ago), another sea spread over the Southwest and deposited a thick blanket of limestone from Canada to Mexico. Small and poker-chip shaped discs, known as crinoid stems, are one of the most commonly recognizable fossils in the aquatic graveyard of this rock layer, known as the Redwall Limestone. Crinoids were small invertebrates related to sand dollars and sea urchins. They resem-

A time of fish and tropical seas

Trilobites became extinct 220 million years ago, followed by yet another gap of missing time, but only a small amount of just 100 million years. At this point in time, the North American continent, which was slowly moving northward, straddled the equator.

A warm, tropical sea covered much of the Southwest and a new group of creatures had begun to make their appearance – fish – although we might not recognize their profile, since a hard coat of bony armor protected their heads. Fossilized scales from these fish occur in a few places in the Grand Canyon.

This span of time, known as the Devonian

bled plants, with a base, a stem, and a flower-like top. Other fossils are solitary corals, looking like a horn or ice cream cone.

Although this fossil-rich period has a red face in the Grand Canyon, it is actually a gray rock covered by coat of red. The red comes from red sediments washing out of the rock layer directly above the Redwall.

Iron is the principal coloring agent of sedimentary rocks in the Southwest. Oxidized iron, which is similar to rust produced on a nail left out in the rain, gives rock its characteristic red color. Sandstone consists of approximately 3 percent iron, mostly as a surface coating on individual grains of sand.

Green layers of rock, especially the ones found in Arches National Park, contain iron that was altered in a low oxygen environment, such as a shallow lake or mud flat.

Dark brown to black streaks, known as desert varnish, cover many southwestern rock surfaces. This micro-thin coating receives its color from manganese oxides (black) and iron oxides (reddish brown). Geologists argue about how the manganese and iron, which are derived from sources outside the rock, are bonded to the rock surface. Some believe the process involves bacteria that oxidizes the minerals and cements them to the rock, while others believe

The Paradox Basin sea probably looked something like the modern Mediterranean Sea with its narrow connection to the Atlantic Ocean. This thin neck created a restricted environment where evaporation of the closed-in Paradox waters left behind vast beds of salt. Evaporation occurred because the North American continent lay in a warm climatic zone, slightly north of the equator. Episodic flooding and evaporation of this sea produced a mile-thick layer of salt.

Salt has an unusual property. Put enough weight on it and salt contorts like Silly Putty. Salt is also less dense than the surrounding

that a purely chemical reaction occurs between iron, manganese and water. The latest evidence points to a combination of both.

Formation of a restricted basin in what is now southeastern Utah was the dominant event of the next geologic period, the Pennsylvanian (320–286 million years ago). Known as the Paradox Basin, this northwest-to-southeast trending trough allowed water from an ocean that lay to the west to flow into the area. This oval-shaped basin extended from northwest New Mexico through Moab up to Price, Utah, 120 miles (193 km) south of Salt Lake City.

ABOVE: the Grand Canyon from Yaki Point.

sandstone, so it has a tendency to rise when it is forced to move. Under the intense pressure of thousands of feet of rock, produced by sediments washing out of nearby mountains, the salt in the Moab-Arches National Monument area began to move and bow upwards, creating mile-long ridges capped by a rock unit known as the Entrada Sandstone. Salt movement continued for about 100 million years.

Now jump forward to about 10 million years ago, when water began to percolate into and dissolve the beds of salt, which led to collapse of salt-created ridges. As the sandstone folded into the void, it stretched, cracked, and produced a series of parallel cracks, which eroded into a system of parallel canyons and fins, or narrow ridges of rock. Good examples include the Devil's Garden and Fiery Furnace in Arches National Park – fin and canyon formation created a perfect environment for the formation of arches in the park. Arches form when water mixes with atmospheric carbon dioxide to form a weak acid, which first weakens the fins and then erodes them. In addition, during winter, water may seep into fractures in the rock, freeze, expand and crack the fins open, thus forming an arch.

Advancing and retreating seas were common across the Southwest during the period following the deposition of salt in Moab. This resulted in intermixed layers of sandstone, shale and limestone. One of the most interesting limestone regions is southeastern New Mexico.

Two hundred and fifty million years ago, a constricted sea covered what is now the area of Carlsbad Caverns National Park and Guadalupe Mountains National Park. The warm waters were an ideal spot for the formation of a reef resembling Australia's Great Barrier Reef, except that algae and sponges built the 400-mile-long by 4-mile wide complex (640 by 6.4 km), instead of corals, which make up modern reefs.

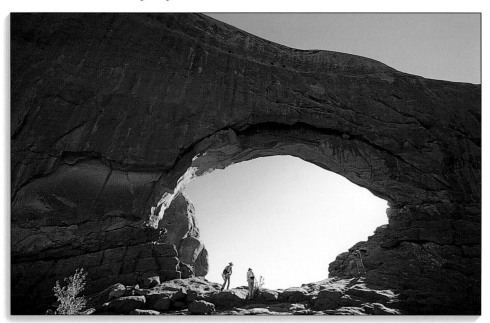

THE FINE STUFF OF SAND

Deserts are often associated with sand, and a visitor to the American Southwest will encounter countless varieties of the stuff, from the fine white gypsum of White Sands to the vibrantly burnt orange of Monument Valley. Sand, as intuition might suggest, is the result of weathering on rock. Wind, water and abrasion grind down rocks into smaller particles that, when wind blown, must eventually gather in deposition, often as sand dunes, the most recognized symbol of the desert but which cover only 20 percent of the planet's deserts. Under the right conditions of time and geology, sand dunes may be subject to forces that turn them into sedimentary stone.

The caverns at Carlsbad began to form roughly 12 million years ago during the uplift of the entire reef complex, which formed the Guadalupe Mountains. Uplift allowed groundwater to percolate down into the limestone and dissolve it. Dissolution of the rock created passageways and caverns, while deposition of the dissolved elements formed stalactites, which hang down, and stalagmites, which rise upwards from the cave's floor.

Petrified trees and uranium

Throughout the time of advancing and retreating seas, the North American continent continued to move north. The climate was generally warm with monsoons and intermittent dry seasons. During one of these periods when no sea covered the land, a purplish, yellow and brown mottled unit, the Chinle Formation, was the most important unit deposited, at least from an economic viewpoint.

The Chinle contains huge reserves of uranium, produced from ground water and most likely leached out of volcanic ash. As it moved through the rock, the uranium-rich water encountered plant remains and replaced the organic material with uranium minerals, which settled out of the water. The Chinle is also the rock unit where one finds the petrified logs at Petrified Forest National Park. Petrified wood forms in a similar process to the uranium but now the ground water was silica-rich, so quartz precipitated out instead of uranium. The logs originally came from streams carrying material from nearby highlands.

Deserts and dinosaurs descend

By 200 million years ago, the southwest portion of the continent had drifted into a climatic zone governed by dry, hot conditions. Deserts began their 40-million-year-long reign over the northern portions of the southwest. The sand dunes of these early deserts have been preserved today as the 200 to 2,000-foot-thick (60–600 meters) cliffs of red and tawny sandstone found in the national parks and surrounding lands of southern Utah.

Non-marine or continental conditions have mostly dominated the Southwest since the time of the deserts. Volcanoes at the edge of the region periodically spewed ash and lava into the lakes and streams. Alteration of these ashes created the green rocks found at Arches National Park. Other rock layers across the Southwest are tan, red, or grayish.

It was during this era that dinosaurs roamed the streams and lakes. When the dinosaurs died, some fell into the streams and washed down into the lowlands, where their bones collected. A good fossil locality is just outside Grand Junction, Colorado. Nearby, paleontologists found the bones of Utahraptor, a 20-foot-long (6-meter) animal with a foot-long killing blade growing out of its foot. Utahraptors were a relative of the cinematic velociraptor.

LEFT: North Window, Arches National Park.
RIGHT: petrified wood fragment, Arizona.

When Steven Spielberg made *Jurassic Park,* he enlarged the velociraptors, which were actually about the size of a golden retriever, to create a more dramatic beast. Coincidentally, Utahraptor, which was about the same size as Spielberg's velociraptors on steroids, was discovered the same summer the movie was released, thus adding a bit of credence to Spielberg's fantasy world. Utahraptor was excavated from the Morrison Formation, the fossil-rich rock unit that makes up Dinosaur National Monument in northern Utah. The extinction of the dinosaurs 66 million years ago occurred as the Rocky Mountains began to be uplifted.

ALL ABOUT MINERALS

While "rock" and "stone" are often used interchangeably, one can't use "mineral" in the same way. In fact, rocks and stones are usually made from minerals, which are inorganic substances with very specific chemical and crystalline structures. Most minerals are either pure deposits called ores, or are blended with other minerals in rock. Many minerals are formed volcanically when magma surging up through the earth's crust forms deposits. The magma then cools and the heavier basic minerals crystallize first and sink. Minerals may also form because of chemical action – heat causes reactions on surrounding rocks, resulting in mineral changes.

Rise of the mountains

Additional mountain building events have occurred several times in the past 66 million years. Numerous small mountain ranges, such as the La Sals, Henrys, Abajos, Sleeping Ute and Navajo dot the Southwest, and were all formed in this time period. Geologists call these mountains laccoliths, while some less serious folk call them "hot humps between the sheets."

Laccoliths form when molten rock or magma cools within the earth. As the magma was rising

> **STURDY FIR**
>
> One non-geologic feature at El Malpais is a 930-year-old Douglas fir, which must have started to grow within a few decades of the cooling of the site's lava.

meter) thick layer of dark volcanic rock, known as rhyolite. Subsequent erosion by water, ice and wind sculpted the rhyolite into columns, balanced rocks and hoodoos.

Between 5 million and 13 million years later, lava and ash spewed out of a volcano at the opposite end of the state. The light and dark rocks make up the Ajo Range and Bates Mountains of Organ Pipe Cactus National Monument. At roughly the same time another flow of lava spread across the Verde Valley area of central Arizona. This was fol-

it reached a zone of weakness and began to spread laterally between sedimentary layers (the sheets). Continued pulses of magma bowed up the sheets and formed a mushroom-like structure (the hump). Over time, the softer sedimentary rocks eroded away, leaving behind rounded mountains that glaciers would eventually carve into jagged peaks.

In some places, though, the magma pierced the surface and erupted. One such volcanic event occurred in southeast Arizona 27 million years ago when six incandescent ash flows shot out of a crater near present-day Chiricahua National Monument. Eruption of the Turkey Creek caldera produced a 2,000-foot (609-

lowed by eruptions 2 million years ago in New Mexico. Pumice (a lightweight and light-colored rock that can float in water), tuff (solidified ash flows) and obsidian (volcanic glass) from these explosions are found in Bandelier National Monument, in western New Mexico.

The most recent eruptions of black lava (basalt) occurred within the past 1,000 years. Known in New Mexico as *malpais* – Spanish for "bad country" – the jagged, fractured flows spread across the northwest corner of the state. El Malpais National Monument is a good place to see these flows. Sunset Crater in Arizona is the youngest volcanic center. The crater first exploded in either 1064 or 1065.

The other mountainous terrain in the American Southwest, known as the Basin and Range province, makes up the landscape of southern Arizona and New Mexico. It did not involve dramatic volcanoes. Instead, movement of the North American plate starting about 20 million years ago caused the crust to stretch and crack along a roughly north-south trend. When the land spread, some blocks of earth started to break and tilt like a stack of upright books tipping over. This forced some chunks of land to rise and others to drop. The ones that dropped formed the basins and began to fill with sediments washing out of the blocks that rose,

fornia. Downcutting still occurs in the Grand Canyon, only at a much reduced rate.

In his classic tome on the region, *The Colorado*, writer Frank Waters sums up the place of geology in the life of the desert Southwest. "Geology here forever dominates life and gives it its ultimate meaning." This is a rather eloquent way of pointing out the interrelationships of plants, animals, humans and geology. For example, soil types affect where plants grow, and elevation differences create climatic variation, with precipitation that varies across the region from less than 5 inches (13 cm) to over 30 inches (76 cm). ❑

which are now the mountain ranges. Some basins contain 15,000 feet (4,600 meters) of fill. Crustal movement along these faults continues to the present day.

Erosion of the Grand Canyon occurred even more recently than the Basin and Range. Surprisingly, the significant downcutting by the Colorado River that created the canyon took place somewhere between 4.7 and 1.7 million years ago, which works out to a rate of about 1.2 to 3.2 feet (1 meter) per thousand years. All of that material ended up in the Gulf of Cali-

LEFT: volcanic cinder cone, Tularosa Basin.
ABOVE: Slickrock Canyon in northern Arizona.

BIG ENCOUNTERS

The first Europeans to see the Grand Canyon were Spanish, in 1540, just a scant two generations after Christopher Columbus' voyage to the New World. These first Spaniards were treasure-seeking members of Coronado's futile expedition in search of the fabulous Seven Golden Cities of Cíbola. One of Coronado's lieutenants, Garcia Lopez de Cardenas, was guided by local Indians to the South Rim of the Grand Canyon.The Spaniards were duly impressed by the size of the place, but they saw the canyon as an impediment to further exploration and left with no recorded regrets. It would be 300 years before the next European visit.

Decisive Dates

BEGINNINGS

circa **500 BC** The Hohokam people develop an intricate system of canals for irrigation in the Salt River Valley.

AD 700 Five distinct groups of people have evolved in the region: the Anasazi, the Sinagua, the Hohokam, the Salado and the Mogollon.

circa **1150–1250** Severe drought hits; Southwestern peoples leave valleys for caves and canyons.

1299 Drought ends; most Anasazi and Mogollon villages have been abandoned.

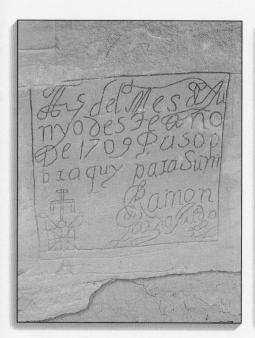

EUROPEAN ARRIVALS

1540–42 Francisco Vásquez de Coronado explores the Southwest.

1598 The first European settlers in the Southwest: Juan de Oñate leads 149 colonists from Mexico to a spot just north of present-day Santa Fe.

1610 Santa Fe is founded as the capital of the Spanish province of New Mexico.

1680 Indians kill 22 Franciscans in New Mexico's Pueblo Revolt.

1692 Father Eusebio Francesco Kino establishes the first mission in Arizona; more soon followed.

1705 Albuquerque is founded.

1775 Tucson is founded by Irishman Hugh O'Connor.

1776 Spanish missionaries arrive in the Utah region.

1778 Construction of San Xavier del Bac mission, south of Tucson, begins.

THE SETTLER YEARS

1822 Settlers begin arriving in New Mexico via the Santa Fe Trail; Mexican War of Independence.

1824 Founding of the Mexican Republic. The Territory of Nuevo Mexico, a vast region that included much of today's Southwest, belongs to the new republic.

1846–48 The Mexican War.

1847 A group of rebels from Taos Pueblo kill the governor of New Mexico Territory and 20 Anglo settlers. Mormons, under the leadership of Brigham Young, begin to settle Utah and Nevada.

1848 Lands north of the Gila River are ceded to the US territory of New Mexico. Wagon trains on the Oregon Trail begin to pass through the area.

1851 Fort Defiance is built to "control" the Navajo.

1853 The Gadsden Purchase secures lands between the Gila River and what is now Arizona's southern boundary; all of Arizona now under US control.

1857 The Utah War briefly pits Mormon settlers – who were repeatedly denied statehood petitions because of their practice of polygamy – again US Army troops. Lt. Joseph Ives leads an expedition into the Grand Canyon and returns with the first geological descriptions and illustrations of the natural wonder.

1858 Silver-rich Comstock Lode is discovered at Virginia City, Nevada, spurring population growth.

1861 A Chiricahua leader, Cochise, is wrongly accused of kidnapping a rancher's son, setting off a vicious cycle of revenge. Nevada becomes a territory.
1863 President Lincoln creates the Arizona Territory.
1863–65 "Kit" Carson is commisioned to move Navajos to a camp in eastern New Mexico; hundreds died along the 300-mile journey known as the "Long Walk".
1864 Nevada granted statehood.
1868 Navajos are allowed to return to their homeland. Phoenix is founded.
1869 Major John Wesley Powell leads the first expedition down the Green and Colorado rivers and through the Grand Canyon. The transcontinental railway is completed at Promontory Summit in Utah.

1888 Copper surpasses gold and silver as an important Arizona export.
1890 The Mormon church repudiates polygamy.
1896 Utah is granted statehood.

A NEW CENTURY

1910–23 The Mexican Revolution takes place.
1910–15 Gold and silver mining are at their peak in the Southwest.
1911 Roosevelt Dam is constructed in Arizona. Las Vegas is incorporated.
1912 Arizona and New Mexico are granted statehood.
1916 Notorious Mexican revolutionary Pancho Villa raids Columbus, New Mexico.

1871 A mob of Tucson vigilantes massacres 85 peaceful Apaches.
1881 Phoenix is incorporated as a city. The Gunfight at the OK Corral takes place in Tombstone, Arizona.
1886 Geronimo surrenders, ending 25 years of Apache wars. Settlement in the region gathers speed.
1887 Congress passes the General Allotment Act, dividing Indian tribal lands into parcels and deeding them directly to individual Indians, to encourage them to become involved in agriculture.

PRECEDING PAGE: Ancient Native American petroglyphs. **LEFT:** Spanish inscription, New Mexico, circa 1709; navigating the Colorado River. **ABOVE:** John Wesley Powell and Paiute guide; lights of Vegas.

1922 Pueblo Indians form the All Pueblo Council.
1931 Gambling is legalized in Nevada; liberal marriage and divorce laws enacted in the state.
1936 The Hoover Dam is completed.
1945 The atomic bomb first explodes at the Trinity site near Alamogordo, New Mexico.
1960 Sun City, west of Phoenix, is invented by the Del Webb Corporation and becomes the blueprint for American planned retirement communities.
1963 A decision by the U.S. Supreme Court increases Arizona's allocation of water from the Colorado River; Glen Canyon Dam completed.
1974–present Construction of the huge Central Arizona project, which diverts water from the Colorado River and carries it across Arizona. ❏

IN ANCIENT TIMES

After arriving across long-submerged land bridges, early migrants to the American Southwest evolved into five main cultural groups, different but similar

In the final stages of the Pleistocene Epoch came the Ice Age. Nearly one-sixth of the earth's surface was blanketed with ice, making possible the arrival of humans in North America across land bridges. Massive glaciers formed from billions of tons of water and the oceans receded. In some areas the sea level dropped by as much as 300 feet (90 meters) and long-submerged fragments of sea bottom were exposed. One of these – a 56-mile (90-km) strip of rocky earth between northeastern Siberia and northwestern Alaska – was an early gateway for migration to this continent.

Exact dates of New World penetration are simply speculation. We can, however, say that aboriginal Asians probably arrived on North American shores between 15,000 and 40,000 years ago. Human arrival was not sudden. Late in the Pleistocene, interglacial sub-ages (warm trends) began to occur, causing sea-level ice to melt. As the climate slowly mellowed, grass and low shrubs flourished – even on the newly exposed land bridge. This forage attracted grazing animals from the Asian continent, and following the mammoth and bison, of course, were the hunters.

When did humans first reach the Southwest? Archaeological evidence – mostly the datable artifacts found with bones of extinct animals – suggests that they were firmly entrenched in relatively large numbers 10,000 or 12,000 years ago. This same evidence has allowed scientists to reach some logical conclusions about early humans. Paleo-Indians were primarily meat-eaters, although they probably gathered wild plants for food as well. Using flint or bone-tipped weapons of their own creation and design, Paleo-Indians could kill animals 20 times their size. In part, early humans were social creatures; they hunted in organized groups in order to kill not just a single animal but an entire herd at one time for the good of the community. Because constant expansion of

hunting range was necessary, fixed habitations were seldom established.

From about 7000 BC for the next 7,000 years, human life styles in the American Southwest were changing significantly. This span of cultural amplification has been named the Desert Archaic period. Among the most important

changes to occur during the Archaic period were: the acquisition of the fire-drill and the grinding stone; the utilization of foods other than meat – mainly seeds, wild grains, tubers and berries; the construction of semi-permanent, seasonal dwelling places – primarily "pithouses," round or rectangular holes in the earth that were covered with brush and mud; and the practice of spiritual ceremonies.

The development of the Paleo-Indian into the Archaic Indian was a sluggish process at best, dependent upon interaction between groups of people sometimes separated by hundreds of miles. This was not true, however, of the next period of cultural expansion – the Pithouse-

LEFT: White House Ruins, Canyon de Chelly.
RIGHT: petroglyphs in New Mexico.

Pueblo Period – which began about 2,000 years ago and ended with the arrival of Europeans in the Southwest in the mid-16th century.

Cultural divisions

By AD 700, five distinct groups of people had evolved and were inhabiting the Southwest. In the north were the Anasazi – an intelligent, artistic, peaceful society of farmers whose cliff palaces and sprawling canyon cities were so well constructed that many have survived nearly intact for a thousand years. To the south,

> **EXPANDING SOCIETIES**
>
> Of changes occurring during the 1,500-year-long Pithouse-Pueblo Period, none was more important than the development of discreet human societies over a wide area.

humans that demanded huge changes in social structures. Because agricultural products could be stored for the winter, dependence upon hunting and gathering was drastically reduced. In turn, habitations became more permanent so that farmers could tend their fields. Permanency demanded security from enemies, and security required a large and stable population.

Whatever the reasons, there arose these five major cultures and many minor ones. Geographically separated by hundreds of miles,

near the San Francisco Peaks area of present-day Arizona, were the Sinagua, an agricultural people whose culture later became a melting pot of building techniques and increasingly complex social development. In the Gila and Salt River valleys near present-day Phoenix were the Hohokam, at their peak perhaps the greatest canal builders in North America. To the east were Hohokam cousins, the Salado, and in the rich mountain country of present-day New Mexico were the Mogollon. We can only guess how and why these divisions of culture came about. One important factor may have been the introduction and development of agriculture – a new concept to primitive

each bore striking similarities to the others. They were all agricultural societies, heavily dependent for survival upon crops of maize (corn), beans, squash and melons. In their early stages of development, all lived in underground pithouses or caves, later moving to above-ground, apartment-style, multistoried homes called *pueblos* by the Spaniards. By 700, they all used pottery extensively and had acquired the bow and arrow. Three centuries later, cotton-weaving implements were in use. More importantly, none developed the aristocracy (as far as can be determined) that marked the Aztec and Inca civilizations to the south.

Similarities among the cultures occurred also

in physical appearance, clothing, and daily activities. From burial evidence, scientists think that most prehistoric Indians were about the same size and build; men averaged 5 feet 4 inches (1.6 meters), women slightly less. They were muscular, stocky people with sparse body hair. Head hair was thick, however. Men wore it long; women preferred it bobbed or fashioned into elaborate coiffures.

The Golden Age

Similarities amongst the differing groups were not coincidental. Throughout the 15-century span of the Pithouse-Pueblo Period, interaction undoubtedly took place among all prehistoric cultures in the Southwest, as well as in northern Mexico, with each contributing something to cultural development.

So rapidly, in fact, did new ideas and methods spread among the five major cultures that by the mid-11th century a "golden age" existed among Southwest Indians. Building techniques and irrigation systems had progressed to a highly sophisticated degree. Frivolities such as ball games and contests with dice were commonplace. In addition, increased rainfall had mellowed the often harsh environment; natural springs and streams ran full, and game and wild plants flourished. Because of the added moisture and new agricultural techniques, farming increased, and with surplus food available, populations grew. New farming projects were started in areas that could hardly have supported cacti a century before. Existing towns grew more complex.

Decline of the good years

This new life of relative comfort was only temporary, however, and although there are many plausible explanations as to why the golden age was cut short, one of the most feasible is that by the middle of the 12th century, weather patterns had once again changed and the region saw the beginning of drought. Where water was permanently available, farmers were little affected; but in areas where agriculture depended upon rainfall and not irrigation, existence once again became difficult. Many towns and outlying family dwellings were abandoned, the inhabi-

tants migrating to larger centers of population that had been constructed near natural groundwater sources. What possessions could be carried were taken along; all else was left behind. This sudden influx of refugees must have created hardships for the already settled population but, in most cases, room was found.

Then a new threat appeared in the Southwest. Shoshone raiders (probably the ancestors of present-day Ute) suddenly arrived uninvited from the north, and local tribes found themselves the targets of continual harassment. Few in number, the Shoshone dared not attack a fully protected town, but they easily raided

LEFT: diorama of a Mesa Verde-area pueblo of around AD 850.

RIGHT: stone arrow points of the Southwest.

ANCIENT FASHION

Clothing varied amongst the five main groups, but variations depended less upon tribal affiliation than upon time of year. In hot weather, most people wore nothing but sandals woven from plant fiber or plaited from yucca leaves. As the seasons changed and the days cooled, skirts and aprons made from vegetable material or animal skins were added. In winter, hide cloaks, shirts and blankets – the latter made from rabbit skin, dog fur or turkey feathers – were probably sufficient to turn the chill. When cotton was introduced and people learned the art of weaving, more elaborate forms of winter clothing – mainly heavy cloaks – came into vogue.

fields, stole harvests and picked off an occasional farmer or his family. In addition, towns and villages had, probably out of necessity, begun to prey on one another.

Sometime during the late 12th century, the combination of harassment, thievery and steadily worsening drought conditions brought about a drastic change in lifestyle for most Southwestern cultures. The people began to leave their traditional valleys or mesa-top homes for the security of isolated caves and protected canyon amphitheaters. Whether the move ended the Shoshone threat or only prolonged it, researchers don't know. They do

know, however, that it did little to ease internal strife or to alleviate the need for water.

Midway through the 13th century, even as the great cliff cities of Mesa Verde, Mancos Canyon, Betatakin, Keet Seel and others were under construction, the drought was reaching its peak. Even permanent water sources began to run dry, and life became a matter of day-to-day survival. The soil was worn out and turned to dust; crops failed year after year. Hunting and gathering had never been fully abandoned, but food supplies in the wild decreased in direct proportion to the decrease in moisture. There was simply not enough food and water for the population. Although we have no idea of its exact

nature, some type of social upheaval undoubtedly took place – perhaps a universal uprising against the blameless but available leadership. Migrations began. By 1299, when the drought finally ended, most villages and towns of the Anasazi and Mogollon had been abandoned. Hohokam, Salado and Sinagua communities (near permanent streams) survived longer; however, they met the same fate within a century.

Migrating peoples

It is here that the real mystery begins. Where did the refugees go? It is believed that some journeyed east to join or start pueblos on the Rio Grande River in present-day New Mexico. Others went east but not as far, stopping at the pueblos of Zuni and Acoma, also in New Mexico. Some may have gone south to Mexico or west to California, and a good many simply changed their lifestyles to meet current requirements for survival and remained nearby, the ancestors of today's Pima and Hopi.

The Hopi mesas in Arizona, in fact, were perhaps a major refuge for both the Sinagua and Anasazi. Hopi people claim ancestral ownership of many of the great population centers such as Mesa Verde, Betatakin, Keet Seel and Wupatki. Prehistoric Hopi clan signs found in these ruins give validity to the claims, though many archaeologists argue the point. Pictographs (prehistoric rock paintings) and petroglyphs (rock carvings) similar to those the Hopi claim as clan symbols were once freely used throughout both North and South America. This certainly suggests widespread interaction among early cultures but not necessarily the traditional ownership of the signs that Hopi legends proclaim. Hopi ancestors were probably an aggregation of several different cultures.

Wherever these early people went, they were gone, for the most part, by 1400, abandoning homes they had so painstakingly constructed. Many of these prehistoric dwellings, preserved by dry desert air and remote locations that prevent desecration, and in some cases by the stabilization and restoration technology of modern science, still exist and may be easily visited. Remember, however, that although old, these ancient dwellings remain fragile. ❏

LEFT: early fire-making through friction.
RIGHT: although many tribes would disappear, others would be converted to Catholicism.

CONQVISTA
ENBARCAROSE ALASINDIAS

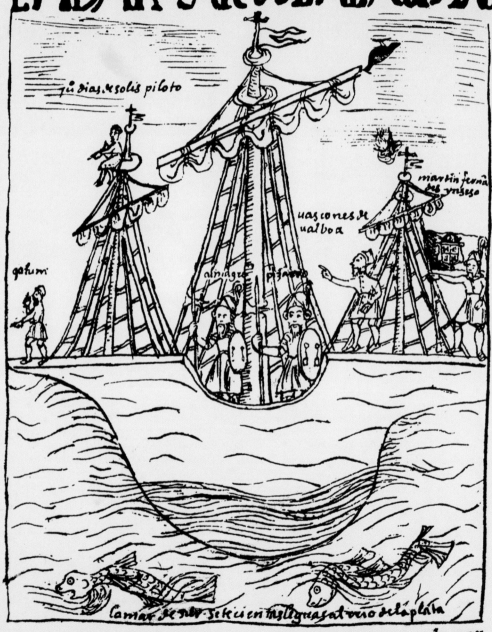

ju dias de solis piloto

martin ferná des yñiseso

uascones de ualboa

gotum

almagro piçarro

lamar de su se cicien mil leguas al rio de la plata

la mar

SPANISH EXPLORATION

First seeking imaginary gold and then lost souls, the Spanish in the New World
embedded their culture into Mexico and the American Southwest

On an autumn day late in November of 1528, four half-drowned seamen – survivors of the ill-fated Spanish expedition of Pánfilo de Narváez – were washed ashore onto the beaches of Texas by the unfriendly sea. Naked, chilled and starving, they were fortunate to be found alive by Indians, who fed and clothed them. These naked conquistadors were the first known Spaniards to set foot in the Southwest. So began one of the most remarkable journeys in American history. The shipwrecked, led by Nuñez Cabeza de Vaca, walked for thousands of miles through the desert until, eight years later, they reached Mexico City.

On the way, they learned to live and adapt like Indians. They adopted not only the clothes but the habits of the tribes they met along the way. The Indians most often feted the men as messengers of the gods, as the Aztecs had regarded Cortés further to the south. Especially welcome in this group of four men was Estéban, the black Moor and a Christianized slave of the Spaniards who was favored by the Indian women even more than the others.

Although no records exist to document the theory, historians conjecture that the first mestizos, half Spanish and half Indian, were born of the lost conquistadors and Indian women. In his memoirs, de Vaca mused wryly about "the possibility of life in which to be deprived of Europe was not to be deprived of too much."

Seeking new conquests

On his arrival in Mexico City, de Vaca told tales of walled cities with houses four and five stories tall and of Indians who were more civilized than the Spaniards. To the conquistadors of Cortés, who had conquered most of Mexico and then fallen into fighting among themselves over the spoils, the reports meant new treasures of gold might be found in the desert to the north. The cry went up: *Otro Mexico! Otro*

Peru! Here is another Mexico! Another Peru!

Enticed by de Vaca's tale, the restless and bored conquistadors polished their rusting armor and prepared themselves for battle. They intended to conquer the entire continent.

The Viceroy of New Spain, Antonio de Mendoza, sent forth an *entrata* – an expedition –

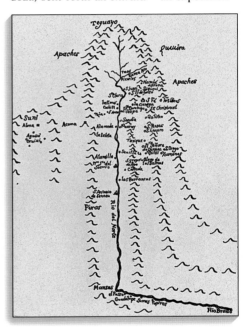

SEVEN GOLDEN CITIES

Las Siete Ciudades Doradas de Cíbola, or the Seven Golden Cities of Cíbola, were the elusive goals of Spanish conquistadores in North America during the 16th century, following the failure to find similar cities in South America. These legendary centers of unbelievable wealth and splendor were first suggested by Alvar Núñez Cabeza de Vaca, who was shipwrecked in 1528 and wandered through Texas and northern Mexico for 8 years. Because of his reports, the viceroy of New Spain sent out an expedition under Estéban, a slave shipwrecked with de Vaca, and Fray Marcos de Niza, who then claimed to have seen them from a great distance.

LEFT: Spanish *conquistadores* departing for the New World, depicted in the chronicles *Waman Puma*.
RIGHT: map of New Mexico region, 1680.

led by Father Marcos de Niza and guided by the black Moor, Estéban. Its aim was to find the legendary Gran Quivira and the fabled Seven Cities of Cíbola that de Vaca had heard about – but never seen.

For months, Father Marcos and his men wandered through the northern desert but clearly found no cities of gold. They returned to Mexico City empty-handed. In the course of their ordeal, Estéban had been killed by the men of Zuni Pueblo, who said he had "assaulted their women." (For

> ### A GOLDEN HELL
>
> "To possess silver and gold, the greedy Spaniards would enter Hell itself," said the Franciscan Father Zarate Salmeron of New Mexico, failing to dissuade them.

ing of the emperor and the viceroy, Coronado marshaled a small army in Mexico and crossed half a continent. He alone among the conquistadors created a romantic legend that would linger.

Coronado was the image of the poor *hidalgo* (gentleman): dignified, handsome and so poor he had to borrow from his wife to fund the expedition. His pretension of courtly nobility in the inhospitable wilderness, epitomized by his wearing armor in the burning desert sun, made him the American Don Quixote; he was one of

reasons no one understands, a statue of now-Saint Estéban was raised in the nearby pueblo of Acoma, where it stands today.)

Despite the failure of Father Marcos's expedition the Spaniards were not discouraged. Deaths, hardships and dangers challenged their sense of adventure and *machismo*, and, when that failed, the promise of great riches spurred them on.

Of all the conquistadors who set forth in search of the Seven Cities of Cíbola and Gran Quivira, none behaved with more grandeur and nobility than Francisco Vazquez de Coronado, the governor of the Kingdom of Nueva Galicia, the "Knight of El Dorado." With the bless-

those rare men who perfectly fit his moment in history, for better or worse.

The men of Coronado's army, on the other hand, were the riffraff, cutthroats and adventurers of Mexico City. It was an epic irony. The image of the conquistadors riding forth in resplendent armor of gold, with flags and plumes proudly flying as in a knightly pageant, is largely a myth, created in retrospect. The contemporary description of Coronado's men is not nearly so grand.

ABOVE: Canyon de Chelly rock paintings show the Spanish arrival. **RIGHT:** Spanish inscription on El Morro Rocky by Don Juan de Odate, 1605.

Most of Coronado's men wore "American" rather than European clothing, said one observer, and another noted that "many more [wore] buckskin coats than coats of armor." And while the majority were horsemen, few were high-born. In Spain, only a gentleman was permitted – by royal decree – to ride a horse, and any knight found on a mule was subject to punishment. But in Mexico, anyone could ride. In 1554, the viceroy Velasco complained of these horsemen: "Very few are *caballeros* (knights) or *hijosdalgos* (sons of gentlemen). They are *gente comun* (common people). In these provinces, the caballero is a merchant."

The nobleman Don Juan Garray added in total disgust, "Even beggars ride horses in Mexico."

For his entrata, Coronado mustered nearly 400 men, almost all of them volunteers. There were officially 235 mounted men and 62 on foot, but unofficially there were many more, ranging from teenagers to old men. It was rather a motley troop.

Not only were the soldiers not conquistadors, some of them weren't even Spaniards. The company bugler was German, and there were two Italians, five Portuguese, a Frenchman and a Scotsman, Thomas Blake, who had changed his name to Tomas Blaque. And there were

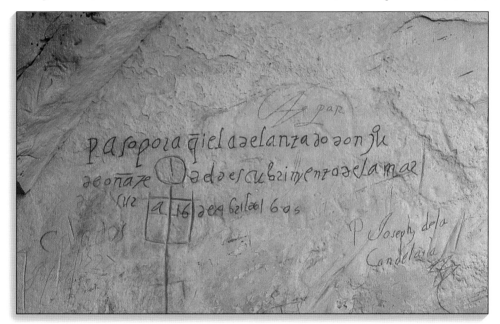

CORONADO'S GOLDEN FAILURE

Francisco Vázquez de Coronado journeyed to the New World, and New Spain (present-day Mexico) in 1535 with the new viceroy, Antonio de Mendoza. Coronado was quick to earn a reputation in the pacification of Indians, and he was soon appointed the governor of Nueva Galicia.

When the expedition ordered by Mendoza – to seek the legendary golden cities of Cíbola – and led by Fray Marcos de Niza returned to Mexico City confirming the richness of these cities, (which were, in fact, Zuni pueblos in present-day New Mexico), Mendoza organized yet another expedition. One part of this expedition, two ships commanded by Hernando de Alarcón, found no cities but

did discover the mouth of the Colorado River, in 1540. The main force, led by Coronado and consisting of 300 Spaniards, probably an equal number of Indians, and herds of livestock, moved overland northward. The pueblo of Zuni was captured but proved to be no city of gold; a secondary reconnaissance group sighted the Grand Canyon. Offshoot expeditions into Texas and Kansas proved futile, and two years later, in 1542, Coronado returned to Mexico.

Coronado was indicted for his failure by an official inquiry but found innocent. After another indictment in which he was fined, he stayed on the Council of Mexico until his death in 1554.

hundreds of Indians. No one knows how many Indians marched with Coronado, but it is known that they were not simply bearers and carriers. Most of them were hired to be scouts, guides, horse wranglers, herdsmen, *vaqueros* (cowboys) and bridge builders. All of them were well armed with lances, spears, and bows and arrows. Were it not for these Mexican Indians and the American Indians who later joined the expedition, it is doubtful that there could have been a successful expedition at all.

Coronado's army traveled north from Mexico for some 1,500 miles (2,400 km) through the Apache lands of what is now Arizona into pre-sent-day New Mexico. On the Rio Grande, Coronado asked directions from a man he called The Turk (because he was dark-skinned), who explained that his people had no gold – it was all farther east in what is now Kansas, where the people were so rich that even their canoes were made of glittering gold.

Coronado headed for Kansas, with The Turk. He crossed the Pecos River into West Texas and went north through Oklahoma. He finally reached Kansas near the present-day town of Abilene, but found no gold canoes there. Frustrated, he turned back to Mexico after first ordering the execution of "The Turk."

A LEGACY OF CONQUEST

From where did *conquistadores* (Spanish for "conquerors"), whose influence lingered in the American Southwest for centuries, come? Where they went was in search of gold.

When Spain sought to colonize the Americas at the beginning of the 16th century, it was the military who led the way, first with the landing near Veracruz by Hernán Cortés in 1519, who then headed inland with 400 soldiers to begin the conquest of Aztec Mexico. He gained an ally with the independent city of Tlaxcala and conquered the Aztec capital at Tenochtitlán, now Mexico City. By 1524, most of present-day Mexico had been conquered by the conquistadores, with the help of the Tlaxcalans.

In South America, Inca Peru was subdued by two Spanish adventurers, Francisco Pizarro and Diego de Almagro, who had first settled on the Isthmus of Panama. In 1531, Pizarro left with 180 men and 37 horses to start his conquest of Peru, which was in civil war at the time. Pizarro captured the Inca ruler and, with the help of Almagro, took Cuzco, the capital, in 1533. Pizarro established a new capital at Lima. In 1538, Pizarro and Almagro were at each other's throats in their own war; Pizarro won but was murdered in 1541. From Peru, the conquistadores extended Spain's control over much of South America – soon replaced by Spanish administrators.

Neither Coronado nor any of the other conquistadors found the gold and jewels they sought. Most of them returned to Mexico City in disappointment, and, after their discouraging reports, few followed them into the desert in search of fabulous treasure. The conquistadors themselves, weary and aging, had come to that time of life when even old soldiers have to settle down and retire. The conquest was over. Even the mighty Cortés lamented, "I am wasted, and exhausted, by all I have done…"

By themselves, the conquistadors could never have conquered the Southwest. In the rugged mountains and deserts, their medieval military tactics and armor were of little use, nor did they have the spirituality – despite the pervasiveness of the Catholic Church in the New World – needed to comprehend the deep religiousness of the Indians. So disillusioned were the latter-day conquistadors that they even forgot their discovery of California. Not until more than two centuries after the voyage of Cabrillo did Juan Bautista de Anza set forth to settle California, in 1777. In the end, it was left to the Spanish missionaries to accomplish what the conquistadors could not: conquer the land.

Missionaries seek souls, not gold

The missionaries came to conquer not by force of arms, but by settlement and religious fervor. Of course, when the Indians rejected "peaceful" conquest, the religious conquistadors set down their plowshares, took up swords, and forced their rule on the native tribes.

The Franciscan padres in New Mexico and the Jesuits in Arizona and Texas did more than baptize and make Christians of these Indians. (From 1591 until 1631, the Jesuits alone baptized 151,240 Indians.) They tried to transform the Indians into Spanish peasants, to "attract the nomadic tribes to a peaceful, sedentary life." As the Jesuit Father Juan Nentuig wrote in 1763, the Christian Indians were "more inclined to work…[and]…to till their lands."

The missions of the Jesuits were more than churches. Into their hands was placed the responsibility for government and the economy. The missions became the centers of farming, commerce and education. To the suspicious Spanish officials, the rather autonomous Jesuits

seemed to be building an ecclesiastical empire within the Spanish provinces. What was worse, many of the Jesuits were not even Spaniards – not with names like Pfefferkorn, Benz, Kino, Stiger and Nentuig. Nevertheless, when Jesuits asked for permission to raise their own army, the Spaniards often agreed. (In one case, prisoners were released from the jails of Mexico City and sent out to protect the missions.)

In New Mexico, the mission churches of the Franciscans were more like fortresses than places of worship. The walls were sometimes 7 feet (2 meters) thick. After the Pueblo revolt of 1680, when Indians killed 22 Franciscans, the

missionaries protected themselves with Indian slaves and mercenaries.

Even so, in 1792 the Franciscan Juan Domingo Arricivita called for the "protection of troops in order to propagate the faith." It was "impossible without them," he said. And from 1744 to 1745, when the Visitador to Sonora, Juan Antonio Balthasar, had visited the San Xavier de Bac mission of the Tohono O'odham at Tucson, he requested "soldiers to force these Indians to live in the Pueblo," as it was clear that "just a hint of soldiering is necessary" to make them go to church.

But not all the missionaries were so eager to take up arms against their parishioners. Father

LEFT: a 19th-century print of the interior of Acoma Church. RIGHT: reenactment of Spanish procession.

Eusébio Francisco Kino, the Jesuit who founded the San Xavier de Bac mission, just south of present-day Tucson, would have objected to such a policy. He wanted the Indians treated as brothers. One of the most courageous of the missionaries, he was said to have made 40 entratas into the deserts and established many missions in the region, no to mention one of the first cattle ranches in present-day Arizona. (There is currently a move to have Kino canonized.)

A true folk hero, Kino was known as the Padre on Horseback. At the age of 70, he died at the mission of Magdalena, in Sonora; his

death bed was made of two calf skins, and his pillow was a saddle. His eulogist, Father Luis Velarde, said Kino died as he lived – as one with the Indians. (His bones are displayed under glass in Magdalena, Mexico.)

Settlers settle down

Shortly after arrival of the missionaries came settlers, mostly people escaping aspects of their past or lives in Mexico. They, more than the conquistadors, were the true explorers of the land. Once settled, they began detailed surveys of the countryside. As farmers, they had to know the flow and direction of every stream and river, the precise rise and fall of every

canyon and valley, the grass and trees of every pasture and forest. The settlers explored the land the ways soldiers could not; the conquistadors, riding swiftly for safety in hostile territory, mapped from horseback. But settlers walked the earth, foot by foot, and explored the territory intimately, surveying every inch of land. The old Spanish land grants, indeed, were measured and so too were the village deeds.

Hard times

Many of the settlers were poor farmers and shepherds, Mexicans from the Sonora and Chihuahua areas of Mexico. Few wealthy noblemen or old conquistadors in Mexico or Spain had any desire or need to endure the desert's severe hardships to establish a new life. As always, the immigrants were poor men and women seeking new opportunities, hoping to escape a life of poverty.

But on the poor lands of the desert, the poor settlers became poorer. The dry farming and small mines they established offered a meager existence. "Not only have the settlers of New Mexico not enjoyed riches, but the scourge of God has been upon them always, and they are the most oppressed and enslaved people in the world," the Franciscan Father Zarate de Salmeron wrote of them in 1626. "As long as they have a good supply of tobacco to smoke, they are very contented and they do not want riches, for it seems as if they have made a vow of poverty."

In the palatial mansions in Mexico City, the American Southwest was known as the "Land of the *Barbarosos*" – the barbarians – and that referred not only to the American Indians but to the "Spanish" settlers as well.

Few of the settlers who came on the entrata of Juan de Oñate into New Mexico were born in Spain. Most were Mexicans and mestizos, half-Indians, who, like de Oñate himself, were born in Sonora; he was married to an Indian woman said to be a granddaughter of Montezuma. Typical of the expeditions of the Southwest, de Oñate's entrata included as many as 1,000 Mexican Indians, outnumbering the Spanish by 10 to one. Having lived on similar land in Mexico they knew the terrain and survived more easily than the settlers. ❏

LEFT: a water carrier typical of the colonial era.
RIGHT: a *vaquero* on a Mexican *hacienda*, or ranch.

ARRIVAL OF THE ANGLOS

Unlike the Spaniards, early Anglos to the Southwest sought only pelts and trade, but they were soon settling and bringing with them a less constrained lifestyle

On the East Coast of the expanding United States, they were contemptuously known as "Squaw Men" and "White Indians." No one quite like them had ever lived on the American frontier before, and certainly no one ever will again. The mountain men who came to New Mexico and Arizona in the early 1800s were "a rare moment in history," wrote the American Indian author Vine Deloria. These men not only crossed the continent, they crossed from one culture to another.

Unlike the Spaniards, the first Anglos to settle in the Southwest came to hunt beaver and to trade, not to conquer. In the mountain wilderness where they made their homes, trappers most often lived in peace with the Mexicans and Indians already in residence.

Paradoxically, the mountain men who went West to escape the civilization of the East brought some of that civilization with them in their saddle-bags and wagons. The trade goods they offered the native people forever changed the wilderness and paved the way for the shopkeepers who replaced them. The mountain men made themselves obsolete.

One of the first mountain men in the Southwest, Baptiste le Land of the Missouri Fur Company, came to Santa Fe, New Mexico, in 1804, the same year as Lewis and Clark began their expedition of the land purchased from France. The first Anglo most Mexicans and Indians had ever seen, Le Land was, in fact, a French Creole who married an Indian woman. He was followed by James Pursell in 1805 and, in 1809, Zebulon Pike, a mapmaker and government agent who first arrived in Santa Fe as a prisoner on his way to trial in Mexico City. Pike built the first Anglo fort, of cottonwood trees, on the Conejos branch of the Rio del Norte, the Rio Grande River.

The empire of Spain then ruled the land, but just barely. It was sparsely inhabited by Spaniards, and the royal authorities were nervous about the Anglo traders and wanderers who had entered their domain.

Between 1812 and 1821, several merchant adventurers were arrested by Spanish soldiers and locked up in Chihuahua's dungeons. Not until the Mexican War of Independence in

GRIZZLED CHARACTERS

By necessity, mountain men were multicultural and multilingual, and by nature they were invariably colorful figures. The flamboyant Pauline Weaver, a hunter and agent of the Hudson Bay Company, was a gun-toting adventurer who is sometimes called the Founder of Arizona. Christopher "Kit" Carson, one of the fathers of Anglo New Mexico and known to most modern-day schoolchildren, began his career as a grizzled mountain man, then became a U.S. Army scout and officer, a respected citizen of Taos and a civic leader. He personally united the three cultures of the territory by marrying, in turn, a Mexican, an Indian and an Anglo wife.

PRECEDING PAGES: first passenger train to the Grand Canyon, 1901. **LEFT:** U.S. Army officers picnic near Fort Thomas, Arizona. **RIGHT:** Kit Carson.

1822, and the founding of the Mexican Republic in 1824, did the atmosphere change. The Territory of Nuevo Mexico was established, a vast territory that included New Mexico and Arizona, and where the Anglo mountain men and merchants were welcomed in a friendlier manner.

In his "Report on Foreigners" in 1825, the Governor of New Mexico, Antonio Narbona, wrote of 20 Anglos arriving in a single month, half of them merchants. By 1827, a similar monthly report listed 36 Anglos, of whom 31

TRAILING WEALTH

From 1822 to 1844, the value of the merchandise carried on the Santa Fe Trail increased from an estimated $15,000 each year up to nearly $450,000.

true spirit of Western enterprise," for these men believed the "many strange and marvelous stories of inexhaustible wealth" that were told about the West.

Becknell's expedition opened the way to the West. In Congress, Senator Thomas Benton introduced a bill to maintain a road to New Mexico. It made more sense. Since the distance was much shorter from Missouri than from Mexico City, goods could be sold more cheaply by the Anglo traders than by the Mexican entratas.

were merchants who "to sell their goods remain for some time in the towns," but have "no intentions of settling themselves."

Santa Fe Trail

With the establishment of the Santa Fe Trail from Missouri, wagon trains and caravans crowded the trails that led West. By 1821, the Missouri frontiersman William Becknell led his "company of men destined to the westward" to New Mexico. Of these traders, George Sibley wrote in 1825 that "the first adventurers were hardy, enterprising men who, being tired of the dull and profitless pursuits of husbandry, were determined to turn merchants and traders in the

The merchant wagons brought with them a new way of life into the Southwest. Not only were luxury itmes such as champagne, beer, whiskey and rum introduced, but also oranges, lemons, cherries, whale-oil candles, tobacco, Epsom salts, straw hats, silk handkerchiefs, dried fish and hundreds of other products became available.

In their dusty wake, the merchant wagons also brought settlers. They homesteaded, planted crops, established ranches and built towns – all on Mexican and Indian land grants to which they had no title. For generations afterward, the ownership of the land would be under dispute. It often still is.

American soldiers arrive

The settlers were soon followed by soldiers. In 1846, President Polk sent General Stephen Watts Kearny to the West to conquer New Mexico, but the anticipated war with Mexico became more an occupation than a conquest. In a treaty signed with Mexico in 1848, the United States paid $15 million for New Mexico, Arizona, Utah, Nevada, California and part of Colorado.

After the Mexican War, few federal troops besides General Kearny's small detachment were stationed in New Mexico and Arizona. With so few troops to defend them, the territo-

ident Andrew Johnson after the Civil War between the American North and South. "Hostilities are therefore kept up (against the Apache) with a view of supporting the inhabitants…" Even that irony was compounded by the sending of the 10th Cavalry, composed largely of former slaves, to subdue and control the Southwest-area Indians.

Arizona presented a dramatic contrast to New Mexico: the settlers who populated the western desert were a different breed to those who had settled in New Mexico. Few people chose to venture into the lands of the aggressive Apache, thus only a small number of trading

ries were nearly lost during the Civil War to the Confederacy, which had seen a vacuum in the Southwest and tried unsuccessfully to exploit it.

The supplying of merchandise and food to the troops became the region's largest and most profitable business. Many an old family fortune was built on government contracts, something of an irony for people who prided themselves on rugged individualism.

"Almost the only paying business the white inhabitants of the territory have is supplying the troops," General Edward Ord wrote to Pres-

centers, farm towns and ranches were established in the Arizona region. The main settlements were mining towns such as Tombstone, Jerome and Prescott – all in the southern part of the territory – that eventually produced billions of dollars in silver and copper ore.

Even in the early centuries of Spanish colonization, few settlers had ventured into Arizona because of the Apache, whose skill in warfare took on near-legendary status. From the 1600s, the Apache, fighting from their mountain strongholds, successfully held back the European invaders. In 1630, Padre Alonzo Benavides called them a "people fiery and bellicose and very crafty in war." In fact, the Apache

LEFT: an 1840 map of the Republic of Mexico.
ABOVE: wagons on the Santa Fe Trail.

were a nomadic people, less interested in conquering places and capturing people than in taking horses and cattle. By the 1760s, in spite of the efforts of the staunch Jesuit missionaries, the Spaniards had to abandon nearly 50 settlements and 126 ranches throughout Arizona. By 1775, Padre Bartolomo Ximeno reported that there were only 10 horses and 56 cows left in the territory that the Apache had not stolen.

Those Anglos who did settle in Arizona were mostly Southerners, and although there were few slaves in the area, there was a lively slave trade in Apache children. During the Civil War, Arizona, unlike New Mexico, sided with the slave states of the Confederate south. The citizens of Tucson voted to join the Confederacy, and in 1862 the Confederate Congress proclaimed Arizona a Confederate territory. Despite their former rebel sympathies, the Anglo settlers in Arizona were happy to welcome the U.S. Army after the Civil War ended. The Indian Wars, fought to open more territory for settlement, were largely conflicts between nomads and settlers, and when faced with modern military campaigns, they often surrendered.

In 1865, the Mescalero headman Victorio told Lieutenant Colonel N.H. Davis that "I and my people want peace. We are tired of war. We are poor and have little to eat and wear. We want to make peace." Davis replied: "Death to the Apache, and peace and prosperity to this land, is my motto." General Edward Ord added his agreement; the Apache, he declared, were "vermin to be killed when met."

Not everyone among the conquering forces agreed. General George Crook, who led the capture of Geronimo, said of the Apache, "I wish to say most emphatically that [this] American Indian is the intellectual peer of most, if not all, the various nationalities who have assimilated to our laws…"

Cowboys and ranches

During the 1870s, ranching became a new way of life in the west. Huge cattle outfits spread out over the territory; ranches such as the vast Matador, King and Lumpkin ran tens of thousands of cattle on hundreds of thousands of open ranges. Not many years after the Civil War and the Indian Wars had ended, the so-called Range Wars began. These were battles between sheepmen and cattlemen over grazing lands. One of the most famous was the Lincoln County War, in New Mexico, where Billy the Kid (born in Brooklyn) earned his reputation as a gunman. In reality, the Kid worked as a busboy and waiter in a café in the town of Shakespeare; he was no more a cowboy than was Wyatt Earp, Bat Masterson or Doc Holliday, the dentist. Few, if any, ranch-working cowboys ever fought in the Range Wars.

On the ranches of the Southwest, the cowboy of English-Irish-Scottish-German ancestry inherited the older Western traditions of the Mexican and Indian *vaquero*. Southerner and Easterner, Mexican and American Indian, Spaniard and Anglo, they all merged into a new

A LONG WALK INTO HELL

Like their Apache cousins – both tribes have common ancestry and cultures – the Navajo people had a fierce reputation. They were like "wolves that run through the mountains," said one U.S. Army general, and they needed removing by force. In 1863, Kit Carson was commissioned by the U.S. Army to round up the Navajos and ship them to a camp in eastern New Mexico. Rather than fighting the Navajo, Carson starved them out by destroying their livestock and crops. By 1865, more than 8,000 Navajo had been sent on the Long Walk of 300 miles (480 km). Some 400 died on the walk while thousands more died in the camp at Bosque Redondo.

and unique figure known as the Westerner. Perhaps more than anything else, it was the earth and sky that shaped cowboy culture. There was nothing in their experience back East to prepare the Anglos for such awesome vistas.

In the beginning, the cattle ranches resembled those of Sonora and Chihuahua in northern Mexico, built in the adobe styles of the Southwest. And during the old days of Spanish rule, the ranches were feudal fiefdoms with *haciendas* that were entire towns. But later ranches of the Anglos were rough frugal buildings, reflecting the pioneer life of their owners.

A COWBOY DITTY

The cowboy's life is a dreadful life
He's driven through heat and cold
I'm almost froze with water on my
    clothes,
A-ridin' through heat and cold.

The buckaroo is born

In time, with the meeting of divergent cultures under the inhospitable desert sun, a new breed – the buckaroo – was created: he was, as the old saying goes, "Tough as a longhorn cow, and just as dumb." The cowboy "yell" was a way of proclaiming one's manhood, and one of the old cowboy yells of the Southwest says it all: "Whe-ee-o, I'm a bad man! Whoopeee! Raised in the backwoods, suckled by a polar bear, nine rows of jaw teeth, a double coat of hair, steel ribs, wire intestines and a barbed wire tail, and I don't give a dang where I drag it. Whoopwhee-ha!"

Ranch women of those days were not about to be outdone by their men, thinking themselves to be as tough as the men. One proper lady described herself in 1887: "My bonnet is a hornet's nest, garnished with wolves' tails and eagle feathers. I can wade the Mississippi without getting wet, out scream a catamount (mountain lion), jump over my own shadow... and cut through the bushes like a pint of whiskey among forty men."

The modest, laid-back, low-key, taciturn style of the 20th-century cowboy was not that of his 19th-century ancestor. The first cowboys of the Southwest were lusty, ribald, raucous men who lived with a gusto that reflected the Victorian appetites of the era. With the passing of the open range and the fencing of the New Mexico and Arizona ranges, the Anglo ranchers and

cowboys were doomed. The turn of the century turned their memories into nostalgia. The last of the old-time cowboys, together with some of the old lawmen and outlaws, joined Buffalo Bill's Wild West Show or Teddy Roosevelt's Rough Riders, and were largely recruited in New Mexico and Arizona.

When the cattle drives ended and the stagecoach trails faded, replaced by the railroad, the desert silence was shattered by the din of railroads and motorcars that brought thousands of newcomers. These were the new

Anglos, the sick seeking the sun, the land developers seeking a tidy fortune, and the artists seeking a new light and new colors.

As the 19th century ended, artists discovered the Southwest. Ernest Blumenschein and Bert G. Phillips settled in Taos, New Mexico, in 1898. In 1916, Mabel Dodge Luhan moved her New York salon to Taos. A few years later, novelist D.H. Lawrence, a temporary resident, was to proclaim, "There are all kinds of beauty in the world, but for a greatness of beauty I have never experienced anything like New Mexico."

The old-timers were to become a part of the artists' scenery and the writers' stories, and even a few legends. ❑

LEFT: Manuelito, Navajo leader during the Long Walk.
RIGHT: the Apache chief Geronimo (lower row, second from left) and other Chiricahua Apache prisoners.

CONTEMPORARY TIMES

Air conditioning and the hot, dry weather gave the Southwest an appeal
that lured people from colder climes to the area's warm embrace

By World War I, the old frontier life was gone – but not quite. Gone were the long-horns and the great cattle drives on the Goodnight Trail. Gone were most of the gunslingers and bandidos, but by no means all. Even so, there was still plenty of the frontier atmosphere left. Many of the old gunfighters,

those who had not died of "lead poisoning," were still alive. Pat Garrett, the sheriff who killed Billy the Kid, was himself dry-gulched in 1908 with a bullet in his head, at a time when such goings-on were presumably a thing of the past. The great gambling saloons of the Southwest closed their doors sometime between 1900 and 1911, outlawed due to an influx of "good women," but in the red-light districts the "soiled doves of the prairie" still did a land-office business.

Mexican bandidos still strayed across the border to raise havoc on the wrong side of the Rio Grande. And trains were still robbed at gunpoint until the outbreak of World War I.

Revolution to the south

The Mexican Revolution (1910–23) brought plenty of excitement, and it actually started on American soil in 1911 when Francisco Madero led a few hundred followers across the Rio Grande to start the civil war that would topple the Mexican dictator, the "Old Cacique" Porfirio Díaz. A decisive battle was fought at Juarez between the revolutionary army, led by Pancho Villa and Pascual Orozco, and the Porfiristas, led by Vásquez Gómez. The rebels won a brilliant victory, while Americans on the El Paso (Texas) side across the river had a grand-stand view, watching the battle from their roofs and the tops of railroad cars.

In 1912, freshly escaped from jail and fleeing for his life, Villa holed up in a fleapit hotel in El Paso's Chamizal district. Soon he was back in Mexico to meet up with Zapata in Mexico City. Relations between the revolutionaries and the American Government fluctuated between good and bad. At a time when they were bad, in 1916, Villa made his famous raid on Columbus, a sleepy New Mexico frontier town where the only previous excitement in the town's history was a plague of rattlesnakes.

The battle in Columbus between the Villistas and Americans grew into one of the greatest shoot-outs the Southwest had ever experienced. It resulted in the death of 16 Americans and a

GERONIMO AND TECHNOLOGY

For American Indians, changes in the new century were bewildering. The Apache chief Geronimo, born in 1829, had grown up as a technologically stone-age man; his first weapons were stone-tipped arrows. Shortly before his death in 1909, as a member of the Dutch Reformed Church, he attended a convention of cattlemen in Tucson. In his hotel room he was confronted by newfangled symbols of civilization – electric lights and the flush toilet, which he did not know how to use. As nobody had told him how to turn off the lamp at his bedside, he simply put his boot over it. Later, he was photographed at the wheel of an early Ford automobile.

punitive U.S. Army chase under "Black Jack" Pershing in a fruitless pursuit of Villa.

The period around World War I has been described as a time of the gringo, a period of racial tension as Anglo newcomers engulfed the Spanish-speaking communities while looking down upon Hispanics. Statehood for both Arizona and New Mexico was held up as lawmakers and preachers alike opposed statehood. One congressman argued, "We don't want any more states until we civilize Kansas!" The Ari-

FROM TWO, ONE

While considering statehood (granted in 1912) for New Mexico and Arizona, Congress considered making one state from both, to be called Montezuma.

God, you are a better looking man than your picture, you old son-of-a-bitch." Teddy, the one-time cowboy, took it as a compliment.

Modern amenities were slow to arrive in the Southwest. Flagstaff got its first telephone in 1900, with 85 subscribers throughout the county. The first steam-powered automobile arrived in 1902. Electricity came in 1904. Teachers were scarce as their salaries were fixed at $75 a month, while room and board cost $40.

Miners had infested the Southwest during the

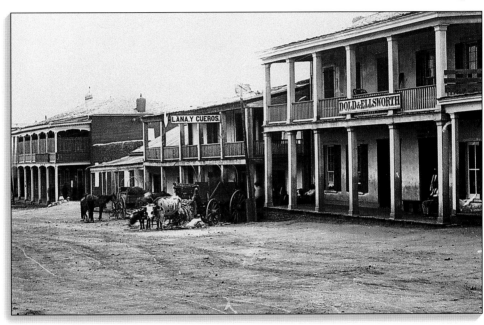

zona Legislature passed a law stipulating that 80 percent of workers in the state had to be American-born, a measure directed against immigrant Mexicans and Asians.

Economic upswings

Development proceeded slowly. After all, New Mexico's state motto is Crescit Eundo – it grows as it goes. Frontier manners remained rough for many years. In Flagstaff, Sandy Donohue, barkeep at the Senate Saloon, greeted President Teddy Roosevelt by declaring, "By

late 19th century, but gold's best year was 1915, when New Mexico produced $1,461,000 worth of what the ancient Indians had called the "Dung of the Gods."

Silver was found in some abundance throughout the region, though never rivaling the famed silver lodes of Nevada and Colorado. The most silver produced in New Mexico was $1,162,200, in 1910. By 1950 this had dwindled to about $100,000 per year.

Luckily, the Southwest had a wealth of other desirable minerals, and copper soon became king. When American industry began demanding copper, mines and mining towns once again mushroomed overnight. Coal also became

LEFT: Zapata (left) and Pancho Villa in the presidential chair. **ABOVE:** Santa Fe in the 1880s.

important, particularly with the ever expanding networks of railroads which needed the black stuff for their engines. After copper and coal came potash, and a number of more exotic minerals such as cobalt, antimony and molybdenum. As one metal was replaced by another, new communities sprang up.

Early Anglo settlers had come to till the region's soil. In 1900, 5 million acres (2 million hectares) of land were under cultivation in New Mexico alone, and by 1910 the state had 35,000 farms. Lack of rain wiped out many of these farmers, and in 1911 the first of the big dams – Roosevelt Dam – was built in Arizona. Irriga-

tion resuscitated much of the farming, although eventually the small farmer was replaced by large agribusiness.

Some 90 percent of Southwest land is unsuited to cultivation, yet is good cattle country. But cattle don't grow fat on Southwest ranches. (They are raised and sold to cattle feed lots in the Midwest and elsewhere.) By 1910 there were 40,000 miles (64,000 km) of barbed wire in Arizona alone.

The end of open ranges meant the end of old-fashioned cowboys. In 1892, a Western writer lamented that "railroads and bobwire *(sic)* spell the demise of that colorful character."

BARBED-WIRE BLESSINGS

Ubiquitous not only in the American Southwest but throughout the country – anywhere land is plentiful but divided – is the barbed-wire fence, silvery threads of metal strung from pole to pole, punctuated with sharp barbs.

There are actually several dozen types of barbed wire in use, though increasingly only one type is seen on America's open ranges: two longitudinal wires twisted together with wire barbs wrapped around the wires at regular spacings. There is a purpose to using two, intertwined wires, as it not only makes the fence stronger but also allows the wire to contract and expand under the West's temperature and weather extremes.

Patents on barbed wire were first issued in the United States in 1867. But barbed wire wasn't widely used until 1874, when Joseph Glidden (after seeing a sample at a fair in 1873) devised a suitable machine for its manufacture. Within 15 years, barbed-wire fences, intended primarily to restrict movement of cattle, had enclosed most of the country's open range.

Although Glidden's patents on his manufacturing process were challenged, he eventually prospered by selling his business.

A modern variation is the electrified fence, which is typically a single strand of barbed wire, electrified.

Shifts in Indian communities

Changes were coming to Indian communities too. In 1919, Indian men who had enlisted in the army to fight the country's enemies became eligible for U.S. citizenship. Oil was discovered on Navajo land, bringing income to the tribe that had wisely invested in education and other projects beneficial to all. In 1922, Pueblo Indians formed the All Pueblo Council to fight the so-called Bursum Bill, legislation that was designed to secure the right to Indian land for white squatters. In 1924, American citizenship was conferred upon all Indians born within the borders of the United States.

In 1934, the Indian Reorganization Act gave the right of partial self-government to the tribes. As a result, tribal constitutions were framed and tribal presidents and councils democratically elected. It was a mixed blessing. The elected leaders often represented the more assimilated, educated and English-speaking sector of the Indian population, while the traditional Indians saw no reason to adopt forms of self-rule patterned after the system of government practiced by non-Indians.

Instead, they adhered to traditional dependence on elders or religious chiefs. This led, in some places, to a simmering conflict between the "Progressives" and the "Traditionals."

Meanwhile, lagging behind the Anglos in economic gains and the professions, Hispanic Americans of New Mexico concentrated on politics and wound up effectively running the state. One author, Francis Stanley, wrote:

"Politics is a religion above the family. It streams into the *niño* (child) from his mother's breasts; it is patted into the tortilla, and ladled with the frijole, masticated with every mouthful of chili, washed down with every glass of beer. Sacred, ingrained, ritualistic, mysterious, it is its race, color, creed – politics."

Gold and silver mining became mostly a distant memory and many unproductive coal mines were shut down. (Still, potash mining started in a big way in 1931.) Natural gas became a source of income in the 1920s, and the Southwest enjoyed a number of moderate oil booms. Large copper mines opened in Arizona and New Mexico.

In 1936, Hoover Dam was completed. Water, or rather the lack of it, was becoming a problem. Many of the old-timers complained that modern industry, farming, ranching, tourists and the increased population were "pumping the West dry." It was true.

Shades of secrecy

In 1942, the U.S. Army took over land belonging to a boys' school at Los Alamos, in northern New Mexico west of Santa Fe. In the words of Erna Ferguson, "No secret was ever better kept than that of Los Alamos.

The schoolboys had it that they were moving out for the Ethiopian Ski Corps or the Scan-

LEFT: on the Grand Canyon's rim in 1914.
RIGHT: Hoover Dam brought electricity to the region.

TIMELESS SOUTHWEST IN ART

The Southwest has lured artists and writers to its embrace in the past century, amongst them the notable artist Georgia O'Keeffe, who arrived in Taos for the first time in 1917 and immediately fell in love with the place. In a letter to photographer – and lover – Alfred Stieglitz, she described the New Mexican landscape as "a perfectly mad-looking country – hills and cliffs and washes too crazy to imagine all thrown up into the air by God and let tumble where they would." By the time she died in 1986, O'Keeffe had painted not the Old Southwest or the New Southwest, but a timeless Southwest of light and colour, and of geology and life.

dinavian Camel Artillery. Santa Feans saw lights against the Jemez peaks, but knew nothing." Meanwhile, a town of 8,000 people was springing up almost overnight in the vicinity of the state capital and without anyone being aware of it.

Landlocked and chronically thirsty, the Southwest at the end of World War II was remote but hardly unknown. Railroads, highways and scheduled flights made access easy. Inhabitants shipped out iron, T-bones steaks and grapefruit, and got back dude ranchers and tourists doing the national-park circuit. Yet each state seemed in a private trance. Arizona, focus

of frantic Air Force activity during World War II, returned to its three Cs: cotton, cattle and copper. New Mexico, with its Pueblo and Hispanic agricultural traditions, changed primarily with the seasons.

Southwest Nevada, in decline since the silver boom of the 1800s, was a polity of sand and collapsing buildings. And southern Utah deliberately stayed out of the postwar mainstream to preserve the isolation and purity of its Mormon culture.

The Southwest in 1945 resembled the Great Basin of Utah and Nevada, whose rivers deadend in separate valleys instead of reaching out

to the sea. Like the Great Basin to its north, the Southwest was facing inward, fixed on its several selves.

Great and mighty dams

A federal role was crucial in developing what all Southwesterners demanded: more and more water. Reclamation was hardly a new idea. The Southwest had received the Reclamation Act in 1902, the Hoover Dam on the Colorado River in 1935 and countless dams by federal, state and private concerns. But with the war effort over, the Bureau of Reclamation could direct its attention westward in a major way, and it made proposals for every watercourse.

Its grandest single monument was Glen Canyon Dam, completed in 1963 near Page and backing water 180 river miles (290 km) into some of the Colorado River's least-known and most spectacular canyons; and its most ambitious scheme is the ongoing Central Arizona Project, to channel water from the Colorado River to Phoenix and Tucson at a cost of more than four times the original estimate of a billion dollars.

Federal stimulation of the Southwestern economy developed a wide spectrum of activities and shifted the balance of power in the Southwest. Much of the driest and least productive land had been allotted to the military

during World War II, and the military kept it. During the 1950s, the salt and alkali basins of Nevada became the site of hundreds of underground nuclear tests, and Hill Air Force Base in Utah became the West's leading missile center. Towns like Yuma and Sierra Vista, in Arizona, are virtual adjuncts to the military, and many of the most empty reaches of the Southwest are off-limits to civilians.

Ironically, much of the land in the hands of the military – scarred by tanks, pounded by artillery, glittering with shrapnel – has remained

LEFT: Kitt Peak National Observatory and dam on the Colorado River. **ABOVE:** potash miner, New Mexico.

SAVING THE GRAND CANYON?

Been to the Grand Canyon lately during the summer months? Was it a serene, contemplative effort, especially when trying to park? Disappointed by how schlockingly commercial it is just outside the park boundaries?

In 1999, the Federal government announced a plan to develop some national forest land just outside Grand Canyon National Park – and environmentalists applauded it as a model for the future. The cooperation, and compromises, between developers, government and environmentalists is rare on these issues. Supporting the plan are state agencies and Arizona's Indian tribes.

The plan is to develop a new village – Canyon Forest Village – on 272 acres (110 hectares) of national forest land at the southern entrance to the park, at Tusayan and at a cost of $330 million. Canyon Forest Village will include 1,270 hotel rooms and more than 250,000 sq. ft (23,200 sq. meters) of retail space. Also included is 20 acres (8 hectares) of housing for people working within the national park. Water for the village would be brought in rather than pumped out of the Grand Canyon. Built with private money, the village will be built with ecological concessions that will assure protection for the Grand Canyon. Moreover, efficient energy systems and intensive recycling programs will minimize the need for landfills.

Plans for a new gateway to the national park were begun by the Federal government in the late 1980s. The planning was not too soon – by the end of the century, over 4½ million people visited the Grand Canyon each year. Four out of five visitors to the park arrived via Tusayan and the southern entrance. Tusayan, a simple town of less than 1,000 permanent residents, fast became overwhelmed by the unstructured and unplanned demands made upon it by the swelling numbers of tourists. One not-so-evident need, for example, was housing for more than 500 of the people who work in the national park.

For those fed up with feeling as if they're driving in lower Manhattan during rush hour, plans for the new village include a light-rail system between Tusayan and the South Rim of the canyon. It is estimated that the trains will cut traffic in the park by 80 percent. (Ironically, it was a railway that first brought tourists to the canyon.)

The plan was made possible by land swaps of national forest land around Tusayan and private parcels. The Forest Service exchanged land at Tusayan for 2,200 acres (890 hectares) scattered elsewhere in Kaibab National Forest, land that could have been developed with no environmental safeguards at all. In this case, everyone involved – the U.S. government, private landowners, developers, environmentalists, Indians – were satisfied and happy with the exchange of land.

relatively intact, while the drive for minerals, timber and cheap energy has caused more lasting devastation.

Mining on federal land was encouraged by minimal fees and scant regulation, while timber contracts didn't – and still don't – make that most basic requirement that a new tree be planted for each cut down. In the early 1950s, uranium prospectors gouged roads at random across southern Utah, leaving permanent scars. Uranium was developed more systematically in northwestern New Mexico in the 1970s, leaving behind carcinogenic mill tailings for the Indian inhabitants.

But it was coal, abundant and often lying near the surface, that became the most coveted resource. In 1957, a Utah coal company made the first contract with the Navajo Tribal Council to extract coal beneath Navajo land. The major oil companies, sensing that the coal beds of the Colorado Plateau were a vital energy source, began acquiring coal companies and turning them into subsidiaries. Cities like Los Angeles and Phoenix badly needed new energy but had to generate it elsewhere. Ample coal in southern Utah and northern Arizona could be burned on the spot. Power would surge through transmission lines to immense cities hundreds of miles away.

In 1974 a consortium of 21 utilities, representing seven states, banded together and proposed a mesh of strip mines, power plants and transmission lines of unprecedented complexity. Not all of the proposed grid came into being, but major coal-fired power plants went up in Farmington, New Mexico, and Page, Arizona. The Page plant, near Glen Canyon Dam, was linked by a company railroad to a strip mine 70 miles (110 km) east on Black Mesa, a formation sacred to the Hopi.

Retirees and real estate

While energy battles were being fought on the Colorado Plateau, the warmer lands to the south were filling up with humanity. With the introduction of air-conditioning during World War II, suddenly no desert was too hot for colonization. Snowbelt retirees settled in vast retirement communities like Sun City, in tracts and trailer parks along the Colorado River from Boulder City, Nevada, to Yuma, Arizona, and even in the small towns of New Mexico.

While traditional industries like copper mining and small-scale ranching fell into decline, high-technology industries in Albuquerque, Phoenix and Tucson drew ambitious young people from elsewhere to the area, balancing the demographics and at the same time inflating the population.

Mesquite gave way to mobile home communities, to pseudo-adobe duplex compounds, to townhouse labyrinths around artificial lakes that obliterated the desert. One developer brought the London Bridge to the Colorado River and ran the world's tallest fountain on subsiding groundwater merely to promote his ventures. Easier on the terrain was outright land fraud, wherein development took place on paper, and the land, if any, was spared.

The 1990s brought unbridled, unfettered extravagance to that odd little city of Las Vegas, with several $1.5-*billion* hotels ushering in the new millennium. The national parks of southern Utah and northern Arizona were buried in tourists, requiring that light-rail trains or bus shuttles be introduced into Grand Canyon and Zion national parks. And through it all, cities in the Southwest continued to be the fastest-growing cities in America. ❏

LEFT: the space shuttle lands at White Sands Missile Range, New Mexico. **RIGHT:** Las Vegas tiki head.

THE MILITARY'S PLACE IN THE SUN

The Southwest's important military bases are used for development of stealth technology, atomic weapons, missiles, aircraft and training

In the wide-open and sparsely populated vastness of the Southwest, the U.S. military has placed a number of installations – depots, attack aircraft training centers, fighter weapons centers, research and development weapons test centers and fighter wings. The cloudless skies certainly make ideal flying conditions. As all pilots know, there are huge restricted air zones, not to be entered by unauthorized aircraft, so as not to be blown to smithereens in a missile test. Given the secrecy that surrounds such activities, and the human thirst for mystery, one must occasionally ponder what goes on in those extremely remote, fenced, and heavily guarded sites. Take Site 51, a restricted Air Force base in the isolation of the Nevada desert. The government even denied the existence of the installation, but eventually issued this statement: "We do have facilities within [Site 51]. The facilities of the Nellis Range Complex are used for testing and training technologies, operations, and systems critical to the effectiveness of U.S. military forces. Specific activities conducted at Nellis cannot be discussed any further than that." The site was selected in the mid-1950s for testing of the U-2 spy plane, due to its remoteness, proximity to existing facilities and presence of a dry lake bed for landings.

ATOMIC SECRETS

In New Mexico in 1942 there was enough room and privacy to cloak housing and laboratories for physics' upper echelon as they developed the world's first atomic bomb. The weapon was tested in July 1945 in the desert region named Jornada del Muerto (Dead Man's Route, appropriately), about halfway between Albuquerque and Las Cruces. The project code name was Manhattan; the test site code name was Trinity. A second bomb was dropped on Hiroshima on August 6; a third on Nagasaki on August 9. Nearly 100,000 people died.

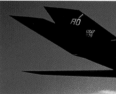

▷ **FLYING PUMPKIN SEED**
The deltoid shape of the F-117, first deployed in 1982, sends a thrill through anyone who sees it in flight. Its proven weapon systems enabled development of the F-22.

▷ **BASIC IS BASIC**
These soldiers at Lackland Air Force Base in Texas find that basic training has not changed with advances in military technology.

◁ **BIRD OF PREY**
The F-22's characteristics, such as reduced radar screen imprint and low visibility, give it the advantage of surprise.

THE 1947 ROSWELL INCIDENT

On June 14, 1947, a rancher in Lincoln County, New Mexico, found unusual debris on his property. He had found weather balloons twice before, but not like this one. On July 7, having heard reports of crashed "flying discs", he reported his find. The military examined the wreckage, a bundle of tinfoil, paper, tape, sticks, and rubber weighing about 5 pounds (2 kg), and determined it was indeed the remains of a weather balloon. All was quiet until 1978 when the drama resumed in books, tabloid print and TV, all crying cover-up. The furor grew until the early 1990s when the government began an investigation into the events, again determining the scraps to be balloon. Just enough discrepancy remained to keep the juicy conspiracy theory alive.

△ **MISSILE PARKING**
The White Sands Missile Range Missile Park displays more than 50 items. The largest, the Redstone, is 69 feet (21 meters) long; the smallest is 42 inches (106 cm).

◁ **HOME BASE**
Edwards Air Force Base has seen more major milestones in flight than any other place on earth.

▷ **WHO? WHY? WHAT??**
Major Jesse Marcel, intelligence officer at Roswell Army Air Field, in July 1947, displaying the mysterious wreckage that many people believe was an alien space ship.

THE NATIVE AMERICANS

Living in this part of the world more than 100 centuries before the Spanish
discoverers arrived, these proud and varied people are the "original Americans"

Whether they are called "American Indians" or "Native Americans" seems to matter less to most individuals than their tribal identity. Native American people tend to think of themselves first as members of a particular tribe, and many tribes further differentiate according to specific locales. Even tribal names such as Navajo, Ute or Pueblo are mere labels attached to the tribes by Europeans who were unable to pronounce – or did not bother to discover – the name each tribe has to identify itself.

The myth that all "Indians" are alike still persists, but nowhere is this falsehood easier to disprove than in the Southwest. For here, often within a few miles, are Native American communities whose cultural and linguistic differences are as pronounced as those between England and Turkey.

Creation or migration?

All tribes in the Southwest have religious beliefs connecting their creation and the creation of the Universe with a higher force or being. Each tribe has its own particular story of Creation, and anthropological theories about origins in Asia or the South Seas are firmly rejected by many Native American people.

Regardless of how the Native Americans came to the Southwest, when the Spanish arrived in 1540, Native American people had already been living there for some 10,000 years. It is within this immense span of time that the tribes of the Southwest have come to understand their intimate relationship with Earth, the Mother Creator for many Pueblo tribes. Mountains, hills, streams and springs are sacred; they can point to them and say, "This is where our people come from." They can point to the ruins of ancient villages and say, "These are the footprints of our ancestors." Even today, there are Indians who can trace the migration of

their ancestors for thousands of years. It is no wonder, therefore, that Native Americans feel spiritually rooted to the land.

It is difficult to gauge the impact of the arrival of the Spaniards and later European settlers upon the tribal cultures of the Southwest. The difficulty lies in the fact that any attempt to

PRECEDING PAGES: Navajo petroglyphs, northeastern Arizona; Mescalero Apache ceremonial dance.
LEFT: Hopi women. **RIGHT:** Zuni with beast of burden.

SPIRITUALITY

Religion is the cornerstone of Native American identity, with many complementing ancient religious traditions with the practice of Christianity. Perhaps the most visible form of contemporary Native American religion, however, is a loosely defined movement that can be termed "American Indian Spirituality", which draws on some very general religious themes in order to forge a common intertribal spiritual identity. It exemplifies harmonious living and spiritual interconnections with the natural world; politically, it is firmly opposed to environmental exploitation and Western materialism. Also appealing to non-Indians, It is a mainstay of the New Age movement.

CLIMATE AND LAND

Whatever the tribe, the determining factors in the life patterns that were (and still are) followed have always been the weather and the terrain. The Native American people of the Southwest, no matter what their linguistic or philosophical differences, have always seen themselves in relation to the landscape around them: they regard the earth as their mother and the sky as their father. Survival, until very recently, has always depended upon powers of adaptation, not change, and upon intimate knowledge of weather patterns, clouds, animals and plants.

In places where annual rainfall and drainage patterns allowed farming, and where nearby hills and mountains offered small game or deer, groups like the Pueblo people of New Mexico and the Hopi of northern Arizona established permanent villages with massive stone-and-mortar walls to ward off the rigors of winter. The Pima and Tohono O'odham of southern Arizona settled in villages near desert springs since water was of primary concern in their locale. Their villages, while permanent, did not require elaborate masonry walls but, rather, cool, airy thatching woven from local cane to provide protection from the sun and to allow the wind to circulate throughout. Although vast cultural and linguistic differences existed between them, these communities, which farmed and supplemented crops with hunting and gathering, shared similar concerns with regard to clouds and rainfall. In religious ceremonies, the focus was always, and continues to be, on adequate rain throughout the year. Prayers for rain and careful surveillance of the sky are activities understood by all cultures engaged in farming without benefit of modern technology.

In Pueblo culture, kachinas are spiritual beings that serve as intermediaries between people and the Great Spirit – and also act as messengers between the Pueblos and the domain of the Rain People. They manifest themselves as clouds and bring life-giving rain to the arid fields. With only 10 inches (25 cm) of rain falling each year on Pueblo land, the main concern of their religion is rain and the growth of corn, their most important crop.

Because the terrain and climate of the Southwest are so unpredictable and the consequences of long droughts irreparable, all Native American tribes of the Southwest have survived here, as one Hopi elder put it, "By prayer... we live by our prayers." Thus, the figure of the Rainbow Woman arching over the Great Seal of the Navajo tribe (displayed prominently on tribal motor-pool vehicles) symbolizes, literally, the sustenance that the Rainbow Woman is believed to provide the Navajo people.

evaluate or compare the "before" of Native American cultures with the "after" is impossible. Furthermore, implicit in such an assessment are Western assumptions about "change" or "loss of cultural purity", which are appropriate only when applied to Western cultures. Western views of life and culture tend to place an inordinate emphasis on material evidence, while the Native American cultures of the Southwest tend to assert the spiritual dimension. No outsider, no matter how "expert", can truly comprehend what lies at the heart of the Navajo or Pueblo or Apache cultures.

What is visible is evidence that deep within

these Native American cultures is the profound philosophical belief in coexistence with all living things, including human beings of other races and cultures. The Native American cultures of the Southwest have continually demonstrated their belief in and respect for many alternative ways and beliefs. This adaptability and intellectual breadth enabled these cultures to survive and even thrive in the harsh Southwestern climate. Within the world view of these Southwestern Indian cultures, the fact that a medicine man has a color television in his house does not necessarily mean that he has rejected ancient beliefs and traditions; what it means is that his curiosity and belief in knowledge about all humanity have prompted him to include within his world this peculiar artifact of high-tech culture. His view is that what he might see, or learn by seeing, can strengthen his traditional healing powers.

While many of the sacred dances and ceremonies are closed to outside visitors (as a result of 150 years of onlookers often displaying boorish behavior), a great many are performed for the renewal of all human beings, and these ceremonies do include outside visitors. In fact, the Zuni Pueblo people of western New Mexico believe that, if they were to bar outsiders from their impressive Winter Solstice Shalako Cere-

who have fought and died for this land in every major war. The overwhelming richness and intensity of tribal identity may occasionally obscure the plain patriotism, also a key ingredient in the identity of a White Mountain Apache or an Isleta Pueblo. The "trusteeship" of the US Government over tribal lands is not a Native American scheme. The Founding Fathers conferred this unique (and, as some Indians see it, paternalistic) legal status upon Indian Tribes in the Commerce Clause of the US Constitution.

The unusual legal status of communities located on federal Indian reservations often

mony, the ritual would have no effect and the world would not be renewed. So the giant carved wooden masks of Shalako Dancers who appear at sundown and cross the Zuni River are witnessed every year by hundreds of people.

No-nonsense patriotism

At the same time, it is important to remember that nearly all Native American people, no matter which tribe they come from, are intensely conscious of being Americans; of being not only the original Americans, but Americans

LEFT: Navajo sand painting. **ABOVE:** reservation school children learn the tribe's history and traditions.

FIGHTING FOR THEIR COUNTRY

Native Americans have the highest record of service per capita of any other ethnic group. It is thought that their distinctive cultural values – particularly a proud warrior tradition – drives them to serve their country. The courage, determination and fighting spirit of Native Americans were recognized by American military leaders as early as the 18th century, and from the War of 1812 right through the Vietnam conflict, their numbers have been strong. One veteran says they go to war because they are "super patriots": "Any pow-wow you go to… after all the American government has done to Indian people, the American flag is still there. Always."

brings strange or interesting results. For example, in Arizona, the New Pascua Tribe of Yaqui Indians can conduct million-dollar bingo games 10 miles (16 km) west of Tucson because Arizona state laws limiting the size of bingo jackpots do not apply to the Pascua Yaqui Reservation, which lies under the federal jurisdiction of the United States Department of the Interior.

The special legal status also means that the Jicarilla Apache Tribe in northern New Mexico may manage their trophy-size elk and mule deer as they see fit, without state intervention. The result is a paradise for big-game hunters and for trout fishermen at the Jicarilla's Stone Lake Resort.

On the negative side, many Native American communities do not have direct control over the leasing or development of their tribal lands. Before these tribes can do anything on their land, they must secure the approval of the Secretary of the Department of the Interior and the Commissioner of the Bureau of Indian Affairs. The results of this 200-year-old policy toward Indian tribes is readily apparent: Native American communities are notoriously lacking in many of the modern amenities other American communities take for granted. Because neither

RESERVATIONS

There are more than 50 Native American reservations in the Southwest. They encompass the modern tribal lands of more or less separate groups. The largest and most culturally intact of these groups are the Pueblo, Navajo, Hopi, Apache, Tohono O'odham and Pima. Smaller tribes include the Havasupai of the Grand Canyon, the Ute of southern Utah, and the Paiute of northern Arizona. The Walapai, Hualapai, Mohave, Yavapai, Chemehuevi, Yuma, Cocopa, Maricopa and Yaqui live in western Arizona, but many have friends or family in Mexico.

The 17-million-acre (7-million-hectare) Navajo Reservation, which dominates the northeast corner of Arizona and spills over into New Mexico and Utah, is the largest reservation in the country, and is arguably the most dramatic and beautiful scenically.

It is important to remember when traveling on Indian reservations that you must obey all tribal laws and regulations. It is advisable to contact tribal councils before your arrival and ask about any rules or prohibitions you need to be aware of. These may include restrictions on photography, travel, fishing, hunting, hiking and carrying or consuming alcohol. If there is one golden rule, it is "Be Respectful": reservations are living, working communities, not elaborate tourist displays.

individual tribal members nor the tribe itself has "ownership" of the land, financing for housing, sewage treatment and solid-waste disposal were in past years impossible for Native American communities to obtain.

Very few of the businesses located on reservations are controlled by Native Americans. Again, until recently, it has been extremely difficult for enterprising Native American businessmen to obtain bank financing since reservation lands cannot be used as collateral. Because of these complexities, in past years tribes in the Southwest had little control over land use and development of natural resources

land. Evidence of these past abuses is visible on many reservations.

For people who trace their origins to Mother Earth, the natural-resource policies of the Department of the Interior have been particularly painful. But in recent years a gradual shift has been taking place, in which young Indian lawyers and PhDs have helped their tribes assert more control over their lands and natural resources. But always there remains a deep conflict between the traditional reverence for Mother Earth and the critical need for jobs and money and housing in communities where unemployment may run as high as 75 per cent,

on tribal lands. Large mining corporations, aided by apathetic bureaucrats in the Department of the Interior, obtained vast mineral and petroleum leases on tribal lands without paying more than token sums for these lease privileges. Although these unfortunate leases were made in the mid-1950s, many have a duration of 40 or 50 years. Equally unfortunate was the policy of the Department of the Interior allowing mining operations to strip-mine coal and uranium without requiring reclamation of the

LEFT: simple place of worship in Cochiti, New Mexico.
ABOVE: dancers mimic the eagle, going beyond the external and becoming eagles in spirit.

MINERAL WEALTH – OR WOES?

When Native Americans in the Southwest were assigned reservations in the late 19th century, many were sent to land thought nearly worthless for mining or agriculture.

That was before uranium became the driving force of the nuclear age. About half the recoverable uranium within the United States lies within New Mexico – and about half of that is beneath the Navajo Nation. Many Navajos, however, have come to oppose the mining – particularly after one morning in July 1979, when tons of radioactive uranium waste spilled into the Rio Puerco, a major source of water in that desert area. The sad repercussions of that event are still being felt.

and woefully scarce housing is often without electricity or indoor plumbing.

Because the tribes of the Southwest remained relatively untouched by Western influences for so long after the arrival of the first Spaniards, the appearance of the modern technological age is quite a shock to the eye. High-tech sewage plants are juxtaposed with sandstone walls built in AD 1000.

This juxtaposition of ancient non-European culture with a high-tech world disturbs because it raises many questions and provides no answers about the multiplicity of cultural identities. Clearly, tribal people living in the South-

west are very much part of the present and its attendant material culture.

Outsiders have often seriously misjudged the visible and superficial evidence. In 1900, Franz Boas, a towering figure in cultural anthropology, announced that the Pueblo tribes faced cultural extinction within a decade. A century later, cultural anthropologists are just beginning to realize that, as "outsiders", they are unable to understand that ineffable core of tribal identity which lies well intact beneath layers and layers of debris left behind by successive waves of explorers and invaders.

But as one old Pueblo woman said, "How much could you expect Franz Boas to know?

The United States of America hasn't even existed 250 years yet. But we have been around 9 or 10 thousand years at least."

In fact, there is a story that people in the Southwest tell about a Hopi elder who was asked if it was possible for traditional Hopi ways to survive the influences of modern American life. "The Navajos came a long time ago and raided Hopi villages," the old man is supposed to have said. "But the Navajos went away, and the Hopis are still here. Then the Spanish came with their horses, guns and Bible. The Spanish disappeared, and the Hopis are still here. Now the Americans come with electricity, automobiles and television. And perhaps, one day, they too with go away. And the Hopis will still be here."

There's no question that the Native Americans will still be here. But the conundrum disturbing middle-aged Indians today is "In what form will we exist?"

Many Native Americans of this generation have become "modernized" for various reasons, largely economic. The dilemma of one Navajo woman was recently featured in a Southwest newspaper: she, a writer for the paper, was torn between her modern world and modern conveniences and her duty – as her people's tradition dictates – to look after her elderly mother, who still lives quite contentedly in a simple hogan on the Navajo reservation in the northern part of Arizona. Most of the reporter's time is spent in her city-based apartment full of modern conveniences; as often as she can she drives the several-hour journey to visit and help her mother at her childhood home.

The end result? A large dose of guilt for not being there full-time for her mother; a feeling of leading two entirely separate lives. Like many Native Americans, she is caught between two worlds – Navajo and Anglo. She finds herself riding the fence, switching back and forth, never able to bring them together. Modern and traditonal worlds overlap, and she is forced to accommodate both as best she can.

Time and again, through centuries of war, epidemics and hunger, Native Americans have proven their resiliency, their ability to adapt. In the end, they will endure. ❑

Left: Zuni jewelry.
Right: Juan, a young Apache, around 1904.

THE PUEBLO PEOPLE

Sought long ago by the Spanish as legendary cities of gold along the Rio Grande,
the villages of the Pueblo are functional and communal towns of the desert

Details may vary from village to village, but the Pueblo people's story of the Creation begins with a single Mind that "thought" the entire Universe into existence. Once the Creation had been completed, the people and animals found themselves in a dimness full of running water, which was the First World, or the Blue World. They journeyed upward into the Red World, then into the Yellow World or Third World, where they rested before climbing upward into the White World, which was full of flowers and grass and beautiful running water. Many wanted to remain because it was a paradise, but they had been told that theirs must be the Fifth World, and a certain way of life that could be accomplished only by traveling there.

The animals, insects and plants decided they must accompany their brethren, the human beings, into the Fifth World. But when the people and creatures arrived at the opening into the Fifth World, they found the hole was blocked by a large stone.

The people tried but were unable to move the stone. The Badger People began digging with their long claws and managed to loosen the stone. But it was one of the Antelope People who decided to butt the stone. The fourth time he struck it with his head, the stone flew out of the hole and Antelope led all the people and the creatures into the Present World.

From the beginning, the Present World was filled with a great many challenges and difficulties for the people. But it is by these struggles that the people realize their spirituality and humanity and, most important, their place with all other living beings in the Universe. Thus, the Pueblo view of the world emphasizes the interdependence of human beings and animals, the lowliest insects, and the plants and trees. Pueblo clans further recognize this familial relationship by calling themselves, say, the Badger Clan or the Corn Clan. Each animal,

plant and tree that the people use to satisfy human needs has always been prayed to and asked to give itself to the people.

Among the Keresan-speaking Pueblo, for instance, a deer brought home by the hunter is placed in the center of the home and treated as a guest of honor. Turquoise is draped on the

dead animal's neck and antlers, and family and guests approach the deer to "feed" it ceremonially by placing pinches of blessed corn meal on its nose. No part of the deer's body is wasted or in any way dishonored. The hunter must participate in the Deer Dance rituals and "dance" the soul of the deer back to the mountains, where the people believe the soul will be reborn into another deer, who will remember the love and respect of the humans and thus choose to once again give its life.

The land the Pueblo people call Mother is beautiful but unpredictable, and extremes of drought or winter cold have made human survival a great challenge. For thousands of years

LEFT: Jose Toledo, noted artist of Jemez Pueblo.
RIGHT: drummers at San Ildefonso Pueblo.

the Pueblo people have met this challenge, but only with the grace of the spirits of all living beings and the love of Mother Earth. The Pueblo people are by necessity among the greatest sky watchers. In ancient Pueblo observatories, winter sun symbols were inscribed on sandstone, and special windows allowed the sun to illuminate the petroglyphs only on the winter solstice. In a land where the sky determines the fortunes of farming, religious devotion to cloud formations, winds, the positions of the sun and the moon and the tracking of the planets gave the Pueblo people the information necessary for successful agriculture.

Dances of celebration

The Present World of the Pueblo Indian people is comprised of around 20 separate Pueblo tribes in New Mexico and the Hopi Pueblo tribe in northeastern Arizona. Although the Pueblo people share similar religious beliefs which reveal a common world view, linguistic differences distinguish each group from the other.

What a visitor may see at a Pueblo today is not nearly so important as what will never be seen. Outsiders may attend a Pueblo dance but it is only part of a longer religious ritual, and certain ritual dances are now off-limits to visitors after years of bad manners by those vis-

THE REVOLT OF THE PUEBLOS

When the Spanish *conquistadores* arrived at Zuni Pueblo in 1540, they found neat, prosperous fields full of corn, beans, squash, melons and cotton, which was woven into cloth. The Spaniards, taking over the pueblos' control, taxed the agriculture. Eventually, the pueblo people got fed up and the agricultural output was barely enough to feed the people of each pueblo.

In 1680, the people of several pueblos organized a military maneuver still marveled at because of the great distances between the pueblos. Under the clandestine leadership of a San Juan Pueblo medicine man named Po Pay, the pueblo staged a great revolt on 10 August in which

Spanish priests, soldiers and settlers were slaughtered and the survivors driven out of pueblo country, to El Paso.

The pueblos were now freed of Spanish influence. But 12 years later, in 1692, the Spanish returned under the leadership of Diego de Vargas and, although the pueblo couldn't manage another military victory, the Spaniards were more cautious. Eventually, even the King of Spain realized he was dealing with governmental entities and pueblo leaders were granted limited powers of self-government and given modest parcels of land.

The Spanish retained power over the pueblo people until 1821, when Mexico gained its independence from Spain.

itors. Dances that are still accessible to visitors are important religious acts, regardless of the apparent informality of the Pueblo crowd around them. Tape recorders, still cameras and video cameras are usually prohibited.

Among the ceremonies open to the public is Taos Pueblo's San Geronimo Festival, in September. For centuries, this event has included an intertribal trade fair. On display are cottonwood drums, undecorated micaceous pottery (a gleaming pinkish ware with occasional smoke spots), and beadwork on moccasins.

In Santa Clara Canyon each July, the Puye Cliff Ceremonial takes place high atop the mesa. A modest craft show accompanies traditional dances performed against a backdrop of stone and adobe ruins. Puye, which is part of the Pajarito Plateau, is a majestic place to see a pair of eagle dancers, resplendently wearing white feathered headdresses.

Indian dances are requests to the spirit world for blessings, and they are often combined with Christian feast days. On Christmas Eve in the Catholic church of San Felipe Pueblo, for example, the spirits of the animal kingdom – as dancers representing deer or buffalo – pay homage to the Christ Child; elaborately dressed women dancers enter the church after midnight Mass. In hushed closeness, onlookers await the arrival of the procession. No one is supposed to see the dancers emerge from their *kiva*. Buffalo dancers, wearing the dark fur and horned headdress of the buffalo, with their exposed skin darkened, stomp on the floor. Deer dancers, who are bent over their sticks and whose headdresses are decked with antlers, move more lightly.

The Corn Dance is held at various times at different pueblos. Santo Domingo holds it in August on the feast of St. Dominic. It's an open-air extravaganza that involves 500 dancers aged from two to 80. Barefoot women have blue-stepped *tablita* atop their glossy black hair to symbolize a mountain with an indication of rain. They each wear a one-shouldered *manta* (woven sash), the best family jewelry, and hold a pine bough in each hand. The men wear short white embroidered kilts, long bold sashes, arm bands and moccasins. Like the women, they carry pine boughs.

In late November or early December, Zuni Pueblo holds the Shalako Ceremonial, among the most spectacular Indian celebrations. The all-night event centers on the coming of 12-foot (3.5-meter) Shalakos and their retinues, who bless new or renovated homes. Pits are dug in the floor to enable the tall Shalako to enter and dance. The costly costumes are draped over a wooden framework, which includes pulleys to move parts like a puppet.

Complex social relationships grow out of the Pueblo world view, in which the well-being of all creatures is tied to the well-being of every individual, and thus the community. ❑

PUEBLO PRIVACY

Wherever the Pueblo, the best time to visit may be during ceremonial dances and feast days. All dances are ceremonial events – prayers for rain, ample crops, a good hunt, or thanksgiving – and should be approached with appropriate respect. Not all dances are open to the public. Most Pueblo people share a deep sense of ambivalence towards tourism; there are powerful factions within most pueblos that consider tourism a threat to traditional culture. Privacy is highly valued. Although gregarious by nature, the Pueblo people may not always be warm to outsiders, often the response to being treated as objects of curiosity or as camera fodder.

LEFT: Anasazi Indian cliff dwellings.
RIGHT: ceremonial dancer in San Juan Pueblo.

THE NAVAJO

In the Southwest for seven centuries, the vigorous and independent Navajo
people have become known for their exquisite jewelry and textiles

White men called them Navajo, but they call themselves Dine – the People – and they came a long way to settle in the American Southwest. Of Athabascan stock, their ancestors came from the forests of northwest Canada, drifting into the Four Corners area – where Colorado, Utah, Arizona and New Mexico meet – as small groups of skin-clad hunters. By 1400, they were well-established in their new homeland, a land of ever-changing colors, of yellow deserts, blood-red mesas and canyons, green fir and aspen-covered highlands and silvery expanses of sage overspread by a turquoise sky. This beautiful land was sacred to them because it had been created by the Holy Ones for the People to live in.

taught them how to plant corn and squash, weave and make pottery. The Navajo were good learners. In time, their weavers even outstripped their Pueblo teachers. Much later, they learned from the Spaniards how to ride horses and raise sheep, introduced by the Spaniards, and, still later, to be superb silversmiths.

They came as hunters, bringing lances, sinew-backed bows and hide shields. Nomadic and warlike, they raided the villages of the Pueblo people, who had lived on the land long before them. They took from the peaceful Pueblo many useful things – and women, who

NAVAJOS AND THE SPANISH

The Navajos did not always enjoy peaceful relations with the incoming Spanish. In the 1770s, the Spanish made brutal forays into Navajo country, beginning a long and bitter period of slave-raiding and land encroachment; at the same time, Catholic missionaries sought to convert souls and diminish local traditions and beliefs. In 1804, the Navajos made war on the Spanish but suffered a bloody defeat at Canyon de Chelly, in the eastern part of present-day Arizona (Kit Carson would later rampage through Canyon de Chelly, rounding up Navajos for the Long Walk). In 1821, at a truce conference with the Spanish, 24 Navajos were stabbed in the heart.

Planting and shepherding turned the roving nomads into sedentary herdsmen with a settled home, at whose core was the beautiful Canyon de Chelly. Then, in 1851, the U.S. Army built Fort Defiance to "defy" and control the Navajo; in 1863, Kit Carson was sent to subdue and remove the People. Carson waged a cruel war. He did not hunt down the small groups of Navajo hidden in the depths of their canyons. Instead, he made war upon their crops and sheep. Livestock was killed and corn supplies

CANYON HEART

Canyon de Chelly, in Arizona, is the very heart of Navajo country. Established by the now-vanished Anasazi, this canyon has been inhabited for over 1,000 years.

Redondo, several hundred during the march, over 1,500 died after settling in the internment camp. After four years, the government relented and let the survivors go back to their homeland. And so the Navajo set out once again on the punishing five-week trek homewards, to the west.

Today, the Navajo tribe is among the largest in the United States, but this speaks only of the tribe's hardiness and resilience. More than 100 years after it took place, the Long Walk still haunts memories.

burned. Winter came and many Indians, isolated in their canyons, starved or froze to death. At last, they surrendered to the army.

They were made to go on the "Long Walk" to Bosque Redondo, over 300 miles (500 km) away to the east in New Mexico. Their destination was worse than the march itself – a flat, inhospitable land with alkali water that made them sick. They had no materials to build shelters and lived in earthen holes. They never had enough to eat, as their crops withered in the hostile soil. Of 8,000 Navajo moved to Bosque

LEFT: old photo of Navajo riders in Canyon de Chelly.
ABOVE: Navajo hogan dwelling in Monument Valley.

The *hogan*

Navajo home life revolved around the *hogan*, or dwelling. The earliest type was the "forked stick" hogan made of three crotched poles interlaced at the top, covered with sticks and plastered over with earth. In the center of the sunken floor was a fire pit below a smoke hole.

The hogan was well-suited to the country – cool in summer and snug in winter. People slept with their feet toward the fire, like spokes in a wheel. Modern hogans are octagonal log cabins with a domed roof, through which the stovepipe rises. Many have electric lights and appliances. They are roomier than the old-style hogan but preserve its original design.

In the oldest of traditions, if a Navajo dies in the hogan, an opening is made in the back of the dwelling; the body is removed through this hole. The hogan and its contents are burned. The place is then considered the haunt of *chindi*, the ghosts of the dead.

Although taboos are sometimes broken, Navajo tend to honor strictly the most serious taboos and, in time of misfortune, try to determine how they have erred and seek to propitiate the spirits.

Communicating with the spirits needs song

> ### TABOOS
>
> Not observing taboos can arouse the anger of powerful spirits, but traditional Navajo life was highly regulated and people inevitably did break a few.

well. Some sand paintings are small and can be finished by one man in an hour or two. Others may be 20 feet (6 meters) long, requiring several assistants. The patient who is sung over sits in the center of the painting and their living body is part of the sacred altar. When the ritual is over, patient and painting are symbolically united when the medicine man dips his wet fingers into the sand painting and transfers some of it (and its power) to the patient. Finally the painting is destroyed, the sand scattered in all the sacred

and a medicine man, the *hatathli* or chanter, who can bring evil under ritual control. His knowledge is not gained easily. Before a sing, he fasts for days, taking sweat baths and communing with the powers. He searches for the cause of evil through listening or trembling. His whole body shakes, and his trembling hands hover over a patch of cornmeal. Finally, the finger traces an ancient design that indicates the cause of the disease and the appropriate ritual to exorcise it.

This tracing, called sand painting, can last several days. If the sing is performed correctly, the song chanted beautifully, and the sand painting properly completed, then all will be

directions. The "sand paintings" on plywood or certain rugs sold to tourists as curios have their roots in this Navajo religious symbolism.

The Holy People's family tree

Navajo religion is complex, and its teachings, legends, songs and rituals are beautifully haunting and poetic. Navajo believe in the Holy People, powerful and mysterious, who travel on the wind, a sunbeam or a thunderbolt. At the head of these supernaturals stands Changing Woman, the Earth Mother, beautiful, gift-giving

ABOVE: traditional Navajo rug weaving.
RIGHT: textile designs are adopted from sand painting.

and watching over the people's well-being. Changing Woman was found by First Man and First Woman as a baby, lying in a supernaturally created cradleboard on top of a sacred mountain. Within four days, Changing Woman grew to maturity. It was She who taught humans how to live in harmony with the forces of nature. She built the first hogan out of turquoise and shell.

The Navajo's chief ritual, Blessing Way, came to them from Changing Woman and other Holy People. Changing Woman was impregnated by the rays of the sun and gave birth to the Hero Twins, who killed many evil monsters and enemies of humankind, but she allowed old age and death to exist because they have their part in the human scheme.

The touchstone of religion

Religion remains an integral part of daily life for many traditional Navajo. Men go into the fields singing corn-growing songs, weavers make a spirit path thread in their rugs, and hide-curers put a turquoise bead on their tanning poles to keep their joints limber. When a woman has a difficult birth, her female relatives and friends loosen their hair to "untie" the baby. A chanter might be summoned to coax

SAND PAINTING

The exact origin of sand painting (once known as dry painting) is lost in the mists of Navajo mythology and legend, although it seems possible that the practice was borrowed from the Pueblo people to the east after the Navajos' ancestors migrated into the Southwest over 700 years ago. (Today, designs have been adapted to weaving.)

Traditionally, sand paintings were made during night-long healing rituals known as "sings". They were created on the floor of a ceremonial hogan by medicine men, who often spent years learning the elaborate prayers, chants and designs. The most common designs of the sand painting feature the Navajo gods, or *yei*, who were invoked through chants during the ceremony to help cure an ill person. At the end of the ceremony, just before dawn, the sacred images are destroyed. The sand is then collected and buried north of the hogan.

Little was known of sand painting until the 1880s, when Washington Matthews, a military doctor stationed on the Navajo reservation, became the first white person to observe and study the ceremony. But it was some 30 years later when a scholar delved into the sand painting rituals. In the 1920s, Gladys Reichard committed herself to learning the ceremonies, first by mastering the complicated Navajo language and then learning the chants themselves.

the baby along with an eagle-feather fan. Twins are a cause for great joy because they are a sign of the Holy People's blessing. The father makes the cradleboard. When the baby is placed in it, a special song is chanted:

I have made a baby board for you, my child.
May you grow to a great old age.
Of the sun's rays have I made the back.
Of clouds have I made the blanket.
Of the rainbow have I made the head bow.

Religious symbolism has influenced Navajo art, which is rich, beautiful and economically important nowadays. Navajo weaving, is particularly impressive. Originally only blankets were woven; the famous Navajo rug was an invention of white traders after the coming of the railroads and tourists. The traders didn't take long to find out that travelers from the East had little use for blankets worn like ponchos. So they called them rugs and gave birth to a new industry.

Different regions of the Navajo reservation developed their own characteristic styles – Ganado Reds, geometric Two Gray Hills and figural Shiprock, and a great many others. Women also weave fine baskets, while men

FROM GIRL TO WOMAN

Coming of age is the occasion for many rituals, typical in most cultures that have retained traditional ties and attitudes to the natural and spiritual worlds.

In the case of Navajo girls, traditional coming-of-age rituals and celebrations are very elaborate. The time of a girl's "first bleed" is a proud moment for her, and she hurries to tell her parents, who joyfully spread the news. The event is celebrated by a ceremony called *kinaalda*.

The girl has her hair washed in yucca suds. For three days, wearing her best jewelry, she grinds corn on the old family *metate*. During each of the three days, she undergoes a "molding" rite. Lying on a blanket, she is kneaded and "shaped" by a favorite female friend or relative to make her as beautiful as Changing Woman.

Each dawn, the girl races toward the east, each time a little faster. Others are allowed to run with her but are careful not to pass her, so that they do not grow old before she does. On the fourth day, older women make a big cake from the corn that the girl has ground, sometimes as big as 6 feet (2 meters) across.

When the cake is ready, after racing for the last time, the girl distributes it to all of the guests. After that, she is considered a woman, ready to marry and to start a family of her own.

excel in creating some of the best silver and turquoise work to be found in the Southwest. (At the tribal capital of Window Rock, one may visit the Navajo Arts and Crafts Center. Rugs, baskets and jewelry are also sold in shops throughout the area.)

The modern Navajo who does not choose to live the traditional life in the hogan might be a lawyer, electrician, policewoman, or telephone operator. He might operate one of the giant cranes at the nearby strip mine or operate one of the complicated Japanese-built machines at the huge tribal sawmill. He might be a newspaper editor on the *Navajo Times* or a professor at

bring in money but also wrenching changes: pollution, dependency on outside forces, an amount of industrialization and the relocation of people.

Depite natural resources, poverty persists and housing and health care are sub-standard. Schools don't prepare students for the problems they will face in an Anglo-dominated world. Religion and language fight against the inroads of a powerful, alien culture. Offered one Navajo: "We have survived the Spaniards, the missionaries and the Long Walk. We still walk in beauty. We will still be here, still be Navajo, a hundred years from now." ❑

Navajo Community College – all glass and steel but built in the shape of a traditional hogan. The modern Navajo man or woman shares some of the advantages and all of the frustrations, problems and anxieties of fellow Americans.

With a population in excess of 200,000, the Navajo comprise one of the largest tribes in the United States. In fact, the Navajo reservation is bigger than New Hampshire, Connecticut, Vermont and Rhode Island combined. It has oil, coal, uranium and timber. These resources

LEFT: Navajo war veteran, and tribal elder and teacher.
ABOVE: herding sheep is a Navajo tradition.

NAVAJO AND HOPI DISPUTES

The Navajo and Hopi tribes have had their differences, especially regarding a long-term land dispute. The Hopi, whose mesa-top homes are completely surrounded by the larger Navajo reservation, had long claimed that the Navajo were robbing their fields and stealing cattle. Tensions escalated to a high point in 1974, when the U.S. Congress passed the Navajo-Hopi Relocation Act. The law, which divided nearly 2 million acres (800,000 hectares) between the tribes, was supposed to compel 11,000 Navajo and about 100 Hopi to leave homes they had known for generations. Many of the Navajo moved to new government housing; others still resist relocation.

THE HOPI

Wedged between the Navajo and Pueblo peoples, the Hopi live in what outsiders would call a desolate place, but the spiritual Hopi believe otherwise

Approaching Hopi country from any direction may be a bleak or nondescript experience for some travelers, but once they meet and mingle with its inhabitants, a visitor generally comes away from the experience with anything but bleak or nondescript impressions. If Hopi people were inclined to describe them-

and custom, but often separated linguistically and politically.

Speech patterns and vocabulary differ from village to village within the same general language structure, providing natural boundaries. These differences also provide a great deal of chauvinistic interplay with words among resi-

selves, which they are not, they would say they aspire to be industrious, hospitable and helpful. Tradition and custom mandate such attitudes and behavior.

Hopi country can be loosely described as high desert supporting little else beside the tenacious Hopi. They manage to coax the most wondrous yield of cultivated farm products out of it, notably an infinite variety of corn. Hopi country is comprised of 11 distinct villages situated along the 35-mile (55-km) perimeter of Black Mesa, in northeastern Arizona. These villages – some settled for centuries, others founded as recently as 1910 – are home to 10,000 people closely knit by tradition, blood

HOPI STEWARDSHIP

The Hopi are, above all, a deeply religious people. Religion is so completely intertwined with the rest of life that isolating it is like unraveling the entire Hopi universe. For the Hopi, spirituality is a universal concern. Hopi elders believe that they have inherited stewardship over Mother Earth, and are obliged to protect her and maintain the religion on behalf of humanity. This stewardship is carried out through priesthood societies called *wuutsim*, which conduct ceremonies to ensure the temporal and spiritual well-being of all people. There are also priestess societies and other religious groups, such as the kachina societies, that form the spiritual foundation of Hopi society.

dents of each village. The traditional governing system also encourages a political distance between villages. However, the differences are not easily discernible to those unfamiliar with Hopi society.

Kinship and family

The kinship system, which is still intact, provides the unity that allows free intercourse between villages in all the important functions of communal living: family relationships, rites and ceremonies. It may be overstressing the point, only a little to say that

VILLAGE PRIORITY

On meeting a Hopi, often s/he will first give the name of their village, and if prodded further, will most likely tell you the clan affiliation followed by the Hopi name.

generation, only the uncle's children are named nephews and nieces. The aunt's children fall into relationships dictated by clan formulas.

Superimposed on biological kinship is the clan system, which sees people within a single relational universe, that of brother and sister. The clan line is also matrilineal.

Legendary tales, guarded by hereditary caretakers within each clan unit, recount the extensive prehistoric migrations of one ancestral group after another over a vast area of the American Southwest,

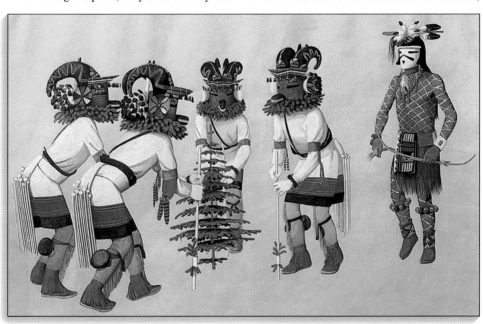

most Hopi growing up and living on the reservation know, if they know nothing else, who they are and from where they came.

The matriarchal kinship system, in which lineage passes through the female line, is crucial in maintaining familial and spiritual unity. All children of maternal sisters and paternal brothers, for instance, become brothers and sisters and share common parent figures, although in lesser degrees of intimacy beyond the immediate family. Paternal sisters and maternal brothers are aunts and uncles, but within the second

LEFT: Hopi girls photographed in the 19th century.
ABOVE: painting of the Bighorn Dance, circa 1930.

southern California and Mexico. The storytellers are able to identify landmarks as far away as central New Mexico, southern Colorado and Utah. Mythic tales of creation provide the basis for a system of beliefs and practices so complex as to mesmerize generations of scholars throughout the world.

Ritual and ceremony

The traveler will find Hopi people naturally open and friendly in the privacy of their home, though somewhat distant at public, social and ceremonial gatherings – unless of course the traveler has "Hopi friends." It is not uncommon to find at least one *pahaana* (white person) among the participants at wedding, natal and *kachina* ceremonial preparation parties.

Hopi are particularly sensitive to the aesthetic tastes of the traveling public, whether these tastes be for art, services or showmanship, such as the dancing kachinas, which have become such a magnetic attraction for countless outsiders. In fact, ritual and ceremony may be the most distinctive aspects of Hopi culture today. A serious issue among them today is how best to preserve Hopi ways that are rapidly changing because of pressures, both within and without, created by modern living and technology. There is no doubt that Hopi do not want to let go of all

the "old" ways of doing things. The specter of losing tradition and custom to modern technology and lifestyles hovers constantly.

The modern Hopi wedding was being discussed around the breakfast table in a Hopi home. One man remarked at the marshaling of a caravan of automobiles to escort the new bride home at the culmination of wedding festivities. He counted 20-odd trucks, each loaded down with gifts to be distributed among the bride's relatives. He was obviously saddened at the blatant ignorance displayed by the relatives about the original significance of the bridal homecoming. "The bride goes back to her mother's house alone to await her new hus-

band's pleasure. When he decides to accept her as a bride he will follow her, bearing appropriate gifts," he said. (Even second-generation Hopi born this century might be hard put to know that the right gift for him to bring is a load of wood, symbol of hearth and home.)

Young people sitting around the table in that modern house were quite surprised and fascinated to hear this; no one had really explained these things to them. Their only experience with weddings consisted of the mixture of Western and Hopi ceremonial activities that has become the modern Hopi wedding: at most, a two-day affair replete with an abundance of foods from the traditional pantry as well as the supermarket, wrapped gifts mingling with the native foodstuffs customarily given to the bride and groom's families, table decor contrasting with makeshift outdoor open fires for cooking.

So it goes. And so it goes in other rites which are still vital, such as natal rites and initiation into ceremonial societies. It is this innovative mixing of the old and new that separates one generation from the other, because, if the truth be told, these hybrids have an ambience of their own, and an appealing vitality.

Kachina dances

This attractive mixture of the old and new can also be seen during one of the many summer weekends on which kachina or other dances are sponsored. Less than a generation ago, kachinas were first introduced to the Hopi child as spiritual beings who come to this world from the Spirit Home, which may refer to either an opening in the floor of a ceremonial room called the *kiva*, or to a shrine on the San Francisco Peaks near Flagstaff, which is a "secret opening."

Kachinas are commonly presented in the dances held indoors in kivas and outdoors in village plazas, depending upon the time of year. These colorful masked beings represent elements, qualities and inhabitants of the universe; they may be cast, in their spiritual state, in roles for various purposes, some didactic and others more inspirational.

Kachina dances are very much taken as a matter of course; there is at least one in each village each year. The kachina and its dancing act as a magnet to a new generation of Hopi

LEFT: an elderly Hopi basketmaker.
RIGHT: Hopi dancer, and a kachina doll, or *tihu* in Hopi.

urban dwellers, increasingly removed from reservation upbringing but who return as spectators and participants.

An upcoming dance mobilizes, as nothing else can, all the combined resources of a village. It is not unusual for Hopi to travel from Los Angeles, San Francisco, Denver or Oklahoma City for these events; coming in from Tucson, Phoenix and even Salt Lake City can be a weekly or monthly habit with some families. When all the relatives have gathered, there may be a fleet of five to 10 vehicles, mostly trucks, in front of each house in that village. Even though these autos may have come loaded with provisions from the supermarkets of the urban centers, the preparation of traditional feast foods is not abandoned.

Corn, the symbolic Mother to the Hopi, is the most visible traditional food, secular and sacred, for this occasion as it is for most rituals and religious ceremonies.

The ceremony consists of a series of dances, usually seven or eight, performed every two hours with 30-minute breaks, beginning about midmorning and ending at sundown. The staging of a kachina dance is an example of the refined sense of the dramatic, a trademark of the Hopi and the other Pueblo peoples. ❏

KACHINA: THE HOPI SPIRIT-BEING

Since time immemorial, Hopi men have carved wooden replicas of the Hopi spirit-beings – *katsinam* – known as kachinas to non-Hopi. Called *tihu* in Hopi, these effigies are given to Hopi children to teach them about religion.

Kachina carving is deeply rooted in Hopi religion, and the kachina spirits are as innumerable as the laws of nature, for that is what they are. Some are the spirits of ancestors hidden by clouds, others make the rain fall and the corn grow. For half the year, from the winter solstice in December until the Niman Kachina ceremony in July, these spirits live among the Hopi in the mesa villages. During these months, they are represented by ornately costumed men – kachina dancers – who perform dances. The rest of the year, the kachina reside in the high San Francisco Peaks, just north of Flagstaff.

It is thought that there are around 350 kachinas depicted in carvings, but no two are exactly alike. Although dolls, kachina are not toys and are, in fact, considered sacred. There are two types: traditional and sculptural. Traditional kachina are crafted from the soft root of the cottonwood tree and were typically carved in rigid poses with legs together and arms to the side. Sculptural kachina are more interpretive and feature the virtuosity of the artist as much as traditional religious symbolism.

THE APACHE

Typically depicted in the media as the most ferocious and warlike of the Southwest tribes, the Apache were traditionally peaceful nomadic hunters

Like most other Southwest tribes, the Apache dispute the anthropological theory that they migrated to North America across the Bering Strait. An elderly San Carlos Apache tells the story handed down for centuries: "Our ancestors tell us that we were created in the area where we now live. In the beginning, there was

no living person upon Mother Earth, only supernatural beings. When our people were created, there were wicked creatures who killed them. During this time, the White Painted Lady gave birth to twin sons. One of these sons went to his father, Sun, and returned to Mother Earth dressed in proper Apache clothing, carrying a bow and arrows and leading several horses. After he taught our people how to use these things, he helped kill the evil creatures. Mother Earth then became a good place to live for our people." All Apache have a creation story with ideas similar to this one.

Before contact with the Spaniards in the middle to late 1500s, Apache bands intermingled freely with each other and with the Navajo. The Apache, like the Navajo, are of the Athabascan-speaking family and have no written history or language.

The Apache called themselves the People, but to others they were the "Enemy." The land the Apache roamed traditionally encompassed present-day Arizona, New Mexico and northern Mexico. While they were, in essence, one family, each group had its own hunting territory and did not encroach on that of its neighbors. The relatively peaceful, nomadic life of the Apache was drastically altered by the appearance of outsiders into the Apache domain: Spaniards, Mexicans and finally Anglos.

Anglo and Spanish colonization

When Coronado made his expedition into the Southwest in the 16th century, he unwittingly introduced a new mode of travel to the Apache, which they would adopt and use more skillfully than any other Southwestern tribe. The horse became a beast of burden, a source of food and a reliable form of transportation that enabled the Apache to expand their geographical range far beyond their original territories.

Apache reaction to Spanish and Anglo colonization was raiding and warfare, which was so effective that twice the intruders were driven out for as long as a decade. Indeed, southern Arizona was one of the last areas of the Southwest to be settled by the Spanish and Americans. Contrary to popular belief, Apache raiding did not include wanton destruction; its aim was generally to steal livestock.

When the Gadsden Purchase was made in 1853, all of Arizona came under the control of the United States. This, and the discovery of gold in western Apache territory 10 years later, brought an influx of Anglo settlers and prospectors. The Arizona Territory Legislature officially decided that the only way to control the Apache was to exterminate them. The Department of War in Washington disagreed with this policy, and the Territory lacked the means to carry out the extermination. This fact, together with the slaughter of 75 unarmed Apache women and children near Tucson by a mob of outraged citizens and a group of Tohono O'odham Indians, led to the implementation of the so-called Peace Policy.

This policy called for rounding up Apache and confining them to reservations, where they would have to make a living by growing crops and raising livestock. This plan required the removal of some tribes from their homelands. The removals were met with ambivalence by the

CURATIVE GIRLS

The sunrise ceremony is the most important ritual for Apache: girls are believed to possess curative powers at puberty and treat the ill by touching them.

Ceremony and celebration

The Apache sunrise ceremony – a girl's puberty rite – can be seen several times a year on the San Carlos, White Mountain and Jicarilla reservations. The Mescalero Apache ceremonies are all performed in summer.

The awesome and colorful masked mountain spirit dancers – *gans* – still perform at the puberty rites of the San Carlos, White Mountain and Mescalero tribes. (The Jicarilla Apache have not used the dancers as part of their ceremonies since the introduction

Apache. Some had become weary of the hardships of war and preferred to settle down in peace. Others, however, waited for a chance to escape. Two of those who bolted were Geronimo and Victorio. But by 1890, the Apache wars were finally over.

Today, the remaining Apache tribes of Arizona and New Mexico have been significantly anglicized. Many, but not all, of the old tribal ways have disappeared. Present-day Apache are struggling to become economically self-sufficient by embracing outside ways.

LEFT: a masked Mountain Spirit dancer.
ABOVE: Spirit dancers perform a puberty ceremony.

of the vaccination program on their reservation. The Jicarilla leaders decreed that anyone who had been vaccinated could not participate as a mountain spirit dancer, and the result was the disqualification of nearly all Jicarilla youth.)

The sunrise ceremony is usually held after a girl has had her first menstruation, assuming that she and her family can afford the costly preparations. The girl, who enters womanhood upon completion of the ceremony, needs strength, patience, good luck and wisdom to help her in life. These qualities are possessed by the White Painted Lady and are acquired by the girl during the four-day ceremony when the White Painted Lady resides in her body. ❑

TOHONO O'ODHAM AND PIMA

Little-known outside of the area, the Tohono O'odham and Pima people live in the sprawling Sonoran Desert and are the most assimilated tribes in the area

A Tohono O'odham may come from any number of small villages dotting the Sonoran Desert of southern Arizona. Tohono O'odham, who make up the community of Sells, (named after an Indian commissioner) came for a specific reason – jobs with the Bureau of Indian Affairs or for government housing, increasingly prevalent on reservations.

Sells is a quasi-urbanized sprawl nestled below the sacred mountain, Waw Giwulk or Baboquivari, the home of the Protector of the Tohono O'odham people. Many Tohono O'odham call this place home, the place where one is from. But the entire reservation is home as well, since all of it was the aboriginal land of the tribe. North of the Tohono O'odham home lies the Pima reservation where fewer than 11,000 Pima Indians live on a little over 3,000 acres (1,200 hectares).

A sense of place

The Pima and Tohono O'odham distinguish one another by placing in front of their tribal name the geographic feature that refers to the place they are from. Tohono O'odham means Desert People. The Pima, who have traditionally lived along the banks of rivers in the valleys of southcentral Arizona, call themselves Akimel O'odham or River People, even though the river that winds through their reservation no longer carries water.

There is no traditional farming, only that which uses water brought from other places in concrete canals or pumped from deep within the ground. But this place along the dry river is home. The other lands that make up the reservation, like the one along the Salt River, are only a small part of what was once the aboriginal land of the Pima. The Salt River Reservation butts against the condominiums of Scottsdale.

Archaeological and anthropological evidence indicates that the Pima and Tohono O'odham Indians were, at one time, the same. They are said to be descendants of the now-vanished Hohokam, or as they are called by the people, Hukukam, "the ones that have gone now." Linguistically the two groups are closely related

and their languages are mutually intelligible. Many of their rituals, stories and songs are similar. The only distinction is place, the area where one is from.

The Pima, and to a lesser extent the Tohono O'odham, are the most acculturated Indian tribes in the Southwest. Since their earliest recorded

contacts with whites, the Pima especially have been looked upon as friendly. During the California Gold Rush of the mid-19th century, the Pima sold provisions to white prospectors and escorted them through Apache territory. At the time of the Apache wars in the 1860s, a large number of the Pima served as scouts for the U.S. Army. Such close contacts with white culture resulted in disintegration of aboriginal culture.

Still, both tribes have retained their language and a few ceremonies, and Tohono O'odham woven baskets are among the finest made. ❑

LEFT: a Pima woman on the reservation.
ABOVE: Tohono O'odham women gather saguaro fruit.

SYMBOLIC EXPRESSION: NATIVE AMERICAN ART

Native Americans of the Southwest have a legacy rich in symbolism, found in Kachina figures, sand paintings, and other creative forms

Native American spirituality can be viewed more as a way of life than a religion. Traditionally their daily lives have not been partitioned; work, play, and worship are all intertwined in experience and belief. Symbols come from all they see and imagine in the world around them: rain clouds, corn, rainbows, animals, spirits. Colors have symbolic meaning relating to the four directions.

HIDDEN MEANINGS

Native Americans do not readily share the meanings of symbols. Therefore, Navajo sandpaintings made for the public always contain one mistake, insignificant to the non-Navajo eye but obvious to a *hatahli*, or medicine man. It may be an altered color sequence or a change of a small detail, but it is enough to avoid trespassing into sacred – and secret – traditions.

Though widely known, rock inscriptions, some of them many hundreds of years old, are poorly understood. They do not represent language, but may mark special occasions, visions, boundaries, prayers, hunts, deities, or other concepts.

Artists do not rely strictly on symbolic images or their own culture. This Ute cuff (above), dating from the early 1900s, shows the influence of Plains Indian horse culture both in the beadwork and subject matter.

▷ **FEARSOME FELLOW**
In traditional Hopi and Zuni cultures, Kachina figures represent beings that carry messages to the gods. This Ogre Kachina makes everyone behave.

▷ **STOPPING PLACE**
Native Americans see habitation sites as stopping places on their journey to the "center" of their spiritual world rather than "abandoned" homes.

△ **DRESSED FOR BATTLE**
When Indians gather for an inter-tribal powwow, the scene is lavish with costume and color. Warrior regalia adorns this Navajo/Yaqui man.

▷ **NEWSPAPER ROCK**
Some images on this Utah panel may be 2,000 years old. The horse-mounted hunter was done after 1540, when horses were brought to North America.

△ **A WAY OUT**
If this Navajo rug was enclosed with a border, an "escape" thread would probably be woven across it so spirits would not be trapped therein.

CREATIVITY IN SILVER AND STONE

Of all American Indian arts and crafts, jewelry must rank highest in demand on the tourist market. It comes at all prices and is widely available. While no group makes only one style, they do have their specialties. Navajo silverwork usually incorporates turquoise, a stone sacred to them. Silver overlay is distinctively Hopi. Zuni are known for designs using small stones, each set in its own bezel. Santo Domingo Pueblo artisans make mosaic jewelry, liquid silver necklaces, and *heishi*. Aside from the customary rings, earrings, necklaces and bracelets, you will find concho belts, hatbands, watch bands, bolo ties, and belt buckles in every style. Modern Indian jewelry usually shows the influence of ancestral Puebloans, but artists continually have new visions for their work and it takes delightful turns.

▷ **HEALING SANDS**
Navajo sandpaintings are created by drizzling sand and ground pigment in complex motifs. They are destroyed after the healing ceremony for which they were made.

◁ **COSMIC PARENTS**
This Navajo sandpainting shows Father Sky and Mother Earth. Corn tassels sprout from their heads and half moons lie between their feet.

▷ **BIRD MAN**
This Zuni shell pendant, made about 1906, depicts Knife Wing Man, inlaid with locally found turquoise and jet and with a painted sash.

THE HISPANICS

The influence of the energetic Hispanic culture not only lingers on, but also permeates nearly every facet of the Southwest, from place names to architecture

In 1598, Governor Don Juan de Oñate led 130 families and 270 single men from Mexico to an area just north of present-day Santa Fe. They were the first European settlers in the Southwest, and the Pueblo Indians who lived along the nearby Rio Grande were linked forever after to the destiny of the new colonists.

For over a century, the Hispanic villages, surrounded by towering mountains, clung to the Rio Grande. Villagers made a living from fields and flocks. The settlers were Hispanos and Mexicanos who had come in search of a new life, while the Catholic friars had come, not surprisingly, for tainted Indian souls to convert. El Paso in modern-day Texas, was the resting point and link between Old Mexico and New Mexico, just as it and Juarez are today.

Heading north from El Paso through an expanse of desert called La Jornada del Muerto, or The Journey of Death, the colonists were rewarded with the high plateaus and mountains of the Sangre de Cristo (Blood of Christ), a topography that reminded some of southern Spain and others of Mexico.

A style in the land

From these first villages the settlers began to extend their influence. Groups of families petitioned the Spanish authorities in Mexico for land grants, and communities spread along the river and into the mountains. When Mexico broke from Spain in 1821, the land-grant system continued, and when Anglo-Americans arrived in the Southwest, they found a communal land system they did not understand.

The land-grant system played a crucial part in the formation of the Hispanic culture and the character of the Hispanos. The original grants provided space for homes, fields, irrigation water, firewood and the grazing of animals. But in 1846, the Anglo-Americans brought a new system of land ownership, and many land grants were lost or greatly diminished. Those that still remain struggle for survival, and as the Hispanic people move away from their villages into larger urban centers, a cultural transformation is underway. Hispanic culture in the Southwest today is one of rapid assimilation into the mainstream Anglo culture.

LEFT: Hispanic woman at El Rancho de las Golondrinas, an 18th-century working ranch near Santa Fe.
RIGHT: chile harvest encourages a spicy cuisine.

LOSS OF HISPANIC DOMINANCE

When Mexico won independence from Spain in 1821, American traders began to trickle in, followed later by settlers. In 1845, the United States annexed Texas, touching off the Mexican War. The U.S. Army captured Mexico City two years later and, under the terms of the Treaty of Guadalupe Hidalgo, the United States took possession of New Mexico (including present-day Arizona) and California, and also solidified its hold on Texas. After more than three centuries of overbearing influence, Spanish – and Hispanic – dominance over the region retreated. With the shift, Spanish-speakers suddenly found themselves as second-class citizens.

Pueblo neighbors

The Hispanos were the neighbors of the Pueblo Indians. A sharing of cultures continued until 1680, when the Pueblo Indians of New Mexico, enraged because Hispanic colonists got preferential treatment and Catholic friars insisted that the Indians give up their traditional religion, took up arms and drove the Hispanos out of New Mexico in a bloody revolt. But in 1692 the Spanish returned, led by Don Diego Vargas. They reconquered Santa Fe and re-established Spanish rule.

> ### EARTH MATTERS
>
> Like many aboriginal inhabitants, the Pueblo Indians were inextricably and harmoniously bound to the elements of "the sacred earth", water and sky.

the sacred earth. Like the Pueblo Indians before them, the Hispanos learned to live in close harmony with their native land. Now that the Hispanic population is mostly urban, this attachment takes new forms: a garden, some trees or flower patch, or just geraniums in an old coffee tin.

Two rivers dominate the Hispanic Southwest. The Colorado River flows from Colorado and through the Grand Canyon in Arizona to the Gulf of California. The Rio Grande originates

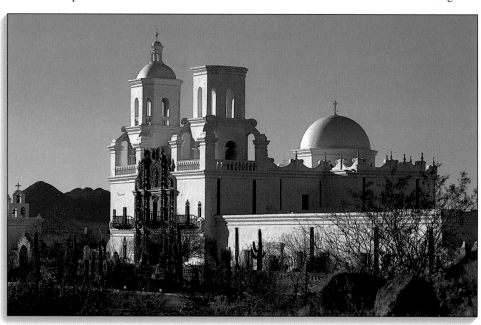

A sense of earth and village

Three elements seem to characterize individuals and communities in the Southwest: earth, water and sky. The Hispanos discovered that Pueblo Indians had a sacred partnership with the earth. They understood the earth and its creatures and knew they needed tending. In Spanish the earth is *la tierra*, and the land that belongs to the community of the land grant or village is to be guarded for the well-being of all. Hispanics love their village; their sense of place is strong. They are honor-bound and loyal to family and community, and this long history of attachment to the land of the village evolved into a close relationship with *la sagrada tierra*,

in southern Colorado and flows through New Mexico on its way to the Gulf of Mexico. Historically, the Hispanic population clung to the life-giving Rio Grande. The river is not only an important source of water, it is a corridor of Hispanic culture that straddles the border between Mexico and the United States. The Rio Grande is to Southwestern Hispanics what the Mississippi River is to the Midwesterner.

Another element in the fragile desert completes the picture: the sky that delivers the light and determines the tone, color and mood. The sky is clear, the air is crisp and the colors sharp. Sunrise and sunset are definite times, and summer's clouds are unrivaled in beauty.

Family and home

Hispanics have lent their unique character and industry to the land. They gave rise to the first mining industry in the Southwest, and they were the original horsemen, the *vaqueros* who introduced the lore and trappings of the cowboy. They learned from the Pueblo Indians how to build humble mansions of adobe, the sundried mud bricks, and how to use the system of *acequia* or canals to water their fields.

Spanish is spoken all over the Southwest, and the place names attest to centuries of Hispanic influence. From San Francisco to San Antonio, the corridor of the border region bears a strong

Family and home are at the center of the value system, as is strong identification with family name. Family relationships are extended by the *compadrazco* network. *Compadres* and *comadres* – godfathers and godmothers – extend the family ties. Godparents are selected for baptisms, confirmation in the Catholic Church, and weddings. This cultural tradition helps to extend the nuclear family into the larger community. A New Mexican family may have compadres as far away as California, Texas or the Midwest, and they are all included in the family. This vast network of communication also helps keep cultural traditions alive.

Hispanic stamp. Santa Fe, Española, Albuquerque, Belen, Socorro, Las Cruces, El Paso – they all sit along the Rio Grande and all were Hispanic settlements.

Hispanic culture was nurtured by Catholic faith, family and community ceremonies, oral storytelling and other folk arts. The Spanish language is still at the core of the culture, but as more activities take place in an English-speaking world, the dilution of the language is inevitable. Still, Spanish is often the first and primary language of many in the Southwest.

LEFT: San Xavier Mission, south of Tucson.
ABOVE: Christmas Eve in Albuquerque's Old Town.

LASTING HISPANIC IMPRESSIONS

The influence of Hispanic culture in the American Southwest remains profound. Much of cowboy culture, for example, has Spanish origins, from the names of clothing – chaparrejos, or chaps, and la reata, or lariat – to old-time cowboy traditions like the roundup and rodeo. Spanish place names, extending geographically from Texas to California, testify to Spanish exploration – El Paso, Santa Fe, Las Cruces, Los Angeles, San Francisco. In Arizona and especially New Mexico, Spanish folk art is still created, and Spanish colonial architecture, with its graceful Moorish and Indian touches, has been emulated by designers around the world.

Likewise, the migration of Mexicans northward into the United States – legally and illegally – reinforces the culture. As workers move north, so does their music, lifestyle, social needs and language. There are millions of Hispanics in the United States, with a considerable proportion – and often a majority – living in the Southwest.

Chicano pride

Of all the border societies, the Hispano has been most actively involved in the development

SLOW CALIFORNIANS

During Spanish colonial times, the towns of Spanish California developed slowly compared with those of New Mexico. Life was austere, but they prospered.

active community. Folk arts, oral storytelling, religious music and the presentation of morality plays during the Christmas season all display a creative imagination kept alive and well by the elders.

The Southwest today is not so much a melting pot as a sharing pot. The various cultural groups try to give and take, share and learn to grow with each other. For Christmas, native people and world travelers attend the festive lighting of the *luminarias*, the lights that illuminate churches and homes. These candles,

of the Southwest. The contemporary social and political movement began in the 1960s with the so-called Chicano movement. Like the parallel black civil-rights movement, it demanded equality in schooling and health care, along with acceptable working and living conditions for all Mexican-Americans. The movement led to a resurgence of ethnic pride, and the word Chicano reflected that pride.

To find their roots, Mexican-American leaders and artists returned to the mother country, Mexico. By asserting their heritage, they reinforced their pride. Political leaders, folk heroes, and the role of Chicanos in mining, ranching, farming and the railroad industry revealed an

burning within brown bags, have become a staple item for Christmas, as have the local foods. Everyone eats *posole*, chili, *carne adovada, natillas, biscochitos* and *enpanaditas* – all traditional Christmas foods. The rest of the year, beans, chili, enchiladas, burritos and tacos are the usual fare for those who like Mexican food. For Chicanos, the kitchen is still the heart of the house.

The Chicano movement inspired a renaissance of artistic expression. Art groups sprang up in every community. A resurgence of ethnic pride and creativity carried the Chicano into new fields: cinema, mural artworks and innovations in music.

An expression of tradition

Traditional art and ritual are at the root of this renaissance. Picture, for instance, a solemn procession winding its way down the arroyo, meandering like a long, colorful ribbon through fields and chaparral, finally coming to a halt on top of a hill crowned by an ancient adobe chapel. There is a ringing of bells, the sound of fiddles and of voices singing. At the head of the procession stands a man holding aloft a gilded cross; by his side the village priest. Behind them four

> ### JEWISH MEXICO
>
> By 1545, more than one quarter of Mexico City residents were admitted Jews, and soon there were more Jews than Catholics in New Spain, or Mexico.

and living museum just south of Santa Fe. The procession heralds a two-day fiesta of music and dance and a gathering of Hispanic craftsmen – *santeros* (carvers of holy images), painters of religious *retablos*, smiths handcrafting objects, women weaving colorful Chimayo blankets, basket makers, and women ladling out devilishly hot chili dishes. All this activity is set against the backdrop of ancient chapels and buildings that underscore the historical roots of today's traditional artists and *artesanos*.

men carry a wooden image representing San Isidro, patron saint of all who till the soil, with his yoke and oxen, his plow and his helper, a diminutive angel – a fine example of traditional wood carving. Behind them follow the worshippers – men in old costumes, devout women in black shawls beneath black umbrellas shading them from the sun, children, and tourists.

The procession blesses the fields in spring and gives thanks for a plentiful harvest in the fall. It takes place at El Rancho De Las Golondrinas, a working 18th-century Spanish ranch

Hispanic artists relied upon their own resources, using materials their environment offered. Even the homes of the ricos, the *gente fina* (fine folks, or well-to-do), were simple, with only essential furnishings. Finery belonged to the rich.

The main piece of furniture in the Hispanic house was the *trastero,* or cupboard, often richly carved and painted. Chests, in which a family's possessions were kept, also served as tables or benches. Fancy chests and boxes had elaborate hand-forged locks and were richly decorated with carved lions and scalloped wheels, less often with designs of Moorish origin. Chairs were sturdy, rough-hewn and thick-

LEFT: traditional Mexican music enriches the U.S. Southwest. **ABOVE:** store-side promotions.

legged. Hanging in the corners of rooms were ornate painted *nichos* to hold the images of saints and other religious objects. Lithographs of saints or biblical figures were displayed in punched tin frames. There were also usually a number of *retablos*, or pictures of saints painted on wooden boards.

Many churches held naive paintings on tin, showing the person who ordered them on his or her knees, giving thanks to some saint for having cured them of an illness. Other such retablos might show a fire, or a fall from a horse that someone had survived, thanks to the intercession of a patron saint.

The religious art of *santos*

Santeros were the men who carved *santos* – figures of the Savior, the Virgin, saints and angels. The images were not anatomically correct but were rather works of faith instead of art. Angels were short-legged; saints were elongated, narrow-waisted and big-footed. Anglos, used to the realistic, formal art of white America, first said santos were "fearful artistic abominations." Today, these abominations are highly prized works of art eagerly sought by museums and serious collectors, who value them for their peculiar charm. One also often encounters tragic figures of the suffering Christ, hollow-

ART IN ISOLATION

Traditional Hispanic art was, and is, homemade – rustic and original, often fashioned by simple farmers who became artists. This art was created with little outside influence, as for centuries the Southwest was all but cut off from the rest of the world. The populous cities of Mexico were more than 1,000 inhospitable desert miles away. Maybe two or three times a year, a mule train or maybe a caravan of *carretas* – clumsy, lumbering ox carts prone to breakdowns and agonizingly slow – made their way to Santa Fe. Yankee goods arrived via the long Santa Fe Trail, but until the railway, the region remained relatively isolated.

cheeked and emaciated, the body chalk-white, hair and beard coal-black, with bright blood trickling from many wounds.

Death and suffering have traditionally played a large part in Hispanic art, possibly as a reminder of centuries of oppression of Spanish Christians by the Moors of northern Africa. They are uppermost in the mind of the mysterious sect called Penitentes, who will scourge themselves until the blood flows and whose prayer is, "Lord, give us a good death." This preoccupation with the inevitability of dying,

ABOVE: waiting for a rodeo, introduced by Spaniards.
RIGHT: the chile is both condiment and decoration.

and with damnation and salvation, shows itself in the most impressive of Southwestern sculpture, the large death cart with its skeleton that admonishes the viewer, "As I am now, so you will be. Repent!" Typical also are statues of La Conquista, patroness of Santa Fe; of Nuestra Senora de Guadalupe, the Indian Virgin; and of the Holy Trinity. More ambitious sculptures are known as *bultos*.

Material used for santos is usually cottonwood and plaster made from locally found gypsum. Colors came out of the native earth – the red and orange from pulverized iron ocher; white and yellow from the abundant clay; black from finely ground charcoal; and green from boiled herbs. Blue had to be imported and was not much used before the 1850s. Santos are an integral part of every household, particularly patron saints after whom family members have been named.

Women excel in embroidering coverlets – *colchas* – using designs of humans, birds and flowers, usually on a white background. Sheep, brought to New Mexico by the earliest Spanish settlers, provided cheap, abundant wool. Women still weave their richly colored thick blankets described as "made in the pattern of a maze of concentric diamonds." ❑

A LOSS OF CRAFTING?

The arts and crafts of Hispanic society were both necessarily functional – whether for food or for worship – and highly aesthetic and personal.

Silversmithing is done by the *platero*, who sometimes still fashions his wares with the help of a homemade mud oven, charcoal, bellows of goatskin and a blow pipe. Often also doubling as blacksmith, traditionally the *platero* melted down silver peso coins to make crosses, necklaces of hollow beads, rosaries, bracelets, earrings, tobacco and powder flasks, silver buttons, head stalls for horses and spurs for the rider. In fact, it was the Spanish plateros who taught the craft to Navajo Indians in the 1850s.

Pottery was simple and made for everyday use, although nowadays some ceramicists make charmingly painted and fired clay figures of Mary, Joseph and the Holy Child in his manger, the three wise kings and praying shepherds – all of them typical Hispanic farmers surrounded by their animals – burros and lambs, oxen and goats. These may be admired and bought in museums and antique shops throughout the Southwest, particularly in Taos and Santa Fe.

Much of what is now sold to tourists as either "art" or souvenirs has its origins in the traditional crafts of yesteryear, though increasingly it lacks personality.

THE ANGLOS

Originally lured southward by animal furs and trade, the Anglo population is increasingly drawn by warm weather, air conditioning and high-tech jobs

So diffused is the Southwestern cultural majority known as the Anglos, that it is difficult to say who is included, except that very few actually descend from the Angles, a small German tribe that invaded England in the 5th century. The label was given currency by Spanish-speaking Southwesterners and it generally includes all white Americans of European descent who do not happen to have Spanish surnames.

The first Anglos to reach the Southwest were explorers, fur trappers and traders who brought long-coveted goods along the Santa Fe Trail and introduced a dominant Anglo cultural trait: free trade and commerce. That small breach through the formerly self-enclosed New Spain soon became a flood. The American military presence began with forts and garrisons to protect trade routes from outlaws and raiding Apaches, but it was soon engaged in the largely trumped-up war with Mexico that resulted in Arizona and New Mexico being ceded to the United States by treaty, in 1848. Before long the Southern Pacific and Santa Fe railroads had opened the Southwest to the American public.

The great move

The enterprising Yankees who built the railroads also built the first grand hotels, and the pleasure-seeking self-indulgent Southwesterner of the future was imported. Within decades, paved highways, air services and national promotion opened the Southwest to tourism. Respiratory patients discovered the clean, dry air and northerners found an ideal – and warm – place to resettle. By the 1960s, a national migration had been launched that organized Southwestern retirement into vast planned communities. By the 1970s, resorts had passed through the grand-hotel and dude-ranch phases to emerge as lavish resort complexes with restaurants, discos and golf, tennis, and national convention facilities. Mobile-home communi-

ties and trailer parks staked out mile after mile, motorcycles and dune buggies roared across the open desert, and motorboats plied the reservoirs. Organized leisure became the Southwest's most visible industry.

Traditional agriculture and manufacturing, meanwhile, went into relative decline. Mining

– subject to falling demand, foreign competition, shrinking deposits and labor disputes – suffered the most, and many smelters and open-pit mines closed. Ranches, faced with expensive mechanization, have further consolidated into large spreads. Cattle are fattened more in feed lots than on the open range and cowboys work machines or they don't work at all.

Water-intensive surplus crops like cotton no longer make economic sense, and municipalities are clamoring for water, a rare and argumentative commodity in this arid land. Ranches, citrus groves and cotton fields increasingly have been bought out by agribusiness or have given way to the walled-in multiplex developments.

LEFT: young sightseer at the Grand Canyon.
RIGHT: cowboy south of Albuquerque, New Mexico.

The trend toward consumerism and resource exploitation finds its strongest opposition within the Anglo community itself. Mormons, powerful in Arizona as well as Utah, have held out for conservative, family-oriented values, though even they have had to strike compromises that allow them, for instance, to own or manage gambling casinos, though not to deal the cards or gamble themselves.

Environmentalism, which grows increasingly passionate as the landscape disappears, is a primarily Anglo movement that runs counter to Anglo materialism. Curiously, environmentalists look to traditional Indians, particularly the

Hopi and Navajo elders, as allies and often join tribal councils in suing outside corporations.

Southwestern retirees

The phrase "retired to the Southwest" invariably conjures up images of the swimming pool and deck chairs, the golf and hot sun of a Snow Belter's afterlife. The reality, while including those items, is fortunately far livelier and far more reflective of the American spectrum.

The terrain itself does not permit uniformity. Much of the Southwest is higher in elevation than outsiders realize and it suffers classic northern winters, particularly Flagstaff – at an elevation of 7,000 feet (2,100 meters) – and

even Santa Fe. A few individuals settle in such mountainous small towns as St. George in Utah and Flagstaff in Arizona, knowing that they will enjoy temperate summers while their contemporaries are holed up with their air conditioning. A few more will strike some compromise in Santa Fe and Taos in New Mexico, or Sedona and Prescott in Arizona, where the summers are slightly too warm and the winters just overchilled. But most of the incoming retirees have spent previous Januaries numb to their very bones, and so they go to the opposite extreme, demanding perfect winters and the summer discomfort be damned.

Given the sunward tilt of the Southwest – high in the north and falling as the Rio Grande and Colorado River basins drain southward – retirement country thickens in southern New Mexico and reaches peak density in the Sonoran Desert of central and southern Arizona, where the winters are mostly celestial.

Most responsible for the popular image of Southwestern retirement is Sun City, west of Phoenix, invented by the Del Webb Corporation in 1960 and the granddaddy of American planned-retirement communities. Around 50,000 people now inhabit this walled-in labyrinth of curving streets, golf courses, single-story dwellings, artificial lakes, recreational centers, churches, medical centers and subdued commercial areas. To own a home, one must be at least 50 years old. Residents gather in travel clubs, bicycle clubs, alumni clubs, even a club for retired union members, and a giant Sundome hosts a symphony of Sun Citians plus visiting celebrities. So calm and safe is the environment that circulation is largely by bicycle and golf cart. With a long waiting list for potential residents, Sun City has spawned such kinsmen as Sun City West, Green Valley, and the euphemistically named Youngtown.

Arizona's over-planned communities offer a bewildering range of activities, yet on streets where nearly identical houses are tinted complementary pastels, and graveled yards are sprayed minutely divergent shades of green, one can't help feeling that individuality is being held onto only lightly.

Far more numerous are the mobile-home communities found outside El Paso and Albuquerque, and along the Colorado River from Boulder City, Nevada, to Yuma, Arizona, and in diminishing perspectives from Tempe through

Mesa to Apache Junction, east of Phoenix. Owing to population density, social life is intense, with evenings of bingo and cards, community meals and dances, and the floating coffee klatsch that slides into a cocktail party.

Forays outside the community are often by recreational vehicle: dune buggies for the hills, motorboats on the reservoir. To give each residence a personal stamp, care is lavished on gardening and decor, but the turnover is far greater than in communities like Sun City or Carefree. Strangers overcome the sense of impermanence with immediate exchanges of life stories and watch over each others' comings and goings.

few hundred residents to tens of thousands of Snow-Belt refugees. A few hook up to utilities in compounds, but most just stake out a spot in the surrounding hard sand.

The town's one thoroughfare, lined with acres of open space, awaits the winter-long flea market. Up go the tables of glassware, antiques, tools, old bottles and campaign buttons collected the previous summer, along with jewelry, ceramics, wood carvings and clothing that the retirees have made. The season climaxes with February's white-man powwow, an annual "rock festival" of minerals and gems that draws more than a million visitors to the town. ❑

Most evanescent and fascinating of all retirement groups are those who converge on the Southwest each winter in campers, trailers and even trucks with homemade cabins to improvise life wherever they pull up. Some retain roots where they spend the summer, but many are too nomadic even for the tax collector. They range throughout southern New Mexico and the Sonoran Desert but can be found in greatest concentration at Quartzsite, a two-café desert crossroads in Arizona, near the California border. During the winter, Quartzsite swells from a

LEFT: a home-garden harvest of squash.
ABOVE: an old-time long in New Mexico.

HIGH TECHNOLOGY AND LIFESTYLES

Two industries increasingly important in bringing white migrants to the Southwest are the high-tech and military research industries. Arizona has a major stake in high-technology, which employs a considerable percentage of the manufacturing workforce. Defense-oriented research into microbiology and particle physics are major employers at research centers such as Los Alamos and Sandia Laboratories. What has become known as the silicon desert has resulted in an upwardly mobile, career-oriented subculture represented by singles bars and club-like apartment complexes, all aesthetically dissected by regional "lifestyle" magazines.

ART IN THE SOUTHWEST

An eclectic range of art and artists, from Pueblo Indian to Europeans

on expedition, give the Southwest an especially rich and satisfying aesthetic

In one of the most ambitious art projects the Southwest has seen, a long-dead volcanic cinder cone in northern Arizona becomes one of the world's largest works of art. Visitors descend to the bottom of the crater bowl and look up to experience the illusion of the sky as a tangible object stretched over the crater, like Saran Wrap spattered with stars. Artist James Turrell's Roden Crater Project is unprecedented in its scale and ambition, yet it still follows the lead of centuries of art in the American Southwest because it is inspired by light and landscape.

No other region of North America is blessed with such extravagant, penetrating, radically changeable light; no other place on our planet has such an astonishing repertoire of land forms and biological zones. No wonder artists never cease to draw inspiration from it.

Awesome images

The artists who first dribbled westward in the mid-19th century were romantics, and the land they encountered sent their imaginations spinning. Exotic Indian cultures and monumental mountains and canyons became epics on their canvases. Paintings such as Albert Bierstadt's *The Rocky Mountains* and Thomas Moran's *The Chasm of the Colorado* took grandeur and raised it to the second power, calling in otherworldly light, Wagnerian storms and impossible peaks and abysses. The Southwest's natural landscapes hardly needed exaggerating, but such paintings were the products of their time.

The whole country imagined the West as something even more awesome than the reality, and the artists gave us what we craved. Commercial interests encouraged them. By the 1880s, the Santa Fe Railway was hiring artists such as Moran to paint the pristine wonders of New Mexico and Arizona, luring tourists and settlers from the over-industrialized East.

Art didn't actually need the patronage of the

railroad industry; the land itself was attraction enough. "Any man who is really an artist," wrote Charles Lummis in 1892, "will find the Southwest... a region where the ingenuity, the imagination, and the love of God are... visible at every turn."

Two academically trained New York artists,

NAVAJO SAND PAINTINGS

Sand paintings were, traditionally, made during night-long Navajo healing rituals. (Nowadays, of course, permanent sand paintings are made specifically for the non-Indian buyer.) Softly singing the various chants of the rite, and depending upon the cure required, the medicine man sifts the colorful crushed stone, corn pollen and other sacred materials through his thumb and index finger, slowly creating the appropriate design – Navajo gods, rainbows, feathers, or representations of animals. Most sand paintings are about 3 feet (1 meter) across, although some reach as much as 20 feet (7 meters) and require helpers to complete.

PRECEDING PAGES: saguaro blooms; painting the Sangre de Cristos. **LEFT:** *Cow's Skull: Red, White and Blue,* by Georgia O'Keeffe. **RIGHT:** sand painting.

Ernest Blumenschein and Bert Phillips, came under its spell in 1898. The two were on a sketching pilgrimage through the Rockies from Denver to Mexico when one of their wagon's wheels collapsed near Taos, in northern New Mexico. Blumenschein later wrote, "No artist had ever recorded the New Mexico I was now seeing... My destiny was being decided." They stayed, and in 1915 along with four colleagues founded the Taos Society of Artists. The Society won national recognition for its work and Taos became a mecca for artists.

Taos today claims some 250 serious resident artists (out of a population of 6,200) and a cen-

tury-long heritage of interpreting the landscapes and cultural stew of its immediate neighborhood. Even the seemingly hackneyed subjects – Taos Pueblo, Taos Mountain, the famous Rancho de Taos church – keep hurling fresh challenges and insights at any artist open to interpretation. A rusty twilight, a dusting of snow, even the sunburn of a bone-dry afternoon in June changes not only their color but also their spirit. In the Southwest, landscapes and architecture have long been acknowledged as living things.

No one understood this better, or made more of it, than Georgia O'Keeffe, who adopted New Mexico as her summer residence in 1929, and

O'KEEFFE: ARTIST AND WOMAN BEFORE HER TIME

Born in Wisconsin and trained primarily in Chicago and New York, Georgia O'Keeffe is the artist most closely associated with the American Southwest. She first came to public notice in 1916 when Alfred Stieglitz, an influential photographer and art collector, exhibited her drawings at his New York gallery. "The purest, finest, sincerest things to have entered (the gallery) in a long while," he said.

Stieglitz and O'Keeffe were married in 1924 in an often tumultuous relationship. An independent woman, she retained her name. "I've had a hard time hanging on to my name, but I hang on to it with my teeth. I like getting what I've got on my own."

At times O'Keeffe felt frustrated by the unwillingness of the male-dominated art world to take her or her work seriously. "Women can only create babies, say the scientists, but I say they can produce art – and Georgia O'Keeffe is the proof of it," wrote Stieglitz.

She wasn't especially comfortable with the elaborate interpretations critics made of her work, once scolding a writer who asked about the meaning of a painting. "The meaning is there on the canvas. If you don't get it, that's too bad. I have nothing more to say than what I painted."

O'Keeffe died in Santa Fe in 1986, aged 92 and one of America's finest 20th-century artists.

moved permanently to the sheepherding village of Abiquiu in 1946. Her art, now properly celebrated in the Georgia O'Keeffe Museum in Santa Fe, is recognizable and yet impossible to categorize. On her canvases, bare hills become voluptuous swirls, flowers bloom with erotic energy, slumping adobe walls exude timeless nobility. The paintings are not quite realistic, not exactly expressionistic and seldom entirely abstract; they are pure, emotional interpretations of what she saw and felt. She explained near-obsessive paintings of bleached bones: "The bones seem to cut sharply to the center of something that is keenly alive on the desert

even tho' it is vast and empty and untouchable... and knows no kindness with all its beauty."

It's in the light

Light teases, probes and reveals O'Keeffe's landscapes. David Muench, the prolific landscape photographer, says that light is "what gives meaning to form," demonstrating with a portrait of white sycamore bark in Arizona's remote Aravaipa Canyon. Muench chose to ignore the sunny side of the trees and photographed the trunks veiled in shadow instead

---

Left: *Sangre de Cristo Mountains*, by Ernest Blumenschein. **Above:** Georgia O'Keeffe in Taos, 1929.

because "It wasn't a mute black shadow. It incorporated the light reflected from a creek, a riparian forest and a desert canyon wall. The whole life of the canyon was wrapped up in the soft shadow on this sycamore trunk."

Since moving to Arizona from Chicago, 30 years ago, painter Lynn Taber-Borcherdt's landscapes have evolved through a fascination with deep, jagged shadows, then iridescence and luminosity, and recently the pure drama of sky. "If I hadn't come to Tucson, none of this would have found its way into my work," she has said. "My paintings in Chicago were dark, dark, dark."

The Southwest's swirl of cultures has also motivated and inspired artists, not always to the good. Western art, while still prized by its devotees, seems, after a 150-year-long run, rather stale and repetitive. But it did (and perhaps still does) play a role in perpetuating the mythology of the noble cowboy, which in turn made the West appear to be a land of adventure, heroism and virtue – and therefore a repository of dreams for many generations of Americans.

Ceramics and pottery

Southwestern pottery has produced and fulfilled a different form of dream for the Southwest's Indian tribes, especially the Pueblo people around the Four Corners region. Their artistic traditions date back more than a millennium but their art suffered hard times, as the people themselves did, beginning with the Spanish *entrada* in 1540. But late in the 19th century, pottery began a spectacular and lucrative revival as the tribes discovered a market for their wares in the enchanted Anglos. Two women, Maria Martinez of San Ildefonso Pueblo, in New Mexico, and Nampeyo, a Hopi from Hano, Arizona, led the way. They studied the pottery of their ancient ancestors that archaeologists had excavated, then layered their own creative force over the traditions.

Today, thousands of skilled Indian potters produce exquisite, immaculately detailed handmade pots, sometimes selling them for thousands of dollars. Each tribe or pueblo maintains a distinctive aesthetic signature. Navajo pottery is generally undecorated, letting the architecture of the vessel form the artistic statement. Acoma jars feature black-and-white interlocking geometric patterns of dazzling complexity. Hopi potters are still inspired by their ancestors' red-and-black-on-yellow designs featuring abstracted feathers, butterflies and shapes that originating from worlds that Anglo collectors will never understand. As one Hopi potter told writer Stephen Trimble, "Most of my designs are from the dreams that I had, from looking at the earth, everything in the universe." Other Indian artists have invented their own traditions, although nearly all have been influenced in some way by the land itself.

R. C. Gorman, the celebrated (and widely imitated) Navajo painter, recalls his first experience in art, drawing in the ruddy mud of

ON VIEW

An excellent place to see some of the best pueblo pottery and ceramics, including those of Maria Martinez, is the Millicent Rogers Museum, near Taos.

in urban *barrios*. Among the most notable Hispanic artists in the are today is Luis Jimenez, whose monumental fiberglass sculptures celebrate people who have been overlooked or downtrodden. His *Border Crossing*, planted outside the Museum of Fine Arts in Santa Fe, depicts a larger-than-life barefoot man carrying his wife across the Rio Grande. This is illegal, according to American law. Jimenez thinks it is full of courage and nobility. Looking up at the sculpture, we are left to ponder the truth.

rience in art, drawing in the ruddy mud of Chinle Wash in Canyon de Chelly. The economical lines of his swirling human figures clearly continue to spring from that well.

Contemporary Indian jewelry frequently borrows the symbolic designs of nature – mountains, lightning, rainbows, clouds, snakes and birds. Whatever the tribe or artistic endeavor, few American Indian artists ever stray far from the inspiration of nature itself. It is an integral part of their tradition, religion and what we outsiders might call soul.

Hispanic art also thrives in the Southwest, from the naive folk-art *santos* – statues of Catholic saints – to politically charged murals

One important genre of southwestern art is often overlooked or scorned by the serious art establishment – Southwestern kitsch. We all know it: the saguaro-in-the-sunset, the mauve coyote launching his arias toward the moon, the prehistoric flute-player Kokopelli gracing earrings, light sconces or toilet-paper holders. Purists will cringe, but the Southwest has always needed simplified symbols. This is an awesome land where reality and mythology are entangled in a complex weave, where nature is often too overwhelming to comprehend and

ABOVE: Zuni pottery and jewelry, and Julian and Maria Martinez, 1931. **RIGHT:** modern Zuni art on a shell.

where many cultures are thrown together in a tense and intricate dance.

The Santa Fe Railroad triggered a cultural exchange when, in 1883, it began to lay tracks from Kansas to Los Angeles. Even regional architecture was affected by entanglement with the railroad. Mary Colter became architect and decorator for the railroad in 1902, and eventually designed and decorated 22 buildings. Her perfectionism and cantankerous manner caused workmen to dread her arrival at a building site, and she showed up often, even to supervise the laying individual of stones. The Watchtower at Grand Canyon is a masterpiece of her "indige-

nous" style and use of local materials. She hired the young Hopi artist Fred Kabotie, who later gained worldwide acclaim, to paint its Hopi Room. Kabotie later related: "She could be difficult, especially when it came to matching colors… one day she kept sending me up in the tower with little dabs of oil colors, too small to match… I finally lost my patience. 'Let me have the tube,' I said [and] squeezed everything out and stirred in the color I felt was right. 'You've ruined everything and you've used up all the paint,' she cried. I took a little dab and ran back up in the tower. Fortunately it matched… saving my life and hers." ❏

OF NOBLE COWBOYS AND GLORIFIED LANDSCAPES

The genre of "Western" art may have become irreversibly stale and tired, but it is almost inescapable for most of us, and that includes the good, the bad, and the schlock.

As for good Western art, not only was the notion of the noble cowboy explored and perpetuated, but often the West's natural splendors were also embellished.

Thomas Moran, for example, was the first artist to celebrate the grandeur of Yellowstone – his work helped to persuade Congress to designate Yellowstone a national park – and later the Grand Canyon with a romantic and glorified atmosphere. Moran didn't intend to make an exact rendering but rather tried to imbue his work with the

emotional power of the landscape. To those critics demanding accuracy, Moran was quick to respond: "I did not wish to realize the scene literally… (but) to preserve and convey its true impression."

For some artists of the late 19th century like Frederic Remington, the Western story was not landscape but the cowboy and his response to his environment. Yet as the 19th century drew to a close, the West of Remington's youth was quickly fading. In 1900, Remington visited Colorado and New Mexico, only to find that the rugged frontier had given way to "brick buildings and derby hats… It spoils all my early illusions, and they are my capital."

LITERATURE

*Writers and travelers have written wondrous things about the Southwest,
grappling with social upheaval, murder mysteries and philosophical musings*

The author of this book," a reviewer once wrote of *The Monkey Wrench Gang*, "should be neutered and locked away forever." The author of the book, Edward Abbey, liked that critical snarl so much that he quoted it in an essay about his own work nine years later. You can almost hear Abbey, the old fox,

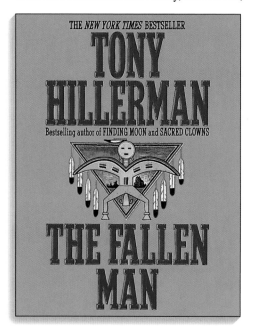

chuckling even now. It was a validation, an assurance that his writing had hit the mark he intended. It had provoked and inflamed – which is what much of the best Southwestern writing has been doing for the last couple of centuries.

The Southwest is a fierce, prickly, obstinate, unforgiving land, replete with natural peril and human conflict. It is only right that its literature reflects this. It is also a place of exotic and delicate beauty, and writers have heaped up mountains of words, often great words, trying to understand and defend it.

"We are learning finally that the forests and mountains and desert canyons are holier than our churches," Abbey wrote in *Desert Solitaire*,

probably his masterpiece. "Therefore let us behave accordingly."

The earliest Southwestern writers were the soldiers and missionaries who came under the Spanish flag, and they kept exhaustive diaries to satisfy the Spanish mania for bureaucratic documentation. A few managed to create literature in the process. The best was Fr. Ignaz Pfefferkorn, an 18th-century Jesuit priest who described in meticulous detail and frequent delight such things as the comings and goings of scorpions, the effects of eating chilis, and the native customs regarding adultery. "Most of them are satisfied with one wife," he deadpanned in *Sonora: A Description of the Province*, "a fact which makes their conversion [to Christianity] easier."

Landmarks in literature

The Anglos who followed in the next century were a motley bunch, mostly amateurs when it came to writing poetry, journalism or fiction, but their work nevertheless forms a fascinating, mosaic-like picture of frontier life. One of the accidental masterpieces of 19th-century Southwest literature is John G. Bourke's *On the Border With Crook*, a painfully vivid account of U.S. Army Gen. George Crook's war against the Apaches. Bourke was an army captain but no knee-jerk defender of his side's campaign. His visionary observations crackle across a century: "Promises on each side have been made only to deceive and to be broken; [and] the red hand of war has rested most heavily upon shrieking mother and wailing babe."

Perhaps the greatest early landmark in Southwestern literature was produced by an even less likely character, an asthmatic New Jersey art professor named John C. Van Dyke, who wandered the Southwestern deserts alone from 1898 to 1901. Van Dyke chronicled their unfamiliar beauty in rhapsodic but accurate detail: "Somehow (the desert mountains) remind you of a clinched hand with the knuckles turned skyward... Barren rock and nothing more; but what could better epitomize power!" After *The*

Desert appeared in 1901, its subject was no longer a wasteland in the American imagination, and this slim book formed a foundation for what would become a flood of interpretive nature writing about the American deserts.

Classic Southwestern fiction

Southwestern fiction of the 20th century has also breathed deeply of the land, as well as from the many human cultures that inhabit it. "I don't believe a person can be born and raised in the Southwest and not be affected by the land," wrote the celebrated New Mexico novelist Rodolfo Anaya. "My earliest memories were molded by the forces in my landscape: sun, wind, rain, the *llano* (plain), the river. And all of these forces were working to create the people that walked across my plane of vision."

Anaya's most celebrated novel, *Bless Me, Ultima*, published in 1972, is a fantastic swirl of violence, familial love, sorcery and faith, and both good and evil are personified in the elements of nature itself. The whirlwinds of summer "carry with them the evil spirit of a devil." The wild herbs have spirits, "and before I dug she (Ultima, the *curandera*) made me speak to the plant and tell it why we pulled it from its home in the earth." Few Anglos have any understanding of the Hispanic world of Anaya's novels, but *Bless Me, Ultima* provides an intimately scaled introduction.

American Indian writers have done much the same for their cultures. Leslie Marmon Silko's classic 1977 novel *Ceremony* tells the story of Tayo, a returning World War II prisoner of war, who struggles to purge his nightmares through the mystical ceremonies of his people. Tony Hillerman, although no Indian himself (and Navajos have been surprised to learn that he isn't), has penetrated Indian society in the Southwest to a remarkable depth within the framework of his page-turner mysteries.

The thorniest cultural novel of the Southwest is John Nichols' *The Milagro Beanfield War*, set in rural northern New Mexico where working Hispanic families are struggling against wealthy Anglo developers. It is hilarious, outrageous, profane – and profound, because it illuminates the real-life epic battle for the little towns and ancient family farms in the orbits of

Taos and Santa Fe. When Nichols first arrived in Taos in 1969, land in the valley sold for about $500 an acre; by the end of the century, an acre was likely to be worth $50,000 and up. An entire culture is evaporating, and in another 30 years *Milagro* is likely to be the most insightful record of this culture that we have.

The classic 20th-century novel about Southwestern development – which is the central story of the land throughout that century – is, of course, the one for which it was proposed that Edward Abbey be neutered. *The Monkey Wrench Gang* is a badly flawed polemic; it reads, in too many places, like the work of a

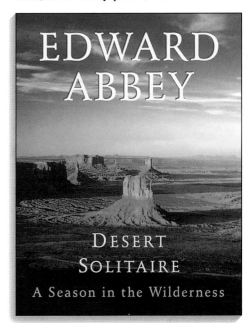

EDWARD ABBEY

DESERT SOLITAIRE

A Season in the Wilderness

"Still, as albatrosses go, I guess this one, ultimately, is fairly benign. I don't know if *The Milagro Beanfield War* is a good book, or just one with a lot of upbeat energy that has captured a certain fancy. To be truthful, though, I do have a few minor regrets. For example, given the opportunity to rewrite the novel, for sure I would cut out two thirds of the cussing, which often seems gratuitous. And believe me, only one character, and just *once* during the entire novel, would dare exclaim, *"Ai, Chihuahua!"* Other than that, I still haven't reread the book in its entirety since the galleys were returned... so long ago."
– John Nichols, 1993

LEFT: one of Tony Hillerman's two dozen books.
RIGHT: Edward Abbey's classic *Desert Solitaire*, 1968.

gifted teenager in glandular warp drive. But its theme of eco-hooliganism seemed to collect and catalyze the outrage and frustration so many Southwesterners have felt (and still feel) about the exploitation and abuse of the land. Abbey always claimed that he wrote it mainly as entertainment, and with an "indulgence of spleen and anger from a position of safety behind my typewriter."

But Abbey's biographer, James Bishop Jr., wrote that *The Monkey Wrench Gang* "comes the closest to reaching that place of Abbey's most steadfast convictions: a romantically idealized world in which the Industrial Revolution

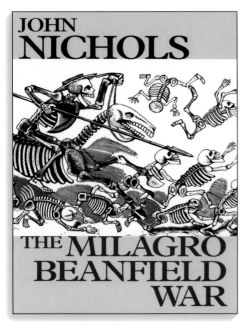

has been aborted, and society has reached a steady-state equilibrium where man and the land can exist in harmony."

With his earlier *Desert Solitaire*, a collection of essays loosely based on an abortive life as a national park ranger in southern Utah, Abbey opened a vein of Southwestern literature that continues to be mined by many superb writers. This genre may resemble nature writing, but at a deeper level it is really about the relationships between humans and the land. And it is far more emotionally charged – and crankier and pricklier – than the work of the pioneer naturalists such as John Muir, Aldo Leopold and Van Dyke.

Charles Bowden summarized it perfectly in the opening lines of his 1986 *Blue Desert*, which picked up where *Desert Solitaire* trailed off. "This is the place where they hope to escape their pasts – the unemployment, the smoggy skies, dirty cities, crush of human numbers. This they cannot do. Instead, they reproduce the world they have fled. I am drawn to the frenzy of this act." Bowden's essays are themselves frenzied – overheated, distinctively styled (some have said "self-indulgent"), often angry, but finally profound.

The finest recent book in this vein, however, is the quizzically titled *America, New Mexico*, by Robert Leonard Reid. In its 10 essays, Reid masterfully paints the natural environment of New Mexico as a stage set – "a time-scented garden where nature is foremost and rocks are truth, and where dawn is a paean to fresh starts and reckless plans" – and then fills in real-life characters who are struggling with issues such as poverty, racism and the weight of the Southwest's tumultuous history.

Reid willingly plunged himself into raw adversity and sinister forces – gang violence in Albuquerque; the remnants of the Trinity Site, where the first atomic bomb was exploded – and found, "standing staunchly against them a quiet and unshakable confidence rooted in the natural world."

The sweeping grandeur and miniature miracles of the land itself seemed to offer, somehow, a redemptive counterpoint to the human frenzy that both Reid and Bowden described. And more than anything else, this is the long, tough thread coursing through more than two centuries of writing about this region. Yes, the land is achingly beautiful and so consequently it is hopelessly fragile. But the land will abide. "When I touch the steel towers of the Sunbelt, they feel like cobwebs soon to be dispersed by an angry wind," wrote Bowden in *Blue Desert*. "When I touch the earth I feel the rock hard face of eternity."

Any bookshelf packed with the best reading on the American Southwest will be hot to the touch, sizzling with pain, passion, fury, violence and moody volatility – all classic characteristics of the Southwest and its people. But under all of these qualities will lie a foundation of deep faith. ❑

LEFT: dealing with the issues of land ownership.

Indian Art

A painted track resembling a roller coaster loops around a clay pot, encircling a flock of lizards, their heads distorted into skewed squares with round, quizzical eyes. Two clowns, part human and part turtle, cavort like circus acrobats in the interior of a bowl.

In what we now know as Utah's Canyonlands National Park, bizarre and chilling mummy figures drift like dark, two-dimensional ghosts across a canyon wall. These art works are as enigmatic as anything hung today at the Museum of Modern Art, but they were created by anonymous artists nearly a millennium ago.

At the peak of prehistoric civilization in the Southwest, from around AD 1100 to 1300, art flowered in dizzying profusion – a sign of people enjoying enough affluence to spend considerable time in creative pursuits. Unfortunately, when these cultures – the Anasazi, Hohokam, Mogollon and others – collapsed and dispersed, most of the stories underlying their paintings and pottery evaporated. Modern people of the Pueblos, descendants of the Anasazi, can sometimes "read" ancient petroglyphs. But they don't agree on the meanings.

Prehistoric Southwestern art mostly falls into three categories: ceramics, body ornaments and rock art. Pottery begins to appear in the archaeological record almost as early as agriculture, around AD 300, but it was several more centuries before it occurred to anyone to paint it. After AD 700, ceramic art blossomed with fantastic geometric and zoologic art.

The Anasazi of the Four Corners canyons and plateaus usually decorated their pots with tense geometric abstractions of checkerboards, triangles, diamonds, zigzags, spirals and mazes. The desert Hohokam of Arizona frequently indulged themselves with chains of dancing figures, sometimes human, sometimes animal or insect. A good Hohokam pot sizzles with joy and energy.

The most sophisticated, and most startling, designs came from the Mimbres people of western New Mexico. Mimbres bowls serve up an astounding mixture of dramatic geometry, phantasmal beasts and pictorial scenes of hunting, fishing or dancing. Pioneer archaeologist Jesse Fewkes believed the pottery depicted the Mimbres' mythological world, a theory that still seems plausible today. A few pieces hint at dark corners in that world: one well-known Mimbres bowl clearly depicts a human decapitation.

Prehistoric art often was designed to be worn as necklaces, pendants, earrings, bracelets or rings. Many pieces were effigies of birds, antelope or mountain lions carved from stone or bone. They likely had religious significance, counterparts to modern Christian cross necklaces or good-luck charms. Other pieces appear (to us) purely ornamental, such as a stunning Hohokam necklace strung with more than 1,200 turquoise beads.

The rock peckings (petroglyphs) and paintings (pictographs) scattered throughout the Southwest's

hillsides, mountains and canyons are the most prevalent remnant of prehistoric art, and also the most bewildering. But the most fundamental question remains to be answered: what were these millions of illustrations intended to do? Depict history, Mark territory? Record a census? Offer pictorial prayers for rain, fertility or successful hunting?

Two things seem certain: rock art was designed to communicate across centuries and cultural lines. Wherever possible, rock artists created their works under erosion-protected natural stone eaves. And many symbols appear throughout the region, forming a *lingua franca* that would have been understood by a speaker of Hohokam, Kayenta Anasazi or Mogollon. ❑

RIGHT: an ancient petroglyph near Zuni Pueblo.

THE SOUTHWEST IN FILM

For decades, film makers have struggled to re-create the old West
"as it really was". The results range from kitsch to memorable Oscar winners

In John Ford's *The Man Who Shot Liberty Valance*, a senator played by James Stewart confesses to a newspaper editor that for decades he has lived a lie. The senator admits that 30 years earlier he did not actually gun down a sadistic outlaw, an act that launched his political career. Having heard the whole story, the editor tosses away his notes and declares, "This is the West, sir. When the legend becomes fact, print the legend."

Duels in the sun

By the time *Liberty Valance* came out in 1962, the makers of Westerns had instinctively followed that creed for nearly 70 years. They portrayed a West of duels in the sun, cavalry charges across desert dreamscapes and savage Indians lined up on ruddy buttes.

These films offer little sense of everyday life, just an idealized world where things usually go according to plan: the bad guy embodies evil, while the hero upholds all that is good, reluctantly resorting to violence to right a world gone wrong. It's a simple scheme, and one that prevailed in countless "B Westerns", those second-billed features at old-time movie houses. Wildly popular, B movies both influenced the public's image of the West and cemented a perception of the Western as simple, light entertainment.

That perspective disregards the artistry of leading filmmakers, from silent-movie star William S. Hart to John Ford and Clint Eastwood. Traditional elements run through their work, but all three take the Western beyond simple formula, an achievement long ignored: Ford won six Academy Awards, but none for his Westerns. Only recently, during a minor revival, has the genre earned greater respect, especially Kevin Costner's *Dances with Wolves* and Eastwood's *Unforgiven*. Both won Academy Awards for best film – the first Western winners since *Cimarron* 60 years earlier.

Western mythologizing was well under way by the time movies flickered into the public consciousness. Even before the Old West rode off into the sunset for good, 19th-century novels, stage plays and Wild West shows had

reshaped it. Film just offered a new medium for an already popular genre.

One of the first movies filmed in Hollywood was also a Western, Cecil B. DeMille's *The Squaw Man* (1913). Originally produced for stage, *The Squaw Man* played another pivotal role in film history. It launched the film career of actor-director William S. Hart, who won Broadway acclaim in the play as a cowboy named Cash Hawkins.

Hart knew and loved the West. Born in New York state in 1865, his family took him to the Midwest, and he grew up playing with Sioux children in the frontier towns where his father set up gristmills. He traveled with his father

---

PRECEDING PAGES: Monument Valley in *Stagecoach*.
LEFT: John Wayne, James Stewart and director John Ford on the set of *The Man Who Shot Liberty Valance*.
RIGHT: Henry Fonda in *My Darling Clementine*, 1946.

deep into Sioux Country before the family returned east. After *The Squaw Man*, Hart began getting more Western roles, such as the lead in *The Virginian*, enhancing his cowboy reputation. None other than Bat Masterson touted Hart's portrayal as "a true type of that reckless nomad who flourished on the border when the six-shooter was the final arbiter of all disputes between man and man."

Committed to an honest depiction (and chronically in need of money), Hart had a revelation while watching a Western movie in 1913. Horrified at its inaccuracies, he likened the film to burlesque. But he also recognized

PAVING THE WAY: THE FIRST WESTERNS

It may be hard to imagine a Western without the sound of gunfire or the thundering of horses' hooves, but some real gems of the genre are the early silent films. Although *Cripple Creek Bar Room* (1898) is considered the "first cowboy film", it was 1903's *The Great Train Robbery* that really gave birth to the genre. The 10-minute-long film was actually shot on the East coast, rather than the Wyoming locale that it portrayed, but all the essential elements of a Western were there: good guys, bad guys, a robbery, a chase and a final showdown. And it all wrapped up with the first-ever close-up of a gunman firing directly into the camera (and delighted audience).

that if this movie succeeded, then his truer vision of the West should be able to capture movie audiences.

A Western revival

By the time Hart arrived in Hollywood, producers were sounding a death knell for Westerns, one of several times the genre seemed to be on its way to the last roundup. Under film pioneer Thomas Ince's guidance, he began his career, and many credit Hart with reviving the Western. His sober face and hunched, two-gun stance became as famous as Charlie Chaplin's Little Tramp.

Unlike the glossy, stunt-filled Tom Mix movies, Hart didn't depict a rhinestone West. His had dust and grit; the plots generally strong and adult. Wild West shows had popularized flashy western duds, more Liberace than Laramie. Hart righted that image with a plaid shirt, simple kerchief and a vest. He prided himself on his vision and in his autobiography wrote, "My pictures of the West in the early days will make that colorful period of American life live forever."

Western expert William K. Everson agreed with Hart and wrote, "His films were raw, unglamorous, and gutsy... the ramshackle Western towns and their inhabitants like unretouched Matthew Brady photographs, the sense of dry heat ever present (panchromatic film stock, developed in the 1920s, softened and glamorized the landscapes in later Westerns), and the clouds of dust everywhere."

Other directors had wetted the ground for a cleaner look. Considered Hart's masterpiece, *Tumbleweeds* (1925) has a documentary feel, especially the scenes of Oklahoma's Cherokee Strip Land Rush. The film is considered by many to be an honest and accurate – even poetic – depiction of an important historical event. Pioneers race across the screen with a sense of urgency and danger, on horseback, in wagons, even on bicycles. Filmed by a semi-buried camera, ground-level shots of thundering hooves and wagon wheels mesmerized audiences and became Western classics.

Hart's character declares, "Boys, it's the last of the West," and indeed *Tumbleweeds* proved to be Hart's final film. Hart pioneered the West-

LEFT: silent-film star Tom Mix.
RIGHT: cowboy philosopher and film star Will Rogers.

ern hero as a loner, the austere good-bad man who finds purpose and redemption in riding to the rescue. There was plenty of good old-fashioned chivalry, and many a rough outlaw became reformed by the love of a good woman. Hart's films often ended by linking the villians with the saloon and the "good guys" with the church. That strict moralistic quality appealed to World War I audiences, but seemed heavy-handed by the Roaring Twenties.

Clashing with the studios, Hart retired to his ranch north of Los Angeles. Over the years, a steady stream of notables, including Charles Russell and Will Rogers, visited him at his Spanish-style home. Hart died in 1946 and gave the Newhall estate to Los Angeles County to be used as a museum. In typical Two-Gun Bill fashion, he explained, "While I was making pictures, the people gave me their nickels, dimes, and quarters. When I am gone, I want them to have my home."

John Ford country

There are statues of John Wayne in California; they even named an airport after him. To the public, John Wayne is the Western. But no man dominated the genre like director John Ford. Within the film community, Ford's legend is as

Will Rogers

ON LOCATION IN THE SOUTHWEST

The Southwest has long provided filmmakers with varied and picturesque settings for their epics. Utah's Monument Valley is probably the most recognizable Western film locale, a favorite of director John Ford. The red rocks of Arizona's Sedona and the Utah sites of Moab and the canyons around Kanab also have their share of film credits.

But probably the most prolific Southwestern "movie studio" was – and still is – Old Tucson. Located about 15 miles (24 km) from Tucson itself, the old walled city of Tucson was actually built in painstaking detail for the 1940 motion picture *Arizona*. More than 20 additional films were shot there in the '40s and '50s, but the site was continually deteriorating until the Old Tucson Development Company leased the locale from Pima County and began restoration. In January 1960, Old Tucson opened with a "new look" – and dual purpose as both a movie location and family-oriented "entertainment park".

John Wayne is particularly associated with Old Tucson; he made four films there, including the acclaimed *Rio Bravo*. The locale also moved smoothly into television, with the series *High Chaparral* shot there from 1966 to 1971.

A fire destroyed a huge portion of the studio in 1995, but the facility was quickly rebuilt and continues to be both a working film location and popular family destination.

big as Wayne's. Ingmar Bergman called him the world's greatest film maker. Orson Welles watched Ford's 1939 *Stagecoach* 40 times and declared his three great influences "John Ford, John Ford, and John Ford."

Born in Maine of Irish immigrants, Seamus Ford (he later changed his name to John) headed west following the Hollywood acting success of his brother Francis. As he explained in an interview with Peter Bogdanovich, he got his chance when a director failed to show for a big

THE DUKE

Marion Michael Morrison, better known as John Wayne, was discovered by director Raoul Walsh and had his first starring role in *The Big Trail* (1930).

Earp on the back lot a few times and based his 1946 O.K. Corral tale *My Darling Clementine* on Earp's accounts, although by that time the old gunfighter was printing the legend, rather than the facts.

Ford rode out to locations and slept under the stars during shooting. In 1938, he headed out to a more distant location than usual – Monument Valley – to film his first sound Western, *Stagecoach*, starring John Wayne. Dubbed "Ford Country," the valley and its towering red rock formations evolved into a famous trade-

scene the same morning that Universal Studios chief Carl Laemmle visited the lot. Someone needed to look in charge, so Ford took control of the action, ultimately burning down the street in a scene he described as "more pogrom than Western." Later, when a new film needed a director, Laemmle said, "Give Jack Ford the job. He yells good."

Yelling good and using his sharp eye for composition, Ford first directed silent two-reelers, then moved on to some of the earliest Western epics, most notably *The Iron Horse* (1924). Like Hart, Ford sought authenticity. He often consulted old-timers and eschewed quick-draw duels and showy costumes. Ford met Wyatt

mark. Ford, Wayne and Monument Valley have grown into a kind of holy trinity of the classic Western. But the West they portrayed was one of considerable complexity. The early Wayne is as different from the icon Duke of later years as Hound Dog Elvis is from Vegas Elvis. Jane Tompkins, in *West of Everything*, writes, "The expression of the young John Wayne is tender... pure and sweet..."

Ford cast Wayne in the roles of men with clashing emotions and loyalties, such as the cavalry officer who is torn between obedience to his commanding officer and his better judgment, in *Fort Apache*. And the classic Monument Valley films often ended ambiguously, allowing audiences to reach conflicting conclusions, something that never happened in good-guy bad-guy Westerns. In *Fort Apache*, Henry Fonda plays the commanding officer, a martinet who leads his troops on a suicidal charge against Apaches. Based on Custer's last stand, the film feels almost like a Vietnam-vintage attack on military incompetence. But as the movie closes, Wayne, whose advice Fonda disastrously ignored, tells myth-seeking reporters of the officer's heroism and eulogizes, "No man died more gallantly."

Critics chastise Ford for his depictions of Indians as bloodthirsty marauders. Certainly in

was *Northwest Passage*, a great adventure saga starring Spencer Tracy as the leader of Roger's Rangers, battling Indians for territory.

"Let's face it," Ford told Bogdanovich, "we've treated them very badly – it's a blot on our shield; we've cheated and robbed, killed, murdered, massacred and everything else, but they kill one white man and, God, out come the troops."

Certainly, if you've seen one Ford film, you haven't seen them all. Ford's West was one of shadings, not unlike the changing play of natural light and shadow found in his movies. It reflects the man himself, who could charm his

Stagecoach they appear as anonymous killers, while in *The Searchers* (1956), the white women captured by Indians have gone insane. Wayne's character is even ready to shoot his captive niece, the one he spent seven years searching for, declaring, "Living with Comanches ain't being alive." Yet in *Fort Apache*, Cochise appears as the man of reason, and it is Fonda who displays the bloodlust and bigotry that draw the Indians into reluctant battle. Yet another anti-Native American picture

---

LEFT: a Colt Peacemaker, perhaps the most ironic name for a handgun ever.
ABOVE: Clint Eastwood as The Man With No Name.

WOMEN IN WESTERNS

Although women were strong heroines (*The Perils of Pauline* types) in the silent era's Western serial melodramas, females in later Western films were either portrayed as good-natured dance hall entertainers or "virginal guiding lights". In many cases, women filled a domestic role; possibly a love interest to be fought over and possessed by the "hero". They were often the motive for male activity. But perhaps the notion of women as less-than-privileged characters stems from the fact that white women were not among the first trappers or hunters to explore the region – they came instead with the establishment of farms, settlements and towns.

actors or, as he did to Wayne, reduce them to tears. As James Stewart said of the director, "Take everything you've heard, everything you've ever heard and multiply it about a hundred times – and you still won't have a picture of John Ford."

Man with no name

Ford filmed his final Western in 1964, while John Wayne continued until 1976 and won an Oscar for his portrayal of Marshal Rooster Cogburn in *True Grit* (1969). But reflecting the social pressures of the 1960s, Westerns underwent major changes. The cavalry song that accompanied an Indian surrender in *The Searchers* was used to ironic effect behind a scene of slaughter in *Little Big Man* (1969). And the new Western man had as much Liberty Valance in him as he did John Wayne.

He smoked a foul little Italian cigar, wore a poncho, sported stubble and a scowl. He was Clint Eastwood as the Man With No Name in a trilogy of mid-1960s Westerns shot in Spain by Italian director Sergio Leone.

The low-budget Spaghetti Westerns helped revive the genre at a time when big-money American epics had bombed. Eastwood told Kenneth Turan of the Los Angeles Times, "When I first went and did *A Fistful of Dollars*, there were a lot of predictions in the trade papers that Westerns were through. And I said, 'Swell, now that I'm doing one they're through,' but that film turned out to have its place in the world."

Eastwood is not exclusively a Western actor, but his career follows some of the genre's trends. His break came in the modern equivalent of a B picture, the television show *Rawhide*, where he played the amicable Rowdy Yates. His appearance in the musical *Paint Your Wagon* evoked the heyday of Roy Rogers and the singing cowboys.

But the Man With No Name had no Hollywood precedent. He subscribed to no moral code like William S. Hart's characters. He and his cohorts did what they had to do in order to survive in a moral and physical desert. In *The Good, The Bad, and The Ugly*, the Eastwood character kills three men before the audience even sees his face – then takes the man he saved captive so he can collect the bounty.

BREAKING NEW GROUND

Kevin Costner's 1990 success, *Dances with Wolves*, was one of the few Westerns to cast Indians in acting roles, use Lakota Sioux sub-titles, and view Native Americans in a sympathetic way and not as bloodthirsty savages.

A cynical loner

In an essay on Eastwood, writer Jim Miller describes the character as "a cynical loner at a time when the mood of the country was shaped in much the same line of thought… he brought a whole new look at the Western hero as a lone wolf, anti-hero that was totally different than characters John Wayne played."

Westerns declined steadily during the 1970s and 1980s; Eastwood went nearly 10 years without making a Western after he directed and starred in the modern classic *The Outlaw Josey Wales* (1976). Then, in 1980, one of the biggest movie bombs of all time, *Heaven's Gate*, convinced Hollywood that, finally, Westerns were well and truly dead.

Westerns today

In the early 1990s, Costner's *Dances with Wolves*, a kind of New Age eco-Western, stunned Hollywood with its success and launched a revival that had everyone from rapper Tone Loc to party girl Drew Barrymore back in the saddle again. And after years of waiting, Eastwood decided that he had aged enough to portray reformed killer William Munny in *Unforgiven*.

Now a widower and hog farmer, Munny tries to convince himself that he is truly a changed man, even as he heads out again as a bounty hunter. He struggles with almost everything – his past, his horse and his shooting – and looks as weary as the Man With No Name looked invincible. When his young partner asks him about what the Old West days were like, Munny replies, "I can't remember. I was drunk most of the time."

Every murder has its consequences, and Eastwood demythologizes killers and sheriffs alike by exposing the fictions of a reporter who would twist their exploits into the kind of dime novels that inspired Westerns in the first place. As in *Liberty Valance*, the genre has turned in on itself, exposing its own false origins. In 1992, Eastwood told the *Los Angeles Times* that *Unforgiven* would be his final Western. "Maybe that's why I didn't do it right away. I was kind of savoring it as the last of that genre, maybe the last film of that type for me." ❏

The Great Equalizer

God made some men big and some small, but Colonel Sam Colt made them equal all." So went a popular saying in Texas, where the Colt revolver made its mark early on. Firearms went by many names: six-shooters, hog legs, peacemakers, belly guns, lead chuckers and equalizers. Whatever the name, they were an essential piece of equipment in the shoot-'em-up West.

In the early days, guns weren't terribly effective for either hunting or protection. An Indian could unleash several arrows in the time it took to reload

surest shooting pistol made." Lt. Col. George Armstrong Custer was said to be carrying a pair of Webley "British Bulldog" revolvers when he fell at Little Bighorn. Wyatt Earp probably drew a Smith & Wesson at the O.K. Corral. And Mark Twain packed a .22-caliber pistol known as a "suicide special" which he claimed had just one fault: "You could not hit anything with it."

Because low-caliber guns were used in much of the Wild West's "gun play", it usually took more than one shot to disable an opponent. That's why shootists came to prefer a revolver of at least .44 caliber, which was often enough to drop a man with one hit. Most Westerners also owned a rifle or car-

a single-shot firearm. And then came Sam Colt in the 1830s with revolving pistols and rifles capable of firing several shots without reloading. Their impact was almost immediate. At Plum Creek in 1841, Texas Rangers armed with five-shot Paterson Colts overcame four-to-one odds against 100 Comanche warriors. By the 1850s the Colt revolver was the gun-of-choice, although the most popular Colt of the frontier era, the .45-caliber Peacemaker, didn't appear for another two decades.

But not every gunman preferred a Colt. After surrendering in 1882, the notorious outlaw Frank James called his Remington "the hardest and

bine because they were far more accurate at long range than handguns. The Winchester rifle was called the "gun that won the West", and was standard-issue among Texas Rangers, who put it to use against outlaws and Indians. As the manufacturer, Oliver F. Winchester, liked to say, "It has become a household word and a household necessity on our western plains and mountains. The pioneer, the hunter and trapper, believe in the Winchester, and its possession is a passion with every Indian."

Lever-action repeating rifles were just the thing to give a man confidence even if he was only a fair shot. More than 300,000 Spencer rifles, personally tested by Abraham Lincoln, were issued to Union soldiers during the Civil War. ❏

ABOVE: life as they knew it – down the barrel of a gun.

SOUTHWEST CUISINE

It may be the choicest culinary offering to hit menus in recent years,
but locals know that food in these parts has always been downright tasty

Southwest cooking traditions became the New Frontier to a host of innovative, and widely celebrated, fashionable chefs. Although neither Texas nor California is really considered "Southwestern" by inhabitants of Arizona and New Mexico – even though they share the cultural and culinary impact of Mexico's rule before they were booted or bought out – they have made their own contributions to "nouveau" Southwestern cuisine.

Among the luminaries in the Southwestern culinary world who have captured international attention are Robert Del Grande of Texas, considered one of the fathers of contemporary Southwestern cuisine (and particularly "New Texas" cuisine); author and innovator Mark Miller of the *Coyote Cafe* in Santa Fe and *Red Sage* in Washington, DC; Vincent Guerithault, who put Phoenix, Arizona on the map for his classic French treatment of New World recipes; native New Mexico chef John Sedlar, who wrote the ground-breaking *Modern Southwest Cuisine*; Native American chef Loretta Barrett Oden, who reintroduced the culinary genius of the "original Americans" at her *Corn Dance Cafe* in Santa Fe; and Mary Sue Milliken and Susan Feniger of the *Border Grill* in California, who are known to television viewers as the "Too Hot Tamales".

Ancient traditions

Most of these star chefs found their inspiration for nouveau Southwestern cuisine in ancient, traditional foods. The basic cooking style derives first from the staples of its indigenous population of Native Americans, who largely had a diet of wild game, including deer, elk, buffalo and wildfowl, as well as wild berries, acorns, piñons and other nuts, herbs (like sage), prickly pear cactus, and especially the ancient, cultivated foundations of life – corn, beans and squash, the legendary "Three Sisters".

PRECEDING PAGES: contemporary Southwestern cuisine is now familiar the world over. **LEFT:** picking chili peppers south of Albuquerque. **RIGHT:** Biltmore Hotel.

Next came the fiery catalyst. Chile was unknown in Europe before the 1492 landing in the Americas by Columbus. The off-track explorer was, incidentally, looking for black pepper, not chile "pepper", and also erroneously thought he was in India, which is why he called the locals Indians. Still, chile became

EDIBLE CACTI

As forbidding as they may look, some cacti provide delicious delicacies to eat. The best known is the fruit of the prickly pear, but also edible is the "vegetable" part of the plant: its "pads", known as *nopales*. Both the fruit and *nopales* are often found in Southwestern grocery stores. As a vegetable, the somewhat tart *nopales* – carefully prepared – can be used in many ways, including in salads, casseroles and soups. Its taste has been compared to a green bean or asparagus. The saguaro, too, produces a fruit that is particularly valued by the Tohono O'odham people of southern Arizona, who labor long hours to produce its syrup and jam.

a great hit in Spain and elsewhere over the next century.

According to widely regarded New Mexico native and author Carmella Padilla in *The Chile Chronicles* (published by the Museum of New Mexico Press), "Chile soon became so thoroughly incorporated into the cuisines of India and Indochina that many early botanists believed the plants originated there, although scholars would eventually designate South America as the plant's ancestral home." Although chile is considered more or less indigenous to the Southwest (thanks to migrating birds), it has been eaten since about 7000 BC in Mexico and grown in South America since about 5200 BC. "It was Mexico, though," writes Padilla, "that would get credit for domesticating the various types of chile that evolved from the (wild) chiltepin into the species *capsicum annuum*.

"By the time Spanish explorers, led by Hernan Cortés, began their invasion of Mexico in 1519, Aztec plant breeders already had developed dozens of cultivars within the species, including poblanos, jalapeños and serranos, as well as other non-pungent chile plants. In its native South American home, the word for chile was *aji*.

The Aztecs, however, used the Nahuatl term *chilli* to refer to various chile cultivars. Perhaps the most sophisticated chefs of their time, the Aztecs laid the foundation for modern Mexican and New Mexican foods by using chile in the preparation of *moles* [made also with the Mexican "spice", chocolate], tamales, salsas, pipian, and other dishes and sauces."

Chile's growth

The Spanish called the plant *chile*. And, between the expedition led by Francisco Vasquez de Coronado in 1540 (who ultimately conquered the inhabitants), and the expediton of Don Juan de Oñate (the last Conquistador) in 1598, chile was already being grown in Northern New Mexico, fed by water channeled through established Spanish *acequias* from the Rio Chama.

It has been a cultural and agricultural staple ever since. In fact, New Mexico (which is sparsely settled and considered economically poor) produces some 60 percent of the country's chile, which has gained even more importance since salsa usurped ketchup as the nation's favorite condiment. Now, native chilies, along with their fiery cousins in other parts of the world, figure prominently in the most sophisticated international culinary circles.

It's ironic, really, because, once upon a time not so long ago, as New Mexico writer Marsha McEuen points out, "chile was humble food, working-class food. It grew in bad dirt and dry weather. And you could buy it for pennies and use it to flavor almost anything. It lent its liveliness to the cheapest cuts of meat and to huge stews of beans and dried vegetables. *Abuelas* loved it for its supposed curative powers and moms for its ability to stretch a budget. But,

A RICHTER SCALE FOR CHILIES

A process known as liquid chromatography determines capsaicin – the chemical compound that produces the heat – levels in chilies, and overall heat is measured in Scoville Heat Units (named after a pharmacist who devised the process). A bell pepper, for example, has 0 Scoville units; a jalapeño can have between 2,500 and 10,000 units. The hottest on record? A Red Savina habanero, which sizzled the scales at 577,000 Scovilles. And don't let anyone tell you that color determines heat in chilies: the heat is located in the seeds and in the placenta. The best rule of thumb is that the thinner and smaller the pepper, the hotter it will be.

in the 1990s, the lowly chile pepper has gotten all dressed up in spangles and high heels and gone to dine with fancy friends like Muscovy duck breast and rack of lamb in some of America's premiere restaurants."

What you'll discover while traveling throughout the Southwest is both. You can dine happily and hotly on the unfancy original, or seek out the culinary innovators in the region's metropolitan areas to sample the exciting tastes and textures of the New Southwestern Cuisine. (Trying to

CHILE BUZZ

The intense burning sensation one experiences when eating hot chilies can trigger the body into releasing morphine-like endorphins, often resulting in mild euphoria.

processed white flour, water and lard; the other of corn (*masa*), water and lard.

In the 1980s, the tried-and-true yellow/white corn tortilla got a "different taste and look" with the commercial introduction of "blue corn" tortilla chips. It was hardly an instant hit. Blue food is bad enough, but when it looks more gray to black... well, it ranked last as the snack food of choice for quite awhile. That is, until the health and fitness craze kicked in. The traditional Native American blue corn,

decipher the menus of haute chile cuisine, however, is quite another story.)

On the traditional side of the menu, foods – including the names they're given – vary widely even between Arizona and New Mexico. There are some dishes, like the *fajita* (claimed by Texas), which is comprised of seared flank steak strips, onions and mild peppers served with salsa, guacamole and tortillas, that are essentially the same throughout the Southwest. The same is true of the flour tortilla and corn tortilla: one a flat bread made of

LEFT: Southwestern soup of the day.
ABOVE: some like it hot; variations on a chile theme.

grown by the Navajo and Hopi in Arizona and the Pueblo peoples in New Mexico (along with other little-known varieties) was healthier and more easily digested, so a large segment of the health-minded public developed a taste for it and simply ignored what it looked like.

On other scores, the differences – and the tastes – are substantial. For example, in Arizona, *enchiladas*, like their Sonoran counterpart, are stuffed with meat and rolled into a tube, topped with cheese and served with a choice of red or green chile. The chile has a softer edge and is definitely milder than that of New Mexico. In New Mexico, *enchiladas* are more likely to made with blue corn tortillas, which are stacked like pancakes and layered with a filling of choice (*carne adovada*, chicken or ground beef). They're topped off with either a blazing green chile, sharp-edged red chile or a "Christmas" chile: red on one side, green on the other.

New Mexico, by the way, prides itself on the nuclear heat of its chile. The secret for chile novices? It's the *sopapillas* (little deep-fried pastry "pillows") and honey that always accompany meals. Don't ignore them. A *sopapilla* drizzled with honey kills the heat instantly. Although once common only in New Mexico, *sopapillas* are now on the menus of Mexican

restaurants throughout the Southwest – but if they're not, you'll have to rely on a cold glass of milk or a packet of sugar to quell the fire.

Burros or *burritos*, like the small pack-animal they're named for, carry within their flour tortilla "pack saddle" everything from beans and cheese, meats and chile to breakfast staples or lunch meat and mayo. Tacos? Soft or deep-fried, they are filled with an amazing number of things... even dessert.

Actually, without writing a culinary encyclopedia, it would be virtually impossible to describe and define the many differences, and interpretations, of the Southwest's traditional regional cuisine.

Nouveau Southwestern cuisine? Well, an American original is Mark Miller and his Coyote Cafe, where the menu is a delicious interpretation of Hispanic/Native American cuisine, sometimes with a touch of Pacific Rim inspiration. The Coyote's tortilla soup is a lush, spicy, tomato-based concoction topped with *creme fraiche* and toasty tortilla strips, and his luncheon special of *tacos al pastor* (grilled pork and pineapple), served with soft corn tortillas in a small stone *metate*, is totally addictive.

Chefs' favorites

Here is a sampling of some of the specialties featured in the PBS program *Savor The Southwest*, hostessed by well-known food editor and culinary entrepreneur Barbara Pool Fenzl of Arizona, which showcases some of the top Southwestern chefs.

Robert Del Grande: coffee-roasted filet of beef and *pasilla* chile broth, served with gratin of Swiss chard and shiitake mushroom garnish.

Robert McGrath: sugar and chile-cured duck breasts; green chile macaroni, *jicama* hash browns, served with an accompaniment with a dried cherry salsa to accompany other smoked or grilled meats.

Vincent Guerithault: shrimp *enchilada* with goat cheese and *chipotle* cream (widely used, the chipotle is the mild outcome of the dried jalapeño chile); baked mussel and corn tortilla; banana and raspberry tortilla tart.

Jay McCarthy: sauteed asparagus with chile glaze sauce; and poached pears with prickly pear sauce.

Mary Sue Milliken and Susan Feniger: chilied fruit; red chile pasta salad; fiery red rice; chipotle cheese bread and duck breasts with raspberry *chipotle* sauce.

Chuck Wiley: grilled Chilean sea bass with Anasazi bean stew; *nopal* (prickly pear) cactus salsa; roasted asparagus with grilled citrus salsa and persimmon shortcake tart.

Loretta Barrett Oden: three sisters stew with corn dumplings; crusted buffalo tenderloin with *chipotle* onions; cranberry piñon sauce; skillet corn cake with easy tomato preserves and Indian pudding.

Many of the above menus may sound exotic, but in fact they are among the easiest Southwestern dishes to understand. ❏

LEFT: rice is also a Southwestern cuisine staple.

Indian Food

I n the 1998 film *Smoke Signals* – the first movie about American Indians to be written and directed by tribe members after more than a century of having their stories told by others – the mother of one of the two young protagonists says to her son, while painfully kneading dough with arthritic hands: "People always tell me I make the best frybread in the world... but I don't make it myself, you know. I got the recipe from your grandmother, and she got it from hers. And I listen to people when they eat my bread."

Frybread as a link between generations, frybread as the foundation of a cuisine and culture connecting Indians across the entire North American continent. Forget about Anglo variations of fried dough. True Indian frybread, just delivered from its scalding, oily bath, is a puffy sensation to be savoured. Remarkably ungreasy, it is, like all food made by the continent's first inhabitants, deliciously earthy and redolent of home and hearth. In the Four Corners, with an overlay of beans, shredded lettuce and tomato, perhaps some meat and a bit of salsa, frybread becomes what's usually a Navajo, or Indian, Taco. As a side accompaniment to a steaming, wholesome bowl of *posole*, or green chili stew, with pork or Navajo lamb stew, fry bread is the perfect utensil with which to sop up subtly seasoned sauces.

Genuine home-made Indian food isn't always that easy to find while traveling through the Southwest. What we think of as Southwestern cuisine, as typified in Santa Fe, Tucson or Phoenix, simply combines elements of Indian cuisine with Spanish and Mexican influences. But there are some exceptions. in Albuquerque, the restaurants at the Indian Pueblo Cultural Center feature marvelous basic dishes and frybread in an attractive museum setting, while in Santa Fe, the Corn Dance Café at the Hotel Santa Fe serves what can only be admirably described as nouvelle Indian cuisine in surroundings that are simultaneously rustic and elegant.

The best Indian food is of course found on reservations. Some of the more famous and visitor-friendly habitations, such as Taos, have small food stands built inside or outside of family dwellings which sell satisfying bowls of *posole* with a side of frybread to adventurous tourists. There's

a Poquaque Pueblo owned shopping center just off the intersections of Highways 84/85 in which you'll find Po-Suwae-Geh restaurant. Nondescript outside, it nonetheless features good Pueblo and Southwestern cuisine. If you're lucky, you may find home-made *tamales* being sold near a pueblo, with the meat fillings spiced with enough red or green chili to send you either to heaven or hell. Also at Taos and other pueblos are the outdoor *hornos*, in which the superb "over breads", cookies and pies are baked. These round loafs, made and baked as nature, and not not chemical companies, saw fit, will remind you of a time when eating bread was a meal in itself. Also emerging from these

ovens are magnificently simple, square pieces of thin pie, the crusts sandwiching fillings of spiced pumpkin or fruit. Another great way to indulge on pueblo foods is to attend the annual Santa Fe Indian Market in August, with stands selling every conceivable variation of these foods.

In Window Rock, New Mexico – the capital of the Navajo Nation – there's a good restaurant inside the Navajo-owned hotel where you can feast on lamb stews and posoles and other typical dishes. Don't refuse an invitation to dine in a pueblo home during one of the feast days open to the public. It will be an unforgettable culinary journey into the heart of a people where tradition has, thankfully, managed to transcend our fast food culture. ❏

RIGHT: corn is held sacred by Native Americans.

FLORA AND FAUNA

The deserts of the Southwest demand that all who dwell there be
perfectly adapted. The resulting ingenuity is fascinating

Diverse though it is, all life in the Southwest is shaped by aridity. This is primarily a rainshadow region of dry desert basins trapped between high peaks and plateaus, which capture what little Pacific-storm moisture makes it over the 14,000-foot (4,300-meter) barrier of California's Sierra

observe the cleverness and the infinite variety of techniques of survival under pitiless opposition," wrote John Steinbeck in *Travels with Charley*. "Life could not change the sun or water the desert, so it changed itself."

And how! The most successful desert plants, cacti, take advantage of infrequent but hard

Nevada. Rain is much prayed for and received with thanks when it falls. It's no exaggeration to say that locating water, trying to hold onto it, and adapting to life without it are the main preoccupations of life.

Human squabbles over water rights are legendary but when the going gets tough people can always leave. That's an option for birds and larger predators like mountain lions and coyotes which, although less visible, travel long distances to find water and prey and call most of the Southwest home. But those with smaller home ranges and specialized niches have to find other solutions. "The desert, the dry and sun-lashed desert, is a good school in which to

rains by employing extensive root networks and conserving water in expandable, gelatinous tissues. Waxy trunks and paddles protected by spines are used for photosynthesis instead of leaves. The cacti lure moth and bat pollinators with bright flowers and produce tasty autumn fruits that are eaten and disseminated by many animals, from piglike Sonoran Desert javelinas to humans. Some trees and shrubs shed their leaves and virtually shut down to conserve water; others close up or tilt fleshy, waxy leaves to keep cool. Most delightful of all are wildflowers, many of which bloom only if summer or early winter rain has been adequate, putting on wave after wave of brilliant Impressionistic color, starting in April in the low deserts and May and June at higher elevations.

The desert seems quiet in the daytime because three-quarters of animals are nocturnal. Take a walk at dusk or dawn to a local water hole if you want to glimpse coyotes, kit foxes, raccoons, bobcats, badgers, perhaps even a rare bighorn sheep. In the day, look skyward to see red-tailed hawks, golden eagles, peregrine falcons, and ravens patrolling the skies from cliff aeries in search of unsuspecting cottontails or ground squirrels in the bushes below. Smaller birds, such as tits, finches, vireos, tanagers, and a variety of hummingbirds, flock in

their time, waiting in the bottom of dried up potholes, or *tinajas*, for the drumbeat of rainfall to signal spawning time. Some animals, such as kangaroo rats and spadefoot toads, have lost the need to drink water at all, recycling it instead from seeds. The desert is certainly not short of miracles.

Deserts

Not one but four types of desert are found here — the Chihuahuan, the Sonoran, the Mojave, and the Great Basin — with all four converging in Arizona, making the Grand Canyon State the most biologically rich of all desert

huge numbers to riparian zones in sheltered canyons, with many Mexican species fraternizing with American cousins along US-Mexico borderlands.

Reptiles keep their body temperature down beneath bushes and rocks, becoming active on trails at twilight and leaving strange slither marks and delicate tracks in sandy soil. Collared lizards, whiptails, and chuckwallas are often seen, along with the huge and colorful Sonoran Gila monster, North America's only venomous lizard. Spadefoot toads simply bide

LEFT: a horned lizard in the Gila River Valley.
ABOVE: coyote are found throughout the Southwest.

LOOK, BUT DON'T TOUCH

Venomous creatures are plentiful in the desert, but use venom only to immobilize prey and aid in digestion or to defend themselves. In fearsome-looking scorpions, size does not relate to potency. The giant desert hairy scorpion, more than 5 inches (13 cm) long, is less poisonous than the inch-long bark scorpion, whose sting can be deadly. Gila monsters are rarely seen, move slowly, and will not bite unless they are cornered or picked up. In addition to rattlesnakes, coral and other snakes, poisonous desert dwellers include an 8-inch-long (20-cm) centipede, black widow and brown recluse spiders, cone nose bugs, tarantulas, ants and wasps.

Southwest states. Each desert has its own distinctive personality. The Chihuahuan Desert, two-thirds of which is in Mexico, stretches north as far as Albuquerque, New Mexico, and into parts of southeastern Arizona. At a mean 3,500 to 5,000 feet (1,000 to 1,500 meters), it is quite high and has relatively long, chilly winters, with occasional snowfalls that disappear as quickly as they came. Summer temperatures often reach into the 100s, but are cooled by short, violent thunderstorms, which drop most of the 8–12 inches (20–30 cm) of annual rainfall for the area.

In Permian times, some 250 million years ago, this area lay under a warm, shallow sea, leaving a legacy of limestone and large cave systems such as those seen at Carlsbad, New Mexico, and Kartchner Caves in southeastern Arizona. Carlsbad is famous for the half-million breeding Mexican free-tailed bats that summer just inside the entrance to the Natural Cave entrance and exit nightly to feed on cactus nectar that will, in the thrifty natural economy of the desert, also pollinate their cactus hosts for another season. Cactus such as prickly pear and cholla do well in these calcium-rich soils along with creosote bush and grasses. Agaves such as lechuguilla are common and

WONDERFUL WETLANDS

Spring runoff promotes a fast call to action for wildflowers in high-altitude country parks like Cedar Breaks in southern Utah, a veritable Monet painting of brightly splashed blooms roused from snowy sleep in early June, along with hibernating bears, pikas, and marmots. Townsend's nutcrackers make fast work of seeds as the season rolls on. Rushing mountain streams spilling to lowlands slow gradually to a trickle and ice up in places as winter arrives. Lack of rainfall and aggressive damming of major courses mean that many smaller southwestern rivers are dry arroyos much of the year, flooded by seasonal runoff. But where mighty rivers such as the Colorado and the Rio Grande run, they form green riparian corridors of cottonwood, boxelder, willow, exotic tamarisk, and other water-lovers that provide a respite from the heat and a habitat for many species. Deep, protected canyons offer cool, moist microclimates in which a Douglas fir might grow across from a pricklypear cactus. Groundwater here percolates through sandstone, attracting brightly colored monkeyflower, columbine, shooting stars, maidenhair fern, and other moisture-loving plants to form luxuriant hanging gardens in unexpected places. Also glorious is the song of the canyon wren: often heard, rarely glimpsed and truly the top of the hit parade of southwestern crooners.

have tall, thick spikes rising from a rosette of fleshy, swordlike "leaves". Yuccas have been particularly useful to desert dwellers, who use the roots for shampoo, the fibers for clothing, and the autumn fruits as a starchy food.

Another evaporite, gypsum, is washed out of surrounding highlands into the basins, where it is picked up by winds and built into dunes such as those seen at White Sands in the Tularosa Basin. Although they look bare, the dunes do support life. Plants like the soap tree yucca stabilize the dunes, growing fast enough and having long enough roots to avoid being buried. Fringe-toed lizards and western diamondback

ico. By a quirk of positioning, the Sonoran receives moisture twice a year – summer "monsoons", as they are known, and winter storms – making it by far the greenest of the deserts. Tough customers like mesquite, creosote bush and blackbrush do well here, but most enchanting are the flame-tipped wandlike ocotillo, the green-barked palo verde with its rain of golden blossoms, and more than a hundred different kind of cactus, including organ pipe, cholla, prickly pear, beaver tail, pincushion, claret cup, hedgehog and – the most recognizable cactus in the world – the many-limbed saguaro.

Symbols of the Sonoran, saguaros are record

and desert massasauga rattlesnakes live here, along with the more ubiquitous coyote and cottontail, hunter and prey, which find ways to thrive in a variety of settings. Birds travel easily between mountains and dunes, with finches, doves, thrashers, and shrikes giving up the night skies to nighthawks and owls whose eerie hoots float across the dunes like strange echoes.

The Sonoran Desert, next door in Arizona, is relatively young at only 10,000 years old, and spans the 3,000-foot (900-meter) lowlands and basins that start just north of Phoenix into Mex-

LEFT: saguaro cactus outside of Tucson; flowering cactus. **ABOVE:** White Sands National Monument.

WONDROUS CACTI

Though not indestructible, cacti can put up with almost anything except too little or too much water. Because cacti, like most plants, use sunlight to make energy, they thrive in the desert sun. And, like all plants, they "breathe" by opening their pores to exhale excess oxygen and inhale carbon dioxide to be used in photosynthesis. Cacti, however, to conserve moisture, hold their breath during daytime heat, and open their pores only at night, when desert temperatures fall dramatically. This peculiar method of photosynthesis causes cacti to grow slowly, and while it enables adult plants to survive, seedlings need a series of wet summers to become established.

breakers in almost every way. They favor warm, south-facing alluvial slopes, or *bajadas*, such as those found around Tucson and often get their start in the shelter of palo verde "nurse" trees. In spring, they sprout large, creamy topknots of blossom to attract pollinating bats and moths, which, if they do their stuff, allow the saguaro to produce bright, globular fruits in late summer. Large cacti like the saguaro and the organ pipe (found in the Sonoran Desert) also provide nesting sites for birds such as elf

> **SONORAN SENIORS**
>
> Some saguaros reach 150 years of age and beyond; they don't even begin sprouting their famous arms until they hit 75 – and then only if conditions are right.

tree, a variety of yucca. In the Kofa Mountains southwest of Phoenix, relict palm trees have found a niche in a protected canyon along with a healthy number of endangered bighorn sheep, which are protected here and in Cabeza Prieta Preserve farther south. Also endangered are desert tortoises, found between St. George and Las Vegas and heavily impacted by development and recreational use of their habitat.

The fourth desert type, the Great Basin, is found in the far northwest corner of Arizona

owls and Harris hawks. Watch for Gambel quail at water holes and the roadrunner – state bird and cuckoo relative – along roads.

The Mojave Desert is mainly found in California, extreme southwestern Utah, and Nevada but extends into the central and northern portions of Arizona. The Mojave is the hottest and most monotone of all the deserts in summer, but with the addition of a small amount of rainfall in winter it is transformed in early spring with stunning wildflower blooms.

Vegetation such as ironwood, desert holly, blackbrush, creosote and bursage distributes itself to make the most of available moisture, with the indicator species the shaggy Joshua

and covers a far larger area than the others, extending all the way to eastern Utah and Oregon. At elevations of 4,000 feet (1,200 meters) and above, this is a cooler desert once dominated by a mixture of lush native grasses that have been heavily grazed over the last century and crowded out by cheatgrass and vast quantities of sagebrush, saltbush, snakeweed, rabbitbrush, and other disturbance species.

The Sky Islands

The Southwest desert is by no means flat, although most newcomers think it is. In fact, elevations range from about 1,000 feet (300 meters) to higher than 12,000 feet (3,600 meters) atop the highest peaks, dubbed "sky islands" because, in the heat haze, they seem to float up from the lower deserts. The mountains of southern Arizona and New Mexico and western Utah and Nevada have been thrust up in typical basin-and-range fashion relatively recently, their craggy faces now softened by mixed evergreen-deciduous forests. In the sheltered canyons of the Chiricahua Mountains, on the Arizona-New Mexico-Mexico boundary, Arizona cypress and alligator juniper mingle with Mexican natives such as Mexican Chihuahua and Apache pine while at higher elevations, lush forests of Douglas fir, aspen, and ponderosa pine provide browse for white-tailed deer and cover for sulphur-bellied flycatchers, Mexican chickadees, and the elegant trogon – found on every birder's list.

The low basins between the mountains – what most of us think of as desert – are a tougher row to hoe for most desert dwellers. They are so hot that runoff evaporates, leaving behind dry salt flats, or *playas*, that attract only salt bush, iodine bush, pickleweed, and other salt-tolerant species. These lowlands often come into their own in winter, when they are flooded by rains and attract migratory fowl like sandhill cranes. Equally unpromising are the sprawling, angry-looking lava flows, some as young as only one thousand years old, that absorb the heat and reflect it into places like the Tularosa Basin's Jornada del Muerto. It may take a hundred years for a few hardy plants to colonize these flows – perhaps a thousand for anything substantial to grow. Jornada Mogollon American Indians used the basalts as blank slates for remarkable petroglyphs, but like earlier Spanish travelers, today's visitors mostly hurry through, bound for the cooler climes of the high country.

The Colorado Plateau

Forming a distinct geologic province to the north is the Colorado Plateau, which covers 130,000 square miles (337,000 sq km) of Arizona, New Mexico, Utah, and Colorado. The Colorado Plateau is a mile high and rising, a largely sedimentary monolith that was squeezed up beginning in the mid-Cretaceous period. It has been locally uplifted by volcanic

forces into peaks, plateaus, and mesas and spectacularly eroded by the Colorado River and its tributaries.

Large, cheek-by-jowl elevation differences are particularly obvious in and around the Grand Canyon, which drops from 8,200 feet (2,500 meters) at the North Rim to 1,300 feet (400 meters) at the Colorado River. Along with these elevation changes are changes in plant types, from desert to montane. This piqued the interest of a young eastern naturalist called C. Hart Merriam, making studies in northern Arizona in 1889. In just 60 miles (100 km), Merriam noted, one passed through landscapes

NATURE'S PAINT

Of the natural phenomena of the Southwest, among the loveliest are the dark curtains of desert varnish that stream down canyon walls and settle on desert boulders. Research shows this to be a biogeochemical process: colonies of bacteria living on the rock surface absorb manganese and iron from the atmosphere. In a process that takes thousands of years, the bacteria and minerals, along with clay particles, form a one-hundredth-of-a-millimeter-thick coating. When manganese is dominant, the varnish is black; iron results in rusty red. When scientists find stone tools that have become covered with desert varnish, they know that they are ancient indeed.

LEFT: young golden eagle about to leave the nest.
RIGHT: ground squirrels are easy prey for raptors.

more usually seen on a trip from Mexico to the Canadian Arctic. Merriam dubbed these Southwest zones: Lower Sonoran 2,000–5,000 ft (600–1,500 meters), or desert scrub; Upper Sonoran 5,000–7,000 ft (1,500–2,000 meters), or pinyon pine-juniper forest; Transition 7,000–8,000 ft (2,000–2,400 meters), or ponderosa pine forest; Canadian 8,000–10,000 ft (2,400–3,000 meters), or sub-alpine spruce-fir-aspen forest, and Hudsonian 10,000–12,000 ft (3,000–3,600 meters), alpine to treeline.

Modern scientists have expanded on Merriam's ideas, now recognizing that slope angle, soil type, exposure to sun and wind, moisture and other variables all contribute to local microclimates.

Great Basin-style vegetation extends onto the Colorado Plateau, covering large tracts of the Navajo Reservation and providing enough rangeland for ranching to remain a popular lifestyle. Starting around 6,000 feet (1,800 meters) is the pinyon-juniper forest. Useful in a multitude of ways – for nuts, berries, firewood, posts, even insulating material – "P-J" is the friendliest of dwarf forests to camp under, offering views of the stars at night and adequate shelter at noon. Cedar gnats, or "no-see-ums", appear when temperatures warm up. Watch out. They give a mean bite.

Forest inhabitants

At about 7,000 feet (2,000 meters), P-J gives way to ponderosa pine forest, which reaches its greatest density around Flagstaff. Sheltered against the cinnamon-smelling, platey trunks of ponderosa are stands of Gambel oak and toothy maples that flare red and bronze in the dying days of fall. Mule deer are often seen here, twitching long ears and jumping away skittishly. The forest is often noisy with disputing Steller's jays and tassel-eared squirrels.

The native Abert squirrel is an interesting link in the ecosystem of the ponderosa forest. It lives on ponderosa pine cones and scrabbles among the roots of the ponderosa for fungi. The Abert's cousin, the Kaibab squirrel, lives only on the North Rim of the Grand Canyon and looks slightly different, having been separated in the past 6 million years by the great chasm of the canyon.

Snow is not uncommon in June on the plateau, so wildflowers are late bloomers here. Watch for explosions of bluebells, lupines, columbines, Indian paintbrushes, gentians, primroses, penstemons, woolly mullein, and numerous asters and sunflowers. Above 8,000 feet (2,400 meters), pioneer deciduous species like quaking aspen take over subalpine meadows in silvery profusion, but they will eventually be overshadowed by spruce, fir, and at higher elevations, lodgepole, limber, Jeffrey, and very occasionally bristlecone pines, the world's oldest tree, often reaching ages of 3,000 to 4,000 years. ❑

DELIGHTS OF THE FOREST

The pinyon-juniper forest contains a gustatory treasure: the delectable pine nut. Birds and animals put it to good use, as do people. Native Americans traditionally depended upon caches of pinyon nuts to see them through the lean winter months. Many Indians still take time to gather nuts, which ripen in the fall. The nuts yield 2,880 calories per pound, almost equal to a pound of butter. Though corn is considered the "staff of life" for many southwestern Indians, the pinyon nut protein contains greater quantities of the amino acids essential for human growth. Gathering and shelling are labor-intensive pursuits, but the reward is in the taste.

LEFT: adult male mule deer on the alert.
RIGHT: member of sunflower family, Monument Valley.

PLACES

A detailed guide to the entire region, with principal sites clearly cross-referenced by number to the maps

After spending time in the American Southwest, most other places will seem cramped. This is a land of endless horizons and big skies, off-the-beaten-track lush green canyons and valleys that rest the eye and provide shelter from the sun. Unexpected pleasures are as much a part of the Southwest as the great masses of red rock and open stretches of desert, but ones which the traveler rushing from national monument to natural spectacle can easily miss.

The Southwest has sometimes been defined geographically to include areas as far east as Oklahoma, as Far West as Southern California, and as far north as Salt Lake City, Utah, and Reno, Nevada. This book defines the Southwest on the basis of cultural and geographical similarities, and so the area can be reasonably explored by car without long detours.

This tour of the Southwest includes the Grand Canyon – one of the most frequently visited natural spots in the world, and also southern Utah, as spectacular in many ways as the Grand Canyon but less accessible, less crowded and on a more human scale.

Near Utah is Indian Country, which spills over from Arizona into New Mexico and Utah, and as the home of the Navajo and Hopi Indians, is an entity unto itself. Pueblo Country includes Albuquerque, Santa Fe and Taos, all in New Mexico. This area represents a mixture of Indian Pueblo and Hispanic villages existing side by side with cities. It is culturally and geographically so rich that a traveler could spend years exploring it. Here is the place to satisfy a fascination for Old Spanish Churches and adobe architecture: to look for Native American and Hispanic arts and crafts in the plazas, pueblos and villages: and the place with the best red chilies to be had anywhere.

Eastern and Southern New Mexico are more spread out, but the deserts, mountains and plains offer equal rewards of a different quality for those who stop and explore. Southern Arizona is border country – the line between the United States and Mexico creating almost a separate country, offering the most interesting desert flora and fauna, as well as the laid-back ambience of Tucson.

Phoenix dominates central Arizona on the map, but the mountains surrounding it to the south, east and north are an outdoorsman's paradise as well as the home of the largest Apache Indian tribes. Las Vegas is an anomaly in the Southwest – a garish non-stop neon city dedicated to entertainment of every imaginable variety. The writers of this section have lived in and written about the Southwest extensively. Rather than attempting the impossible and covering everything, they have concentrated on their favorite spots. ❑

PRECEDING PAGES: Dinetah Petroglyphs; near Mexican Hat, Utah; homestyle restaurant near Albuquerque.
LEFT: contemplating Petrified Forest National Monument.

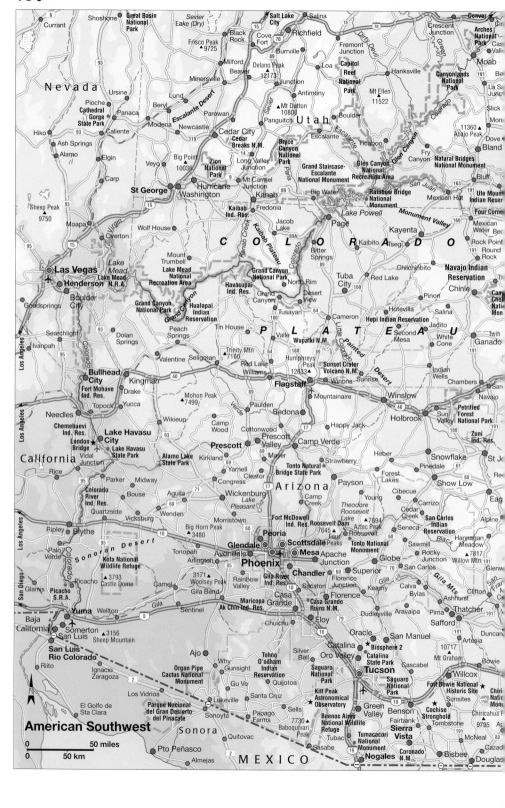

American Southwest

0   50 miles
0   50 km

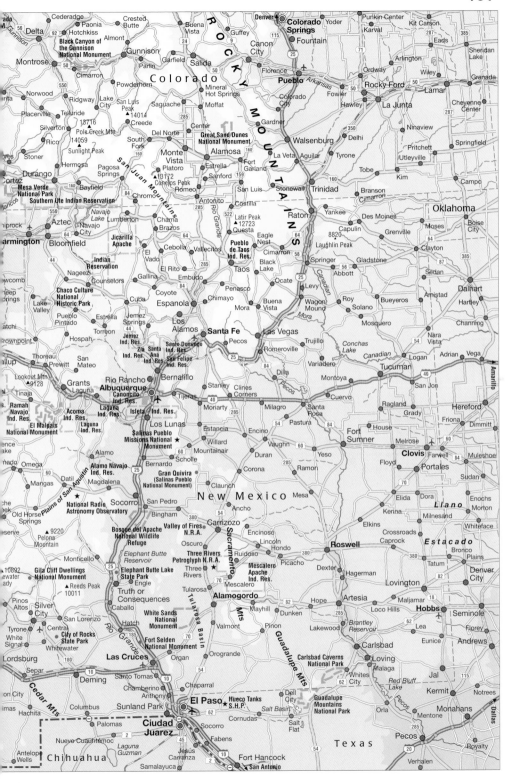

THE BORDER

From stunning national parks and monuments, to mown lawns and skyscrapers, the Border region has it all

People have managed to make homes here for at least 2,500 years – the ancient Hohokam (who mastered the use of canals to bring water to their fields), the O'odham, and the Apache. The Spanish entered the region in the mid-1500s, and Jesuits forthwith established missions. European-Americans began to show up on a larger scale in the latter half of the 1800s. There were also the cowboys and outlaws whose rootin'-tootin', gun-totin' wild-west image is etched upon the silver screen. Of late, retirees seek repose here during the mild winters.

The region is rife with state and national parks, and monuments where one can absorb the natural and cultural histories of a land that is beautiful but, in reality, harsh. Several Indian reservations are within easy reach.

The general low levels of air and light pollution make the border country a good place for astronomical observatories, and the Very Large Array Telescope of the National Radio Astronomy Observatory in New Mexico stands poised to receive communications from outer space. The wide-open spaces are also perfect for aircraft and weapons research and development. White Sands Missile Range occupies 3,200 sq. miles (8,300 sq. km) of southern New Mexico desert and they tell us "we still are not large enough for some test scenarios".

Phoenix, Arizona's capital city, in defiance of its desert setting, sports green lawns and spouts water fountains. It is a bustling business city with the automobiles, freeways, and air pollution to prove it. Although the population is culturally varied, it doesn't seem to come through as such. The farther south of Phoenix one goes, the richer the cultural mix: American Indian, Mexican, and general 21st-century amalgam. Tucson is more northern Sonoran than southern Arizonan. The mowed lawns disappear; exquisite native plants taking their place around homes.

Architectural jewels, from Spanish-colonial missions to the creations of Frank Lloyd Wright and Paolo Soleri, stand proud in their desert mounting. Rustic frontier buildings and Victorian houses grace Tombstone, and New Mexico's silver mining towns and ghost towns contribute to the romance of the Old West.

Excellent roads take you to all of these engaging places. Interstate 10 crosses the Continental Divide about 35 miles (56 km) east of the Arizona/New Mexico border; the summit here is 4,585 feet (1,398 meters) above sea level. As you travel in border region, pay attention to your fuel gauge; it can be a long way from one gas station to the next, and summer's heat can take its toll on radiators. ❏

PRECEDING PAGES: rich and varied cactus growth at Saguaro National Monument.
LEFT: cactus against adobe backdrop, Tuscon.

PHOENIX

In summer, the dry heat of Phoenix can purge the mind of lucidity. But air conditioning – and golf courses – have made the Phoenix area one of America's fastest-growing metropolitan areas

Maps:
Area: 188
City: 165

When Frank Lloyd Wright first saw the Salt River Valley in the late 1920s, it struck him as a "vast battleground of Titanic natural forces." Like a revelation to Wright were its "leopard spotted mountains… its great striated and stratified masses, noble and quiet," its patterns modeled on the "realism of the rattlesnake." Here, thought Wright with the zeal of someone moving in, if Arizonans could avoid the "candy-makers and cactus-hunters," a proper civilization could be created that would "allow man to become a godlike native part of Arizona."

Wright's architectural work in Arizona sought that lofty aim, though it has hardly happened. But aggressive irrigation – which has been in use both in ancient and modern times in this area – and air conditioning have nurtured a city of nearly 3 million people – **Phoenix ❶**, America's sixth-largest city. Unfortunately, their nearly total dependence on automobiles results in both traffic headaches and smog. Water is sucked up from deep aquifers to keep green the metropolitan area's 190 golf courses, upon which 2 million tourists and half a million locals play 11 million rounds of golf each year.

A civilization that adapted people to the Salt River Valley preceded Wright's idealistic visions by some 2,500 years. As early as 500 BC, the Hohokam people developed an intricate system of canals for irrigating fields of corn, beans, squash and cotton. Remains of that ancient system were absorbed and expanded in 1868 by the Swilling Irrigation Canal Co., the first Anglo organization to stake claims in the long-deserted valley. The following year, their settlement was named Phoenix by an Englishman who saw a new civilization rising like the mythical bird from the ashes of the vanished Hohokam.

What rose from the ashes was an aggressive ranching community that catered to miners and military outposts. Canals were extended through the alluvial valley, watering fields of cotton and alfalfa, pastures for cattle, and rows of citrus to the horizon's edge. Water storage commenced on a grand scale with the construction, in 1911, of Roosevelt Dam, still the world's largest masonry dam, on the Salt River some 90 miles (145 km) upstream from Phoenix. Three more dams on the Salt, and two on its major tributary, the Verde, allowed agriculturalists to send water where they liked. The Salt River became the driest place in the region.

Residents with long memories recall the 1930s as a Phoenician golden age. Those who couldn't afford the Biltmore found it too snobbish anyway and frequented a lively downtown that still retained a Spanish-American flavor. In summer, when temperatures climbed over 120°F (50°C) and daytime highs did not

LEFT: Phoenix's expansion is fed by deep aquifers.
BELOW: living a dream of yesterday.

dip below the hundreds for months, locals complained less of the heat than they boasted of trick ways to stay cool. It was common sport to be pulled on an aquaplane along the canals, holding a rope from a car.

Phoenix was transformed forever by World War II. The open desert was ideal for aviation training, and much of Phoenix became something of an extension of nearby Luke Air Force Base. Aviation equipment companies moved into the valley and even the cotton fields turned out silk for parachutes. It is less known that Phoenix had internment camps for German prisoners of war, and many of the prisoners, as susceptible to the desert's allure as anyone else, remained in the area after the war to become a part of the community.

The military revolutionized Phoenician life with a device called air-conditioning. The city had previously seen minor use of the evaporative or "swamp" cooler, but now there was genuine refrigeration. Suddenly Phoenix was a year-round possibility for those who couldn't stand the heat. The great migration was on. Camelback Mountain, at whose feet lay the most elegant dude ranches, was engulfed by suburbia. To the east, greater Phoenix swallowed up the once-isolated communities of Scottsdale, Tempe, Mesa and Apache Junction. Golf courses replaced dude ranches and resort hotels sprouted like desert grass after a thunderstorm.

The stereotype newcomer over the past decades has been the snowbelt retiree living in rule-bound planned communities of upscale houses or proletarian acres of mobile homes. In fact, however, the more recent influx of career-oriented young people in high-tech industries has so altered the population in the past couple of decades that the average resident within city limits, contrary to popular belief, is younger than the national average.

BELOW: Washington Street long ago.

Downtown Phoenix

The geographical setting of Phoenix is impressive, especially when the air is not veiled with smog. To the east soar the massive Four Peaks and the formal flank of the Superstition Mountains, while the Sierra Estrella rides the southeast horizon in dorsales of blue silk. Hemming in the city north and south are lower ranges of Precambrian gneiss and schist, framing the Phoenix trademark of Camelback Mountain – a freestanding, rosy, recumbent dromedary with a sedimentary head and granitic hump.

And what of the city itself? In a country of young cities, it is a young American city, and like many, it lacks a strong local character or personality, seeming at times to be rather sterile in ambiance, especially when many of its residents retreat into the air-conditioning in summer. Most of downtown is not a place that encourages casual strolling and people watching, especially in the scorching heat of summer, and at night one may find more happening at the motel than downtown. And unlike other older cities and towns in the Southwest, Phoenix lacks an Old Spanish undercurrent. Still, like many other cities with the same downtown identity problem, Phoenix has invested considerable energy in locating museums and cultural venues in the downtown area.

Heritage Square Ⓐ (open Tuesday–Saturday 10am–4pm, Sunday from noon; tel: 602-262 5029; free), a block east of the **Civic Plaza**, is what remains of this city's Victorian heritage and is part of downtown's **Heritage and Science Park**. Most striking of Heritage Square's 11 buildings – some of them, like the Lath House Pavilion, quite modern – is the **Rosson House** (admission fee), built in 1895 and once one of the most prominent homes in Phoenix. Some of the other houses here, dating from the early 1900s, were moved from other

Map below

Temperatures in the Phoenix area exceed 100°F (37.8°C) on more than 90 days a year, with an average scorching high in July of 106°F (41°C).

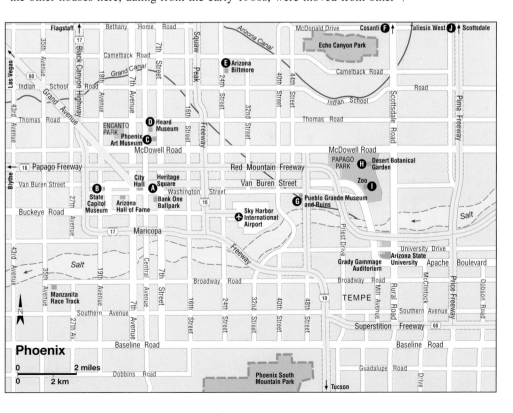

Frank Lloyd Wright left an indelible mark on the Phoenix streetscape.

locations to save them from demolition. Also part of Heritage and Science Park are the **Phoenix Museum of History** (open daily 10am–5pm, Sunday from noon; tel: 602-253 2734; admission fee), with interactive exhibits of the city's development, and the **Arizona Science Center** (open daily 10am–5pm; tel: 602-716 2000; admission fee), which is a $50 million hands-on funhouse of science, embellished with a planetarium. In particular, the center highlights Arizona's contributions to technology and the sciences. A flight simulator, virtual reality and fascinating exhibits on flight make this a choice for antsy children tired of the mundane.

Arizona's modest state capitol building lies 1½ miles (2.4 km) to the west of downtown, along Washington Street. The **Arizona State Capitol Museum** **B** (open Monday–Friday 8am–5pm, Saturday 10am-3pm; tel: 602-542 4581; free) uncovers some of the building's secrets, if one is interested. The capitol building was constructed in 1899 to house the territorial government; its dome was covered in 1976 with 15 tons of copper donated by the state's mining interests. Atop the dome is *Winged Victory*, a quarter-ton statue dating from 1899 – and decidedly Greek Revival – that turns with the wind. Much of today's governing is done in adjacent modern structures, but the restored Senate and House of Representatives chambers are open to visitors. Furnishings and ornamentation throughout the building date from 1912, when Arizona became a state.

The **Phoenix Art Museum** **C** (open daily 10am–5pm except Thursday and Friday, to 9pm, closed Monday; tel: 602-257 1222; admission fee) at Central Avenue and McDowell Road, 1 mile (1.6 km) north of Heritage Park, supplements a sometimes obscure permanent collection with splendid rotating shows and owns a choice group of recent Mexican works. Galleries include American

BELOW: swimming pool, the Biltmore.

and Asian works, and a decorative arts gallery exhibits ceramics, metalwork, furniture and glass covering a diverse spectrum of cultures and time periods. Art of the American West is represented by the works of Thomas Moran and Frederic Remington.

The exceptional **Heard Museum D** (open daily 9.30am–5pm, Sunday noon–5pm; tel: 602-252 8848; admission fee) is the one essential museum in Arizona to be visited, even if one doesn't like museums. It was founded in 1929 to house the Heard family's collection of American Indian art and artifacts, and it was – and is – an exceptional collection. The 1999 revamp of the museum, located on Central Avenue a few blocks north of the Phoenix Art Museum, enhanced the visitor experience.

Contemporary art of the last few decades is displayed in the Edward Jacobson Gallery of Indian Art, while the Crossroads Gallery has on-going exhibits of today's new artists. Also on the courtyard level (the original museum, just one-eighth of the size of today's, encircled the modest courtyard) are the Native Peoples of the Southwest Gallery and Katsina (Kachina) Doll Gallery, which help to place the Southwest tribes in a historical and cultural context. Everywhere in the Southwest visitors will see kachina dolls in souvenir shops, but for the authentic, the Katsina Doll Gallery features almost 500 dolls, a number of them from the collection of Arizona's late senator, Barry Goldwater. Many of the nearly dozen galleries have rotating exhibits. An excellent book and gift shop is worth a look, and the Ironwood Cafe is convenient for a break.

A great monument to another period is the **Arizona Biltmore Hotel E** (tel: 602-955 6600), 5 miles (8 km) northeast of downtown and Heritage Park. With a slack economy to begin with, Phoenix hardly noticed the Great Depression of

Map on page 165

BELOW: details at the Biltmore.

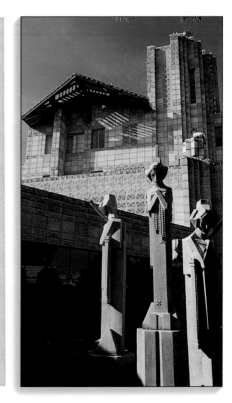

FRANK LLOYD WRIGHT

When Frank Lloyd Wright (1869–1959) was in his 60s, and at an age when other men are retiring, he was designing buildings that continued to revolutionize architecture, dismissing the stagnation found in much architectural design. Indeed, the older he got, the more innovative and revolutionary his designs became. His Guggenheim Museum in New York City, for example, was completed in 1959, the year he died aged 90. From his earliest days as an architectural student in the Chicago area in the 1890s, Wright remained true to his philosophy of "organic architecture", in which a building should rise from the nature of its natural surroundings.

"We must recognize the creative architect as poet and interpreter of life," he wrote. "This enrichment of life is the cause of architecture, as I see it." Wrote Lewis Mumford in 1929: "Wright has embodied in his work two qualities which will never permanently leave it – a sense of place and a rich feeling for materials." Wright's works in Phoenix, including the Biltmore and Taliesin West, revealed his deep belief that architecture should enhance both person and environment. Taliesin West, Wright's winter home and architectural studio from 1937 to 1959, was also a school that encouraged students' experimentation.

the early 1930s, living off its own agriculture and catering to those tourists who had kept their money in fine style. Built just before the financial crash of 1929, the Biltmore sailed in splendor through the bleakest of times. It is to the Biltmore that Phoenix owes the arrival of Frank Lloyd Wright. The hotel was originally designed by Albert Chase McArthur, a former student of Wright, who found himself in trouble and summoned the master for help. Wright came, and then stayed to create Taliesin West.

To see more of the work of the Hohokam and their canals, visit the many sites along the Salt River, including those in the path of a long-planned cross-town freeway held up, in part, by research work on the canals.

Wright probably gave more help than required, for the result was a masterpiece of textile block construction from Wright's middle period and is a delight for the eye – geometrically tidy, quietly whimsical and aesthetically inspiring. The Biltmore's 250 acres (100 hectares) are restful if somewhat Republican.

Gutted by fire in 1973, the interior was refurnished with furniture and textile designs from all periods of Wright's career. The visitor who enters no other building in Phoenix should make it to 24th Street and Missouri to inspect the Arizona Biltmore.

A contemporary architect today who has caught world-wide attention is Paolo Soleri, an Italian who has lived in Arizona since 1956. In Scottsdale, Soleri's **Cosanti** ❼ (open daily 9am–5pm; tel: 602-948 6145; free) offers a broad-brush overview of Soleri's architectural philosophy and of a grander site 65 miles (104.6 km) north of Phoenix, Arcosanti. Cactus and olive trees are scattered amidst Cosanti's earth-formed concrete structures, designed and constructed to maximize both ecological efficiency and use of space.

BELOW: *one of the nearly 200 courses in the Phoenix area.*

Pueblo Grande Museum and Archaeological Park ❼ (open daily 9am–5pm, Sunday from 1pm; tel: 602-495 0901; admission fee) is sited just outside of the central city, wedged in between an interstate highway and the inter-

national airport. It is a confounding juxtaposition, but this ancient pueblo site is worth a look. A wheelchair-accessible trail, just over half a mile long, encircles the ruins and has numerous, well-written interpretive displays. The visitors center has artifacts from the Hohokam culture and this pueblo site.

The Hohokam people lived in southern Arizona until around AD 1450. Experts at cultivation, the Hohokam developed a complex system of irrigation canals extending hundreds of miles; some of these canals remain today. Bad weather and internal conflicts resulted in the abandonment of the Salt River Valley, home to Phoenix, in the 1400s.

The Pueblo Grande mound is actually two smaller mounds dating from around AD 1150. Less than 200 years later, the two mounds were combined into a mound the size of a football field and about 30 feet (9 meters) high. Many of the buildings once on top of the mound were probably used for other purposes, including ceremonial. Immediately north of the mound, accessible by a walkway, is an excavated ball court used for ancient sports.

East and north of downtown

To the west of downtown, increasingly surrounded by the expansion of the greater metropolitan Phoenix, the **Desert Botanical Garden** ❶ (open daily; tel: 602-941 1225; admission fee) is said to be the world's largest collection of desert plants living in a natural environment. Several trails lead through the plants, displays and invigorating air. The garden emphasizes, as one might expect, the Sonoran desert of southern Arizona. Not far away on the same road, the **Phoenix Zoo** ❶ (open daily; tel: 602-273 1341; admission fee) offers the Arizona Trail with both flora and fauna of the Southwest.

Map on page 165

Pants full of hot air.

BELOW: Youth of Tularosa Basin

Maps:
Area 188
City 165

TIP

Wright's works in
Phoenix include half a
dozen homes, the
Arizona Biltmore, First
Christian Church on
North Seventh Avenue,
Grady Gammage
Auditorium in Tempe
and Taliesin West.

BELOW: fresh catch
from a stream.

Taliesin West ❶ (open daily 9am–5pm; tel: 602-860 2700; admission fee), in northeastern Scottsdale, was the personal residence and architectural school of architect Frank Lloyd Wright. In fact, most of the buildings and facilities were intended to be an on-going, hands-on educational exercise for architectural and design students. New techniques in the use of natural materials were developed here, often after many failures considered part of the educational process by Wright. Rocks from the desert and sand from dry washes were melded into foundations, walls and walkways, all the while following geometrical proportions that stayed constant from the smallest ornamental detail to the dimensions of the buildings themselves. Some of Wright's trademark techniques, such as the squeeze-and-release of a cramped entranceway opening into an expansive room, are apparent here. But from a distance, the buildings are barely apparent.

Around Phoenix

Development leapt to the northwest when **Sun City**, America's first fully-planned retirement community, was pitched by the Del Webb Corporation in 1960. More recently, cactus forests to the north of Phoenix have been bulldozed for a realtors' bonanza, and Phoenix and Scottsdale have competed in annexing the area under the pretext that they are trying only to control development. Expansion has taken such forms as trailer parks to the east, tract housing to the west and walled-in mazes of simulated adobe ranchettes in the newly populated areas to the northeast.

For those preferring humanity untrammeled by nature, there are the sumptuous resorts north of Scottsdale – itself rich with resorts – and the three mountainside Pointe resorts on the north and south edges of Phoenix. Gone is any pretense of the dude-ranch culture common before World War II, and the only reference to cactus may be worked into the macrame in the lobby. Offering golf, tennis, saunas, pools with underwater bar stools, French restaurants, nightclubs, discos, refrigerated suites and a clientele armored in platinum credit cards, these are not desert hideaways but total-concept luxury resort complexes.

Of the desert drives outside Phoenix, the most spectacular is the **Apache Trail**. One must endure the drive 25 miles (40 km) eastward through trailer parks and roadside businesses to **Apache Junction ❷**, where the western flank of the Superstition Mountains rises like a crumbling mansard roof. The road from there to **Roosevelt Dam ❸** weaves through 50 miles (80 km) of volcanic ash spewed millions of years ago and settled into rhyolite and tuff swirling like brains. Here and there, lakes of the dammed Salt River form blue calms in the riot of cactus and disordered stone. The Superstition Mountains themselves are protected by wilderness status and offer labyrinthine trails for hiking, horseback riding and backpacking.

The extremes of dude-ranch living still survive in obscure corners. The Wigwam in Litchfield Park west of Phoenix, for example, began as a corporate retreat by the Goodyear Corporation in the late 1920s. It is now a quiet contemporary resort with plush leather and copper-flecked adobe interiors. ❏

Water Issues

"Too thick to drink, to thin to plow." That's what they used to say about the Colorado River. Not anymore. The 1,450-mile-long (2,330-km) Colorado, rising in the Rocky Mountains and draining an area the size of France, has been tamed – dammed, diverted for irrigation and power, and so heavily used by the states it flows through that it is no longer a river by the time it passes over the border with Mexico and into the Gulf of California. The river once known as the Grand, which less than 6 million years ago carved the mile-deep Grand Canyon, is now a managed resource, not the wild, churning, seasonally flooding Great Unknown that so intimidated John Wesley Powell's 1869 and 1871 river expeditions.

Historically, the Colorado was a warm river that swelled into a red, silty, roaring froth when snow in the high country melted. Two thirds of its volume comes from the Green River, which confluences with the Colorado in what is now Canyonlands National Park. Twice mighty, the Colorado then rages in a series of whitewater rapids through the narrow confines of Cataract Canyon.

Plants and animals in the Grand Canyon, carved by the river, evolved to deal with seasonal surges in the river. Humpback chub appeared in the warm waters of the Colorado some 3–5 million years ago, when the river first cut through the layer-cake strata of the uplifted Colorado Plateau. Now, warm-water fish like the chub and razorback sucker struggle to survive in the colder waters exiting Glen Canyon Dam, which has created Lake Powell. The Grand Canyon is now a "naturalized" environment rather than a natural one, in the words of an environmental analyst, Stephen Corothers, meaning that the environment has changed to suit new conditions.

The greatest challenge today is to provide for the needs of a burgeoning Southwest population in the nation's fastest-growing region while conserving its natural habitats, such as those of the Grand Canyon. Daily surges in demand for power in large metropolitan centers like Phoenix once drove dam releases, creating damaging high- and low-river levels. This has been improved by the 1992 passage of the Grand Canyon Protection Act, which requires the dam's operators, the Bureau of Reclamation, to smooth out flows to ensure the natural habitat downstream is not subjected to extreme fluctuations.

On the other hand, infrequent great floods were once a feature of the Colorado and may have a place in the downstream environment. In 1996, the floodgates at Glen Canyon were opened to allow the river to run unchecked through the Grand Canyon. Beaches were quickly renewed, old vegetation whisked away and habitat improved in the week-long flood.

As Secretary of the Interior Bruce Babbitt put it: "When the dam was going up in the 1950s, it never occurred to anybody that they needed to think about what would happen a hundred miles downstream because we tended to see the landscape as fragments and each one of them independent. What we've learned... is that nature doesn't operate that way." ❏

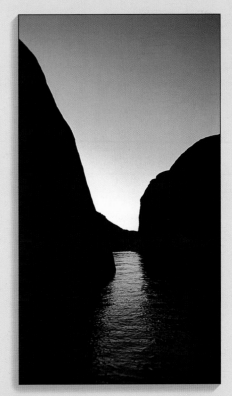

Right: Lake Powell resulted from the damming of the Colorado River.

TUCSON

Once perceived as a dusty town ringed by cacti and still air,
Tucson is increasingly becoming Arizona's coolest city,
grounded in Hispanic tradition and full of fun

Maps:
Area 188
City 176

Examining the emigration patterns of people over the centuries into the area around the southern Arizona city of **Tucson ❹** is one of the best ways to understand the culture of Tucson and its surrounding environs. The first surge of people into the region began over 2,000 years ago when a group of people known as the Hohokam (from a Piman word meaning "those who have vanished") moved into the area from what is today northern Mexico. When the Hohokam arrived, they found a lush valley with water flowing in the now-dry Santa Cruz River. As an agricultural people, the Hohokam built an extensive canal network to supply water to their fields of corn, beans and squash. By 1450, however, weather changes forced the Hohokam to abandon the villages.

The next group to emigrate into the Sonoran desert was the O'odham people, descendants of whom still live in the area. Two groups make up the O'odham: the Tohono O'odham (formerly known as Papago) and the Akimel O'odham (also known as the Pima). Akimel means river and refers to their village locations along the Gila and Salt rivers, near Phoenix. Both groups built small villages, one of which, at the foot of a low hill, was called Stjukshon.

The pronunciation of Stjukshon ("spring at the foot of black mountain") was modified over time to Tucson. The black mountain anchoring the city is now called Sentinel Peak or "A" Mountain, referring to the University of Arizona. (freshman have painted the letter on the mountain every year since 1915.)

The third wave brought the Spanish, led by Jesuit missionary Father Eusébio Francisco Kino, who established missions at Tumacacori, south of present-day Tucson, in the late 1600s.

The gold rush

In 1821, Tucson came under the control of Mexico when it gained independence from Spain. Mexican rule did not last long, however. Only 33 years later, Tucson became a territory of the United States through the Gadsden Purchase. (Arizona did not become a state, however, until 1912.) The 1860s brought the first wave of American citizens, who came in search of gold. Although little gold was actually found, mountains of silver and copper were extracted, creating a frantic migration of miners, prostitutes and their associates.

Tucson remained small until the military moved here and built Davis-Monthan Air Force Base in 1925. This brought thousands of military personnel, many of whom returned to Tucson as civilians following the end of World War II. The military presence is still strong and numerous aircraft from the base crisscross the skies above town.

A hot, dry climate has contributed to the most recent migration, mostly of retirees. This has helped lead to

PRECEDING PAGES: colors on an adobe house, Tucson. **LEFT:** Tucson's old courthouse dome. **BELOW:** roadside reflections.

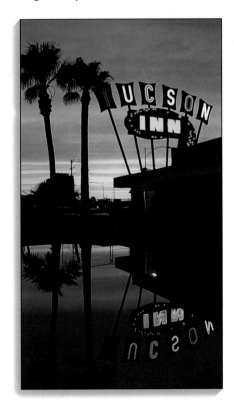

the massive housing developments that consume vast acres of desert landscape across the valley of Tucson. If you ever wonder what was there before the boom, just check out the names of the developments.

All of these emigrants still contribute to creating Tucson's dynamic urban environment. Like few other cities, Tucson's historic populations still play a role in forming a culture that mixes Spanish, Mexican, Native American, Old West and New West peoples.

Downtown Tucson

Several downtown Tucson locales highlight regional history. The first is in an area known as **El Presidio** and the adjacent mosaic-domed **Pima County Courthouse** Ⓐ (115 N. Church St.). Tucson's modern history winds back to 1776, when the Spanish built the walled Presidio of San Augustin del Tucson. The soldiers constructed adobe walls 12 feet (4 meters) high and 750 feet (230 meters) long to protect themselves and other immigrants from the Apaches, who also lived in the region. One small remnant of this wall can be seen in the Pima County Courthouse.

The **Tucson Museum of Art** (open Monday–Saturday 10am–4pm, Sunday noon–4pm; tel: 520-624 2333; admission fee) is west of El Presidio a few blocks. The museum contains over 5,000 pieces of art ranging from pre-Columbian to Western American. A dozen traveling exhibits each year add to the diversity. (None of Tucson's museums are world-class, but taken as a whole they provide an informative and eclectic mix of art, science, and history.)

Just to the northeast of the museum and one of Tucson's oldest houses, **Casa Cordoba** (open Monday–Saturday 10am–4pm, Sunday noon–4pm; free) was

TIP

Every October El Presidio plays host to the Tucson Heritage Experience Festival, a melange of food, dance and music. Scottish highland dancers follow old-time fiddlers; Burmese performers are sandwiched between a mariachi band and Polish singers.

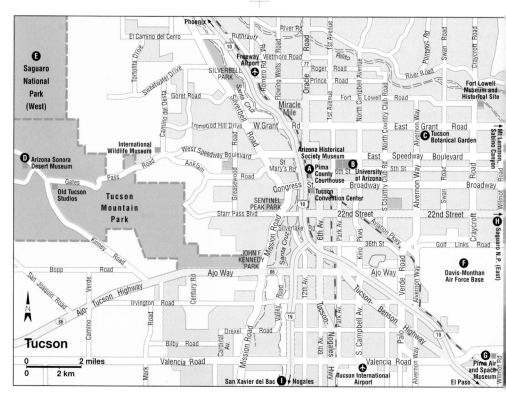

built in 1848 and is managed by the Tucson Museum of Art. Casa Cordoba displays the classic Mexican adobe construction of thick walls, interior courtyard and flat roof. The inside ceiling consists of pine beam vigas and cactus rib latias. A diorama shows the evolution of El Presidio.

East down the block from the museum is **Old Town Artisans** (186 N. Meyer; open daily), which offers arts and crafts by 150 artists representing southwestern and Latin American cultures. The building is a fine example of adobe construction. "Downtown Saturday Night" is a good way to experience the myriad cultures of Tucson. Every first and third Saturday night of the month, Tucson's downtown vibrates with street performers, musicians and vendors.

Most of the urban action centers on Congress Street, the city's most eclectic thoroughfare with tattoo parlors, an art-movie house and second-hand shops. At the eastern end is the legendary **Hotel Congress** (tel: 520-622 8848), on East Congress and built in 1919 to serve the railroad. The hotel achieved a bit of notoriety in 1934 when police apprehended the outlaw John Dillinger and his gang. The entire building still reflects its heritage, although nowadays one can also surf the Internet at the Library of Congress Cybar.

Also on Congress Street is the **Ronstadt Transit Center**, east of El Presidio at 6th and Pennington and a transit station that honors a well-known Tucson family. Federico Ronstadt, the grandfather of singer Linda Ronstadt, founded the F. Ronstadt Company in 1901, starting out as a manufacturer and repairer of wagons and carriages before evolving into an all-purpose hardware store, which closed in 1985.

The final downtown spot to investigate is **El Tiradito**, the Wishing Shrine, due south of El Presidio on South Main and the **Tucson Convention Center**.

Map on page 176

BELOW: Wishing Shrine, El Tiradito.

TIP

Tucson is a golfer's heaven, and one of the best courses is in town at 6125 E. Speedway. The 36-holes of Magic Carpet Miniature Golf feature a replica of Easter Island, a 20-foot-tall dinosaur, and a golf-ball-eating skull.

The small shrine, rumored to be the only one in the country dedicated to a sinner, commemorates the spot where Juan Olivera was killed by his father-in-law. It seems that the young Lothario was having an affair with his mother-in-law. Because of his sins, he could not be buried in consecrated ground. Despite this, town residents lit candles for his soul. This custom evolved into the modern practice where people come to the shrine and light a candle. If it burns all night, one's wish will be granted.

Around the university

East of El Presidio and downtown, the **Arizona Historical Society (AHS) Museum** (open Monday–Saturday 10am–4pm, Sunday noon–4pm; tel: 520-628 5774; donation) on East 2nd Street, focuses on area history, emphasizing the non-American Indians with exhibits on 1870s Tucson, transportation and mining. The mining display has a full replica of an underground copper mine.

The **University of Arizona B** is across the street from the AHS Museum. The **Arizona State Museum** (open Monday–Saturday 10am–5pm, Sunday noon–5pm; tel: 520-621 6302; free), at Park Ave. and University Blvd., is housed in two buildings just inside the west entrance. The museum provides an overview of the past 2,000 years with information on the Hohokam in the south building. Particularly interesting is the "Paths of Life" multimedia exhibit devoted to 10 cultures of American Indians in the southwest.

At the opposite end of campus is the **Flandrau Science Center** (open daily 9am–5pm, Wednesday–Saturday 7pm–9pm; tel: 520-621 4515; admission fee), which contains hands-on science exhibits suited to both children and adults. The planetarium shows feature a variety of science and cultural topics. A min-

BELOW: reflection of St. Augustine Cathedral.

eral exhibit in the basement entrances with a dazzling range of gems and minerals found throughout the state. The museum also has a world-class collection of meteorites, including a model of the Tucson Ring, a 1,400-pound (635-kg) chunk used unknowingly as an anvil in the 1860s, until scientists realized its extraterrestrial origins.

The University of Arizona is also home to the **Center for Creative Photography** (open Monday–Saturday 11am–5pm, Sunday noon–5pm; tel: 520-621 7968; free). Originally conceived by well-known landscape photographer Ansel Adams as a safe location to store his photographs and archives, it is now one of the world's great photography and research centers. Exhibitions are held year-round. In addition, the archives and library of Adams – known for black-and-white images of Yosemite and the Southwest – are open to the public, so one can examine, up close, the photographer's work and his especially wondrous black-and-white prints.

The university's **Museum of Art** (open Monday–Saturday 9am–5pm, Sunday noon–5pm; tel: 520-621 7567; free) is across the road, off Speedway Blvd. at Park Avenue. The Museum of Art displays a good survey of art extending from the Renaissance to contemporary. Of particular interest are 15th-century Spanish altar pieces and *Adventures in the Painted Desert: A Murder Mystery*, by Roland Reiss. A series of oversized metal chairs by local artist Barbara Grygutis was installed in 1999 outside the museum.

The **Tucson Botanical Garden** ● (open daily 8.30am–4.30pm; tel: 520-326 9255; admission fee) is also on the east side of town on N. Alvernon Way. Several gardens comprise this 5-acre (2-hectare) gem. Vanilla, coffee and bananas grow in the Tropical Greenhouse, while the Herb Garden encourages

Map on page 176

A famous symbol of the Southwest.

BELOW:
video store with a religious collection.

Tarantulas – not so unfriendly.

hands-on and noses-on sensory experiences. A third section contains a vast array of cacti and succulents, including a primitive cactus that has leaves. The five-acre location also houses the offices of Native Seeds/Search, a non-profit organization that works to encourage the traditional crops, seeds and farming methods that have sustained native people throughout the southwestern U.S. and northern Mexico. (They have a well-stocked store at 526 N. 4th Avenue.) In October, the garden plays host to the La Fiesta de Los Chiles, a two-day festival celebrating the life-sustaining (at least for some) fire-hot chili.

West of downtown

For anyone who has ever wanted to know more about the desert, Tucson has the world-famous **Arizona Sonora Desert Museum ◗** (open daily 8.30am–5pm in winter, 7.30am–6pm in summer; tel: 520-883 2702; admission fee). Located on N. Kinney Road west of central Tucson, the museum is part natural history museum, part zoo and part botanical garden – the museum is both entertaining and educational. Exhibits and displays include a hummingbird aviary, where hummers buzz around just inches from visitors; a desert grassland with a small, but active, prairie-dog town; several "cat" canyons inhabited by bobcats, jaguarundis and cougars; a plant-pollinator garden, with humorous signs explaining why we need to be concerned about the birds and the bees; and the museum's newest habitat showcase, the Arizona Uplands, where javelinas (also known as collared peccaries – they are not pigs) and coyotes roam freely behind "invisible" fences.

BELOW: Saguaro National Monument.

Just north up Kinney Road is the best place to learn about the great symbol of the desert, the saguaro cactus. The interpretive displays at the western unit of

Saguaro National Park ⑤ (open daily 8.30am–5pm; tel: 520-733 5158; admission fee) clearly show the importance of this massive succulent plant to desert inhabitants. Saguaros provide homes for numerous animals, including Gila monsters, woodpeckers, screech owls and honey bees, while both animals and humans eat the fruit.

Saguaros grow best on the rocky slopes (*bajadas*) at the base of the desert mountains. They don't grow in valleys because the air that settles down below at night is too cool for them.

This land was set aside in 1933 to protect the cacti and is broken into two halves that total 87,000 acres (35,200 hectares); the other half is east of Tucson (*see page 175*). Both units have excellent visitor centers. The much lower Tucson Mountains are found in the western area. Scenic drives and a network of trails provide excellent access in both districts.

East and north of downtown

Tohono Chul (open daily 7am–sunset; tel: 520-575 8468; donation) – or "desert corner" in the Tohono O'odham language – consists of 37 acres (15 hectares) of trails, gardens and exhibits, including a rock wall depicting the geology of the nearby Santa Catalinas, a demonstration garden and an ethnobotanical garden. The small preserve on North Paseo del Norte is a nonprofit park. Inside the grounds are an exhibit house and a tea room and garden cafe, offering excellent food.

Established in 1925, **Davis-Monthan Air Force Base ⑥** is home to the **Aerospace Maintenance and Regeneration Center** (AMARC), known locally as "the boneyard" and where the U.S. military takes advantage of the dry climate

Map on page 176

A large, many-armed saguaro cactus may be 175 years old. In the 1970s and 1980s, cactus rustling was a serious problem as homeowners in the southern deserts sought the saguaro for their yards.

BELOW: fancy and hot 1946 Chevy.

Map on page 176

and hard ground surface to store over 5,000 mothballed planes and helicopters. These aircraft will be junked, separated into parts, stored indefinitely or sold to friendly foreign governments.

One-hour tours are offered Monday through Friday and begin at the **Pima Air and Space Museum G** (open daily 9am–5pm; tel: 520-574 0462; admission fee). This museum houses and displays over 200 aircraft ranging from the 6-foot-wingspan (1.8-meter) Bumblebee, to Pres. John F. Kennedy's presidential airplane. Other highlights include models of the rocket-powered X-15 and the Wright Brothers' plane, as well as numerous helicopters. The museum showcases the phenomenal variation on the theme of wings and propulsion.

The eastern unit of **Saguaro National Park H** (open daily 8.30am–5pm; tel: 520-733 5153; admission fee) off Old Spanish Trail is nestled against the Rincon Mountains, which rise to over 8,400 feet (2,500 meters) and dominate the eastern section of the park.

Further to the northeast of central Tucson are **Sabino Canyon** (open Monday-Friday 8am–4.30pm, Saturday–Sunday 8.30am–4.30pm; tel: 520-749 8700; fee for tram) and **Mt. Lemmon**, at 9,157 feet (2,791 meters). Sabino offers excellent access into the foothills of the Santa Catalina Mountains. Trams travel continuously up the 3.8-mile-long (6-km) road and provide interpretive narration during the trip. The canyon's 50-foot-tall (15-meter) gnarly cottonwoods seem out of place in the desert, but a perennial stream, which has numerous swimming holes, provides the necessary ingredient for the trees to survive.

The road up to Mt. Lemmon begins just a few miles from Sabino. The 40-mile (65-km) drive up the mountain side threads through five of the seven life zones in the United States – from cacti through oak woodlands to Douglas fir forests. The same visual result driving north would require driving all the way to Canada. The temperature drops by 4°F for each 1,000 feet (300 meters) of gain. Mt. Lemmon is the southern-most ski area in the U.S. and annually receives over 120 inches (3 meters) of snow.

Biosphere 2 (open daily; tel: 520-896 6200; admission fee), about 35 miles (56 km) north of Tucson, was intended to study earth's biosphere – the zone in which all life exists – with its opening in 1991. Glass-enclosed and isolated from the outside, this 3.5-acre (1.4-hectare) facility was intended to be completely self-sustaining in food, air and water. Controversy involving the initial researchers tainted the experiment, but the effort is still admirable. Visitors are welcome; tours investigate the complete facility.

South of Tucson

South of Tucson is the brilliantly painted **San Xavier del Bac I** (open daily 8am–6pm), 9 miles (14 km) southwest of Tucson on Interstate 19. *Bac* is a corruption of the Piman word *wak*, which means "where the water emerges." Construction of the spectacular white church, also known as the White Dove of the Desert, was begun in 1778 by Franciscan missionaries, who moved into the area after the Spanish kicked out the Jesuits in 1767. Restoration of San Xavier (*see photograph opposite*), which began in 1991, has revitalized the beautiful and colorful interior. ❑

BELOW: Jose Galvez, Hispanic photographer.
RIGHT: Mission San Xavier del Bac.

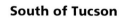

SOUTHERN ARIZONA

The broad Sonoran Desert of southern Arizona, hot and typically lacking in air conditioning, is often overlooked by visitors. But it is rich in flora and fauna, and complexity

Map on pages 188–9

Southern Arizona lies almost entirely within the Sonoran Desert, a land surprisingly lush with plants, birds and reptiles. Of course, cacti are the premier desert denizen. Low intensity, long-lasting winter storms and violent, quick-burst summer thunderstorms combine to foster this diverse plant and animal life. Add to this the geology of the Basin and Range province, once described as resembling a horde of "giant caterpillars marching northwest out of Mexico," and one has what many consider to be the most beautiful desert region on the planet. Southern Arizona is also well known as one of the premier birding regions in the country. A convergence of four biotic communities – Rocky Mountains, Chiricahuan desert, Sonoran desert and Mexican Sierra Madre – creates ideal habitat for plants and animals. Birders and non-birders can find species that occur nowhere else in the United States.

Most human desert-dwellers may not always enjoys the 100°F (38°C) days but they like to point out that it is a dry heat. This basically means it is cooler in the shade and that temperatures can drop by 40°F at night. You will still sweat but you won't notice it as it evaporates immediately, so drink lots of water to stay cool. Drinking water will also help prevent headaches.

The lower half of the state can be divided easily into a western and eastern part. Few people live in the western half of southern Arizona. It is, however, home to the Tohono O'odham Indian Reservation and vast acres of federal land. Stark beauty is its main asset.

Southeast Arizona is a land of legends: Cochise and Geronimo, the Earps and Clantons. Vast fortunes were made in the late 1800s and early 1900s but the area faded quickly after the mining booms. The towns languished until tourism came along and propped up the economy. Now the area offers anything – world-class outdoor activities to gunfight reenactments.

PRECEDING PAGES: San Xavier Mission. **LEFT:** saguaro and the Sonoran desert. **BELOW:** truck driver, sartorial style.

West of Tucson

As noted earlier, the western half of southern Arizona contains few people. A lack of people means a lack of civilization and, consequently, lights, – ideal for those who want to peer up into the night sky. The largest optical observatory in the world, **Kitt Peak Astronomical Observatory ❺** (tours daily; tel: 520-318 8600; donation) sits atop the 6,875-foot-high (2,095-meter) Quinlan Mountains about 45 miles (72 km) west of Tucson. Astronomers chose the site after a three-year-long investigation of 150 mountain ranges. The lack of artificial light combined with nearly 300 days and nights of cloud-free viewing, make it the perfect choice.

Twenty-two optical and two radio telescopes, including the world's largest solar telescope with its

O'odham boy at a reservation festival.

500-foot-long (150-meter), liquid-cooled viewing channel, scan the heavens. Each of three daily tours visits a different telescope. The gift shop sells the usual array of astronomy-influenced material, along with high-quality Tohono O'odham handicrafts at fair prices.

Kitt Peak also offers good views of the surrounding region, including the spectacular 7,730-foot-high (2,356-meter) **Baboquivari Peak** to the south. Baboquivari is a sacred peak to the Tohono O'odham, as it is the home of I'itoi (Elder Brother), the god who created them. The familiar motif of the Man in the Maze shows the path I'itoi took to his home beneath the mountain.

The observatory is located on the eastern edge of the **Tohono O'odham Indian Reservation**, once called Papago Indian Reservation. The O'odham, who at first objected to the observatory being built on their sacred land, lease the peak to the astronomers. Tribal elders changed their opinions after seeing the telescope at the University of Arizona. They call the astronomers "the people of the long eyes." The O'odham reservation, at nearly 2.8 million acres (1.1 million hectares), is the second-largest Indian reservation in the nation. About 10,000 people live on the mesquite- and cactus-covered land.

For years the O'odham were called the Papago, which translates to "Bean People." Beans were an important part of their diet, along with amaranth, mesquite and cacti. They also used native plants such as creosote as a remedy for a variety of illnesses. A change in diet has had unfortunate effect on the O'odham: adult-onset diabetes. Ethnobotanists believe that changing to a diet of fast-food has altered the O'odham insulin metabolism, as well as made many overweight. This is a perfect combination for adult-onset diabetes, which in O'odham people is 15 times the rate found in Anglo-American communities.

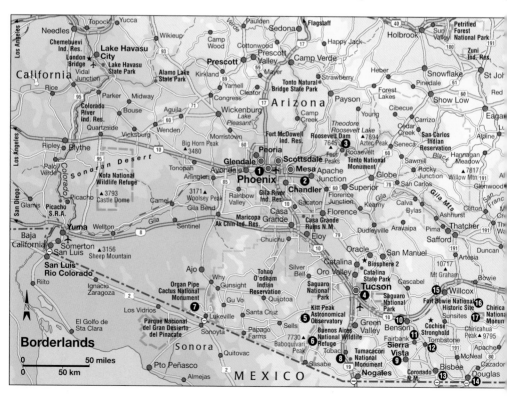

The **Buenos Aires National Wildlife Refuge** is near **Arivaca**, south of Tucson on U.S. Route 286. More than 115,000 acres (46,500 hectares) of grassland, cienaga (wetland) and riparian ecosystems acquired in 1985 is now protected in the Altar Valley. Overgrazing in the late 1800s destroyed once-lush grasslands, which have slowly begun to return.

Ornithologists recognized that the grasslands would be an ideal location for the masked bobwhite, a bird thought to be on the verge of extinction until a small population was found in Mexico, in 1964. Reintroduction began in the 1970s and continues to this day. Several hundred pairs now nest in the refuge. Pronghorn also range across the grasslands and may be encountered on the 8-mile-long (13-km) Antelope Drive. The wildlife refuge also includes Arivaca Creek and Arivaca Cienaga, home to gray hawks, vermilion flycatchers and green kingfishers. Short trails wind through both areas.

Organ Pipe Cactus National Monument ❼ borders the western edge of the Tohono O'odham reservation, on the border with Mexico. The name refers to the many-limbed plant that reaches its northern limit in the 330,000-acre (120,000-hectare) monument. Organ Pipes can grow to 25 feet (7.6 meters) in height and have more than a dozen arms. In June and July, bats pollinate the abundant white blooms that open at night. Other cacti in the monument include teddy-bear and chain-fruit chollas, senitas and saguaros.

Two loop roads provide access through the monument. The 21-mile (34-km) Ajo Mountain Drive circles the foothills of this range and takes about two hours. For those with more time, the 53-mile (85-km) Puerto Blanco Drive winds deeper into the monument and passes near the desert oasis of Quitobaquito. Both roads are windy, bumpy and unpaved, making them more interesting.

Map on pages 188–9

Madera Canyon is the closest avian hot spot to Tucson, 48 miles away. Over 175 species of bird have been sighted in the river canyon. Look for 14 species of hummingbird, the red and green elegant trogon, and nine varieties of owl in the rich, riparian-zone oak woodland.

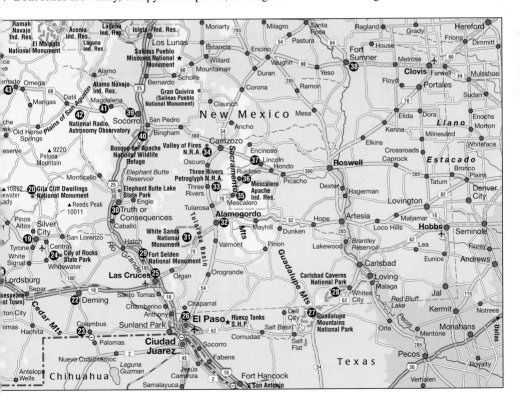

South of Tucson

Less than an hour south of Tucson, on Interstate 19 and east of Buenos Aires National Wildlife Refuge, is the hamlet of **Tubac ❽**. Its motto of "where art and history meet" is a fair description of the town. In 1691, the legendary Jesuit missionary Father Francisco Eusébio Kino was one of the first Europeans to enter the Santa Cruz Valley. The Spanish established the Tubac Presidio in 1752, a year after the Pima Revolt. Twenty four years later the Presidio was moved north to Tucson, leaving Tubac unprotected. When Tubac became American territory in 1853 after the Gadsden Purchase, it was mostly in ruins.

Almost a hundred years later the town began its foray into the arts with artist Dale Nichols' establishment of the Artists School. Numerous small shops now sell artwork ranging from copper saguaro fountains to vintage costume jewelry. Tubac's artist community, kindly, does not have the trendy feel of Santa Fe.

Four miles south is **Tumacacori National Historical Park**, which preserves three Spanish missions established by Father Kino in the 1690s. Only Tumacacori is open to the public. The present church was built by Franciscan missionaries between 1800 and 1822. It is a quiet place dominated by the ruined church with its brick bell tower, white-domed sanctuary and circular mortuary chapel. The ranger-guided tours offer good insights into the history of Tumacacori and the Spanish missions in Mexico and Arizona.

For those who are more adventurous, the **Juan Bautista de Anza National Historic Trail** runs for 4½ miles (7 km) along the Santa Cruz River between Tumacacori and Tubac. This sandy route crosses the river three times. The trail commemorates de Anza's 1775–76 expedition from Nogales, Mexico, to San Francisco. Three hundred immigrants and soldiers walked for 80 days with one

BELOW: church at Tumacacori.

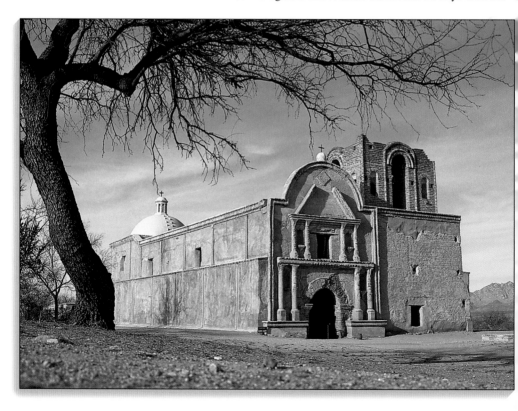

Map on pages 188–9

death and three births. The goal is to eventually create a 600-mile-long (960-km) trail following the old route. Only a few short sections are open at present.

Over the Santa Ritas to the east is the **Patagonia-Sonoita Creek Preserve**, owned and managed by The Nature Conservancy. Some of the tallest – over 100 feet (30 meters) – and oldest – 130 years old – Fremont cottonwoods grow in the preserve. It is one of the last places to see a healthy cottonwood-willow ecosystem, as well as a good spot for finding Arizona black walnut, velvet mesquite and velvet ash. Over 275 bird species – including northern beardless-tyrannulet, rose-throated becard and thick-billed kingbird – visit the area. Other animals include cougar, coatamundi, rattlesnakes and toads.

Another great birding spot of southern Arizona is **Ramsey Canyon**, located in the Huachuca Mountains just south of **Sierra Vista** ❾. Another Nature Conservancy preserve, Ramsey is pierced by a perennial stream that provides habitat for many amphibians. Fourteen of the 19 species of hummingbird known to inhabit or visit the United States have also been recorded in the canyon. It is also a splendid place to find butterflies. Be forewarned, though, that the preserve has only 12 parking spaces. Advanced reservations are recommended.

East of Tucson

To get a good feel for the landscape, head east out of Tucson on Interstate 10 about 40 miles (65 km) to **Benson** ❿, home to one of the least commercial spots in the West, the Singing Wind Bookshop. Located in the front couple of rooms of proprietor Win Bundy's ranch, the store contains an excellent collection of southwestern books addressing Native Americans, geology, history and mystery. **Kartchner Caverns State Park** is located 16 miles (26 km) south of

TIP

Just west of Sierra Vista is Fort Huachuca, established by the U.S. Army in 1877 to protect the region from Apache attacks. The fort today houses the U.S. Army Intelligence Center and Electronic Proving Grounds. An historical museum is open to the public.

BELOW: pronghorn antelope.

Benson off State Route 90. Although designated a state park in 1988, the caves were found in 1974 but kept secret until they could be protected. The extensive cave system includes two massive galleries and 2.4 miles (4 km) of trails. Unlike the nearby Colossal Cave, which is a dry system, Kartchner is wet and still forming and changing. It opened in late 1999 and the expected crowds have already led to the construction of a nearby fast-food restaurant.

The **San Pedro Riparian National Conservation Area** protects 56,000 acres (22,600 hectares) along the San Pedro River, between Benson and Tombstone. One of the best ways to see the area is on the San Pedro and Southwestern Railroad. A four-hour round-trip adventure parallels the river. The narration is a bit hokey, with an emphasis on the dramatic Old West, but the scenery is well worth the tour. Over 250 species of bird have been sighted along the San Pedro. If desiring to access the river by foot, information is available in the historic town of **Fairbank** ⓫ at the Bureau of Land Management (BLM) headquarters.

This is funny.
— JOHN "DOC" HOLLIDAY
MOMENTS BEFORE DYING
OF TUBERCULOSIS IN 1887

In addition, archaeologists have found North America's densest concentration of Clovis sites in this area. The Clovis Culture, which ranged across the area around 11,000 years ago, was one of the earliest groups to inhabit this continent. Well excavated locales are the Lehner Kill Site and the Murray Springs Clovis Site. Bones found here include camels, mammoths, lion and wolf. One exciting aspect of the Murray Springs site is that the tools and bones were found in situ, providing a wealth of information about these prehistoric desert dwellers.

On Route 80, between Benson and Bisbee, is the town of **Tombstone** ⓬. Originally known as the "town too tough to die," a better modern appellation might be "the town too tacky to die." Tombstone has exploited its niche – the Hollywood image of the Old West – like no other town. One is never far from

BELOW: U.S. Border Patrol on the Mexican border.

an historic site or out of ear shot of a reenacted shoot-out. Even if you have no desire to buy tombstone-shaped shot glasses, pay $1.50 to see the largest rose tree in existence (at the Rose Tree Inn), or be waited upon by waitresses dressed as 19th-century trollops.

Most of the commercial action takes place on Allen Street, the town's main thoroughfare. The **OK Corral** (open daily; tel: 520-457 3456; admission fee) is the best-known attraction on the block. One can cross into the restored grounds and see where, in October of 1881, Wyatt, Virgil and Morgan Earp, along with the erstwhile Doc Holliday, battled Billy and Ike Clanton, Tom and Frank McLowery, and Billy Claiborne. History was made in a scant 30 seconds after the Earp gang emerged victorious. (*See box on page 194.*) The same fee also includes an historic reenactment of the gun fight. If time is too short for the battle, mosey next door to the Historama and see a 26-minute multimedia presentation about the town, narrated by Vincent Price.

Further down Allen Street are the **Bird Cage Theatre**, once-home to prostitutes, drinkers and gamblers; **Oriental Saloon**, once part-owned by Wyatt Earp; and the **Crystal Palace**, still a fine location to find a cold drink in a dusty town. Allen Street is also a good place to see historical characters dressed in 19th-century clothes haunting the town. Striking up a conversation with them is a real treat, at least for the kids.

For those who want a less commercial perspective, amble over to **Tombstone Courthouse State Historic Park** (open daily; tel: 520-457 3311; admission fee), on Toughnut Street. Built in 1882, the brick Victorian structure houses the history of the town. Exhibits discuss the numerous lynchings and shootings that made the town famous. The original courthouse is also visible, although

Map on pages 188–9

Wyatt Earp.

BELOW: storefront in Tombstone.

Girl with her horse.

one wonders how much more "justice" took place outside the building. The courthouse also has a display addressing the two most popular theories about what actually happened on that legendary October day of 1881 at the OK Corral. And as you head off into the sunset, don't forget to stop by **Boothill Graveyard**, just north of town and the burial ground for the Earps' victims. Characters interred here include Red River Tom and Dutch Annie, as well many other lesser known victims of the vicissitudes of the Old West.

Of additional interest is the **Jewish Cemetery** located down the hill from the main section of graves. According to regional history, enough Jews lived in the town to establish the Tombstone Hebrew Association in 1881. Furthermore, a Jewish mine superintendent, Abraham Hyman Emanuel, was mayor from 1896 to 1900, and Wyatt Earp's third wife was Jewish.

Bisbee and the open-pit mines

About 25 miles (40 km) south of Tombstone is the mining town of **Bisbee** ⓮. Like many small former mining towns, Bisbee is trying to recreate itself as a tourist destination. Artwork ranging from the truly tacky to skillful, creative pieces is displayed in the many galleries that have appeared in recent years.

After the discovery of copper in the mid-1800s, the town grew in a few years from a nefarious mining camp to a phenomenally rich, well-heeled town with Victorian brick buildings. An air of respectability, as well as more money, came when Judge Dewitt Bisbee and a group of San Francisco investors bought the Copper Queen Mine in 1880. They consolidated a year later with Phelps Dodge and basically controlled the town from that point forward. This new concern built the **Copper Queen Hotel**, the town's most famous structure and the Phelps

BELOW: Lavender Pit, a copper mine near Bisbee.

SHOOTOUT AT THE O.K. CORRAL

Hollywood likes to depict it as an epic shootout between good and evil, but the famous gunfight at the OK Corral in Tombstone was really little more than a small-town grudge match between two factions that wanted things their own way. On one side were the Earp brothers and their friend, dentist-turned-gambler John "Doc" Holliday. On the other side was a gang of cattle rustlers and thieves, including Ike and Billy Clanton, the McLaury brothers and Billy Claiborne

The Earps became one of the most powerful families in town after they arrived in Tombstone in 1879, soon making the town marshall and deputies a family affair. The Earps, and friend Holliday, quickly made enemies, especially of the Clantons and McLaurys. After months of bad blood, the grudge turned violent in 1881 at the O.K. Corral. The Earps got off the first shots. In all, the gunfight lasted half a minute. Billy Clanton and the McLaurys were dead or dying, two Earp brothers were badly wounded, Holliday barely scratched, and Wyatt untouched.

Holliday and Wyatt stood trial for the shootings and were exonerated. But the grudge – and killings – continued for years, and only Wyatt Earp died of old age, in Los Angeles in 1929 at the age of 81.

Dodge General Office Building, which now houses the impressive **Bisbee Mining and Historical Museum** (open daily; tel: 520-432 7071; admission fee). Here one can learn about the geologic history of the mine as well as read about the infamous Bisbee Deportation, when, in 1917, Phelps Dodge rounded up at gun point 1,000 striking miners of the Industrial Workers of the World – known as the Wobblies – and loaded then into rail cars and shipped them like cattle to Columbus, New Mexico.

Around the corner is Brewery Gulch, once home to 50 saloons and now home to tourist shops and the Muheim Block, where the Bisbee Stock Exchange was built. The original stock tote board is still in the bar.

Much of the area's copper came out of the **Lavender Pit**, a 340-acre (137-hectare) and 900-foot-deep (275-meter) hole, visible from highway US 80, just before Bisbee. Despite the pit's color, the name honors a former mining executive, Harrison Lavender. The rest of the ore came from the nearby **Copper Queen Mine**, where there is an entertaining and educational underground tour led by an ex-miner, who will offer insights into the whys and hows of mining. Claustrophobes may want to bypass this subterranean sojourn, of course. Over 2,000 miles (3,200 km) of tunnels bisect the hills of Bisbee.

Visitors venturing far off the main roads will find remnants of the glory days of Bisbee. Some of the fine Victorian houses have been restored, but many show clearly what happens when a boom busts and the outside money interests abandon "their" town.

When the Phelps Dodge Company decided the Bisbee smelter was too small they built a new one in **Douglas** ⓰, 25 miles (40 km) east of Bisbee and on the Mexican border, naming the town after the company president, Dr. James Douglas. The

Map on pages 188–9

BELOW: Chiricahua National Monument.

Map on pages 188–9

twin smokestacks that loom over town stopped polluting in 1987. All that truly reveals the glory days of Douglas is the five-story-tall **Gadsden Hotel**, with its marble columns topped in 14-carat gold leaf, white marble stairs and a 42-foot-long (13-meter) Tiffany stained glass mural of desert scenes.

East through Apache land

Further along Interstate 10, around 80 miles (128 km) from Tucson, is **Willcox ⓕ**, which calls itself the fruit-and-nut-picking capital of Arizona. In summer, one can pick apples, peaches, pecans and pistachios. Although winter lacks the excitement of fruit-picking, the nearby Willcox playa is home to 10,000 sandhill cranes. Country-and-Western buffs may also want to peruse the **Rex Allen Cowboy Museum** (open daily; tel: 520-384 4583; admission fee).

The final refuge for the Chiricahua Apache chief Cochise on his run from the U.S. Army is about 25 miles (40 km) south of Willcox in the Dragoon mountains. He and his band of Apaches remained in the rocky confines of what is now called **Cochise Stronghold** for many years. A beautiful and quiet campground sheltered by oaks now marks Cochise last hideout.

Fort Bowie National Historic Site ⓰ (open daily; tel: 520-847 2500; free) is a good location to learn more about the Apache. The site preserves the ruins of an Army outpost built near the Butterfield Stagecoach stop to protect travelers from the Apache. The hostilities were precipitated by false accusations made by the military of Apache kidnapping and theft. Little remains of the outpost, but it contains good historic information.

BELOW: modest turquoise-and-silver jewelry.

Chiricahua National Monument ⓱, south of Fort Bowie, was known as the Land of Standing Rocks by the Chiricahua Apaches who formerly inhabited the mountains. The Chiricahuas were a refuge for the Apaches, led in later years by Geronimo and Cochise.

After the U.S. Army's forced relocation of the Apaches in 1886, the Erickson family moved into the area. They lived at Faraway Ranch for nearly a century and were influential in obtaining National Park Service designation for the land they called a "wonderland of rocks." Visitors can still see the ranch house, located a few miles from the national monument's western entrance.

The land was set aside in 1924 to protect this fantasyland of rocks, which formed 27 million years ago when a nearby volcano exploded. Eruption of Turkey Creek caldera produced a 2,000-foot-thick (600-meter) layer of dark volcanic rock, known as rhyolite. Subsequent erosion by water, ice and wind sculpted the rhyolite into columns, balanced rocks and hoodoos. The Chiricahuas have many miles of trails and good backcountry camping, especially near Booger Springs.

Like many ranges in southern Arizona, the Chiricahuas are called "sky islands." They receive significantly more precipitation and experience far cooler temperatures than the surrounding Sonoran desert. Many unusual plants and animals – including Chiricahua fox squirrels, tanagers, and Chiricahua and Apache pines – intermingle with more the more usual desert denizens one typically finds. ❏

Geronimo

I n 1905, while a prisoner of war at Fort Sill, Indian Territory, Geronimo recounted the Apache creation story: "In the beginning the world was covered with darkness," he said. "There was no sun, no day. The perpetual night had no moon or stars. There were, however, all manner of beasts and birds. Among the beasts were many hideous, nameless monsters... Mankind could not prosper under such conditions, for the beasts and serpents destroyed all human offspring."

But there was one boy who was not eaten by the monsters, Geronimo said. His mother, White Painted Woman, hid him from a dragon who ate human children. When the boy grew up, he went hunting and met the dragon in the mountains. He shot three arrows into the dragon's scales, and then, with the fourth arrow, he pierced the dragon's heart. "This boy's name was Apache."

It must have seemed odd to the men who heard this tale that the old storyteller was once the most feared warrior in the American Southwest. Geronimo was a war leader of the Chiricahua Apaches, the most truculent and fearsome of the Apache bands. Between 1876 and 1886, Geronimo and his warriors terrorized settlers and frustrated soldiers with lightning raids, elusive retreats, and repeated escapes.

Geronimo's early life was subject to raids and warfare. As a young man he married and had children, but his entire family was wiped out by Mexican troopers. He launched bloody raids against the Mexicans in revenge, and emerged as a leading warrior. He later fought alongside Chochise and Mangas Colorado in engagements against American and Mexican soldiers.

Geronimo joined Cochise in 1874 on his newly created Chiricahua reservation, but when the reservation was dissolved two years later, he escaped and returned to raiding. He was captured in New Mexico in 1877 and brought to San Carlos, where many Arizona Apaches were being confined and encouraged to take up farming. It had no appeal for Geronimo. He broke out of San Carlos in 1881 and the raiding started again.

Twice more Geronimo agreed to return to San Carlos, and twice he bolted. Finally, in 1886, with some 5,000 soldiers and 500 Indian scouts chasing his band of 24 warriors, Geronimo surrendered for the last time.

Back home in Arizona, whites wanted him tried for murder and executed. Newspapers across the country painted him as a savage killer. Even President Grover Cleveland suggested that he be hanged. But Geronimo's punishment may have been worse. He and the Chiricahuas – even many who had served as army scouts – were shipped in chains to a prison camp in Florida, and then, one year later, to another in Alabama. They were ravaged by tuberculosis, homesickness, despair. Within a few years, more than 100 died.

In 1894, after much lobbying by friends, Geronimo and his people were relocated to Fort Sill, Indian Territory. Throughout his imprisonment, Geronimo begged to go home, but his request was not granted. He died of pneumonia in 1909. He was still a prisoner of war at Fort Sill. ❑

RIGHT: Geronimo, a feared war leader.

SOUTHERN NEW MEXICO

Top-secret military bases, vast dunes of white gypsum, one of the world's richest horse races, a mountain resort of the Mescalero Apaches and the shooting grounds of Billy the Kid

Map on pages 188–9

Southern New Mexico is a study in opposites: snowcapped 11,000-foot (3,400-meter) peaks abutting the torrid 3,000-foot-elevation (900-meter) Chihuahuan Desert; sleepy historic copper and ranching communities alongside Space Age towns, telescope arrays and military installations; irrigated fields planted with corn, beans, squash and chilies within sight of the empty barrens of Texas's Llano Estacado (Staked Plains) and dark lava flows; ruined Spanish missions poking up from lonely grasslands and Indian dwellings in countryside so remote one wonders how anyone could make a living there.

People do make a living here – in agriculture, ranching, mining, aerospace, defense and education – but feel unjustly neglected and maligned by the more glamorous northern part of the state. That's a shame. This is a great place for adventurous backroad drives and introspective walks, where the friendliness of the people is surpassed only by changing landscapes and the juxtaposition of the truly ancient with the world of tomorrow.

Southwestern New Mexico

A couple of miles south of **Lordsburg ⑱**, in the far southwestern corner of New Mexico on Interstate 70 about 20 miles (30 km) east of the Arizona-New Mexico border, is the classic ghost town of **Shakespeare** (open on weekends for tours), where Billy the Kid used to be a dishwasher. Now part of a family-owned working ranch, the town (originally named Mexican Springs) boomed and died through successive silver strikes and a great diamond hoax, witnessing its share of hangings and brothels. In 1879, it was bought by an Englishman who rechristened the town Shakespeare and its main street, Avon Avenue.

Also caught up in the silver boom, **Silver City ⑲** was born in 1870 just 40 miles (65 km) northeast of Lordsburg. Unlike most mining boom towns, it never died. Like Bisbee, Arizona, it has transformed into an artist's community of refurbished Victorian houses, bed-and-breakfast places and boutiques aplenty. Today, it's also the gateway to Gila National Forest and Gila Wilderness and is the largest town in southwestern New Mexico.

To learn more about the local history, especially that of the Mogollon, pay a visit to the **Western New Mexico University Museum** (open Monday–Friday 9am–4.30pm, Saturday–Sunday 10am–4pm; tel: 505-538 6386; donations) in Silver City, where there is a large exhibit of black-on-white pottery decorated with birds, snakes and other dramatic motifs, produced by the Mimbres branch of the Mogollon people between AD 900 and 1100. Six miles (10 km) north of Silver City is **Pinos Altos**, the oldest mining town in the dis-

PRECEDING PAGES: White Sands National Monument. **LEFT:** black beetle on white sands. **BELOW:** always time for a chat.

trict with a museum housed in the old school. Across the street is the Buckhorn Restaurant and Saloon and **Opera House** (open Monday–Saturday for dinner; tel: 505-538 9911), with its whitewashed adobe walls, heavy-beamed ceilings, carved furniture and velvet draperies adding a touch of Spanish elegance. Although not the original building, the Opera House has excellent exhibits of historic photographs and Mimbres pottery, and in the summer it often provides entertainment such as theatrical melodrama or old movies.

Highway 15 continues north through the mountains to **Gila Cliff Dwellings National Monument ㉑** (open daily 8am–4.30pm; tel: 505-536 9461; admission fee) in a secluded canyon. The Mogollon lived here for a thousand years before they apparently folded into the greater Ancestral Pueblo culture that was burgeoning to the northwest. A mile-long trail leads up the canyon and into the dwellings, 180 feet (55 meters) above the canyon floor.

Other trails lead from the visitor center into the 790,000-acre (320,000-hectare) Gila, Aldo Leopold and Blue Range wildernesses within 3.3 million-acre (1.3-million hectare) Gila National Forest. The Gila Wilderness was established in 1924, the first in the country. The Aldo Leopold was named for the pioneering forester whose classic book *Sand County Almanac* was one of the first to promote the idea of wilderness. Trips into the wilderness require backcountry permits and must be made on foot.

Sixty miles (100 km) northwest of Silver City, on US 180, is the village of **Glenwood ㉒**, another headquarters for pack trips into the wilderness. There are a couple of small motels, restaurants and a district ranger station here. Three miles (5 km) north of Glenwood a road turns east toward the ghost town of **Mogollon**, 9 miles (14 km) up in the mountains. Relics of mines, tailings dumps

BELOW:
Gila Cliff Dwellings National Monument.

and foundations on the hills show the prominence of gold and silver mining in this area from 1875 until World War II. About 20 people live in Mogollon now, mostly along Main Street, which follows Silver Creek. The buildings are weathered gray, the metal rusted red. Some were built years ago for a Henry Fonda movie, but built so well most people can't tell the old from the new.

Towards the border

Thirty-five miles (55 km) south of **Deming ㉒**, the border with Mexico is marked by the border towns of **Columbus ㉓** on the American side and **Las Palomas** on the Mexican side. **Pancho Villa State Park** (open daily 8am–5pm; tel: 505-531 2711; admission fee) at Columbus commemorates much more than the revolutionary figure for whom it is named. In 1916, Pancho Villa led a band of rebels across the border in an attack that killed eight civilians and soldiers at Columbus and nearby Camp Furlong. This was the only time since the War of 1812 (against Britain) that the continental United States had been invaded by foreign troops. It is also the first time in American history that air power was used in war. General John J. "Black Jack" Pershing led a pursuit party into Mexico after Pancho Villa. Pershing's troops were given air cover by eight small single-engine planes from Fort Sam Houston in Texas.

Twenty-eight miles (45 km) northwest of Deming is **City of Rocks State Park ㉔** (open daily; tel: 505-536 2800; admission fee). Like a Stonehenge on the desert, boulders rise 50 to 60 feet (15 to 18 meters) high. Some look like skyscrapers, others tilt at crazy angles. In a state where prehistoric ruins are common, one might suppose these to be ruins but they are actually the products of erosion on ancient rhyolite outcroppings. This was a favorite lookout place for

Map on pages 188–9

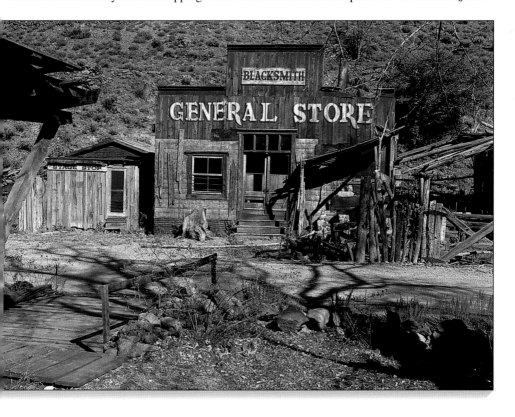

TIP

The Inner Loop, a paved, 100-mile (160-km) scenic drive (state roads 15, 35, and 90), goes from Silver City to Gila Cliff Dwellings National Monument, then returns through the Mimbres Valley past lakes and farms.

BELOW: Mogollon.

Adobe building door.

Apache waiting to ambush stagecoaches on the Butterfield stagecoach route. Camping and picnic areas are among the rocks and sheltered from heat and wind by gnarled alligator juniper trees.

Fifty miles (80 km) on Interstate 10, east of Deming, **Las Cruces 25** is New Mexico's second-largest and fastest-growing city with about 75,000 people. It took its name from a forlorn cluster of crosses that marked the place where Franciscan missionaries were killed by Apaches in the early 1800s. The town itself was not established until after the area became a U.S. territory in 1849, but the Spanish El Camino Real (Royal Road) between Mexico City and Santa Fe passed through here. Today, it's an important transportation hub and agricultural center noted for its chilies, pecans and cotton – a history that is examined in the **Farm and Ranch Heritage Museum** (open Memorial Day to Labor Day, Wed-Sat 9am-6pm, Sun noon-5pm; tel: 505-522 4100; admission fee). Las Cruces is also home to **New Mexico State University**, with a student population of 24,000 and noted in particular for its schools of engineering and agriculture.

Sleepy little **Mesilla**, just south, was built about the same time as Las Cruces but has none of its big city feel. The Gadsden Purchase was signed here in 1853, fixing the boundary between the United States and Mexico and ceding the U.S. vast areas of the Southwest that had once been Mexican territory.

Slipping into Texas

BELOW: Guadalupe Peak, in Guadalupe Mountains National Park.

To the south of Las Cruces about 50 miles (80 km), over the state border in Texas, **El Paso 26** was originally a place where Spanish trails crossed the Rio Grande. Travelers called it El Paso del Norte, the Pass of the North. In 1659, a small colony was established on the south side of the river and in 1827 another began on the northern side. After the war with Mexico, when the border was set, the two colonial villages became El Paso, on the north side of the river, and Ciudad Juarez, Mexico, on the south. The two today comprise an international city home to more than a million people.

El Paso used to be a tough, gunslinging border town and a bit of that flavor persists in the number of cowboy boots and Stetson hats – strictly for fashion, in most cases – seen on the streets. In fact, five major cowboy-boot factories are located in El Paso.

Traces of three Indian villages lie within 10 miles (16 km) south on the Rio Grande. During the Pueblo Revolt of 1680 in New Mexico, refugee Spaniards and non-hostile Indians fled to El Paso, where they established new villages. After the reconquest 12 years later, many chose to stay and these villages – Ysleta del Sur, Socorro and San Elizario – are the vestiges of those settlements.

Caverns and canyons

One hundred miles (160 km) east of El Paso is **Guadalupe Mountains National Park 27** (visitors center open daily 8am–6pm; tel: 915-828 3251; free), where the ancient Permian Reef has been exposed as limestone crags and deep canyons. Texas' highest mountain, 8,749-foot (2,667-meter) **Guadalupe Peak**, towers at the center of the park, which also preserves

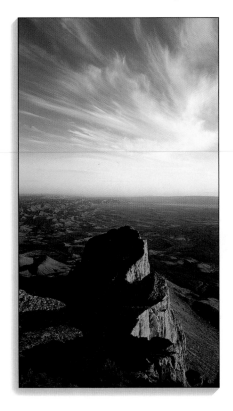

Texas' largest wilderness. More than 80 miles (130 km) of trails crisscross the desert lowlands into the high country, and although there are no services here, there is a visitor center and small campground. Try to time a visit in early October and hike **McKittrick Canyon**, famous for the autumn brilliance of its Texas madrone, oak and other deciduous trees, which cluster along the only year-round creek in the park. The trail leads to the quaint Pratt Cabin, built by oil-field geologist Wallace Pratt, who fell in love with the Guadalupes and helped establish it as a national park in 1972.

For surreal juxtapositions, it doesn't get much better than **Carlsbad Caverns National Park** ❷ (visitors center open daily 8am–5.30pm; tel: 505-785 2232; admission fee), tucked into the southeastern corner of the state, just northeast of Guadalupe and on the Texas border. The tour into the caverns descends into a strange, discreetly lit underground parallel universe, far from harsh desert. The temperature remains a steady 56°F (13°C) and silence reigns, broken periodically by the *drip drip drip* of water. As eyes adjust to the gloom, what emerges is a limestone fantasia, where popcorn flows across walls, soda-straw stalactite and helectite curtains drape from the ceiling, stalagmite pillars rear up from the floor as if holding up the earth, and one must glide on slippery trails around pools filled with nests of calcite "pearls" and floating "lily pads."

You have to wonder: How did all of this get here? The process began 250 million years ago in a warm, shallow sea inhabited by marine sponges and calcareous algae, which died and piled up on the sea bottom, eventually forming a 400-mile-long (650-km) limestone reef, long ago exposed by a receding sea.

The oldest of the 80 known caves at Carlsbad Caverns (more are discovered all the time) formed 12 million years ago (and as recently as 200,000 years

Map on pages 188–9

BELOW:
Carlsbad Caverns.

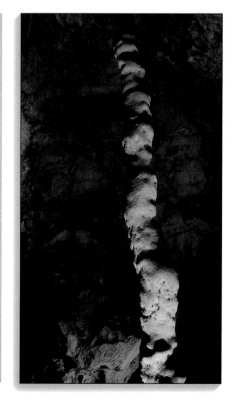

BILLY THE KID, A.K.A. HENRY

Whatever he was like as a real kid in the Irish slums of New York City is lost to history, but his bloody exploits as a teenager in New Mexico are infamous. Billy the Kid was born Patrick Henry McCarty in 1859, in lower Manhattan. A childhood in Wichita – using the name Henry – was followed by a move to Santa Fe for his mother's tuberculosis, and then Silver City, where his mother died. Henry was 15.

A year after his mother died, the Kid was arrested for stealing clothes from a Chinese laundry. He escaped by climbing up a chimney and heading for Arizona, where he stole livestock and killed his first man, in a saloon fight. He fled back to New Mexico, where he joined a gang of thieves near Silver City and took the name William Bonney. He moved to Lincoln County to gain notoriety during the Lincoln County War, a violent clash of commercial and political interests. The Kid was later captured by Lincoln County Sheriff Pat Garrett, convicted of murdering a sheriff and sentenced to be hanged.

The Kid shot two deputies and escaped. Two months later in the early morning and in a dark bedroom in Fort Sumner, Billy awoke to the shadow of a man – Garrett – who then put a bullet into Billy the Kid's chest, killing him.

ago), when slightly acidic groundwater started percolating through the limestone reef, hollowing out caves. Corrosion was greatly accelerated by sulfuric acid from hydrogen sulfide gas seeping into the reef from the Permian Basin oil field in nearby western Texas.

Carlsbad is known for an outside experience: bats. More than 300,000 Mexican free-tailed bats raise young in the Bat Cave passage during spring and summer. They exit in a black cloud at dusk and return at dawn. Seating for people is at an outside amphitheater.

After the caves had formed, it was only a matter of time before groundwater exiting to air-filled caverns caused precipitation of limey water. Much later, pools of water sustained prehistoric people. Their thirst sated, they used leisure time to carve inscriptions on the base of the cliffs, most commemorating their passage. The earliest carvings are petroglyphs left by people living atop the mesa in the large Atsinna Pueblo, an ancestral home of the Zuni people, whose present Pueblo lies 30 miles (50 km) to the west. One of the most significant carvings relating to New Mexico's later history is the inscription of the territory's first Spanish governor, Don Juan Oate, who passed through the region in 1605.

A visitor center, pleasant little campground, summer campfire programs and well-maintained trails over and around the mesa and bluff make this lesser-known national monument a special place to visit. Here is the essence of New Mexico: space, sparkling air, mountains and the ever-present signs of co-mingling cultures.

BELOW: high noon at a trading post.

If you only have a short time or cannot walk far, access the main cavern, the Big Room, via elevator from the visitor center. But the best approach is on foot, descending 830 feet (250 meters) into the caves along the steep, 3-mile (5-km) Natural Entrance trail. Far below, the Big Room opens up like some kind of great Hall of the Mountain King, 22 stories high, the size of 14 football fields and filled to the rafters with a weird assembly of limestone formations that

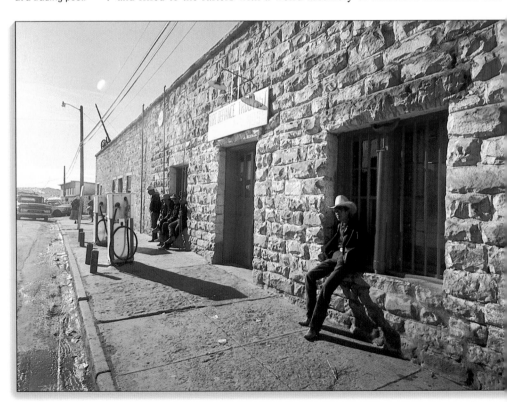

glow luminous in the low lights. Guided tours of caves leading off the Big Room – such as King's Palace, the Queen's Chamber and the Papoose Room – offer a closer look at the eerie formations, but it's the off-trail tours that offer the best caving introduction. The helmet-and-headlamp tour of Lower Cave and the easier candle-lit tour of Left Hand Tunnel are easily tackled by anyone of moderate fitness, while the popular Slaughter Canyon Cave tour (limit 25 people), 23 miles (37 km) south of the visitor center, requires a strenuous one-mile hike to enter the undeveloped cave using flashlights. Experienced rangers make these tours safe, fun and educational and always offer a few minutes of absolute darkness – definitely something everyone should experience once in a lifetime.

North of Las Cruces

Twelve miles (19 km) north of Las Cruces lie the ruins of **Fort Selden National Monument** ㉙ (open daily 8.30am–5pm; tel: 505-526 8911; admission fee), built in 1865. The fort played an important role in protecting the pioneers and miners who traveled along the overland trail to California. Continue north on Highway 195 or Interstate 25 and turn off at **Hatch**, which calls itself the Chili Capital of the World. The annual Hatch Chili Festival over Labor Day celebrates the year's crop of chilies.

The Rio Grande is dammed at **Truth or Consequences** ㉚ (known as T or C), north of Las Cruces, to form **Elephant Butte Lake State Park** (open year-round; tel: 505-744 5421; admission fee), one of the state's most popular boating, fishing and watersports spots. This small town on the central highlands changed its name from Hot Springs to T or C in 1948, in response to an offer from Ralph Edwards, who originated a popular radio show of the same name.

Map on pages 188–9

BELOW: cattle branding.

*Space Center in
Alamogordo.*

Tularosa Basin

Nestled between the Sacramento and San Andres mountains in the **Tularosa Basin** northeast of Las Cruces is **White Sands National Monument** ③ (in summer 8am–7pm, rest of year 8am–4.30pm; tel: 505-479 6124; admission fee), off Highway 70 and just outside of the town of Alamogordo. These white "sands" are really a 50-mile (80-km) expanse of fine gypsum that has shed from the mountains and then been picked up on the prevailing winds and dropped into dunes of many different types, some as high as 200 feet (70 meters). Stop at the visitor center for an orientation, then take the 8-mile (13-km) drive through the dunes. Interpretive signs and trails tell the story of their formation. You can also stop and picnic in the Heart of the Dunes for a dining experience in perhaps the world's strangest setting.

Surrounding White Sands are two giant military installations, **Holloman Air Force Base**, home to the B2 or Stealth bomber, and **White Sands Missile Range**, the latter best known for its Trinity Site, where the world's first atomic bomb was detonated in 1945. (The Trinity Site is open to visitors on the first Saturdays in April and October; tel: 505-437 2840).

The history of space exploration is the focus of the **Space Center** (open daily 9am–6pm; tel: 505-437 2840; admission fee) in **Alamogordo** ㉜. Inside are exhibits on rockets, missiles, satellites, space programs such as the Apollo and Skylab missions, and milestones in astronomy. Former astronauts are inducted annually into the International Space Hall of Fame in a special October ceremony. Outside the Space Center are actual rocket stages.

A 20-mile (32-km) drive east of Alamogordo on US 82 leads to the mountain resort of **Cloudcroft**, in Lincoln National Forest. The road climbs abruptly

Map on pages 188–9

from 4,350 feet (1,325 meters) at Alamogordo to almost 9,000 feet (2,700 meters) at Cloudcroft. Several sections of the road offer panoramic views of the White Sands National Monument to the west. Cloudcroft has a family-oriented ski area; old logging roads make good cross-country ski trails, while summer visitors seek cool days and chilly nights. Situated at an elevation of 9,000 feet (2,700 meters), the golf course at Cloudcroft Lodge is the nation's highest.

Heading north on Highway 54 from Alamogordo, turn off and drive 5 miles (8 km) east to **Three Rivers Petroglyph National Recreation Area** ❸ (open daily; tel: 505-525 4300; admission fee), where a 0.8-mile (1.3-km) trail leads past more than 20,000 carvings carved on basalt boulders by the prehistoric Jornada Mogollon. It is one of the best rock art sites in New Mexico.

Four miles (6 km) west of **Carrizozo**, off Highway 380, is **Valley of Fires National Recreation Area** ❸ (open daily; tel: 505-648 2241; admission fee), which preserves one of the youngest and best lava fields in the United States. The thousand-year-old lava erupted from a small peak near the northern end of the *malpais* (badlands) and flowed 44 miles (70 km) down into the valley. It offers a stark contrast with the shimmering white sands in the southern part of the Tularosa Basin.

Image at Three Rivers Petroglyph.

These mountains, buttressing the eastern flank of Tularosa Basin, were the last stronghold of the Mescalero Apache before they were forced out by American westward expansion. The **Mescalero Apache Indian Reservation** (tel: 505-671 4494) occupies almost a half-million acres (200,000 hectares) in the Sacramento Mountains. The wealthy tribe makes a good living in cattle ranching, lumber and tourism. A popular annual powwow is held every 3-4 July in the town of **Mescalero** ❸, also the location of the tribal **Cultural Center** (open

BELOW:
Space Center,
Tularosa Basin

TIP

The Inn of the Mountain Gods is in a beautiful setting, high in the mountains of the Mescalero Indian Reservation, one of the most economically successful – not counting gambling – reservations in the country.

Monday–Friday 8.30am–4.30pm; admission fee), with exhibits on the history and culture of the Mescalero Apache. At the northern end of the reservation is the tribe-owned **Inn of the Mountain Gods**, a luxury resort and casino, complete with golf course, of course. The grounds are situated at the base of 11,973-foot (3,649-meter) Sierra Blanca, the tribe's sacred mountain. The Ski Apache Resort in Lincoln National Forest draws skiers from Texas and the Midwest.

Just northeast of the Mescalero reservation is **Ruidoso** ㊱ (Spanish for noisy, referring to its lively stream), a year-round vacation town favored by Texans. With horse races every weekend from May through Labor Day, Ruidoso Downs is one of the most popular racetracks in the Southwest. World-class quarterhorses are bought, sold and raced here, and the world's richest quarterhorse race – the multimillion-dollar All-American Futurity – is run here each Labor Day.

Equines are also the focus of the **Hubbard Museum of the American Southwest** (open daily 10am–5pm; tel: 505-378 4142; admission fee), which has 10,000 horse-related exhibits, including a horse-drawn fire engine, an 1860 stagecoach, and paintings and sculptures by famed western artists.

Billy the Kid's turf

Over the mountains, 37 miles (60 km) northeast of Ruidoso, is **Lincoln** ㊲. A hundred years ago this was the scene of the so-called Lincoln County War, a brief but bloody battle pitting ranchers, merchants, cowboys and politicians against each other – with the outlaw Billy the Kid gunning on the side of the good guys. The entire town (pop. 100) is now preserved as **Lincoln State Monument** (open daily 8.30am-5pm; tel: 505-653 4372; admission fee), with the Old Courthouse, now a museum, the site of a daring jailbreak by the Kid; the

BELOW: Inn of the Mountain Gods, Mescalero Indian Reservation.

bullet holes from that breakout remain. During the first weekend in August, the citizens of Lincoln stage a colorful "Last Escape of Billy the Kid" as part of Old Lincoln Days, which features arts, crafts and an authentic Pony Express race from the ghost town of White Oaks to Lincoln, with the riders carrying mail specially cancelled to mark the event.

Map on pages 188–9

Billy the Kid was eventually killed by Sheriff Pat Garrett in **Fort Sumner ㉘**, northeast of Lincoln off Highway 285, where the Billy the Kid Grave and **Billy the Kid Museum** (open Monday–Saturday 8.30am–5pm, Sunday 11am–5pm; tel: 505-355 2380; admission fee) are popular destinations. **Fort Sumner State Monument** (open daily 9am–5pm; tel: 505-355 2573; free) commemorates the end of a sadder and longer trail that led thousands of Navajos and Mescalero Apaches to federal internment here, at Bosque Redondo, in the 1860s. Particularly cruel was the 400-mile (650-km) enforced march of Navajos (Dineh) from their homeland in 1864, dubbed "The Long Walk". Nine thousand Navajo and Apache were held here, with 3,000 dying from exposure, starvation, alkaline water and diseases. It was a miracle that anyone was still alive when the experiment was finally deemed a failure and the Mescalero Apache and Dineh allowed to return to designated reservations in 1868.

Billy the Kid's tombstone in Fort Sumner.

To the north

Socorro ㉙ (*succor*, or "help", in Spanish) received its name by early Spaniards for its helpful Indian residents. The first church was built in 1628, but the village was abandoned during the Pueblo Revolt of 1680 and not resettled until 1815. Socorro is in the middle of a rich mining district and was a boom town during the last two decades of the 19th century. When the railroad arrived in

LEFT: Lincoln shop.
BELOW: a common sight in these parts.

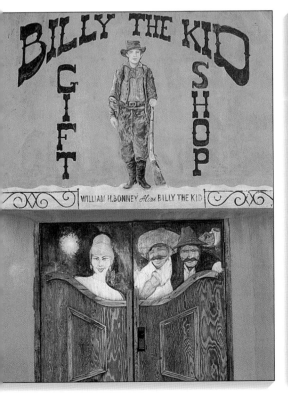

Map
on pages
188–9

1880, Socorro quickly grew into a ranching headquarters town. The original plaza is a block off the main street and several buildings around it are designated historic landmarks. Socorro's premier institution is the **New Mexico Institute of Mining and Technology** (tel: 505-835 5011), a few blocks west of the town plaza and which has been training geologists and engineers since 1889. Geology is also the draw at the **Mineral Museum** (open Monday–Friday 8am–5pm, Saturday–Sunday 10am–3pm; tel: 505-835 5140; free), run by the New Mexico Bureau of Mines and Mineral Resources. It houses the largest geological collection in the state.

Continue north along the Rio Grande Valley, where old Spanish settlements, small farms and wildlife refuges cluster along the river. Twenty miles (30 km) south of Socorro, on old US Highway 85 (which parallels Interstate 25), is **Bosque del Apache National Wildlife Refuge ⓴** (open Monday–Friday 7.30am–4pm, 8am–4.30pm on weekends; tel: 505-835 1828; admission fee). Here, November through February, thousands of waterfowl – most spectacularly snow geese, sandhill cranes and whooping cranes – make a winter home.

West 30 miles (50 km) of Socorro, along Highway 60, is **Magdalena ⓵**, railhead for the old Magdalena Livestock Driveway. Cattle were driven here from Arizona and western New Mexico to be shipped to market as late as the 1950s. A few remnants of wooden windmills mark the famous cattle driveway.

The highway continues west across the Plains of San Agustin, the setting of Conrad Richter's novel *Sea of Grass*. In the middle of this ancient sea-floor valley, completely encircled by mountains, is the **Very Large Array Telescope** of the **National Radio Astronomy Observatory ⓶** (open daily 8.30am–sunset; tel: 505-835 7000), where 27 huge antennae mounted on a Y-shaped railroad track probe the skies in search of intelligent life, work that was fictionalized in the 1997 film *Contact*, based on Carl Sagan's book.

Catron County, in west-central New Mexico, is the least populated part of the state – about 3 square miles (8 sq. km) for every person. The county seat and largest town is **Reserve**, population 400. About 80 miles (130 km) west of Magdalena is the county's second-largest town, **Quemado ⓷**, with a population of around 200.

About 30 miles (50 km) north of Quemado is the *Lightning Field*, a work of land art that is the essence of isolation. In 1970, artist Walter de la Maria won a commission from the Dia Center for the Arts in New York City to create the work, which is made of 400 thin, pointed stainless-steel poles, arranged in a mile-long grid, 16 rows by 25. In the flat light of midday, the poles almost disappear, but in late afternoon, early morning and even by full moonlight light catches on the poles like spots of gold or silver shining in perfect symmetry to a diminishing point that seems to vanish into eternity. Visitors may experience the *Lightning Field*, but only six people at a time during summer. Leaving cars and cameras behind, they are driven by pickup from the foundation's office in Quemado to an old homesteader's cabin in the field, which becomes home for the next 24 hours until the manager reappears to drive guests back to Quemado. ❑

BELOW: cowboy on the trail.
RIGHT: three of 27 antennae of the Very Large Array Telescope.

WATER RATIONING: A WAY OF LIFE

Perhaps somewhat surprisingly, the lack of water has not hampered the Southwest's wildlife, but shows us how truly adaptable nature can be

The Southwest's landscape is much varied – grass and shrublands, high and low mountains, high and low deserts, mesas, arroyos, and deeply cut canyons. In one particular way, these features are similar: all are bereft of moisture.

Everything that lives here, whether it has feet, wings, roots, or crawls on its belly, must get by on what little there is. Their methods go right to the basics of existence. Roadrunners' breeding corresponds with seasonal rains when food is plentiful. In the Sonoran Desert, which has both summer and winter rains, they often breed twice. Kangaroo rats do without water altogether, getting all the moisture they need from their food. To retain burrow humidity, they seal the entrances. Burrowing owls (above) will take up residence in abandoned rat burrows, and astonishingly, will join prairie dogs in theirs. Prairie-dog-like, they keep watch outside, bobbing up and down. Living underground makes it easy for predators to visit, and young burrowing owls try to throw them off with a call that sounds like a rattlesnake.

In the desert, when temperatures are high, rattlesnakes become more active at night. Rattlesnakes have no control system for their body temperature and cannot handle excessive heat, so they remain underground during the day hidden in burrows, under rocks or in the shade of shrubs. When temperatures become milder, rattlesnakes can be seen sunbathing on rocks or hunting for food during daylight hours.

△ **GOLDEN EAGLE**
The eagle's magnificent profile and 7-foot wingspan qualify it to represent courage and power. Its passing shadow sends desert creatures running for cover.

▽ **RATHER RUN THAN FLY**
The non-migrating roadrunner must cope with both heat and cold. It warms itself by spreading its wings and exposing its black skin to the sun's rays – and "pants" for evaporative cooling.

▽ **OOOWWW, IT'S HOT**
Desert coyotes have made physical adaptations for survival. They have shorter, thinner, paler fur, and weigh about half as much as other coyotes.

△ **FAIR WARNING**
Rattlesnakes, generally heavy and slow, rely on resistance to protect themselves, and warn of their presence with an unmistakable sound.

SYMBOL OF THE DESERT

Though we may see the saguaro as being representative of all deserts, they grow only in the Sonoran. They can become 50 ft (15 m) tall, weigh several tons, and live for 175 years. They do not begin to put on arm buds until they are almost 70. The pleats of this columnar cactus expand as it absorbs up to 95 percent of its total weight in water after a good rain. It could live several years on that supply. In late spring creamy white blossoms appear, a few opening each night over about a month's time, and develop into red fruits. Each ripened fruit splits to reveal about 4,000 tiny black seeds. The few that survive predation of hungry animals will strike roots and take up their sentry posts in the desert.

△ **LIVING LARGE**
A Gila monster can live several years on fat stored in its tail if drought limits the availability and number of small animals that make up its diet.

◁ **TOUGH GUY**
Scorpions can withstand the loss of 40 percent of their body weight to dehydration.

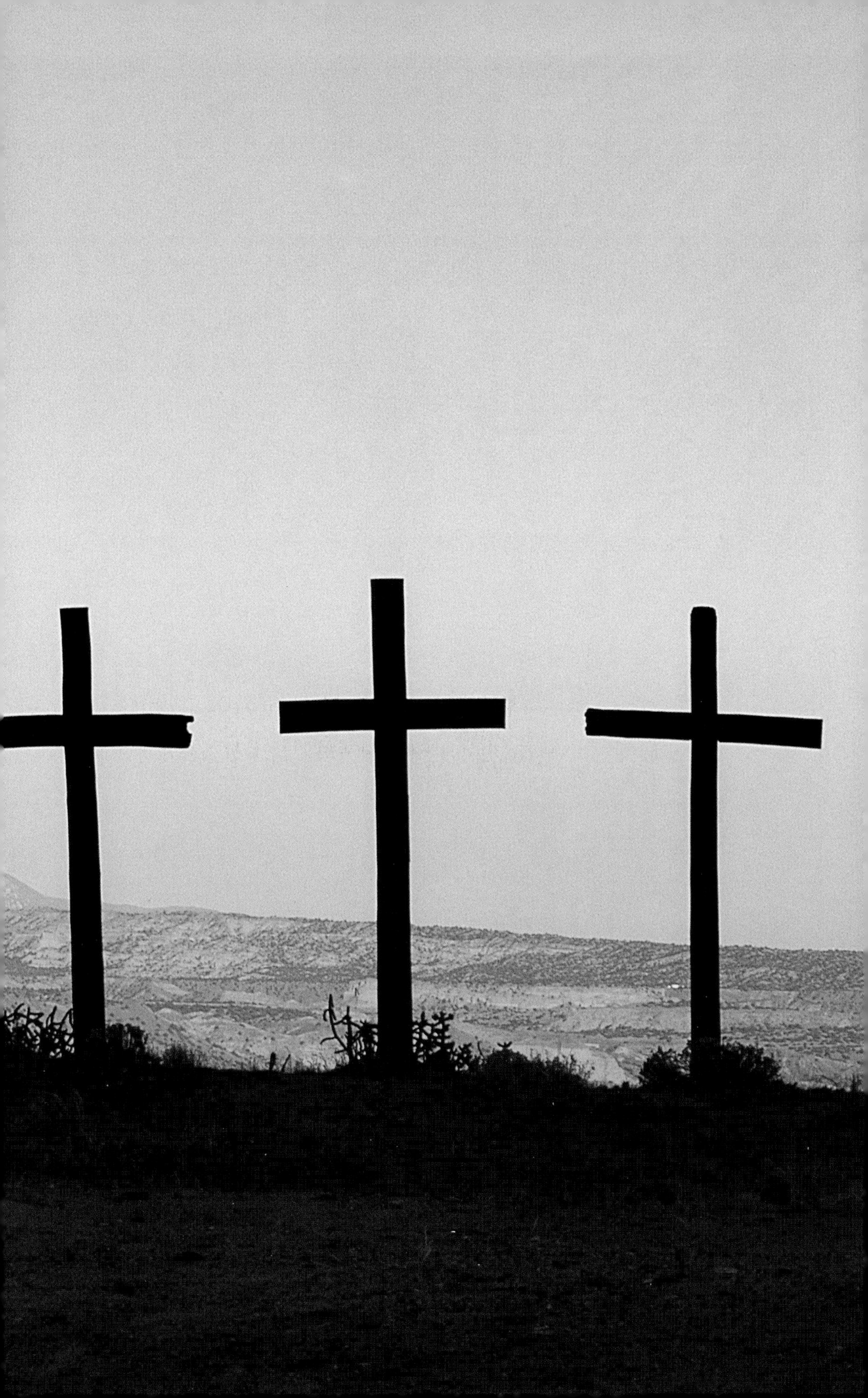

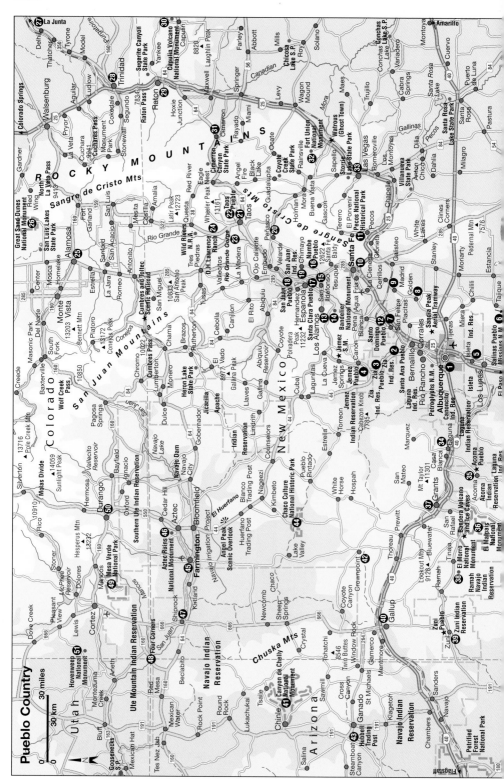

Pueblo Country

PUEBLO COUNTRY

Echoes of Spain and Mexico persist in this region, and there are treasures for lovers of Native American art

Primal landscape and ancient cultures are the main attractions in the golden light of the Southwest's Pueblo Country. Though the Puebloans were here long before the Spanish came in search of wealth and converts, the Hispanic influence now takes its share of the spotlight: town plazas, lovely Catholic churches, Mexican food in the New-Mexican way, pinatas, Saltillo tile, and flat-roofed adobe houses are among a thousand other echoes of Spain and Mexico.

When Spaniards in the mid-1500s beheld the Zuni pueblo of Hawikah in the cast of the setting sun, they were convinced they had discovered a city of gold. Truth, disappointment, and fury came soon enough. Today there are 19 aged Indian pueblos in the region, each with its own strong identity. In some, mission churches still hold regular services, but, for the most part, the Pueblo people hold fast to their old spiritual ways. Christmas celebrations are often a mixture of ancient Indian and Catholic pageantry. The capital of the Navajo Nation is at Window Rock, and landmarks and mountains sacred to the Navajo punctuate the Four Corners region. The Navajo Reservation is the largest in the US, with a population of 210,000 on its 17½ million acres (7 million hectares).

Native Americans, as a group, are one of the most artistically endowed peoples on the planet. From their rich cultural roots they draw upon symbol and design to create stunning arts and crafts and, if you are enthusiastic about their work, you might imagine you've found paradise. Every town has galleries and shops. The pueblos and villages that are open to the public have shops. There are multitudinous trading posts, some lying an astonishing number of miles off the beaten path. Every facet of Indian arts and crafts, from baskets to beadwork and back, is available.

Most national park sites in this region interpret Indian culture. Petroglyph National Monument, as its name implies, is dedicated to rock inscription, but can you imagine 15,000 of them? Canyon de Chelly, Chaco Culture, and Mesa Verde are among the park service's most significant cultural sites, but the area's numerous less discovered sites are equally informative.

Landform takes a backseat to culture in this the heart of southwestern Indian country, yet it is hard to overlook volcanoes and their residue. Along Interstate 40 in the vicinity of Mount Taylor, you will drive through an enormous lava flow, its black and broken countenance present alongside for many miles. Several park sites focus on volcanism, and Shiprock, a Navajo sacred site, is the lava core of an extinct volcano. Culture and landscape are quite clearly entwined in an ageless embrace. ❑

PRECEDING PAGES: Prickly Opuntia bigelovii cacti find homes in Southwest deserts; a classic scene from the Southwest.

ALBUQUERQUE

Maps:
Area 220
City 225

*New Mexico's largest city is not the state's capital,
but it retains some of its Spanish heritage, dating from 1598,
while embracing high-tech industries and Pueblo cultures and arts*

t all began in 1706 as a cluster of mud huts near a simple mud chapel, where the Rio Grande makes a wide bend – leaving rich bottomlands for settlers to plant corn and orchards. The provincial governor of New Mexico named the small outpost in honor of the Viceroy of New Spain (modern-day Mexico), the Duke of Alburquerque. (In the early 19th century, the first *r* disappeared form the spelling.) For a century and a half, **Albuquerque ❶** was a Spanish farming community and military outpost on El Camino Real, the road of government from Santa Fe to Chihuahua and on to Mexico City.

For over a century and a half, Albuquerque's center was what today is called Old Town. But when the railroad arrived in 1880, Albuquerque's commercial center moved 2 miles (3 km) east, where downtown is today, leaving Old Town to enjoy a long siesta – but without losing any of its identity. In the four centuries since the Spanish first arrived, four flags have flown over Albuquerque's old plaza: Spain, from 1598 to 1821; Mexico, 1821 to 1846; the Confederacy, in 1862; and finally that of the United States.

Today, Albuquerque is the largest city in the state of New Mexico, with some half a million people in the metropolitan area. Its growth has been phenomenal, like many cities in the American Southwest: in 1860 there were less than 2,000 people, and in 1950 less than 100,000.

It is the trade center of the state, headquarters for regional governmental agencies, a medical center of some renown, home of the state university and a private college and, since World War II, a center for space-age research and development. (Contrary to expectations, Albuquerque is not the state capital; Santa Fe, to the northeast, is the government center.) Slightly more than a mile above sea level, it has a dry, crisp climate and a relaxed life style.

Old Town

Any visit to Albuquerque begins with **Old Town Plaza ❹**, a community focus since 1706. Galleries here (and in other parts of town) represent some of the most prestigious artists in the state. Jewelry, pottery, rugs and weavings are good buys and of dependable quality. There is also a significant amount of absolute garbage being touted to passing tourists.

In the plaza are the replicas of cannon left behind by Confederate troops in 1862; they buried them behind the church before retreating from Albuquerque. The original cannons are in the Albuquerque Museum.

Most activity in Old Town revolves around **San Felipe de Neri Church**, which hasn't missed a Sunday service in more than 275 years. The church was originally erected on the plaza's west side but was moved to its present north-of-the-plaza spot in 1793.

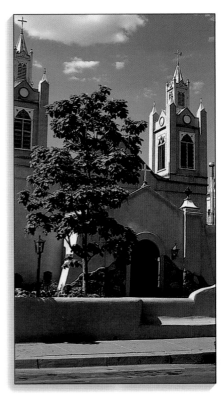

LEFT: Albuquerque's annual balloon fest.
BELOW: San Felipe de Neri Church in Albuquerque's Old Town.

TIP

Although historically
significant, remember
that Albuquerque's
plaza, like those of
Santa Fe and Taos, is
increasingly a place
for extracting money
from tourists – gift
shops, schlock shops
and "art" galleries
abound in the area.

In May, the church is the scene of the Blessing of the Animals and, in June, the Old Town Fiesta. For nine days before Christmas, Las Posadas processions circle the plaza in candlelit reverence, reminding the faithful how Mary and Joseph sought shelter for the birth of baby Jesus. On Christmas Eve, the plaza glows with thousands of *luminarias*, an Old Spanish custom to light the pilgrim's way to the Christ Child. Original luminarias were small bonfires of crossed sticks called *farolitos*; today's version is a small brown paper bag with a votive candle inside, held steady by a fairly thick layer of sand in the bottom.

Albuquerque Museum (open Tuesday–Sunday 9am–5pm; tel: 505-243 7255; donation) two blocks north of the plaza, is a modernistic, solar-heated adobe building with changing exhibits in art, history and science. The major permanent exhibit covers 400 years of New Mexican history. The museum is positively kid-friendly, with hands-on exhibits ranging from weaving to old-fashion toys.

Two blocks east is the **New Mexico Museum of Natural History and Science ❸** (open daily 9am–5pm; tel: 505-841 2800; admission fee), another favorite with kids but positively entertaining – and educational – for adults, too. The walking route through the museum leads through the geological and natural history of New Mexico, from tropical times to the ice ages to recent volcanism. There is a working fossil research facility where one can watch scientists identify and preserve actual fossils, many of which are beautifully displayed. A naturalist's center allows children to learn, hands on, some of the techniques that biologists and naturalists use to explore and identify the world.

Just south of the plaza is the dubiously named **American International Rattlesnake Museum** (open daily 10am–6pm; tel: 505-242 6569; admission fee). Strictly a commercial effort to empty your wallet in its overwhelming gift shop, it is still interesting if you're keen on snakes. It claims to have the largest collection of rattlesnake species in the world. True or false, the cramped displays reveal a lot about rattlesnakes.

The **Indian Pueblo Cultural Center ❸** (open daily 9am–5.30pm; tel: 505-843 7270; admission fee), a few blocks to the north of Old Town and just north of Interstate 40, is owned by the 19 pueblos of New Mexico, each of which has an exhibit area showing its own unique arts and crafts. It is a good place, for example, to see the difference between Zuni and Acoma ceramics. One floor is devoted to the history of the Pueblo Indians, and there is a shop and small restaurant that serves pueblo fare. On summer weekends, members of different tribes perform dances on the patio, where photography is permitted free.

To the south is **Albuquerque Biological Park** (open weekdays 9am–5pm, weekends to 6pm; tel: 505-764 6200; admission fee). The park's entrance opens onto a main plaza, with cafe and outdoor seating. To the right is the entrance of the **Rio Grande Botanic Garden ❹**. The botanic garden offers unfettered strolling paths through a number of gardens, including one of Spanish-Moorish design. Also within the grounds are two enclosed conservatories, one with Mediterranean flora and the other with a comprehensive collection of desert flora. To the left from the main plaza is the **Albuquerque Aquarium**. Salt

BELOW: fine detail of Zuni jewelry.

marshes, the Gulf Coast, coastal zones and the open ocean are all beautifully represented in the aquarium. Outside is an actually shrimping boat, the *Candy M.*

Part of Albuquerque Biological Park but on separate grounds south a bit along the Rio Grande, the **Rio Grande Zoo** is a pleasant place for both animals and people. In addition to the expected menagerie, all of it displayed with the idea that zoos are for animals first and human visitors next, the zoo has special displays for Asian elephants, Komodo dragons from Indonesia, and Australian wildlife, including the popular koala.

Map below

Contemporary Albuquerque

Downtown Albuquerque has made a successful comeback in recent years after almost succumbing to that common illness, suburbia exodium. The civic plaza now sparkles with flowers and a fountain, serving the same purpose as the plaza in any Spanish town, that of a communal gathering spot. The old buildings on Central Avenue are becoming a center for art galleries and studios, and the Ki Mo Theater, a marvel of ornate Indian-style art of the 1930s, was restored to its former glory by the city.

The architecture at the **University of New Mexico E**, farther east along Central Avenue, shows how adaptable the basic Pueblo style is. Traditional buttressed walls with protruding *vigas* (rafters) sit happily beside modern angular lines with lots of glass. In the center of the campus are the seven-story library and the president's home, both outstanding examples of Pueblo architecture. Also on campus are the Maxwell Museum of Anthropology, the Fine Arts Museum and Popejoy Hall, which has a full schedule of symphony, light opera, Broadway shows and many other forms of live entertainment.

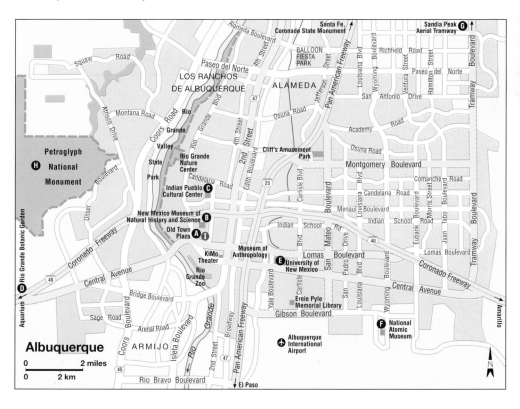

The **National Atomic Museum** **F** (open daily 9am–5pm; tel: 505-284 3243; admission fee) – located on Kirtland Air Force Base, with a shuttle bus ferrying visitors from parking lots – is one of those museums that may sound not worth the effort, but most visitors find some aspect of the museum fascinating. Yes, some parts of it promote (and with bias) all that has gone into atomic and nuclear research, but it remains interesting. The emphasis is on nuclear weapons – full-size replicas of atomic weapons through the decades and explanations of various delivery systems – but there are also displays on nuclear medicine and the history of basic atomic research. Outside are a complete B-52, Minuteman and Polaris missiles, and a cannon for firing atomic shells.

Sandia Peak Aerial Tramway is the world's longest cable car route.

Albuquerque environs

The Sandia Mountains – of granite, topped with limestone and hard against the east side of Albuquerque – dominate the region aesthetically, recreationally and climatically. The mountainsides facing the city are rugged and steep; the other side is gentler, with forested slopes. Both sides offer miles of hiking trails.

Sandia, 14 miles (22 km) north of Albuquerque, has fertile river bottomland for farming and has capitalized on its proximity to Albuquerque by encouraging tourist-related industries. The reservation extends to the top of the Sandia Mountains. On the road to the Sandia Peak Tram is a large arts and crafts center selling the work of many tribes.

Sandia Peak Aerial Tramway **G** (open daily 9am–10pm; tel: 505-856 7325; admission fee), the longest in North America, goes up the west (city) side of the mountains. By day one can see mountain ranges a hundred miles to the north, west and south. At night eat at a restaurant at the top while the lights of Albu-

BELOW: country music performance.

querque, Santa Fe and Los Alamos twinkle like stars below. In winter, skiers take the tram to the top of Sandia Peak Ski Area or drive up the other side.

Built in 1966 by a Swiss company, the double-reversible, jigback aerial tramway spans 2.7 miles (4.4 km) along two towers between the terminals. Climbing 3,819 feet (1,163 meters) to the top terminal, which is at an elevation of 10,378 feet (3,163 meters), the tram moves 20 feet (6 meters) a second to cover the distance in about 15 minutes. The land is rugged directly beneath the tramway, especially along the 7,720 feet (2,353 meters) of free space between the second of the two towers and the top.

West of Albuquerque just a few miles is **Petroglyph National Monument** (open daily 8am–5pm; tel: 505-899 0205; free). Established in 1990, this national monument contains land that is considered by the Pueblo people to be sacred land. There are several trails in three main areas: Boca Negra Canyon, Rinconada Canyon and Volcanoes, which is accessed on the opposite side of the monument. The 15,000-plus petroglyphs here – the earliest over 2,000 years old – are etched on stone contained within a greater 17-mile-long (27-km) table of land west of the Rio Grande. This table surfaced 110,000 years ago as lava emerging through a crack in the earth.

Pueblos north of Albuquerque

Of special interest geologically and historically is a drive through the Jemez Mountains northwest of Albuquerque. The sights on this tour range from red and saffron cliffs to mountain streams, from forested slopes and alpine meadows to Indian Pueblos. It covers 200 miles (320 km) and can be done in a day, but two would be better. The first stop is **Coronado State Monument**, 20 miles (30 km)

Map on page 225

Each of these rocks is alive, keeper of a message left by the ancestors... There are spirits, guardians. There is medicine...
— WILLIAM F. WEAHKEE
PUEBLO ELDER

BELOW: hiking in the Sandia Mountains, east of Albuquerque.

RETURNING TO AN ANCIENT HOME

After nearly 75 years of study and storage at Harvard University, the bones of almost 2,000 Pueblo Indians were returned to New Mexico, in 1999. The bones were met by 200 Indians from the pueblo of Jemez *(see page 228)* who had walked three days for the private rendezvous and mass reburial of the bones, which were taken from an excavation of the pueblo of Pecos, in Pecos Valley. The Pecos Pueblo, for 500 years a regional trade center, was thought by the early Spaniards to be one of the sought-after cities of gold. In 1838, the pueblo's importance gone, the people of Pecos merged with the pueblo of Jemez.

Excavation of the Pecos pueblo was a touchstone in modern archaeology, setting standards for archeological techniques. Research on the bones provided invaluable historical, cultural and sociological information.

In 1990, the U.S. Congress passed the Native American Graves Protection and Repatriation Act, which mandates that skeletal remains, along with sacred objects, be returned by museums to the various tribes. When the law was passed, there were an estimated 100,000 skeletons at museums around the country; so far, 10 percent have been returned, 40 percent of those from the National Museum of Natural History alone.

BELOW: caretaker at Salinas National Monument.

north of town where you leave Interstate 25 and turn northwest on State Route 44. These are the ruins of a large prehistoric Indian pueblo, thought to be the spot where Coronado's expedition headquartered during the winter of 1540–41. The Indians never reoccupied it after Coronado's departure. Of special interest is a *kiva* (underground ceremonial chamber) with rare restored murals. This is probably the only chance to enter a kiva.

Santa Ana ❷, 30 miles (48 km) northwest of Albuquerque, keeps the entrance to the pueblo chained except on special feast days, when visitors are permitted to enter. Most of the people live in three smaller villages down by the river near Bernalillo and return to the old pueblo only on feast days. Photography is not permitted. Traditional polychrome pottery almost became a lost art until Endora Montoya undertook teaching the younger women. This has revived the art. Coronado State Monument preserves the ruins of a pueblo said by the Santa Ana Indians to be their ancestral home.

The pueblo of **Zia** ❸, 36 miles (58 km) northwest of Albuquerque, sits on a volcanic mesa, its mud-plastered houses blending so well with the landscape that they are easily missed. Zia pottery, usually earth tones painted with stylized figures of birds and flowers, and well-fired, is sought by collectors; especially prized are the pots made by Candelaria Gauchpin. Zia is a small pueblo and conservative; photography is not allowed. Zia watercolor paintings are also prized. The ancient Zia sun symbol appears on New Mexico's state flag as a symbol of "perfect friendship." The pueblo's feast day is August 15, with a corn dance.

Jemez ❹, situated 48 miles (77 km) northwest of Albuquerque, is a pueblo set among the red and ocher cliffs of the Jemez Mountains. The people of Jemez were one of the last tribes to capitulate to Spanish rule after the reconquest,

and many of its people went west to live with the Navajo. Even today, at any feast day in Jemez, a surprising number of Navajo will be present. A craft cooperative on the highway sells Jemez pottery, usually reddish-brown and tan, painted black.

About 12 miles (19 km) up the canyon, just beyond the resort village of Jemez Springs, **Jemez State Monument** preserves the ruins of a mission church built by and for the Jemez people around 1617. It was gutted in a 1680 rebellion and never rebuilt. Jemez celebrates its patron San Diego on 12 November, and in August the Pecos Bull Dance is performed to honor the Pecos people who moved in with them in 1838. The highway follows the Jemez River past the camping and picnic sites, and the hiking trails of Santa Fe National Forest.

Pueblos south of Albuquerque

The pueblo of **Isleta** ❺ is only 13 miles (21 km) south of Albuquerque but manages to retain a strong identity nevertheless. Its people farm the bottomlands along the river and hold jobs in Albuquerque. Most of the Isletans remained friendly with the Spaniards during the revolt of 1680 and fled south with them, returning with de Vargas in 1692–94. Their magnificent mission church, built around 1615, was gutted during the rebellion and restored on their return. It is still in use, one of the most venerable in New Mexico. San Agustín, the patron saint, is honored on 4 September but other dances are held in fall and summer.

Head east from Albuquerque on Interstate 40 and turn south on State 14, which follows the east side of the Manzano Mountains. In the early 1600s, the Spanish built missions to serve the Pueblo Indians on the eastern face of the mountains, but within 50 years raids from the fierce Plains Indians became

Map on page 220

Protection from New Mexico's sun.

BELOW: ruins at Gran Quivira of Salinas National Monument.

Map on page 220

unbearable and the peaceful Pueblo abandoned their mountain homes for the Rio Grande Valley. Together three of these missions make up **Salinas Pueblo Missions National Monument ❻**, headquartered at **Mountainair** on US 60. At the missions of **Quarai** and **Abó**, part of the national monument, stand high walls of red sandstone, like primitive cathedrals open to the sky. Farther south along State 14, **Gran Quivira**, built of gray limestone, stands lonely on a high, windswept hill. Most of the pueblo, also part of the national monument, has been excavated, as have the ruins of two large mission churches, one of which was abandoned before finished. There are visitor centers at Gran Quivira and Quarai.

The Turquoise Trail to Santa Fe

Twenty-eight miles (45 km) north of Albuquerque, **San Felipe ❼** is one of the most conservative pueblos, never permitting photography under any circumstances. The lovely 18th-century mission church is open only during religious services. On Christmas Eve, spirits of the animal kingdom pay homage to Jesus as dancers representing deer or buffalo. Elaborately dressed women dancers enter the church after midnight mass. In hushed closeness, onlookers await the arrival of the procession. No one is supposed to be around to see the dancers emerge from their kiva. Buffalo dancers wear the dark fur and horned headdress of the buffalo, with their exposed skin darkened, and stomp on the floor. Deer dancers, their headdresses bedecked with antlers, move more lightly. One by one, the dancers move to the altar to greet the figure of the holy infant.

BELOW: desert cactus.
RIGHT: rope handler.

The scenic road from Albuquerque to Santa Fe goes around the back (the east side) of the Sandia Mountains, through ghost towns and Hispanic villages. The **Turquoise Trail**, otherwise known as State Route 14, begins at the Tijeras-Cedar Crest exit from Interstate 40, east of Albuquerque. To continue on the Turquoise Trail, return to State Route 14 at San Antonio and turn north again to **Golden ❽**, an inhabited "ghost town." But it's a ghost of what it used to be. Nearby, the first gold strike west of the Mississippi was made in 1826. Look sharply and you'll see the ruins of foundations in the narrow canyon. At the north end of Golden, on a hill beside the road, stands St. Francis, a mission church built in the 1830s and restored in 1958. The church and cemetery still serve the parish. The gate is usually locked but one can drive up to the gate.

Eleven miles (18 km) beyond is **Madrid ❾**, once a coal mining town of thousands. Its days were numbered in 1952 when diesel fuel started to replaced-coal on the railroads. Many of the cottages have been restored but abandoned houses in all stages of decay still line the road.

The turquoise mines of **Cerrillos**, the last town on the Turquoise Trail, gave its name to this back road. In the early 1600s, Spaniards found Indians already working turquoise mines here, but when the veins played out, the Indians left. Cerrillos turquoise is a rare and expensive collectors' item today. Several small and interesting shops are clustered around the plaza, and quite a few movies and television series have been filmed in this colorful little village at the end of the Turquoise Trail. ❏

SANTA FE AND TAOS

Of all the towns and cities in the American Southwest,
Santa Fe and Taos have become the prime destinations – Santa Fe
for its increasingly trendy image and Taos for its ancient pueblo

Officially established in 1610 as the capital of the Spanish province of New Mexico, **Santa Fe** ⑩ today has become one of the trendiest addresses in the west. This has been a mixed blessing in New Mexico, one of the poorest states in the country. Driven by money from southern California and other higher-income origins, land values in Santa Fe have reached the point where most locals can't afford to buy land in their hometown, where some families have lived for tens of generations.

Indeed, downtown Santa Fe has become so hip that it teeters on becoming a mockery of itself, a theme park with a real mayor and its own Zip code – trendy boutiques are a few too many, cuteness in souvenir shops assaults ad nauseum, and it's difficult to find good art amidst the surplus of third-rate "art galleries." Still, beneath the adobed veneer, there is an historical foundation to Santa Fe that gives it a depth and richness found in few other American towns.

Of Spanish heritage, Santa Fe is anchored by a central plaza. The governor's residence and official buildings were on the north side of the Plaza. Spanish colonization in the New World left a ruling triumverate of clergy, military and aristocracy, which often resulted in intrigue of epic proportions. In the early days of Santa Fe, there was much internal bickering between secular and civic officials, with the Indians caught in the middle.

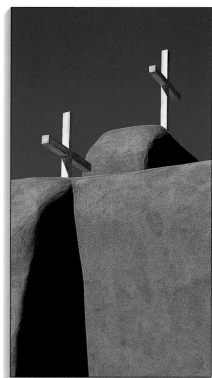

In 1680, the Indians rebelled against heavy-handed missionaries and taxes, gleefully burning all administrative records, books and churches, smashing bells and religious accoutrements, and torturing and killing Spanish colonists who couldn't get away fast enough. This Indian revolt, a defining touchstone of history in the American Southwest, was put down by Gov. Diego de Vargas, who reconquered the province in 1692 without firing a shot. The Spaniards had learned an important lesson – the indigenous population could not be bullied, and so they permitted the Indians' ancient ceremonies, so long as they went to Mass first.

Santa Fe remained the capital during the Mexican period (1821–46) and after the Americans took over. Today, its population is less than 100,000. The city sits at 7,000 feet (2,100 meters) at the base of the Sangre de Cristo Mountains, the southernmost part of the Rockies. The sun is bright and warm, the air cool.

Around the plaza

Santa Fe's **Plaza** is increasingly a commercial venue, although there are remnants of earlier times. The **Palace of the Governors** Ⓐ (open Tuesday–Sunday 10am–5pm; tel: 505-827 6483; admission fee), now a museum, runs the length of the north side of the Plaza. Indians from around the region spread jewelry on blankets along the portal outside, selling to passing

PRECEDING PAGES: Taos Pueblo. **LEFT:** historic inn near Santa Fe. **BELOW:** Santa Fe adobe detail.

tourists. Exhibits in the museum relate to the history of New Mexico's Indian, Spanish, Mexican and Territorial periods, although much of the Indian collection is now at the Museum of Indian Arts and Culture (*see page 239*). In one area, the original walls of the palace are exposed under glass, showing adobe almost 400 years old. Excavations have uncovered pits beneath the floor that were dug by Pueblo Indians for food storage during their short time in control at the palace. The Spanish later used the excavated holes for trash dumps. In fact, the Palace of the Governors has been in continuing public use for a longer time than any building in the U.S.

Surrounding Santa Fe, the Sangre de Cristo, or Blood of Christ, mountains received their name when a martyred missionary prayed that his death not be in vain, turning the surrounding mountains blood red.

Across the street to the west is the **Museum of Fine Arts** (open Tuesday–Sunday 10am–5pm, Friday to 8pm; tel: 505-827 4455; admission fee). Built in 1917, this branch of the state museum is a classic example of Pueblo Revival architecture. The permanent collection features painters whose art has been synonymous with New Mexico for more than half a century, including Georgia O'Keeffe and Ernest Blumenschein. Other exhibits are changed frequently as a showcase for outstanding New Mexican artists.

The world's largest collection of works by O'Keeffe is at the **Georgia O'Keeffe Museum** (open Tuesday– Sunday 10am–5pm, to 8pm Friday; tel: 505-995 0785; admission fee), in a renovated adobe church a block and a half from the Plaza. Well-known works by O'Keeffe are on permanent display. O'Keeffe was seduced by the New Mexican desert on her first visit in 1917; she settled here permanently in 1949 in the small village of Abiquiu, west of Los Alamos, living there for four decades before moving to Santa Fe. A couple of years later she died at 98 years old, in 1986. About New Mexico she wrote, "All the earth colors of the painter's palette are out there in the many miles of badlands."

BELOW: Museum of Fine Arts, Santa Fe.

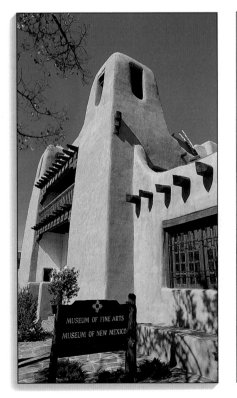

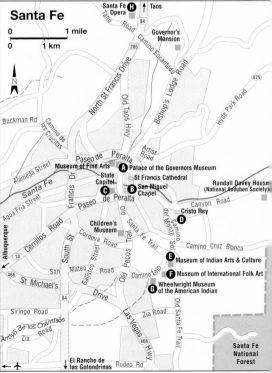

The best people-watching in town is had at **La Fonda Hotel**, on the Plaza. Sit in the lobby and you might see movie stars, politicians, Native Americans, artists, poets and maybe your next-door neighbor – and other tourists. In fact, there has always been a hostelry here at the end of the Santa Fe Trail. The present establishment dates from well before World War II and is built like a multi-storied Indian pueblo, with protruding vigas, smooth, flowing lines, flagstone floors, interior patios, colored glass, carved corbels and furniture. The lounge is a place to sit in comfortable dimness, listen to classical guitar, sip margaritas and crunch nachos.

The **Cathedral of St. Francis** stands in Romanesque grandeur a block east of the Plaza. Actually, its look is quite out of place here in the Southwest – of French design it is a monument to the efforts of Jean Baptiste Lamy, Archbishop of Santa Fe. Constructed between 1869 and 1886, the cathedral has a decidedly European look. This cathedral was built on the spot where Santa Fe's original church was erected in 1610. Willa Cather's novel, *Death Comes for the Archbishop*, immortalizes Lamy's work in the Southwest.

North on Bishop Lodge Road is the Bishop's Lodge, one of Santa Fe's most luxurious resorts and centered on Bishop Lamy's private chapel, open to the public. The lodge, however, is closed in winter.

On the opposite side of the street from the cathedral is the **Institute of American Indian Arts Museum** (open daily 9am–5pm; tel: 505-988 6281; admission fee), a private museum that displays a fine collection of contemporary Indian art.

To the south of the Plaza is **Loretto Chapel**, also known as Our Lady of Light, housing a locally famous spiral staircase built without visible support. Legend says an itinerant carpenter appeared at the convent of the Sisters of

Map on page 236

Santa Fe's Cathedral of St. Francis.

BELOW: selling Indian jewelry at the Palace, and souvenir shop.

Loretto in 1878 in answer to a novena and built the circular, freestanding stairway. The carpenter disappeared, but the sisters believed he was St Joseph.

San Miguel Chapel ❸, on the Old Santa Fe Trail two blocks east of the Plaza, is sometimes called "the oldest church in America." It isn't, but it stands over the foundations of a church built around 1636 and burned during the Pueblo revolt of 1680. It has been rebuilt and remodeled five times since then, most recently in 1955. This part of old Santa Fe was once known as Barrio Analco and was where Tlascalan Indians from Mexico settled in the early 1600s; Spanish colonists, on the other hand, settled to the north of the river where the Plaza is today. The original chapel was built by the Tlascalans, for a long time important allies for the Spaniards – they helped Cortes conquer Mexico – and who had accompanied the Spaniards to New Mexico in 1598. The Spaniards had no church of their own at first and so they celebrated mass in San Miguel Chapel.

Across the street is "The Oldest House in America," housing a gift and souvenir shop. There are actually adobe houses that are older but this one nevertheless serves as a good example of ancient construction.

While New Mexico has the oldest capital – Santa Fe, of course – in the United States, the **State Capitol** ❸ (tel: 505-986 4589) is perhaps one of the newest. Dedicated in 1966, it is in the New Mexico territorial style – which is to say, an adaptation of the Greek-revival style with pueblo adobe influences. From the air, it is in the round shape of the Zia Indian sun symbol, also the symmetrical symbol found on the state's flag. In the floor of the rotunda is the Great Seal of the State of New Mexico, done in brass and turquoise.

Canyon Road, once a crooked trail used for hauling wood and where artists could rent adobe houses for $10 a month, is now Santa Fe's other hip shop-

Effigy jars at the Museum of Indian Arts and Culture in Santa Fe.

BELOW: gallery on Canyon Road, and what is said to be the oldest house in the United States.

ping area, a string of gallery after gallery after gallery between Garcia and Camino Cerrito roads. The once-cheap huts are now pricey condominiums and the finest shops, galleries and restaurants in Santa Fe.

Cristo Rey Church ⓓ, at the east end of Canyon Road at Camino Cerrito, holds the most remarkable piece of Spanish colonial art in the U.S. a huge stone altar screen, or *reredos*, carved with saints and intricate designs. Measuring 40 feet (12 meters) wide, 18 feet (5 meters) high and weighing many tons, it was made in 1760 for an older church on the Plaza and kept in storage for over 200 years before a church big enough to hold it was built.

On piñon-dotted Museum Hill at the southeast edge of town (too far to walk) is a complex of three eminent museums. Nearby, the **Museum of Indian Arts and Culture ⓔ** (open Tuesday–Sunday 10am–5pm; tel: 505-827 6344; admission fee) has excellent displays of pottery, kachinas and other Native American artifacts. Videos of storytellers sharing creation stories and a walk-through Navajo hogan enrich one's knowledge of the Southwest.

The **Museum of International Folk Art ⓕ** (open Tuesday–Sunday 10am–5pm; tel: 505-827 6350; admission fee), a state museum, exhibits religious and other folk art, highlighted by the Girard Exhibit, a collection of 120,000 pieces of folk art from around the world. Of the many museums in New Mexico, this is perhaps the most distinctive and, if possible, it should not be missed.

Also on Museum Hill is the **Wheelwright Museum of the American Indian ⓖ** (open Monday–Saturday 10am–5pm, Sunday 1–5pm; tel: 505-982 4636; admission fee) a privately endowed museum once devoted exclusively to Navajo ceremonial art but now including culture and art from other tribes, often focusing on one particular artist or craftsperson.

Map on page 236

BELOW: the Harvest Procession at Las Golondrinas.

Over 25 years, the **Santa Fe Opera**  (tel: 505-986 5900) has built a worldwide reputation for excellence. The season is July and August, and performances are usually sold out. Those without reservations can try at the gate for standing room. The open-air Opera House, a spectacularly impressive structure, is in the hills some miles north of town. With the sides and part of the roof open to the stars, the setting is part of the performances.

Beyond Santa Fe

El Camino Real, or The King's Highway, carried travelers from Mexico City to Santa Fe for over three centuries. Another notable Camino Real followed the coast of California north to San Francisco.

El Rancho de las Golondrinas (Ranch of the Swallows; open Wednesday–Sunday 10am–4pm in summer; tel: 505-471 2261; admission fee), 10 miles (16 km) south of town, is a reconstructed 200-acre (80-hectare) Spanish colonial village of the 18th and 19th centuries, once a stopping place on El Camino Real. There are working blacksmiths, wheelwrights, a winery and molasses mill, a schoolhouse and chapels. Fiestas are held on the first weekends of June and October, with colonial folk art demonstrations and activities. The village of La Cienega grew up around the hacienda.

Earliest Spanish records mention a large Indian pueblo in the mountains east of Santa Fe. Lying in a high green valley watered by the Pecos River, the pueblo of Pecos had communal dwellings four or five stories high with over 700 rooms. There were five separate plazas and 23 kivas, attesting to the size and importance of the pueblo. Around 1620, the Spaniards built a large mission church there with thick adobe walls, mortared and solidly buttressed, with fine carved corbels. The Pecos Indians joined the revolt of 1680 and burned the church. Pecos was resettled after the reconquest and a smaller adobe church was built inside the burnt foundations. But Pecos was dying, and in 1838 the last two

RIGHT: deer dance at San Juan Pueblo.

dozen inhabitants went west to live with the Jemez Indians, the only other tribe that spoke their language. The ruins of both the churches and the pueblo are preserved at **Pecos National Historical Park** ⓫ (open daily 8am–5pm; tel: 505-757 6414; admission fee).

Map on page 220

The drive to Pecos from Santa Fe on Interstate 25 follows the old Santa Fe Trail. State Route 63 goes north from the monument for 20 miles (32 km) until it dead-ends at Cowles, a summer home area and trail head for horse and backpacking trips into Santa Fe National Forest and Pecos Wilderness.

You can continue east on Interstate 25 past the Pecos turn off for another 15 miles (24 km) to State Route 3, which goes through several villages as pastoral and quiet as they were a hundred years ago. At **San Miguel**, 3 miles (5 km) south of Interstate 25, one can still see where travellers on the Santa Fe Trail forded the Pecos River. In the Mexican period (1821–46), San Miguel was the portal to New Mexico, where wagon trains stopped to pay duty. **Villanueva State Park**, 9 miles (14 km) south of San Miguel, has picnic and camping facilities on the Pecos River. This narrow valley, where the stream is bordered with small fields and villages, lies at the heart of rural Hispanic New Mexico.

The pueblo of **Santo Domingo** ⓬, 30 miles (50 km) southwest of Santa Fe and 39 miles (63 km) north of Albuquerque, is best known for its jewelry, particularly *heishi*, small shells polished to a silky smoothness. These Indians are born traders and most of the artisans you will see selling on the portals of public buildings in Santa Fe and Albuquerque are from Santo Domingo. Theirs is a large pueblo, and the people are active in Indian affairs and conservative about pueblo life, strictly forbidding photography.

Santo Domingo holds its Corn Dance on August 4, the feast of Saint Dominic, an open-air extravaganza involving 500 dancers aged two to 80. Each barefoot female dancer has a blue stepped tablita painted to symbolize a mountain with an indication of rain. She wears a one-shouldered *manta* (a woven sash) and the best family jewelry, and holds a pine bough in each hand. The men wear short white embroidered kilts with long bold sashes, arm bands and moccasins, and they too carry pine boughs. The entry of two long files of dancers into the plaza is pageantry at its finest, but the purpose is sacred: to raise the spirits of rain and fertility, to stamp the earth, beat the drum, and chant and raise the vibrations of the earth to ensure a fine harvest in the autumn. At Christmas and Easter, some dances last several days.

Los Alamos ⓭ is a large town – a true company town – built secretly during World War II for scientists developing the atomic bomb. It is now an open town with attractive residential and business areas, in addition to the still-secret nuclear research laboratories, which include development of nuclear weapons.

Where the road turns east is **Valle Grande**, a lush, grassy valley 12 miles (19 km) across, cupped in high mountains. A few million years ago this was the seething innards of a volcano that, layer by layer, gradually built up the entire 50-mile-long (80-km) mountain range. Finally the volcano collapsed, creating Valle Grande. The volcanic ash and dust from

BELOW: Bandelier National Monument.

BELOW: race day at San Juan Pueblo.

this cataclysmic event added another 1,500 ft (450 meters) to the basalt plateau. Erosion cut the plateau into deep canyons, and where layers of volcanic ash were exposed, natural caves were hollowed out by the wind.

Eons later, Indians used the caves for cliff dwellings, now preserved at **Bandelier National Monument** ⓲ (open daily; tel: 505-672 3861; admission fee), together with a large circular pueblo on the floor of the canyon, probably occupied by the Pueblo Indians before they moved into the Rio Grande Valley.

Santa Fe to Taos

The road northward from Santa Fe to Taos is peppered with a number of pueblos that are active communities today. If stopping at a pueblo, remember that there may be restrictions on photography or other activities. Please heed the local residents' requests. **Tesuque**, 10 miles (16 km) north of Santa Fe, is a small pueblo but it has some excellent potters, usually working with earth-colored clay in animal figures. Its patron saint day, November 12, celebrates San Diego. Pueblo residents perform animal dances in winter.

San Ildefonso ⓯, 20 miles (32 km) northwest of Santa Fe, is best known as the home of the famous potter Maria Martinez. Inspired by ancient Anasazi pottery, she and her husband, Julian, developed San Ildefonso's trademark black-on-black ware and sparked a new interest in Pueblo pottery of every style. Julian died in 1943 and Maria's son, Popovi Da, took up the painting chores. His son, Tony Da, also an artist, became well-known for integrating turquoise, incising techniques and unconventional shapes into his pottery designs. (Examples of the Martinez ceramics can be seen at the Millicent Rogers Museum, in Taos (*see page 246*). San Ildefonso has a large, clean plaza for the performance of an

exciting dance on January 23. It is an animal or hunting dance and it begins at daylight and continues throughout the day.

Pojoaque, 16 miles (26 km) north of Santa Fe, shrank almost to extinction. It was reorganized and now has a tribal structure. On December 12, there's a tribute to Our Lady of Guadalupe, patron saint of New Mexico and Mexico.

Nambe ⑯, 21 miles (34 km) north of Santa Fe, has been largely Hispanicized but its impressive mission church is well-maintained and dominates the area. San Francisco is celebrated on October 4, and on July 4 there's a popular festival at the foot of Nambe Falls, where many dances are performed and photography is permitted. A campground is near the falls.

Thirty miles (48 km) northwest of Santa Fe, **Santa Clara** ⑰ has several outstanding potters, including the well-known Lonewolf and Medicine Flower, members of the Naranjo family. Red or black ware is polished and incised with intricately carved designs. In Santa Clara Canyon each July, the Puye Cliff Ceremonial takes place atop the mesa. A craft show accompanies traditional dances performed against a backdrop of stone and adobe ruins. Puye, part of the Pajarito Plateau, is a majestic place to see a pair of Eagle dancers, in white-feathered headdresses, with feather wings strapped to their arms, swooping and gliding in solemn mimicry of the eagles whose aeries are on the cliff tops.

Across the river from the place chosen by Juan de Oñate as the first capital of New Mexico, in 1598, **San Juan** ⑱ is 46 miles (75 km) north of Santa Fe. Only a cross on the mound of an unexcavated pueblo marks the spot today, but the modern pueblo is large and active. Their feast day is celebrated on June 24, and on Christmas Day pueblo members perform the Matachines Dance, an adaptation of a Spanish morality play.

Boy on feast day at San Juan Pueblo.

BELOW: dancers at Santa Clara Pueblo.

Map on page 220

*Altar of the church of
San José de Gracia.*

An alternative high road to Taos

The high road to Taos, State Route 76, winds through colonial New Mexico and mountain villages like Chimayo, Las Trampas and Peñasco. During the 1700s, small villages away from the capital were isolated, and customs became so ingrained that they linger today, a relic of New Mexico 300 years ago. From Santa Fe go north on US 84/285 to **Santa Cruz** and then onto State Route 76. Holy Cross Church in Santa Cruz was built in the 1740s and is one of the largest of the old mission churches. Its buttressed walls are 3 feet (1 meter) thick and sheltered the villagers when Plains Indians came through the mountains to steal crops, women and children.

El Santuario in **Chimayo** ⑲ is called the Lourdes of America. During Holy Week (the week before Easter), pilgrims from miles around drive, walk and even crawl toward it. The altar, screen and Stations of the Cross are fine examples of religious folk art. To the left of the altar a room is hung with crutches, poems, letters and other offerings from the devout. In a small adjoining room is a hole in the dirt floor, where pilgrims get a pinch of the holy earth of Chimayo, said to have healing powers. Several families of Chimayo weavers have achieved national fame for their tightly woven, brightly colored blankets. The Chimayo Weavers Showroom in town is open to the public.

The village of **Truchas** sits high on a timbered plateau beneath the snow-covered Truchas Peaks. On the main street are a morada – a church of the Penitente sect – and a plastic-roofed Pentecostal church. Truchas is not known for its hospitality, but the setting is superb.

A few miles on is **Las Trampas**, best known for its church, said to be the finest example of Pueblo architecture in the state. The village was founded in

1760 as a buffer for Santa Cruz and Santa Fe against marauding Comanches. The church, San Jose de Gracia, is on the state and national historic registers. Find the kindly neighbor who keeps the key and he will let you inside.

At **Peñasco ㉑**, the next village on the way to Taos, the route divides. Turning right 6 miles (10 km) to State Route 3, travelers drive through the mountains into Taos. Alternatively, turning left onto State Route 75 leads to State Route 68, the main road to Taos.

If choosing the second route, stop at **Picurís**, 20 miles (32 km) southwest of Taos. This pueblo is believed to have been founded around 1250 AD by a group of Taos Indians – the two tribes speak the same language. (Overall, the 19 pueblos speak six distinct languages.) Their annual feast day and corn dance is 10 August, in honor of San Lorenzo. Women potters produce utilitarian cooking pottery that is reddish brown, with highlights of mica and is not decorated.

Picurís was once much larger than it is today, but being on the eastern edge of the pueblo world, it was subject to attack by Plains Indians more than any other pueblo.

The **San Francisco de Asis Church** at **Ranchos de Taos** (1722), on the southern edge of Taos, though not one of the oldest in New Mexico, is probably the best-known and most-photographed because of its classic Pueblo architecture. Georgia O'Keeffe and other artists have captured the flowing lines that seem to be part of the earth.

Taos

The light glows with a physical radiance, white sunlight and lavender shadows, blue distance and golden earth. In 1912, this light drew to **Taos ㉑** eight

Map on page 220

BELOW: interior of El Santuario.

young artists from the East Coast who formed the Taos Society of Artists, the start of a legacy. Whether the spell lies in the physical beauty, the legends or the history of the area, few people visit Taos without feeling its magic.

Taos was settled by the Spaniards in the early 1600s, close to the Taos Indian Pueblo. The **Plaza** of Taos has seen a lot of history go by – Indians, Spanish conquistadors, mountain men and merchants. The American flag flies 24 hours a day in the plaza, a special honor commemorating the bravery of Kit Carson and other frontiersmen during the Civil War; when Confederate sympathizers tried to replace the American flag with the Confederate flag, Carson and friends nailed the stars and stripes to the tallest pine tree they could find and stood armed guard until the Confederates had been driven back to Texas.

Window of the Kit Carson Home.

The first American governor of New Mexico, Charles Bent, was murdered in his Taos home in 1847 during an Indian rebellion a few months after the American occupation. His family escaped by tunneling through the adobe wall to the next door house. The **Governor Bent House Museum** (open daily 9am–5pm; tel: 505-758 2376; admission fee) preserves this historic site. Kit Carson, the famous scout and soldier, lived in Taos with his Mexican wife for 25 years until they both died in 1868; their house is now the **Kit Carson Home** and **Museum of the West** (open daily 8am–6pm; tel: 505-758 4741; admission fee). The cemetery where he and other Taos notables, including Gov. Bent, are buried is part of Kit Carson Memorial State Park, off the main street of Taos.

Taos Pueblo

BELOW: the layers of Taos Pueblo.

Two miles (3 km) north of the town of Taos, **Taos Pueblo** ㉒ (open daily 8am–5pm; tel: 505-758 1028; admission and photography fees) is the most

photographed and familiar of all Indian pueblos, with its large, multi-storied structures facing each other across the plaza. In summer, the parking lot at the pueblo (the road leading to it now is embellished with a casino) is crowded and patroled by security guards who will corner you the moment it looks like you're lingering too long for a look without paying, even if still sitting in the car. While the pueblo is the home for many members, it is also now clearly a commercial commodity and source of income.

Taos marked the northern frontier of Spanish colonial control, and it was here that the Comanche and other Plains Indians came to trade with the Spaniards and Pueblo Indians. Most of the year, the Plains people often raided and plundered the Pueblo tribes, but during the trade period a truce prevailed.

Even today, Taos Indians show traits of their Plains contemporaries: long braids, beaded moccasins, aquiline noses, high cheekbones. The Plains war dances sometimes performed at Taos are unlike the traditionally quieter dances of the other pueblos. Taos potters produce a good red-brown micaceous pottery, like that at Picurís, not ornamental but useful.

On September 29 and 30 they pay homage to San Geronimo with dances. At dawn, male members of North House race against those of South House; at the end of the race the teams are showered with Crackerjacks and oranges by Taoseños from the stepped roofs of North House. The Chifonetti are male clowns painted with black and white stripes and adorned with cornhusks in their hair, who cavort through the onlookers, cart off children and tease the crowd. (In other pueblos similar figures are known as Koshares.) Their joking has a moral purpose – chastising miscreants and warning others.

Immediately after the races, an inter-tribal trade fair begins. Selected arti-

Map on page 220

Jar by Maria and Popovi Da of San Ildefonso Pueblo displayed at the Millicent Rogers Museum.

BELOW: crafts of northern New Mexico.

sans show their wares in booths set up on the wide dirt plaza between North House and the stream that divides the pueblo. Except for a few special feast days, photography is permitted in Taos only after paying a steep fee for a still camera, twice the steep fee for a video camera. A visitor center is at the entrance to the plaza to collect fees and issue permits.

North from Taos

An important stop for those interested in American Indian arts – weaving, ceramics, jewelry and painting – is 4 miles (6.5 km) north of Taos at the **Millicent Rogers Museum** (open daily 10am–5pm, closed Mondays in winter; tel: 505-758 2462; admission fee). The collection is more extensive than can be displayed at one time: Colcha embroideries, Hispanic *santos* (religious icons), Navajo and Pueblo jewelry, contemporary works, Hopi and Zuni kachina dolls, basketry and, for the knowledgeable, ceramics by Maria Martinez. As for Millicent Rogers, she came from a notable New York family and lived in Europe for years, socializing with the likes of Ayn Rand and Noel Coward. She came to Taos in 1947, where she lived until her death. During her time in Taos, she gathered one of the best collections anywhere of Southwestern aesthetic creativity. Time in this museum is time superbly spent.

The **Rio Grande** flows a few miles west of Taos through a deep gorge. Its first 50 miles (80 km) south of the Colorado border make up the nation's first officially designated Wilderness River Area. The **Rio Grande Gorge ㉓** is accessible by hiking down from the rim of the steep volcanic mesas which confine it. In May and June white-water rafters find this part of the Rio Grande a real challenge with some rapids classed Grade VI, the most dangerous kind of white

BELOW: skiing the snow of Taos.

water. Nine miles (14 km) west of Taos on US Highway 64, a dramatic bridge spans the green and white ribbon flowing between black basalt walls 650 feet (200 meters) below. South of town at Pilar, a road leads down to the river to **Rio Grande Gorge National Recreation Area**, a favorite spot for trout fishermen.

During the 1920s, the flamboyant Mabel Dodge Luhan brought many artists to Taos, including D. H. Lawrence. She married a Taos Indian and built a rambling adobe home (now a bed-and-breakfast inn) on the edge of the reservation where she entertained talented and famous people in great style. She gave the Lawrences a ranch in the Sangre de Cristo Mountains about 15 miles (24 km) north of town. After his death in Europe, Lawrence's wife brought his ashes back and built a shrine for him on the ranch, which she willed to the University of New Mexico. The **D. H. Lawrence Ranch** ㉔ 10 miles (16 km) north of town along Route 522, isn't open to the public, but you can visit the nearby shrine.

Skiing in Taos

Taos Ski Valley, 20 miles (32 km) northeast of town, is the best known of New Mexico's 12 ski areas. The runs are on the slopes of Wheeler Peak, over 13,000 feet (4,000 meters) high and New Mexico's tallest peak, and the ski area has dozens of powder bowls, glades and chutes. The season usually lasts from at least early November into April. Ernie Blake, a Swiss transplant known as The Godfather of the Slopes, developed Taos Ski Valley over many years, earning a reputation for high standards. Miles of hiking trails lead from the ski valley into the forests and wilderness areas fringing Taos.

Alamosa ㉕ is in the San Luis Valley of Colorado, a productive farmland 50 miles (80 km) wide between the San Juan Mountains to the west and the San-

Map on page 220

The U.S. Congress rejected the efforts of New Mexico to become a state several times, before admitting it to the Union in 1912, along with Arizona. Congress even thought of combining the two territories into a single state, Montezuma.

BELOW:
Great Sand Dunes
National Monument.

gre de Cristo Mountains eastward. **Great Sand Dunes National Monument ㉖** lies 35 miles (56 km) northeast of Alamosa against the base of the Sangre de Cristos like piles of soft brown velvet. Prevailing winds blow across the valley from the west, picking up particles of sand and dust and dropping them when they reach the solid barrier of the mountains. The dunes are over 700 feet (215 meters) high and 10 miles (16 km) long. A visitor center has exhibits describing the history, plants and animals of the area. There are no trails on the dunes, so you walk where you please. When storms sweep in from the northeast, the winds reverse the pattern of the ridges.

Santa Fe Trail country

Starting in 1821 the Santa Fe Trail was the channel of commerce and communication between the Spanish Rio Grande and the United States. Because of the social and business relationships that had already been established, commerce made victory easy when the United States took the Southwest in the Mexican War (1846–48). Forts protected settlers, pioneers and miners as they fulfilled the nation's "manifest destiny." The main branch of the trail came across southeast Colorado into New Mexico over Raton Pass, through Cimarron, Las Vegas, and then around the southern end of the Rocky Mountains to Santa Fe.

Strangers sometimes doubt it, but you can still see parts of the Santa Fe Trail in northeastern New Mexico. Wherever the ground has not been plowed, as in the areas north of Las Vegas and Fort Union, the grass-grown ruts are plainly visible from the train or from Interstate 25 in Apache Canyon. **Bent's Fort**, 8 miles (13 km) east of **La Junta ㉗** in Colorado on US 350, was built by the Bent brothers in 1833 and became one of the most famous forts and trading posts in the West, doing brisk business with both pioneers and Indians. It has been authentically reconstructed and is today a national historic site, open year-round except twice a year – Christmas and Thanksgiving.

BELOW: mountain man at Bent's Fort.

The fur trappers

Bent's Fort was the meeting place for fur trappers from all over the Rockies, the most famous of whom was Kit Carson. Military and government surveying parties, wagon freighters and stagecoaches stopped for supplies, food and rest. Indians came to trade buffalo hides and furs for food and tobacco. Charles Bent became the first American governor of New Mexico Territory, which at that time included southern Colorado. He was murdered in 1847.

Another stopping place on the Santa Fe Trail was on El Rio de las Animas Perdidas en Purgatorio (River of Lost Souls in Purgatory) – generally shortened to Purgatory or Purgatoire – just before it crossed over the mountains into New Mexico. Today the town of **Trinidad ㉘** is on that spot, a coal mining and trade center with many brick buildings dating back to the last century. The Baca House, built of adobe in 1869, was the home of a prominent rancher and merchant of Spanish ancestry. Bloom Mansion was built in 1882 by a pioneer merchant, cattleman and banker.

The Pioneer Museum is in a 12-room adobe building behind the Baca House.

Across the mountains from Trinidad, a good spring provided another stopping place on the trail, and here the town of **Raton** ㉙ grew. A historic district on First Street preserves several old buildings which now house specialty shops, a theater museum and the Palace Hotel, which does not rent rooms but has a fine restaurant. Raton Ski Basin is really in Colorado, but the only way to get to it is through Raton. It is a small, family-oriented ski area.

One of the colorful men in Raton's past, Uncle Dick Wootton, trapped beaver, and hunted and scouted for the Fremont Expedition with his close friend Kit Carson. He is best remembered for his toll road over Raton Pass. He moved boulders and trees from 27 miles (43 km) of extremely rough terrain to make what was, for the time, a fair wagon road. He built a home and way station at the summit, and not many people argued with this 6-foot 6-inch (198-cm) tall frontiersman, rifle in hand, when he stood at his toll gate and asked $1.50 a wagon, or a nickel or dime a head for livestock. Anyone who chose not to pay could go around the mountains, a detour of more than 100 miles (160 kms). He never charged Indians. He sold his road to the railroad, and the site is marked today. The Santa Fe Railroad still follows the same route, and Interstate 25 is on the hillside just above it.

Capulin Volcano National Monument ㉚, 34 miles (55 km) east of Raton on US 64/87, is a perfectly shaped volcanic cone that served as a landmark on one of the branches of the Santa Fe Trail. At the base there is a visitor center with picnic area, and a road circles the cone to the top where the view reaches into Colorado, Oklahoma, Texas and Kansas. Trails lead into the crater.

Cimarron ㉛, 35 miles (56 km) southwest of Raton, was another stop on

Map on page 220

Active about 10,000 years ago and rising more than 1,000 feet (300 meters) above its base, Capulin, (named after the Spanish word for chokecherry), was one of the last gasps of a period of regional volcanism.

BELOW: ranch kitty on a shoulder.

Map on page 220

the Santa Fe Trail. Cimarron was started by Lucien Maxwell, another trapper-trader-scout-freighter friend of Kit Carson. Through inheritance and purchase he became sole owner of the 1.7 million-acre (694,500-hectare) Maxwell Land Grant which covered most of northeastern New Mexico and some of southern Colorado. Maxwell became a legend of the Santa Fe Trail, entertaining lavishly in his baronial adobe mansion in Cimarron. Weary stagecoach travelers were drawn into gambling at cards or on horse racing when they stopped at Cimarron. Maxwell paid his rare losses from a chest of gold coins. He sold the grant in 1870 and it was subsequently broken up into ranches and town sites.

The past in museums

The Old Aztec Mill Museum is the four-story gristmill Maxwell built in Cimarron in 1865. The St. James Hotel (sometimes called the Don Diego) was built around 1872 by a French chef from Lincoln's White House and has been restored as a museum. The tin ceiling of the original bar, now a gift shop, is pierced by 30 bullet holes, reminders of Cimarron's wild past.

Four miles (6 km) south of Cimarron on State Highway 21 is **Philmont Scout Ranch**, where as many as 17,000 Boy Scouts and their leaders have visited every summer for many decades for their famous Scout Jamboree. The 127,000-acre (51,000-hectare) ranch was given to the Scouts by the wealthy oil baron Waite Phillips. It contains grassy valleys, timbered mountains, streams and a mansion with a 14-room guest house.

BELOW: interior of St. James Hotel, in Cimarron.

Visitors are welcome at Philmont, especially to visit its two museums. One is the Kit Carson Museum, a home he rebuilt and enlarged, where he lived briefly in the 1850s. The other houses a library and art collection which contains much of the work of the famous naturalist, Ernest Thompson Seton, one of the founders of scouting. The museums are open to the public daily throughout the summer, and there's no admission charge.

Fort Union ㉜, 9 miles (14 km) off Interstate 25 and 19 miles (30 km) north of Las Vegas, used to be one of the largest and most important forts in the West. Built in 1851 (two replacements were built during the next 30 years), it was a supply depot for other forts throughout the Southwest. Almost at the end of the Santa Fe Trail, many a Conestoga wagon thundered through its protecting walls barely ahead of the Comanche. Fort Union was closed in 1891 and is a national monument today.

Las Vegas ㉝ (not to be confused with the more significant town of the same name, the Nevada gambling center; *see page 319*) was the capital of New Mexico for two months during the Civil War when the Confederates held Santa Fe, and today it is still a major trade center for the big cattle and sheep ranches in the area. Much of the older part of town around the plaza has been designated a historic district.

Las Vegas began as a land-grant village during the period when the region was part of Mexico and it was an important stop on the Santa Fe Trail, as well as a division point on the railroad. When the railroad bypassed the old plaza by 2 miles (3 km), a new Las Vegas quickly materialized. ❑

The Santa Fe Trail

It's amazing how far a man will travel to find his pot of gold. Take one William Becknell, an Indian fighter and war veteran from Missouri with a pile of debt and not much to lose. When Mexico threw off two centuries of oppressive Spanish colonial rule in 1821 and began courting foreign trade, Becknell was well positioned to take advantage. Directly out of Franklin, Missouri, was an 800-mile (1,300-km) overland trail leading to Santa Fe – a route that crossed rivers, endless prairie and rugged mountains. Buffalo and elk were plentiful enough to keep a man alive, but grizzlies, hostile Indians, violent prairie storms and rock slides could put him six feet under. The risks were great, the potential profits greater. Undeterred, Becknell loaded his wagons and set off.

The journey took two and a half months and passed without serious incident. Any reservations Becknell had about his reception in New Mexico evaporated when the caravan pulled into Santa Fe (whose adobe buildings, one later trader said, reminded him more of "a prairie dog town" than a capital city). Citizens swarmed around the wagons and the governor himself welcomed Becknell, expressing "a desire that the Americans would keep up an intercourse with that country." Becknell sold all he had brought and returned the following fall, bringing with him 22 men driving wagons loaded with goods. They blazed a southern desert route that was hot, dry and liable to flash flood, with hostile Comanches threatening at every turn, but shorter than the mountain route.

Becknell and other traders formed large caravans of 100 wagons. One 1824 wagon train left with $35,000 in merchandise and returned with $180,000 in gold and silver. It was said New Mexico nearly ran out of silver pesos in the 1820s, so many went east. Each "prairie schooner" was heavily laden with soap, cloth, shawls, pots, pans, wallpaper, ribbons, molasses, shoes, cider, coffee, flour, sugar, whiskey, cured meats, tools, farm implements, even window glass. There seemed to be nothing the Americans couldn't sell to a Southwest long isolated from the rest of the world.

In 1833, the Bent brothers and Ceran Verain built Bent's Fort, near La Junta, Colorado, along the northern route of the Santa Fe Trail, and the fort quickly became a major rendezvous for Plains tribes, mountain men, traders and travelers.

Exotic though it was, New Mexico could not remain for long unaffected by America's plans for the West. In 1846, war with Mexico led to the bloodless handover of New Mexico, and just two years later, Mexico ceded vast tracts of the West to the U.S. Citizens of the Southwest were now American, and traffic along the Santa Fe Trail increased, peaking with the California Gold Rush in 1849 and the Civil War in the 1860s. Soldiers stationed at forts along the route protected settlers, traders and travelers from Indian attack.

After the Civil War, the trail remained an important link, with stagecoaches carrying mail from Missouri to Santa Fe, but soon the railroad replaced the Santa Fe Trail. ❑

RIGHT: wagons carried up to two tons of goods along the Trail, taking more than two months.

FOUR CORNERS

Where the states of Utah, Arizona, New Mexico and Colorado meet is a region of astounding geological grace, ancient Pueblo cultures and dwellings, and a good amount of infinite expanse

Map
on page
220

The desert people are bonded fast to their dry lands, and these ties are sacred and as old as the Hopi people themselves. Two stories demonstrate these facts. The first story is from the dark night when the Hopi emerged from the underworld in what is now northern Arizona. The people who emerged from the womb of the Earth were greeted by Maasaw, deity of this Fourth World. "You are welcome," Maasaw said. "But know this land offers scant food or water. Living here will not be easy." The Hopi still chose to stay.

The second story is set at Bosque Redondo, in New Mexico, in 1868 and is taken from the record of the Peace Commission named to establish a reservation for the Navajo. Gen. William Tecumseh Sherman offered the Navajo three options: the tribe could remain at Bosque Redondo and where the Army held it, move to fertile river-bottom land in Oklahoma, or return to their homeland – the arid canyon country on the borders between Arizona and New Mexico. Sherman said he doubted that this wasteland could support the tribe but that since it was worthless, the Navajo should be safe there from the greed of white men. It was, Sherman told Pres. Andrew Johnson, "far from our possible future wants."

It was the same choice the Hopi faced in their ancient myth. The Navajo spokesman that day was Barboncito, a noted fighter and not an orator, who replied to Sherman: "If we are taken back to our own country we will call you our father and mother. If there was only a single goat there, we would all live off of it… I hope to God you will not ask us to go to any other country but our own. When the Navajo were first created, four mountains and four rivers were pointed out to us, outside of which we should not live… Changing Woman gave us this land. Our God created it for us."

The 7,300 Navajo who were being held by Sherman at Bosque Redondo voted unanimously to turn down the relatively lush Oklahoma reservation and return to their desert. It was, as Barboncito told Sherman, "the very heart of our country."

It is still the very heart of America's Indian country, this high, dry southeastern side of the Colorado Plateau known informally as the Four Corners, in the only place in the United States where the boundaries of four states meet at a common point (in this case, Colorado, Utah, Arizona and New Mexico).

West from Albuquerque

Traveling west from Albuquerque along Interstate 40 about 45 miles (75 km), one encounters the pueblo of **Laguna 34**. A turnout gives travelers a good view of the pueblo – a church and squat, square adobe homes on a low hill a few hundred yards away. For a better view, drive into the pueblo. This is one of the largest

PRECEDING PAGES: pueblo moment. **LEFT:** cliff dwelling, Mesa Verde National Park. **BELOW:** woman of Laguna pueblo.

Church at the Pueblo of Laguna

pueblo groups, with almost 5,000 members living in seven villages on the reservation. Uranium mines there provided much employment until the last decade. Once again, cattle ranching and other jobs in Albuquerque provide a livelihood for most families nowadays.

Often called Sky City, **Acoma** ❸ is 65 miles (105 km) west of Albuquerque off Interstate 40. Perched on a 400-foot-high (125-meter) rock mesa, the old pueblo had a strong defensive position. Most Acomans today live in two newer villages below, raising cattle and sheep, operating highway businesses or working in nearby towns. Some are chosen each year to live on top of the rock and keep the old village and church in good repair. Most of the tribe returns to the hilltop for special feast days each year.

An overwhelming sense of history pervades Acoma's church, **San Esteban del Rey**, built in 1629 of flagstone and adobe mud. Every timber had to be carried from the distant mountains, and water and mud for the adobe were carried up the steep trail to the mesa top. The high ceiling, hand-hewn beams, thick walls, square towers and adjoining priests' quarters are a masterpiece of Pueblo architecture. A visitor center is located near the base of the mesa, where tourists must board a bus to visit the village. An Acoma guide conducts them through the pueblo. Photography is permitted for a fee.

Acoma pottery is thin, well-fired and watertight. It is usually white and painted with black geometric designs; a newer style is all white with fingernail marks pressed into the wet clay.

West of Albuquerque is a black and angry river of lava now protected as **El Malpais National Monument** ❸ (open daily 8.30am–4.30pm; tel: 505-385 4641; free). The *malpais* (badlands), pronounced locally *mal-pie*, are composed of five distinct lava flows, which began erupting in the vicinity of 11,300-foot (3,400-meter) **Mount Taylor** around a million years ago. The last eruption, more than 500 years ago, was apparently witnessed by local Zuni and Acoma people, whose legends tell of rivers of fire in the region.

BELOW: church tower of Acoma.

The best place to appreciate the form and magnitude of the lava flow is at the northern end of the monument, 10 miles (16 km) south of Interstate 40 at a designated viewing point and picnic area. Along State Route 117 there are places to explore along the edges, but be wary of walking far on the lava, as it quickly shreds shoe leather.

At the western edge of **Grants** ❸, State Route 53 turns south down the west side of the Malpais. More timber and grass grow on this side, and one or two dirt roads go to the edge of the flow. Signs point to **Bandera Volcano and Ice Caves** (open daily 8am– sunset; tel: 888-423 2283; admission fee), which are privately owned but an integral part of the Malpais. Bandera Volcano, a perfect cinder cone, was one of the sources of the lava flow. Trails go to the top of Bandera and steps lead into the ice caves.

State Road 53 continues to **El Morro National Monument** ❸ (open daily 9am–7pm in summer, 5pm in winter; tel: 505-783 4226; admission fee), 50 miles (80 km) southwest of Grants. The sandstone mesa juts up from the plateau like the prow of a ship.

Zuni ㉝, in the far western part of New Mexico, 40 miles (64 km) south of Gallup, was the first New Mexican pueblo seen by Spaniards. In 1539, soldiers and priests leading an advance party for Coronado's expedition saw the cluster of flat-roofed adobe buildings and immediately went back to report that they had seen the "Seven Cities of Gold," long sought by the Spanish. Although gold cities were lacking, today the Zunis are superb jewelry and pottery craftsmen. The silver inlay jewelry is usually made with small pieces of turquoise, jet, coral, mother-of-pearl and tortoise shell set in intricate patterns. Their crafts are available at a cooperative store and trading posts just outside the old village.

The most famous Indian dance in the Southwest is the Shalako Dance at Zuni, held in late November or early December. Beginning at sundown, towering, grotesque figures come into the village to dance and sing all night at certain designated homes. The costly costumes are draped over a wooden framework with pulleys to move parts like a puppeteer. The covering is of feathers, paint, animal skins and other materials. The head is bird-like, the body is conical. To be chosen as a Shalako is an honor, and the role demands training, both physical and spiritual. As Zuni is at an elevation of over 7,000 feet (2,100 meters), the night of the Shalako is almost always bitterly cold and snowy.

Map on page 220

El Morro Rock.

Canyon de Chelly and Chaco Canyon

The town known as **Gallup** ㊵, New Mexico, calls itself the "Indian Capital of the World," and it is America's most Indian off-reservation town, the trading center for the eastern Navajo and Zuni reservations. Along downtown Gallop's Railroad Avenue walk Hopi, Laguna, Acoma and possibly Jicarilla Apache. It's a ramshackle, unkempt and lively town, a good place to prowl the pawnshops

BELOW: pueblo of Acoma perched atop a mesa.

for Zuni jewelry, Navajo silver, rugs and other artifacts. But first there's an essential and highly recommended side trip.

Thirty miles (50 km) north of Ganado is **Canyon de Chelly National Monument ④**, where three great gorges have sliced through the plateau under the Chuska Mountains. Generations of cliff dwellers – Hopi and Navajo – have lived along the sandy bottoms of these washes, under cliffs which in places tower 1,000 feet (300 meters). There's access by vehicle tours from Thunderbird Lodge or by a foot trail down the cliff. The ancient dwellings were declared a national monument in 1931.

It is believed that the earliest dwellers here, the Pueblo, settled 1,000 years ago; only later did the Navajo replace them. Some of the more than 60 ruins at the site today date from AD 300. The more spectacular ones have been given names – Mummy Cave, White House and Antelope House. While the White House, for example, is accessible to visitors, most of the ruins are not, although they are spectacularly visible from viewpoints.

In a way these canyons sum up this heartland of America's Indian country. They offer spectacular sculptured stone – and they offer a sense of the silence, space and great beauty that encouraged Navajo, Hopi and their ancestors to choose this hard, inhospitable land as the heart of their country.

From Gallup, head into the **Checkerboard Reservation**, so named because the Navajo tribe once owned only alternate square miles – an oddity now partially corrected. **Crownpoint ④** has a school, medical center, Navajo tribal police station and the offices of the Navajo bureaucrats who administer 3 or 4 million acres (1.5 million hectares) of the tribe's eastern territory. Like all Navajo communities, it has a temporary, government-built look as if tomorrow

Sheep, along with horses and cows, were brought to the Southwest by the Spanish in the 1600s. Today, Navajo sheepherders mix goats in with their flocks, as the smarter goats make good leaders.

BELOW: White House dwelling, Canyon de Chelly.

the tumbleweeds will reclaim it. Crownpoint is the site of a rug auction that, six times a year, attracts scores of Navajo weavers and hundreds of buyers for the sale of the fruit of Navajo looms.

State Route 264 winds back to Gallup via the old Hopi government town of Keams Canyon and through Ganado, where a trader named John Hubbell, known to the Navajo as "Double Glasses," opened his historic **Hubbell Trading Post** ⑬ in 1870. It's maintained as a National Historic Site and shouldn't be missed. **Window Rock**, capital of the Navajo Nation, is also on this route.

From Crownpoint, State Route 57 jogs northeast 37 miles (60 km) to the mysteries of **Chaco Culture National Historic Park** ⑭. In this shallow canyon, a great civilization flourished and fell between the 10th and 12th centuries, leaving the ruins of its multi-storied houses and myriad unsolved anthropological puzzles. Satellite photography has confirmed that Chaco Canyon was the center of a network of at least 250 miles (400 km) of improved roads, arousing speculation that the Chaco pueblos housed a religious and administrative center. The visitor center and the ruins offer a rare look into America's past.

Thirty miles (48 km) north, State Route 57 joins State 44 at Blanco Trading Post. Two miles up the highway toward Farmington is Dzilth Na O Dith Hle Navajo Boarding School and beyond it rises **El Huerfano**. This great mesa is the center of an area rich in sacred places for the Navajo. The mesa was the home of First Man and First Woman and other Navajo Holy People. From it one can see other landmarks of the Navajo Genesis.

The blue shape of **Mount Taylor** looms on the horizon 50 miles (80 km) to the south. It is Tsoodzil, the Turquoise Mountain, one of the four sacred peaks that First Man built as corner posts of the Navajo universe. Northeast of Mount

Map on page 220

TIP

Window Rock is the site of Navajo pow-wows. These events renew and sustain Indian pride with feasting, dancing and sometimes rodeos. Dancers from all around compete for prize money.

BELOW: Casa Rinconada and Pueblo Bonito in Chaco Canyon.

Taylor, the basalt thumb jutting into the sky is Cabezon Knob. In a cloud covering its crest one mythical day, First Man and First Woman found the infant White Shell Girl. According to the traditions of the eastern Navajo clans, it was somewhere on the rolling sagebrush hills north of El Huerfano where Talking God, Black God and the other Holy People held the first puberty ceremonial, converting White Shell Girl into Changing Woman.

Eight miles (13 km) northeast of El Huerfano, a right turn leads to **Angel Peak Scenic Overlook**, offering a spectacular view across the wilderness formed by the Blanco Wash and Canyon Largo. Here, the Holy People hung out the stars, and Changing Woman, made pregnant by sunbeams and mist from the San Juan River, bore Monster Slayer and Born for Water, the Hero Twins who were to purge this "Glittering World" of its monsters.

Just before State Route 44 drops into the San Juan Valley, it passes one of the West's most spectacular examples of the human power to modify nature. The endless silver-gray of sage and rabbit brush abruptly gives way to the dark green of corn, potatoes and alfalfa – 44,000 acres (18,000 hectares) of the Navajo Irrigation Project.

Into the Navajo Nation

The "capital" of this San Juan River country is **Farmington** ㊺. Its economy is based on oil, gas, farming and coal – with tourism and Indian trading secondary. About 35 miles (55 km) up the river is **Navajo Dam**, which forms a blue-water lake in a network of drowned canyons backed across the Colorado border. The lake is popular with trout and coho salmon fishermen, and on several miles of the river below the dam is the best fly-fishing in New Mexico.

BELOW: Shiprock.

Aztec, just 13 miles (21 km) east of Farmington, is the site of **Aztec Ruins National Monument** ❹ (open daily 8am–5pm, summer to 6pm), a wonderfully preserved example of how people lived in the Golden Age of the Pueblo. Visitors can walk into the living quarters of these ancient people and into a huge *kiva* – the underground "church" of one of the pueblo's religious societies.

Farmington is also the gateway to the Navajo Nation or the "Big Reservation," a term that requires explanation. The Navajo Tribe, the nation's largest with more than 200,000 members, controls 16 million acres (6.5 million hectares), an area larger than New England. The biggest chunk is on the borders between New Mexico, Arizona and Utah in an area the size of West Virginia. Also covered is the "Checkerboard Reservation" and the Alamo, Ramah and Canoncito reservations. On this Navajo Nation, an elected tribal council operates its own courts, police force and other services. More than 1,100 miles (1,770 km) of paved road, and another thousand which range from quality gravel to tracks impassible in wet weather, tie the reservation together.

The lowest Navajo deserts get only a few inches of rainfall annually, while the forested slopes of the Chuska Mountains at 10,416 feet (3,174 meters) get 25 inches (160 cm). Surrounded by these Navajo lands is the 60,000-acre (250,000-hectare) Hopi Reservation.

It's a huge place, and one of the best ways to visit its interior is by driving west out of Farmington to **Shiprock** ❹, which, like Crownpoint, is a Navajo bureaucrats' town. Driving west on US 64, the sky over the San Juan is smudged with plumes of whitish smoke. The pollution (sharply reduced by millions of dollars worth of soot precipitators in the towering stacks) is from the **Four Corners Generating Plant**. Coal from the adjoining Navajo Mine, the nation's largest

Map on page 220

Rodeo bull riding.

BELOW: Cliff Palace ruins, Mesa Verde National Park.

Map on page 220

Generating power at Four Corners.

BELOW: Stronghold House, Hovenweep National Monument.

open-pit operation, rolls directly into the furnaces, and thence over electrical transmission lines to warm Californian swimming pools. Only the ashes and pollution veiling the previously pristine air are left behind. A side trip through the farming town of **Kirtland** offers a look at this mind-boggling operation. Pollution from this plant is also blamed for the considerable degradation of visibility at the Grand Canyon.

Four Corners National Monument ➍ has virtually nothing going for it except for the thought that one might stand in four states at once. There's a parking lot and a slab on the ground where the state boundaries of Utah, Colorado, New Mexico and Arizona intersect. It's good for a photo, though.

A short drive north of Farmington leads to **Mesa Verde National Park** ➍ (some gates close at sunset). The cliff dwellings here are deservedly among the West's most popular visitor attractions. Most visitors tend to focus on Cliff Palace, a 200-room apartment house high on the wall of a cliff, or else on the Spruce Tree House, a 114-room structure under a massive stone overhang. But the sight of numerous, myriad smaller houses in cracks and crevices begs the question why the Anasazi placed their homes in such dizzying places, and how they raised children where a toddler's misstep meant death.

East of Mesa Verde, **Durango** ➎ was once described by Will Rogers as out of the way and glad of it. No longer. In the 1990s Durango came into its own and is now a favored destination in both summer and winter. Once a place for miners and cowboys – and skiers in the winter – Durango is now taking on flashes of Aspen chic, for better or worse. In any season, it remains a refreshing escape.

Consider taking US 666 for 16 miles (26 km) south to **The Rock With Wings** – the ragged blue shape of **Shiprock** has been visible for miles but only now is its size apparent. It is the core of a volcano, the cinder cone cut away by 15 million years of wind and rain. This core towers 1,450 feet (440 meters) above the grassy prairie – 20 stories taller than the Empire State Building – suggesting an immense black Gothic cathedral. In Navajo mythology, it was the home of the Winged Monster, slain by the Hero Twins with the help of Spider Woman.

Chinese Walls of basalt radiate for miles from its base, 20 or 30 feet (6 to 9 meters) high in places but only 3 or 4 feet (1 meter) thick. They formed when volcanic pressure cracked the earth and molten lava squeezed upward like toothpaste.

One of the most out-of-the-way places to visit in the Four Corners region is also one of the numerous ruins that pepper the area. **Hovenweep National Monument** ➎, established in 1923 and straddling the Colorado-Utah border, requires travel over substandard roads, but the journey is worthwhile. These dry lands north of the San Juan River were once home to the Pueblo people until the 1300s, when they moved on. Six major groupings of ruins are included in the monument's 780 acres (315 hectares), with walls 20 feet (7 meters) high and towers overlooking the desert. The most famous of these towers is **Square Tower**, the best preserved and accessible by car. Information is available at the modest ranger station, along with primitive camping. ❑

Adobe's Magic

Adobe, unbaked clay bricks made from earth, has long been the traditional building material of the Southwest. Structures made from it are undulating and sculptural in nature, yet their mass lends them a sense of permanence and timelessness. The word *adobe* comes from Arabic and was brought to the U.S. by Spanish colonists at the end of the 15th century.

In New Mexico, archaeologists have discovered remnants of adobe walls built by the Pueblo Indians that date back to AD 1200, 400 years before the Spanish arrived. There is evidence of two types of earthen wall built between the 13th and 15th centuries. One was coursed adobe, using a stiff mixture of mud blended with anything from stones to pottery shards. The mud was applied by the handful, course on top of course, until the desired height was reached. A more sophisticated method made use of hand-formed, unbaked clay bricks. Mud mortar cemented the bricks.

The Spanish colonists brought with the word adobe a new brick-making method. Wooden bottomless molds were made with a handle on each end that could hold from one to eight bricks. The molds were set on the ground and filled with a mixture of mud and straw. The straw helped dry the bricks by conducting moisture from the center of the adobe and kept the bricks from cracking as they dried. When the bricks were dry enough not to sag, the forms were lifted, moved to a new spot and the process repeated.

These were the two primary methods of building with adobe until the coming of the railroad in the 1880s, which almost eliminated the use of adobe for several decades with the introduction of new technology. Red-fired brick, board and batten, concrete block and frame-stucco were just a few of the construction materials and methods that dominated the Southwest landscape. Elaborate ornamentation and new rooflines gave the simple, flat-roofed buildings a face lift.

Not until after World War I was there any significant reemergence of adobe architecture. Decreasing natural building materials and excellent passive solar properties made adobe a newly viable material once again. Adobe has the ability, when properly oriented to the sun, to retain its temperature for long periods of time.

With the reemergence of adobe came commercial adobe yards, which are now producing a stabilized adobe block. As the word implies, a stabilizer is an additive, such as an asphalt emulsion, that when mixed with mud produces an unbaked clay brick that resists moisture penetration, adobe's worst enemy. A traditional adobe structure must be re-adobed every so often because of erosion.

Unfortunately, the amount of labor required in adobe construction often makes it too expensive for the average home buyer, though its use by owner-builders is steadily increasing. Solutions are slowly being found. Recently architects and builders have been looking for more innovative methods that will increase productivity and decrease the dollar margin between adobe and conventional building materials. ❏

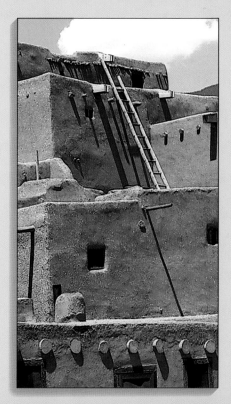

RIGHT: adobe walls at Taos Pueblo.

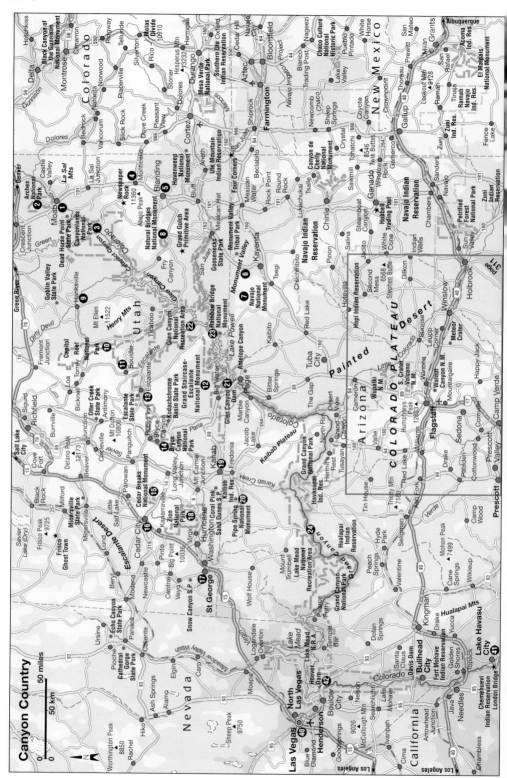

Canyon Country

page 311

CANYON COUNTRY

The weather has sculpted the rocks in this region into a variety of magnificent shapes, culminating in Monument Valley

High, cool desert for the most part, the Southwest's canyon country almost defies description, but that doesn't keep anyone from trying. The slickrock and gray-green desert scrub blend in and out of pinyon-juniper forests as elevation rises and falls. Heated by relentless sun, gusts of wind gather sand into swirling dust devils that dance across the sparsely vegetated countryside. Following summer thunderstorms, the scent of sagebrush and wet rock permeates the air. Winter brings dustings of snow that define every dry leaf and rock ledge. Always stark; always beautiful.

There are arches and natural bridges, standing fins of rock, and more gulches and gullies than can be numbered. There are also magnificent mesas and mountain ranges. For sheer spectacle of standing rock, Monument Valley is in a class by itself.

The population is sparse, the few towns many miles apart. Members of the Church of Jesus Christ of Latter-Day Saints, or Mormons, a devout people, are numerous in Utah. Their forebears founded Salt Lake City and underwent extreme hardship and danger to colonize an intended religious state. Then there were the outlaws, robbers, cattle rustlers and horse thieves. The inconceivable labyrinth of canyons and jumbled rock made perfect cover for the likes of Butch Cassidy, who was raised nearby and knew his way around.

This is country where the getting there can be more exciting than the destination. One outstanding scene leads to another and natural spectacles are too numerous to list. Fortunately, there are plentiful state and national park sites where one can delve until satisfied with the whys and wherefores.

One of the country's largest stands of ponderosa pine cuts a swath across the higher elevations of the Colorado Plateau, including Grand Canyon's south rim area, the volcano-formed San Francisco Peaks, and the Flagstaff region. South of Flagstaff, Highway 89A delivers you, in an exciting 2,000-foot (600-meter) drop in elevation, to Sedona's red-rock country and on to the Verde Valley, replete with ancient American Indian and US military history.

The Colorado River carries its tributary waters into Lake Powell, behind Glen Canyon Dam, flows through Grand Canyon and is again trapped, this time by Hoover Dam and Lake Mead. Both dams are spectacles of engineering. Perhaps it is not so ironic that the canyons channeling the river, made less wild and natural by dams, should lead right to a most unnatural place: Las Vegas. In casinos where the sun neither rises nor sets, you might strike it rich or lose every cent, but the people-watching is fabulous, and pretty much free. ❑

PRECEDING PAGES: stunning vista from Bryce Point in Utah's Bryce Canyon National Park; the many colors of Zion National Park.

SOUTHERN UTAH

Map
on page
270

Arguably one of the country's most spectacular regions, southern Utah offers ethereal light, spellbinding colors, a look into ancient geological history and some of America's finest national parks

I n 1869, after a two-month journey down the Green River from Wyoming, an expedition led by explorer Major John Wesley Powell reached the confluence of the Green and Colorado rivers, one of the most inaccessible spots on the North American continent. Here, in the heart of what Powell called "the Great Unknown," both rivers lay deep within the earth, imprisoned by sheer cliffs of their own making. Climbing to the rim, Powell was amazed by what he saw. "What a world of grandeur is spread before us!" he wrote. "Wherever we look there is but a wilderness of rocks; deep gorges, where the rivers are lost below cliffs and towers and pinnacles; and ten thousand strangely carved forms in every direction; and beyond them, mountains blending with the clouds."

Today, travelers can drive across southern Utah in a matter of hours on paved roads, but there remains no fast route to appreciating the beauty and scope of the geography Powell described: you simply need time, and plenty of it—anywhere from a week to a year to a lifetime. Nature, pure and simple, rules here in a continually metamorphosing landscape whose predominant feature is bare sedimentary rock rearranged by volcanism along deep-seated faults and erosion by water, weather, and time.

LEFT: Delicate Arch at Utah's Arches National Park.
BELOW: redrock climbing in Zion.

Moab and Arches National Park

Few towns in the Southwest have as beautiful and dramatic a setting as **Moab ❶**, southeastern Utah's commercial center and a logical place to begin a trip. Sheer redrock cliffs form fortress-like walls on all sides, enclosing the town in a private world of sandstone, verdant riverbanks and tidy houses fronted by ditches irrigating colorful gardens. Moab has a typically Mormon, grid-like layout in its quaint historic downtown but has burst its confines to the south, spilling into Spanish Valley and other farmlands near the turnoff for the La Sal Mountain Loop.

The town's history is unusual. Members of the Elk Mountain Mission – one of many colonizing efforts in southern Utah in the 1850s and 1860s by the Church of Jesus Christ of Latter Day Saints (or the Mormons) – briefly built a settlement here in 1855 but were driven out by hostile Utes. By the time another group of Mormons succeeded in founding the town in the 1870s, a motley crew of homesteaders, ranchers, rustlers, drifters and grifters had settled.

Moab became a sleepy hamlet, miles from nowhere. And it might have stayed that way if it hadn't been for the atomic bomb. At the onset of the Cold War after World War II, the former U.S. Atomic Energy Commission (AEC), as part of a nationwide search for uranium, established a generous fixed price for the ore as an incentive to miners.

The first big strike was Charlie Steen's. In an area south of Moab that the AEC had deemed "barren of possibilities," Steen discovered his Mi Vida mine, from which he was able to ship $100 million of uranium-235. Overnight, Moab became the "Uranium Capital of the World."

Mining today takes a very different form: that of mining for tourist dollars, following the huge recreational boom of the post-war years that saw surplus army rafts converted to river-running boats, four-wheel-drives to recreational vehicles, then in the 1980s the mounting popularity of mountain biking on slickrock trails around town. This boom appears to be here to stay. Between 1995 and 1999, the resident population of Moab doubled – to more than 5,000 – with thousands more descending on the town from spring break all the way through October.

Moabites, always free with their opinions, grouse that with real estate prices and property taxes what they now are, they can barely afford to live there anymore. And the growing number of motels, fast-food outlets, overpriced eateries, microbrew pubs, espresso joints and T-shirt boutiques that have sprung up in town certainly signals major changes. But one can't argue with success. Moab is perfectly located for trips to Canyonlands and Arches National parks, the Manti-La Sal National Forest and Bureau of Land Management-administered lands nearby. For books and maps, stop in at the federal **Moab Information Center** (MIC) on Center Street and Main (open daily 8am–9pm; tel: 435 259 6111), where rangers will help with trip planning, then head to the enjoyable little **Dan O'Laurie Museum** (open summer Monday–Saturday 1–8pm, in winter Monday–Thursday 3–7pm, Friday–Saturday 1–7pm; tel: 435-259 7985; admission by donation) to learn more about the history of the area.

BELOW: Moab cafe and jogging on a sandstone fin.

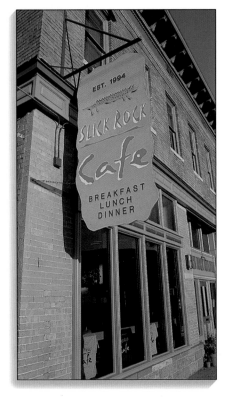

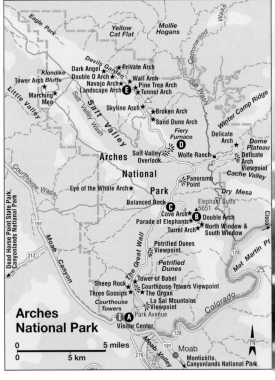

For most folk a trip to **Arches National Park ❷**, a few miles northwest of town, is *de rigueur*. Nowhere in the world are there as many natural arches – some 2,000 at the last count – all clustered together in a setting of such glorious whimsy, satisfying to both geologists and casual sightseers. Moreover, would you believe that all this was caused by salt? The **Visitor Center ❹** is open daily 7.30am–5.30pm (tel: 435-259 8161; admission fee).

Maps:
Area 270
Park 274

Arches National Park sits in the northeastern corner of the huge Paradox Basin, an ancient, faulted depression that formed here 300 million years ago below the Uncompahgre Uplift (in the vicinity of the present-day La Sal Mountains). In Permian times, a warm inland sea was trapped in the basin, then when the climate dried, the sea evaporated, leaving behind huge quantities of salt, gypsum, and other evaporites, which were then buried beneath sediments carried down into the basin by high-country rivers. Thousands of feet of sediments put pressure on the underlying salt, which became plastic and flowed away from the overburden. As it encountered deep fault blocks, it was forced upward into salt domes that eventually cracked, allowing groundwater to enter joints and dissolving the salt. Erosion then began widening the joints, leaving deep red Entrada Sandstone fins that weathered into arches. You can see their linear nature, if you look closely. They seem to dance in formation like chorus lines of bandy-legged showgirls on a tilted stage of sandstone.

*Courthouse Towers,
Arches National Park.*

Many arches are visible along the paved scenic drive, which begins at the visitor center, 5 miles (8 km) north of Moab, or within easy walking distance along well-maintained trails. If pressed for time, visit the Windows Section to view **Double Arch ❸** and **Balanced Rock ❹**. On the other side of Salt Valley, a mile-long trail winds into the **Fiery Furnace ❹**, a spectacular jumble of fins

BELOW: Fiery Furnace at Arches National Park.

separated by sandy corridors that radiate vast amounts of heat in the late afternoon. For safety reasons, visitors can only enter the Fiery Furnace on a ranger-led tour, available twice a day between April and October. Sign up well in advance at the visitor center.

Arches form when erosion and weather sculpt parallel fractures within sandstone into tall walls. Continual thinning of the wall then perforates it, creating an arch.

Popular **Devil's Garden Campground**, 18 miles (29 km) north of the visitor center, fills fast, so get to the visitor center early to preregister for a site. From the campground, a 6-mile (10-km) loop trail leads to seven different arches, including 291-foot (89-meter) **Landscape Arch ❺**, the second-longest known arch – 310-feet-long (94-meter) Kolob Arch in Zion National Park is the longest). Midsummer temperatures often exceed 105°F (41°C) throughout southern Utah, so it's essential to wear sunscreen, sunglasses, a hat, and drink a gallon of water a day, especially when hiking.

Canyonlands National Park

If you think Arches is spectacular, wait until you meet its neighbor, **Canyonlands National Park ❸** (visitor centers open daily; tel: 435-259 7164; admission fee). This 527-square-mile (800 sq. km) park is the piece de resistance of Canyon Country and should not be missed. Planning is everything here, as each section of the park is a long way from the others and there are no roads across the abyssal canyons that divide them. There are three main "districts": Island in the Sky, near Moab and a 2,000-foot (600-meter) headland cut by the confluencing Green and Colorado Rivers; the Needles District, just northwest of Monticello and east of the Colorado; and the remote, undeveloped Maze on the east side of the river, south of the town of Green River. The Colorado and Green rivers make up a fourth, unofficial River District. River trips above and below the confluence of the Colorado and Green rivers allow access to the three primary units from below.

RIGHT: another friendly Utah cactus.

For a raven's-eye view of Canyonlands, head to **Island in the Sky**, 40 miles (67 km) from Moab. Grand View Point offers 100-mile (160-km) views of the entire basin, including the Needles directly ahead, Cedar Mesa and Comb Ridge, the Bear's Ears, Navajo Mountain, and the encircling La Sal, Abajo, and Henry Mountains. Immediately below is the 100-mile-long (160-km) White Rim Trail on the White Rim Sandstone slickrock, halfway up from the river, which offers thrills and spills for off-road vehicles, mountain bikers and hikers and is accessed by the precipitous dirt Shafer Trail. (Four-wheel-drive tours and rentals can be arranged in Moab.) Scenic hiking trails here are short and enjoyable and lead to overlooks and natural features such as elegant Mesa Arch and the unusual Upheaval Dome, once thought to be a collapsed salt dome but now generally believed to be a meteor impact crater, where salt has domed up and broken the surface.

Dead Horse Point State Park (open daily; tel: 435-259 2614; admission fee), which has the only developed campground on the Island, is the only place where one can see the Colorado River, trapped in a huge hairpin bend more properly known as an entrenched meander. Several stories tell of historic ranchers using this point and the Neck of Island in the Sky to corral horses, which then starved when their captors were themselves detained in distant parts.

Allow more time to visit the **Needles**. Return to Moab on Highway 191, load up on gas, food and water, and then head south, turning off just north of **Monticello** and then east across BLM-administered rangelands. The road drops into shady Indian Creek and passes **Newspaper Rock**, a well-preserved rock art panel close to the road and with petroglyphs from archaic, Ancestral Pueblo, Navajo, Ute and pioneer times. Just beyond is the historic **Dugout Ranch**, which once stretched from the San Juan River to the Colorado border but is now run by the Redd family under the aegis of the Nature Conservancy. You'll need to camp at the Needles, so arrive early to snag a campsite at Squaw Flat, the jumping-off point for several trails. Supplies, gas, campsites, and most importantly, showers are available at Needles Outpost just outside the park boundary. Dispersed primitive camping is also allowed within the **Canyon Rims National Recreation Area** surrounding the Needles. Remember: the desert ecosystem is fragile and takes a long time to mend. Pack out what you pack in and leave no trace of a campsite.

The Needles themselves are 500-foot-high (150-meter) eroded cream-and-red-banded pinnacles of Cedar Mesa Sandstone, a rock composed of 250-million-year-old white beach sand and reddish river sediments. When the park was set aside in 1964, the lush meadows of native gramma, Indian rice and other grasses among the rocks were mainly used by ranchers and cowboys for grazing, and one can see a number of cowboy camps in this area. Much earlier occupation by Ancestral Pueblo people is evident in the many small cliff dwellings, granaries and rock art found in four canyons – Davis, Lavender, Salt and Horse. Deep

**Maps:
Area 270
Park 274**

Newspaper Rock contains images of horses – indicating that these particular petroglyphs were made after the late 16th century, when the Spanish introduced them to North America.

BELOW: fording a canyon river.

within Salt Canyon is Angel Arch, perhaps the most sublime arch in Canyon-lands, with its humorous sidekick Molar Rock.

The best day-hike in the Needles is the 7-mile (11-km) Chesler Park Trail, which leaves from Elephant Hill. This moderately strenuous trail heads into the Needles, with side hikes to Druid Arch and the Joint Trail. Longer back-country treks head along Lower Red Canyon Trail to the river via the Grabens – downfaulted valleys shaped like shoe boxes that have slumped due to salt movement and erosion – directly across from the Maze. The Grabens may also be accessed via four-wheel-drive vehicle over Elephant Hill, the most chal-lenging off-road route in the park. Drivers must at one point turn around com-pletely while perched on a flat rock teetering on the edge of a cliff and negotiate a 30-degree switchback – in reverse! Not surprisingly, passengers often decide to forsake the vehicle in favor of their feet.

The undeveloped **Maze District**, 250 road miles (400 km) from the Needles, is best left for a later visit when you're comfortable driving difficult four-wheel-drive tracks and hiking over and into unbelievably confusing slickrock canyons. For a taste, though, sign on with one of the raft companies in Green River or Moab for a four-to-seven-day whitewater trip through 14-mile (22-km) Cataract Canyon; on most trips time is set aside for hiking into the Maze. Green River trips begin at the town of the same name. Don't pass up one of the town's famous melons, if you're here in summer. They're delicious. Nor should you miss the **John Wesley Powell River History Museum** (open daily 8am–8pm; tel: 435-564 3427; admission fee), a huge, modern facility with terrific exhibits bringing to life epic river trips of the past. If you do decide to drive into the Maze, stop at Hans Flat Ranger Station for more information and route planning.

BELOW: Butch Cassidy etched in name in stone.

Shortly before getting there, you'll pass **Robber's Roost Ranch**, the remote 19th-century hideout of two of the West's most famous outlaws, Butch Cassidy and the Sundance Kid, and their gang, the Wild Bunch. The ranch is now owned by the Ekkers, who run tours retracing the steps of Butch and pals.

Map
on page
270

To the south

South from Moab is the small town of **Monticello ❹** on the flanks of the snow-clad Abajo (Blue) Mountains. The Abajos provide a pleasing counterpoint to the slickrock country – and an escape from the summer heat. A quiet back route into the Needles district leads through the mountains from the center of town, then drops down onto BLM land outside the park.

Leave no footprints.

Between Monticello and Blanding there's a refreshingly cool campground at Devil's Canyon. Backpackers wishing to explore **Grand Gulch Primitive Area** should get hiking permits and information from the BLM office (tel: 435-587 1532) in Monticello. Grand Gulch is particularly rich in Ancestral Pueblo buildings, typically built under south-facing overhangs to shield them from the weather. Don't forget that archaeological sites are protected by law. The BLM patrols Grand Gulch by helicopter to intercept illegal activity and will not hesitate to prosecute offenders. Learn more about the Ancestral Pueblo and later Ute, Navajo, and Anglo cultures of the area at the **Edge of the Cedars State Park** (open daily 8am–8pm; tel: 435-678 2238; admission fee), in **Blanding ❺**, site of a large pueblo occupied between AD 770 and 1200. The museum's innovative displays include a superb pottery collection excavated from the area.

A few miles south of Blanding is a highway junction. If bound for Monument Valley and northern Arizona take a short detour to see the world-class entrenched

BELOW: relaxing amidst the redrock.

Gooseneck bend in the San Juan River.

meanders of **Goosenecks State Park**, and then continue south to Bluff and Mexican Hat, the main put-in points for San Juan River float trips. You can double back on the breathtaking Moki Dugway scenic route across Cedar Mesa.

In the winter of 1879–80, this corner of southeastern Utah witnessed a remarkable journey by Mormon colonists "called" to settle the San Juan River. Believing the southern route the most direct, more than 200 pioneers left Escalante in the autumn for southeastern Utah. They soon ran into difficulties negotiating the unforgiving, broken landscape of these rugged canyons and cliffs. What had started out as a six-week journey took six months as colonists labored over what is now dubbed Hole-in-the-Rock Road in Grand Staircase-Escalante National Monument. They were forced to spend the winter near Dance Hall Rock and blast a route out of sheer, 500-foot (150-meter) cliffs to let their wagons down to the Colorado River. Exhausted, they founded a settlement at the first suitable spot on the San Juan River, which they named Bluff, and planted crops and began building homes, many of which can still be seen on a historic loop through the village. After persistent flooding ruined the harvest, some Hole-in-the-Rock pioneers moved north and founded Blanding and then Monticello, towns that retain strong associations to these early colonists.

Monument Valley and Navajo National Monument

Thirty thousand acres (12,000 hectares) on the Arizona-Utah border, south of Blanding, **Monument Valley Navajo Tribal Park** embraces the truly monumental **Monument Valley ❻** and its punctuated horizon of graceful mesas, spires and red buttes. Monument Valley, familiar to those who've watched director John Ford's many Western films, requires a Navajo guide if going off the

BELOW:
Monument Valley.

main road; finding one is absolutely no problem and guided tours are a vigorous – and highly promoted – business in the area. But even from the highway, the otherworldly vistas of Monument Valley are truly breathtaking at any time of the year. **Navajo National Monument** ❼ (visitor center open daily; tel: 520-672 2367; free) contains three of the largest prehistoric, pueblo-type cliff dwellings in Arizona, in three different areas. The most accessible of the three is near **Betatakin**; access to the pueblo ruins is only via guided tours, which are available on a first-come, first-served basis. The 5-mile (8-km) hike is not easy and can be tiring in summer's heat.

National Bridges Monument and Capitol Reef Park

From Blanding, a right turn on State 95 (which figures so prominently in Ed Abbey's novel, *The Monkey Wrench Gang*) leads directly to **Natural Bridges National Monument** ❽ (open daily 8am–6pm; tel: 435-692 1234; admission fee). Although bridges and arches are similar in appearance, only the former have been carved by a stream, in this case by a tributary of the Colorado River. Each of the three bridges in the monument – Sipapu, Kachina Bridge and Owachomo – can be seen from a paved loop road that originates from the visitor center and by making a 10-minute hike to the base of any of the three.

The town of **Hanksville** ❾ is the access for the Henrys, the last discovered, named and explored mountain range in the continental United States. These mountains offer solitude aplenty, but don't head into them without first checking in with the BLM office (open daily 7.45am–4.30pm; tel: 435-542 3461) in town. Forty miles (65 km) west of Hanksville is **Capitol Reef National Park** ❿ (open daily; tel: 435-425 3791; admission fee), whose central attraction is the Water-

Map on page 270

TIP

Be careful when hiking in the desert backcountry. Two killers are dehydration and flash floods, which can fill a bone-dry gully with a raging torrent in minutes, from an out-of-sight thunderstorm miles away.

BELOW:
Monument Valley.

WHEELS IN THE BACKCOUNTRY

Increasingly popular throughout the Southwest, both for residents and visitors, is the mountain bike. "The self-powered thing is cool," says Lou Warner, who runs a bike-touring company in Moab, Utah, which is considered by freewheelers to be the mountain bike capital of the world. Located in the redrock country of southeastern Utah, the area is crosshatched with thousands of miles of dirt roads left behind by miners and ranchers, giving bikers plenty of spare room.

"The riding is excellent because the scenery is excellent," Warner says. "You can go from an elevation of 4,000 feet (1,200 meters) at the Colorado River to almost 14,000 feet (4,000 meters) on the snow-capped peaks of the La Sal Mountains."

Mountain biking combines the best aspects of hiking and skiing – access to the hills and downhill speed – and leaves behind slow travel. In national parks, biking is allowed only on paved or dirt roads and a few designated and marked trails. Although knobby treads on mountain-bike tires can eat up soft earth and cause considerable erosion, on the correct surface it can allow visitors to reach remote locations that one might otherwise miss, and without noise or pollution.

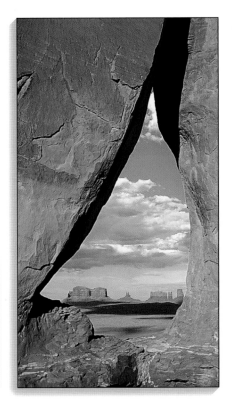

Indian paintbrush.

pocket Fold, a 100-mile-long (160-km) flexure in the earth's crust and dubbed a "reef" by Mormon polygamists who fled here in the 1880s to avoid prosecution by federal agents for their non-traditional – with more than one wife – lifestyle. After it was uplifted about 65 million years ago, the reef was eroded into narrow canyons interspersed with giant domes of creamy Navajo Sandstone. Perhaps residents had government on their minds when they said the domes reminded them of the U.S. Capitol in Washington, D.C. Either way, the name stuck.

The northern portion of the fold is transected by scenic Highway 24 (open sunrise to sunset), which runs beneath soaring cliffs of red Wingate Sandstone alongside the Fremont River. This was the home of the Fremont culture, people who had much in common with Ancestral Pueblo neighbors like the Kayenta and Virgin River cultures but who continued to live in pithouses and hunt and gather. They fashioned unique moccasins of hide heeled with a deer claw and created clay figurines, perhaps for use in rituals. Most distinctive, though, were the huge red pictographs they left on the rocks, displaying large triangular anthropomorphs with ear bobs, headdresses, and other unusual adornments.

Because the Waterpocket Fold is nowhere more than 15 miles (25 km) wide, most of the hikes in the park are short, around 2 to 4 miles (3–6 km). Grand Wash Narrows passes through 500-foot-high (150-meter) canyon walls less than 20 feet (6 meters) apart and where inscriptions left behind by early settlers are visible. Chimney Rock Trail makes another great day hike, particularly if you walk a mile or two into the upper reaches of Spring Canyon. Be careful here in summer. This extremely rugged terrain sizzles under extreme heat and water can be found in only a few places. Inquire at the visitor center for information on

BELOW: cowboy shack in Capitol Reef National Park.

hiking Hall's Creek or Muley Twist Canyon in the southern section of the park, off the Burr Trail, an old ranch trail that switchbacks precipitously over the southern section of the fold between Boulder and the Notom-Bullfrog Road.

Map
on page
270

Grand Staircase-Escalante National Monument

After leaving Capitol Reef, continue west on Highway 24 then drop south on Highway 12 and cross 10,000-foot (3,000-meter) Boulder Mountain, exiting near the little ranching community of **Boulder ⑪**. Stop at **Anasazi State Park** (open daily 8am–6pm; tel: 435-335 7308; admission fee), which preserves a 12th-century pueblo with 87 rooms, the largest such site found west of the Colorado River.

Boulder offers access to **Grand Staircase-Escalante National Monument ⑫**, set aside in 1996 by President Bill Clinton to protect 1.7 million acres (690,000 hectares) of spectacular Utah wilderness from coal mining of the Kaiparowits Plateau. The proclamation provoked a storm of controversy in southern Utah, with communities like Boulder worried that they would lose their traditional ranching and farming ways of life to invasion by recreationalists and environmental extremists. So far this has not happened, although visitation has increased in the area and several lodges, bed-and-breakfasts, motels, restaurants and outfitters now serve travelers' needs.

This large national monument is split roughly into three units: Grand Staircase, Kaiparowits Plateau and Escalante Canyons. Stop at the **Escalante Multiagency Center** (open Mon-Fri 7.30am–5.30pm; tel: 435-826 5499) to plan your trip with a Bureau of Land Management (BLM) ranger. This is truly a wild place, with almost no developed trails and only two modest campgrounds. The BLM deliberately emphasizes personal discovery, so you need to take the initiative

BELOW: Sky lights
Taos, New Mexico

on where you want to go, then ask for help planning your route. It's not that hard to get into the outlying areas of the monument off Highways 12 and 89, using the Burr Trail (paved to Capitol Reef National Park), Hole-in-the-Rock Road, the Cottonwood Road, Johnson Canyon and Wolverine Loop Road. It's a lot harder once you park the car and start hiking. Start with hikes along known routes and major river canyons like the Escalante and don't hike cross-country unless familiar with route finding through narrow, winding desert canyons and rim country. High-clearance, four-wheel-drive vehicles are advised on many unpaved roads, which shouldn't be attempted during inclement weather when the road turns to gumbo mud, stranding vehicles for days at a time.

Bryce Canyon National Park

The limestone layers of Bryce Canyon are from the gradual settling of sediments on an ancient lake's bottom 50 million years ago.

The drive from Boulder to **Escalante** ⓭ along the hogbacks of Highway 12 above the Escalante Canyons is one of the region's most scenic drives, taking in swirling knobs and buttes of pale Navajo Sandstone slickrock, pierced by labyrinthian canyons flaring green with cottonwoods, willows and other deciduous trees that warm to autumn hues in October.

Crossing the Escalante River and its trailhead, the road climbs out of the canyon, with the lonely, remote Kaiparowits Plateau off to the south. An equally dramatic graded road travels 40 miles (64 km) over Hells Backbone Road to Escalante, climbing to 11,000 feet (3,400 meters), and crossing Box-Death Hollow Wilderness via a narrow 1930s bridge near two glorious alpine campgrounds before dropping into Escalante. Until 1929, Boulder got its mail by pack mule over this route – a feat readily appreciated by anyone driving along it.

BELOW: near Sunset Point, Bryce Canyon National Park.

From Escalante it's a couple of hours to **Bryce Canyon National Park**
(open daily 8am–4.30pm; tel: 435-834 5322; admission fee). The Paiute made
their home in the region called Bryce, the place where "red rocks stand like
men in a bowl-shaped canyon." An apocryphal story has Mormon settler
Ebenezer Bryce complaining that the canyon was "a hell of a place to lose a
cow!" If not looking for cows, you can afford to be charmed by Bryce Canyon,
with its Fantasia of pastel-washed hoodoo limestone marching off the east side
of the 9,000-foot-high (2,700-meter) Paunsaugunt Plateau. Technically, Bryce
is not a canyon but a series of 14 amphitheaters eroded into an escarpment
whose beauty can best be appreciated from overlooks along its 17-mile (30-
km) scenic drive.

But why stay on the rim when a variety of colorful and unusual hikes among
the hoodoos beckon? One of the easiest is Navajo Loop Trail, which passes
Douglas firs that have found a protected spot in narrow corridors of shifting
Wasatch Formation. Save your energy to hike out – you're climbing a hill in
reverse. Fairyland Loop Trail or a horseback trip on the Peekaboo Loop offer
more strenuous outings, but one can just as easily stroll the Rim Trail between
any two viewing points, return by shuttle, then relax at historic **Bryce Canyon
Lodge** (open April–October, reserve a year ahead; tel: 303-297 2757).

On a clear day from Yovimpa Point, visibility is over 100 miles (160 km) to
the Grand Canyon, where the rocks are 160 million years older than those of
Bryce – the top "step" in a "grand staircase" with the gray, white and vermilion
cliffs below, and the Buff Kaibab Limestone of the Grand Canyon making up
the bottom stair. Leaving Bryce, head west on Highway 12 through Red Canyon,
Bryce's pretty little sister, then south at the junction with Highway 89.

Map on page 270

Thor's Hammer, a type of formation – hoodoo – said by Paiutes to be evildoers changed to stone by a god.

BELOW: limestone pinnacles of Bryce.

Cedar Breaks National Monument

Twenty miles (32 km) ahead, turn west onto Highway 14, a scenic high country route across the Markagunt Plateau above Zion National Park that leads to **Cedar Breaks National Monument** ⓕ (visitor center open daily, June–late September; tel: 435-586 9451; admission fee), a higher, steeper and more pristine eroded amphitheater of Wasatch Formation rocks surrounded by basaltic flows barely one million years old.

Between June and September, when snows in the high country have melted, visit Cedar Breaks for its spectacular wildflower shows, then descend a scenic back route across the Markagunt Plateau onto the Kolob Terrace section of Zion National Park, picking up Highway 9 to Zion National Park via the hamlet of Virgin, in the Virgin River valley. Some of the park's most interesting and challenging backcountry trails begin or cross at the Terrace, offering a unique bird's-eye view of the tops of Zion's 2,000-foot (600-meter) cliffs, buttes and natural temples. The west side of the Markagunt Plateau marks the edge of the Colorado Plateau and the beginning of the Great Basin Desert 6,000 feet (1,800 meters) below.

Continuing on Highway 14, the road descends sharply to **Cedar City** ⓖ, home to Southern Utah University and the popular nine-week summer Utah Shakespeare Festival, and a good overnight stop. Founded in 1852 as part of the Iron Mission, it's also headquarters of the Cedar City Paiute, one of several bands of Southern Paiutes living on small reservations in Utah and Nevada. Beautiful examples of Paiute basketry, collected by a Mormon in the early 20th century, are on display at **Southern Utah University**. The tribe also holds an annual Paiute Restoration Gathering to celebrate its 1980 official reinstatement.

BELOW: fall colors in Zion National Park.

The **Daughters of Utah Pioneers Museum** (open Monday–Saturday 10am–5pm; tel: 435-628 7274; free) is a good place to start a historic walking tour of **St. George** , home of the historic Cotton Mission and the largest town in southern Utah. Known as Utah's Dixie for its moderate winters, St. George was chosen by Brigham Young as the site of his winter home.

Here, Young oversaw the construction of the dazzling white **St. George Mormon Temple** (visitor center open daily 9am–9pm; tel: 435-673 5181; free) and the sandstone **Mormon Tabernacle** (open daily for guided tours 9am–6pm; tel: 435-628 4072; free), both completed in the 1870s. Note that only Mormons in good standing may enter the temple; visitors may visit only the adjoining visitor center. The Tabernacle, however, is open to all. The historic buildings are within easy walking distance of Ancestor Square in the heart of downtown, which also houses excellent restaurants serving Greek, Chinese and other foods. Located on the northern edge of the Mojave Desert (with its characteristic Joshua trees), St. George gets pretty hot in summer but it's a good base for explorations of the surrounding region.

Zion National Park

Drive west to **Santa Clara**, known for its fruit, and take a tour of the **Jacob Hamblin House** (open Memorial Day–Labor Day 9am–9pm; tel: 435-673 2161; free), built in 1862 by Mormon missionary Jacob Hamblin, a friend of John Wesley Powell, who explored the Colorado River.

Continue north to **Snow Canyon State Park** (open daily 6am–10pm; tel: 435-628 2255; admission fee) for some dramatic lava-and-sandstone scenery and terrific hiking, camping, and horseback riding in an area used as a backdrop in a number of John Wayne cowboy films.

St. George is just 40 miles (64 km) from **Zion National Park** 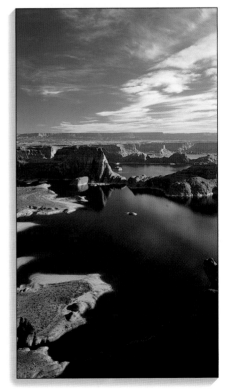 (visitor center open daily; tel: 435-772 3256; admission fee) via Highway 9. Here, in narrow Zion Canyon, is the most dramatic exposure of Navajo Sandstone in the West – some 2,400 feet (730 meters) at the Temple of Sinawava below the Zion Narrows – carved into a stunning array of sheer cliffs, twisting buttes and craggy temples by the busy little North Fork of the Virgin River.

One of the classic hikes in Zion leads from the canyon floor at the Grotto Picnic Area, up 1,500 feet (450 meters) of cliff and side canyon, to the vertiginous precipice of Angel's Landing, using only cables and nerves to steady you. For those wanting to keep their feet firmly on the ground, shady trails on the flat floor of the canyon lead to the Gateway to the Narrows, Weeping Rock and Emerald Pools. Most memorable along these shady trails are seeps, where water percolating down through Navajo Sandstone meets impervious Kayenta shale and is forced out of the rock as horizontal springlines, fostering hanging gardens of yellow columbine, red monkeyflower, acid-green maidenhair fern and purple shooting stars. It is truly spectacular.

Highway 9, which passes through the park, is especially beautiful in spring, when cottonwood, oak, and other deciduous trees leaf out along the Virgin River

Map on page 270

Zion's Virgin River can carry away more than one million tons of sediment and rock each year en route to the Colorado River, at Lake Mead.

BELOW: Lake Powell near Padre Bay.

Map on page 270

The bobcat usually prowls under the cover of darkness.

and its tributaries, and again in fall, when the golden rain of turning leaves becomes breathtaking against ruddy sandstone. The road climbs from the valley floor via a series of breathtaking switchbacks, then continues through the mile-long Zion to Mt. Carmel Tunnel, built by the Civilian Conservation Corps in 1930 to provide a faster roadlink to parks east of Zion. On the higher, cooler, moister east side of the park is the best evidence of the dune-formed 175-million-year-old Navajo Sandstone in the strangely cross-hatched surface of Checkerboard Mesa and the whirling surfaces of barely petrified sand dunes.

Turn south at Mount Carmel and head to the historic town of **Kanab** ⑲, at the junction of Highways 89 and 89A. Kanab is a fine place to find overnight lodging, have a meal and explore spectacular redrock canyons surrounding the town. Pick up information and permits for the Grand Staircase-Escalante National Monument (*see page 283*) from the BLM office downtown (open Mon-Fri 7.45am–4.30pm; tel: 435-644 2672). Most vehicles can reach the historic Pareah Townsite and movie set off Highway 89 (but avoid it in the rain when the dirt road through the colorful Chinle badlands turns to mud).

A different experience can be had by heading south of Kanab to **Fredonia**, Arizona, then east through the Arizona Strip toward Hurricane, Utah. This remote area, a section of Arizona between the North Rim of the Grand Canyon and the Vermilion Cliffs, offers a hypnotically beautiful drive through quiet rangelands, ranches and tiny, old-style Mormon communities that have barely changed in a century. Don't bypass little **Pipe Spring National Monument** ⑳ (open daily; tel: 520-643 7105; admission fee), 14 miles (23 km) southeast of Kanab. Surrounded by the Kaibab Reservation, this monument preserves the beautifully maintained buildings of an historic 1870s-period, fortified Mormon cattle ranch around a perennial spring and yet another link to John Wesley Powell, who used local Paiute guides and lived in one of the cabins here while exploring the region.

Lake Powell and Glen Canyon

The 180-mile-long (290-km) **Lake Powell**, named for the explorer, is the second-largest and most spectacular artificial lake in the United States. The lake is formed by the 710-foot-high (215-meter) **Glen Canyon Dam** ㉑, downstream at **Page** and which generates 1,200 megawatts of hydroelectricity for the megalopolises of Phoenix and environs – and ample controversy. When it was begun in 1956, the dam had the blessing of almost everyone concerned. By the time it was finished in 1963, conservationists had belatedly recognized that Glen Canyon, "the place no one knew," was comparable in grandeur to anything – including the Grand Canyon – on the Colorado Plateau. Today, many people believe that the drowning of Glen Canyon was an unspeakable ecological tragedy, and are working to eventually dismantle the dam and instead use generated power from Hoover Dam in Nevada.

That said, Lake Powell, administered by the National Park Service as **Glen Canyon National Recreation Area** ㉒ (open daily, 8am–7pm; tel: 520-608 6404) is a stunning place to waterski, fish and explore. At Page, there's a visitor center near the dam offering frequent tours of the facility and the small **John Wesley Powell Memorial Museum** (open Monday–Saturday 8am–6pm; tel: 520-645 9496; donation). Miles of blue water and a shoreline of carved cliffs make the lake a photographer's dream. Houseboats, popular with vacationers, may be rented at any of the five marinas, along with fishing tackle and power boats. Don't miss visiting 290-foot-high (188-meter) **Rainbow Bridge National Monument** ㉓, the tallest natural bridge on the planet and a site sacred to the Navajo, whose reservation adjoins the area. ❑

RIGHT:
the special light of Bryce Canyon National Park.

GRAND CANYON

Words, photographs, premonitions, a rich imagination,
astral projection, Imax films, New Age music and even poetry
fail to convey fully the essence of the Grand Canyon

Maps:
Area 270
Park 301

Having heard so much about the **Grand Canyon** ㉔, most visitors are ready to find it breathtaking. Another typical response, however, is unanticipated. The inhuman scale of the chasm can be profoundly disconcerting. What should one make of this gulf of space or of the unfathomable span of time that it represents? To put it more graphically, how does a human being, cradling a small black rock from the Inner Gorge, come to grips with the fact that the canyon is 2 billion years old? So old, in fact, that it dates from a time when life, in any of its miraculous forms, had not yet appeared on the planet.

Those layers that define the canyon walls, descending a mile to the river below that carved them, represent shifts in the region's geography that are difficult to grasp. The upper layers of Kaibab and Toroweap limestone, for example, were formed by ancient oceans, while the lower layers of sandstone were created even earlier by a desert covering more than 32,000 square miles (51,500 sq. km). A desert preceded by an ocean preceded by yet an earlier desert.

Various people who have lived in the canyon for at least 2,000 years must have struggled with the quandary of what is seen and felt within the canyon even today, despite having seen photographs and heard much about it already. In those early days of modern exploration, those trained to put words and descriptions to paper often failed, as did Lt. Joseph Ives in 1857. Hualapai Indians guided Ives and his military expedition into the Grand Canyon via Diamond Creek. (Powell passed Diamond Creek eleven years later.) After reluctantly acknowledging that the landscape promotes a "wondering delight," Ives managed to evade the usual visitor's predicament by protesting that "the region is, of course, altogether valueless. It can be approached only from the south, and after entering it there is nothing to do but leave. Ours has been the first, and will doubtless be the last, party of whites to visit this profitless locality."

Perhaps Ives felt intimidated by his inability to grasp the Grand Canyon, which he called, simply, the Big Canon. Still, Ives returned with the first geological descriptions of the Grand Canyon, along with the first illustrations.

PRECEDING PAGES: typical Grand Canyon view. **LEFT:** view from Bright Angel Point. **BELOW:** mule ride from North Rim.

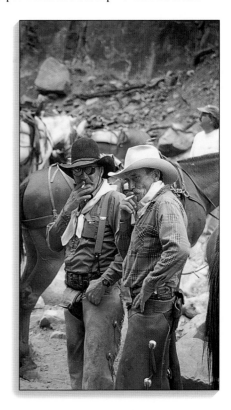

Explorations of Powell

In 1869, 10 gaunt men in three battered boats drifted out of Glen Canyon. Ten weeks earlier they had left Green River, Wyoming, 500 miles (800 km) to the northeast, with four boats and 10 months of supplies. After repeated upsets they were down to rancid bacon, musty flour, dried apples and coffee.

The men were getting mutinous but the man in charge, Major John Wesley Powell, was unperturbed. "If he can only study geology," grumbled one of the

John Wesley Powell and Indian guide.

hands, George Bradley, "he will be happy without food or shelter, but the rest of us are not afflicted with it to an alarming extent." For three months Powell and his expedition traveled 1,000 miles (1,600 km) down the Colorado River, which in this region threads 277 miles (445 km) through a continuous gorge, from Lees Ferry to the Grand Wash Cliffs. The final 215 miles (345 km) are within the Grand Canyon itself.

Years later, as the head of the Geological Survey and the Bureau of Ethnology, Powell would become one of the most influential men in Washington D.C. At the time of the expedition, however, he was unknown, simply a one-armed Civil War veteran and a self-taught scientist who, on the strength of curiosity, intuition and discipline, would make fundamental contributions to the budding sciences of geology and anthropology.

The major was also a gifted writer, as revealed by this passage, often quoted by modern boatmen carrying visitors down the Colorado: "August 13th 1869 – We are now ready to start on our way down the Great Unknown. We are three quarters of a mile in the depths of the earth, and the great river shrinks into insignificance as it dashes its angry waves against the walls and cliffs that rise to the world above; the waves are but puny ripples and we but pygmies running up and down the sands or lost amongst the boulders."

Two weeks after writing that passage, Powell and five of his men safely completed the exploration of the Colorado River. Three men on the expedition, however, unwilling to risk their lives at an unusually nasty rapid during the journey through the canyon, had abandoned the expedition two days earlier – only to be killed by Indians while struggling overland toward Mormon settlements in Utah.

BELOW: rafting on the Colorado River.

The South Rim

Today, the Colorado River has been dammed both upstream and downstream of the Grand Canyon: Lake Powell, upstream of the canyon and mostly in Utah, is formed by Glen Canyon Dam, near Page, Arizona. Downstream, Lake Mead is formed by Hoover Dam, near Boulder City.

One popular misconception is that the Grand Canyon, geologically speaking, is an open book. Geologists know better. For more than a century they have carried on their investigations and yet many of the most basic questions about the great abyss still lack definitive answers. There is, for example, a lively debate among geologists over how (and how long ago) the Colorado River came to be established in its current course.

Ninety percent of visitors to the Grand Canyon visit the canyon's southern side, and most of those visitors pass through **Flagstaff** (*see page 307*). A few miles north of Flagstaff on US Highway 180 is the **Museum of Northern Arizona** (open daily 9am–5pm; tel: 520-774 5213; admission fee), which sponsors much of the scientific research taking place in the Grand Canyon. It's worth stopping at the museum to inspect its geological exhibits and admire a splendid collection of Indian rugs and pottery.

Nearly all visitors to the Grand Canyon see it from the **South Rim**. One might expect the approach to something like the Grand Canyon to build up gradually, as do mountain peaks. Yet as one drives north across the Coconino Plateau through ponderosa pines, flanked by the San Francisco Mountains (the highest in Arizona), there are few geographical cues as to the wonder that lies ahead. Of course, the convoy of tourists suggests a collective purpose, and as one passes through the small town of **Tusayan Ⓐ**, the rampant commercial-

Map on page 301

TIP

On any hike, tell someone where you are going, and don't hike alone. Bring plenty of water, high-energy food, insect repellent, and clothing that will protect you in exposed desert conditions and brushy canyon terrain.

BELOW: onlookers at Mather Point.

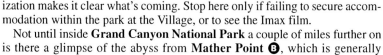

ization makes it clear what's coming. Stop here only if failing to secure accommodation within the park at the Village, or to see the Imax film.

Not until inside **Grand Canyon National Park** a couple of miles further on is there a glimpse of the abyss from **Mather Point ❸**, which is generally crowded. A mile west of Mather Point is **Grand Canyon Village ❻**, tourism central for the park since 1901, when the railroad arrived. Nowadays, tourists spend as much time looking for a parking space here as at the canyon vistas. The park headquarters and **Visitor Center ❶** (open daily 8am–6pm; tel: 520-638 7888) offer extensive information and help, ranging from displays explaining the canyon's geology to an extensive collection of books. The park rangers here are probably the National Park Service's most patient and easy-going, no small feat given the five million tourists who visit the park annually.

Once colored by silt – the name Colorado is Spanish for "reddish colored" – the Colorado River is often clear and blue-green, the silt retained by the Glen Canyon Dam upstream of the Grand Canyon.

Across the road from the visitor center are Mather Campground and Babbitt's General Store, as well as a gas station, post office, bank, public showers and laundromat. Most of the park's lodges are located here, including the venerable **El Tovar Hotel** and the **Bright Angel Lodge**, built at the turn of the century when most visitors arrived by train. But times change and – especially during the summer months – one may want to avoid congested traffic by walking between all these places along the Rim Trail. (The section between the visitor center and Grand Canyon Village is a self-guided nature trail).

Immediately adjacent to Bright Angel Lodge is Bright Angel Trailhead. Since the Bright Angel and the Kaibab are the only two maintained trails that descend into the Grand Canyon, the Park Service recommends hiking one of them before venturing onto any of the unmaintained trails. There is no water along the Kaibab, so most visitors choose to take their introductory hike on the Bright Angel, which has water in three places. Because of the heat – temperatures routinely exceed 105°F (41°C) in summer – hikers should still carry water, at least a gallon per person per day.

BELOW: mule ride on the Kaibab Trail.

Below the Rim

Stepping below the rim of the Grand Canyon changes the experience of it – the quiet and the grandeur of the landscape are measured against each descending footstep. A logical destination for an all-day hike is **Indian Gardens**, a verdant oasis about 4 miles (7 km) and 3,100 vertical feet (945 meters) below the rim. Follow the cue of avid hikers by rising early; the colors are most radiant and the heat most merciful shortly after dawn. Plan on watching the sunrise while eating a leisurely breakfast at El Tovar.

Day hikes will satisfy most people, but others will want to stay out overnight, perhaps on a hike to the Colorado River and back. Backpacking in the Grand Canyon is hard but rewarding work. Consider joining a mule train. To stay overnight below the rim you must have a reservation at either Phantom Ranch or a designated campground. It's sometimes necessary to make arrangements for camping and mule rides several months in advance, particularly in the summer. Travelers visiting the Grand Canyon in autumn or early spring will have an easier time, though it will also be a cooler one.

West Rim Drive

From Grand Canyon Village, one road – the West Rim Drive – extends to the west and another – the East Rim Drive – to the east, appropriately enough. During the summer, the 8-mile (13-km) **West Rim Drive** is closed to private vehicles and a free shuttle bus is provided. You can get on or off the bus at a half-dozen viewpoints; this makes it possible to take the 10-minute hike between **Pima Point ⑤**, which offers one of the best views of the Grand Canyon and the Colorado River and **Hermit's Rest ⑥**, terminus of West Rim Drive.

The hermit was Louis Boucher, one of many prospectors who arrived in the late 1800s and who was one of the South Rim's first white inhabitants. Deposits of copper, asbestos, lead and silver were found, but the costs of transporting ore by mule train were so astronomical that none of the ventures, including those of Boucher, proved profitable.

We do, however, have the miners to thank for most of the unmaintained trails that enter the canyon, including the Hermit Trail, west of Hermit's Rest. There are two good day-hikes on the Hermit: a 5-mile (8-km) round-trip to **Santa Maria Springs** and a 6-mile (10-km) round-trip to the less frequently visited **Dripping Springs**. Constructed in 1912 for mule riders staying at El Tovar Hotel, the trail is in good condition, though unmaintained, and rarely congested. Nearly 15 miles (24 km) later, the trail reaches the **Colorado River**.

Although the paved road ends at Hermit's Rest, it is possible, via the Rowe's Well road, to venture farther west along the rim, although a topographical map and a few gallons of water are essential. The Bass Trailhead is beautifully situated on a narrow peninsula jutting into the canyon and is one possible destination. Backpackers find the Bass one of the most scenic and

Map on page 301

Traditional river dories, an alternative to the raft.

BELOW: rafting in the Grand Canyon.

*Into the Canyon
with all who are sick
with megalomania!
As a guest in the
abyss the dwarf will
quickly understand
that he is a dwarf.*

– YEVTUSHENKO
RUSSIAN POET

easy-to-follow of the unmaintained trails, and the trailhead itself makes a fine picnic or camping site for anyone anxious to escape the relative pandemonium of Grand Canyon Village.

Even farther west is the Topocoba Hilltop Trail, which leads 8 miles (13 km) to **Havasu Canyon** Ⓖ, home of the Havasupai Indians – "people of the blue-green water" – since AD 1300 and now the Havasupai Reservation, with a population of around 500. Tourism sustains the people. Until this century, the Havasupai, in addition to tilling their fields, spent part of each year roaming throughout the canyon in search of game and edible plants.

Once a rarely visited Shangri-La, Havasu Canyon is now visited by an average of 100 people daily, though in actuality the numbers are considerably larger in summer (and fewer in winter).

Thirty miles (50 km) west of Grand Canyon Village, Havasu Canyon's lure is **Havasu Creek**, a blue-green stream tinted by algae that plunges over three stunning waterfalls, one of which, Mooney Falls, is almost 200 feet (60 meters) high. These waterfalls spill over rippled dams made from travertine, formed by calcium carbonate that has been deposited over the centuries. (Calcium carbonate is the same stuff from which a limestone cave's stalactites and stalagmites are formed.)

While the area receives less than 10 inches (25 cm) of precipitation each year, the Havasu Creek is the drainage for thousands of square miles. In 1990 and 1993, flash floods surged through Havasu Creek. Boulders and silt-thickened water caused residents of Supai to climb to safety.

BELOW: blue waters at Havasu Falls.

Havasu is the most stunning of the side canyons that drain into the Colorado, and despite the crowds it is still worth visiting – particularly during the off-

season, late September through early April. Access is difficult. Most visitors walk or ride horseback along the 8-mile (13-km) trail from Hualapai Hilltop, 67 miles (108 km) northeast of Peach Springs on US 66. There is also a limited helicopter service to Supai. There is a small lodge in Havasu, but most visitors stay at a campground.

Map on page 301

East Rim Drive

East from Grand Canyon Village through fragrant forests of ponderosa pine on the 23-mile (37-km) **East Rim Drive**, the road passes the Kaibab Trailhead, near **Yaki Point** ⓗ, and after 20 miles (32 km) arrives at **Tusayan Ruin** ⓘ and **Tusayan Museum**. Anthropologists believe that the Anasazi Indians who built this small pueblo came to the canyon around AD 500. The Anasazi were not the ancestors of the Havasupai, but rather lived a similar life raising corn, squash and beans on the rim during the summer, moving down to the warmer canyon floor in the winter. The Anasazi abandoned Tusayan and a number of other sites around AD 1150, possibly as a result of a long period of drought.

But the Anasazi were not the first people to inhabit the canyon. Anthropologists have discovered split-twig willow figurines pierced by small spears that date to 2000 BC. What, one wonders, did these people think of the Grand Canyon? Perhaps Hopi religion offers a clue. Each year, Hopi holy men make a pilgrimage to a sacred site in the canyon, from where they believe their ancestors emerged from the underworld.

The last viewpoint on East Rim Drive is **Desert View** ⓙ. Here, the **Watchtower**, a beautiful stone tower that rises 67 feet (20 meters) high, offers excellent views of the Colorado River 4,000 feet (1,200 meters) below. There is a

Kayaking in the Grand Canyon.

BELOW: sunset at the Watchtower.

Map
on page
301

End of a rafting trip.

BELOW: mud break
from water rafting.

campground at Desert View, as well as a little-known road that soon deteriorates to a trail leading to Comanche Point. This secluded spot with its marvelous views is ideal for seekers of solitude.

The North Rim

From Desert View, continue east on State Highway 64 to **Cameron**, where there is a trading post. Stop for gas and what connoisseurs say is a "respectable Navajo taco," a local dish that is a hybrid of Indian frybread smothered with refried beans, lettuce and cheese.

The road forks south to Flagstaff and north to Page and the North Rim. An hour's drive west of **Lees Ferry** is **Jacob Lake**, the turnoff point for the North Rim. The North Rim is 1,000 feet (300 meters) higher than the South Rim and as such is closed from late October to late May due to snow. But during summer and fall, it offers a cooler and less crowded alternative.

Drive south through lush forests of ponderosa pine, spruce, fir and aspen trees, interspersed with wide meadows edged by lingering snowbanks and dotted with duck-filled ponds. After 45 miles (70 km) is **North Rim Village ⓚ**, whose centerpiece is the Grand Canyon Lodge. This handsome structure, a masterpiece created in beams and stonework, was built by hand in 1928 and is best appreciated while eating a piece of pie in the lodge restaurant, perched on the edge of the abyss.

Drive to **Point Imperial ⓛ**, offering views of the eastern Grand Canyon and the Painted Desert, and to Cape Royal. Day hikes along the rim include the Widforss Trail and the Ken Patrick Trail. The only maintained trail into the canyon from the North Rim is the North Kaibab Trail. Allow a full day to hike to **Roaring Springs** and back, a 9-mile (15-km) round-trip. More experienced hikers might want to backpack the Thunder River Trail to Deer and Tapeats creeks, gorgeous trout streams that plunge full-born from springs at the base of the Redwell Limestone.

West of the North Rim is the least visited section of Grand Canyon National Park – **Tuweep ⓜ**, reached over 60 miles (100 km) of dirt roads from either Fredonia or Colorado City. Heed the Park Service's advice: "A trip into this area, one of the most remote in northern Arizona, should not be attempted without ample gasoline, water and food."

Despite restricted access, it's surprising that Tuweep is so rarely visited. Research suggests that within the last million years the Colorado has been damned 11 times by molten lava. The largest lava dam was 550 feet (165 meters) high and backed water 180 miles (290 km) upstream. "What a conflict of water and fire there must have been here!" wrote John Wesley Powell on his pioneer voyage. "Just imagine a river of molten rock running down into a river of melted snow. What a seething and boiling of the waters; what clouds of steam rolled into the heavens!"

There are two points of interest at Tuweep. **Toroweap Overlook ⓝ** offers unrivalled views of the lava flows that cascaded into the canyon. Then there's a short but extraordinarily rugged trail to **Lava Falls ⓞ**, the most violent rapid in the canyon. ❏

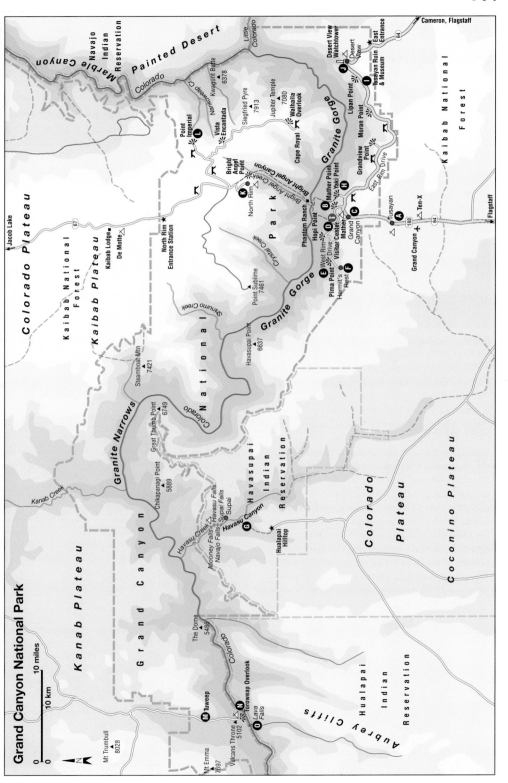

Grand Canyon National Park

Navajo Indian Reservation
Marble Canyon
Painted Desert
Little Colorado
Colorado
Kwagunt Butte 6378
Natwoawp Cr.
Siegfried Pyre 7913
Jupiter Temple
7080
Walhalla Overlook
Cape Royal
Vista Encantada
Point Imperial
Bright Angel Point
Bright Angel Canyon
North Rim
Phantom Ranch
Bright Angel Creek

Desert View Watchtower
Desert View
Tusayan Ruin & Museum
East Entrance
Cameron, Flagstaff
64
Lipan Point
Granite Gorge
Grandview Point
Moran Point
Yaki Point
Mather Point
East Rim Drive

Colorado Plateau
Jacob Lake
67
Kaibab Lodge
De Motte
North Rim Entrance Station
Kaibab National Forest
Kaibab Plateau

Kaibab National Forest

Mather
Grand Canyon
Hopi Point
West Rim Drive
Visitor Center
Pima Point
Hermit's Rest
Point Sublime 7461
Crystal Creek
Shinumo Creek

Tusayan
Grand Canyon
Ten-X
180
64
Flagstaff

Granite Gorge
Park
National
Havasupai Point 6637
Steamboat Mtn 7421
Granite Narrows
Great Thumb Point 6749
Colorado
Chikapanagi Point 5889
Kanab Creek

Havasupai Indian Reservation
Supai
Mooney Falls
Havasu Falls
Supai Falls
Navajo Falls
Havasu Creek
Havasu Canyon
Hualapai Hilltop

Colorado Plateau
Coconino Plateau

Kanab Plateau
Grand Canyon
The Dome 5486
Colorado

Mt Trumbull 8028
Mt Emma 7697
Tuweep
Toroweap Overlook
Lava Falls
Vulcans Throne 5102

Hualapai Indian Reservation
Aubrey Cliffs

10 miles
10 km

N

RAFTING THE COLORADO RIVER

On its 277-mile (445-km) course through the Grand Canyon, the Colorado River provides a world-class rafting adventure

From its headwaters in the state of Colorado to the Gulf of California, the Colorado River is 1,440 miles (2,300 km) long. Through the Grand Canyon, the Colorado River averages 300 feet (90 meters) wide and 40 feet (12 meters) deep. It is famous for its whitewater rapids.

FAST WATER

Rapids form where the canyon narrows, forcing the same volume of water to pass through a restricted channel, where debris from side canyons has tumbled into the river bed, or where elevation drops abruptly. From Lees Ferry to the Grand Wash Cliffs, the Grand Canyon portion of the river, it loses almost 2,000 feet (600 meters) in elevation. In that stretch, rapids account for 90 percent of the river's elevational drop, but only 10 percent of its length. The river lies a heart-stopping 3,000 feet (900 meters) below Toroweap Overlook (above). And from that lofty perch, the river looks pretty tame – except that Lava Falls Rapid's thunder still reaches your ears.

◁ **RIVER GODS**
Guides on the Colorado must have superb skills to negotiate the treacherous rapids.

◁ COLD SHOWER
Even a dousing in the frigid waters can't dampen the spirit of adventure for most rafters. Rain gear helps (a little). Life vests are required.

△ FLEET FEET
Seen more often these days, bighorn are entirely unhindered by terrifying terrain and sometimes peer at boaters from rocky overlooks.

◁ OVER THE EDGE
Mule riders, who will be bow-legged when they dismount, enjoy imposing views. They probably hope the critters live up to their sure-footed reputation.

▽ RAPID RESPONSE
Hermit Rapid, formed by debris washed into the river from Hermit Creek, has waves that make a big raft feel insignificant.

△ NANKOWEAP
Ancestral Puebloans farmed this river delta and stored corn in cliff-face granaries high above the river.

▷ SMILE, ALL
Now that silt drops out behind the dam, trout thrive in the river's clear, cold water. People – and eagles – enjoy the fishing.

THE DAM ON A DESERT RIVER

Glen Canyon Dam, which impounds Colorado River waters in Lake Powell above Grand Canyon, generates as much controversy as hydroelectric power. It may have given us the "world's most beautiful reservoir", but it has altered the river's character, and the ripple effect upon the environment has been weighty. From this strange new river many native species fled or died; odd plants grew; riverbanks eroded. People who knew and respected the old river raised the alarm and in 1992 George Bush signed the Grand Canyon Protection Act, which mandates that the dam be managed to enhance the natural environment in regions both upstream and downstream of the dam.

CENTRAL ARIZONA

Centered around Flagstaff, a tidy town that gets its share of deep snow in winter, and buttressed by the Grand Canyon and Sonoran Desert, this region is a good base for desert rambles

Map on page 311

The journey from Phoenix up to the high country of northern Arizona offers a rare combination for the traveler: an easy two-hour drive along a well-maintained freeway (Interstate 17) and a dramatic introduction to Arizona's changing geology and natural history. The road climbs out of the searing lowlands of the Sonoran Desert, up over the 2,000-foot-high (600-meter) barrier of the Mogollon Rim that transects Arizona and onto the mile-high Colorado Plateau, a 130,000-square-mile (340,000-sq-km) geological province spanning parts of Arizona, New Mexico, Utah, and Colorado.

Leaving the overheated desert basin of Phoenix to the south, the landscape changes from cactus and desert vegetation to sagebrush range bordered by mountains and narrow valleys, dotted with ranches and roads leading to colorfully named places like Bloody Basin. The highway crosses the broad Verde River valley and on through pale limestone road sections that stand out against the dark volcanic escarpment of the Mogollon Rim. In no time, one is up on the Rim itself, motoring through a verdant ocean of pygmy pinyon-juniper forest. Off to the west, the red rocks of Sedona appear, then the road ascends into the cool, fragrant domain of the largest ponderosa pine forest in the Lower 48 at an elevation of 7,000 feet (2,000 meters). Up ahead, lit by a subtle sunset glow, are the San Francisco Mountains and 12,633-foot (3,854-meter) **Humphreys Peak**, Arizona's highest point. Wrapped around the base of the mountains is Flagstaff, the northland's main commercial center.

Flagstaff is not only surrounded by strong contemporary Indian cultures but the preserved remains of those who preceded them – ancestral Puebloans like the Kayenta and the Sinagua, the Cohonina to the west, and the Mogollon, whose culture was centered in southwestern New Mexico but which spread into the White Mountains of Arizona. Flagstaff and environs as far south as Verde Valley were primarily home to the Sinagua (Spanish for "without water"), pueblo-building farmers who made fine, red-hued pottery.

Flagstaff

A few years ago, **Flagstaff** ㉕ earned city status when it topped 50,000 residents, but it started life as a sheep camp. Sheepman Thomas McMillan was the first official settler in 1876, a few months after a group of colonists from Boston passed through and stripped a pine to serve as a flagpole for the July 4th centennial celebration – and thus giving the town its name in 1881. The arrival of the railroad in 1882 allowed meat as well as wool to be sold to markets back east, giving Flagstaff the boost it needed to grow into a lively boardwalk town next to the tracks. Businessmen joined sheepherders, railroad workers and cattle

PRECEDING PAGES: badlands of the Painted Desert. **LEFT:** blossoms near Flagstaff. **BELOW:** tight weave of Indian blanket.

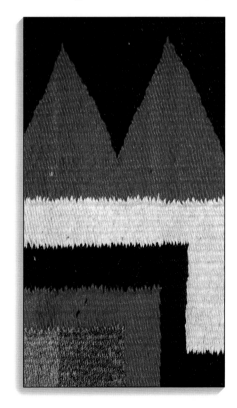

ranchers making (and losing) small fortunes financing business ventures and opening banks, saloons, hotels, stores, restaurants and other services.

By the turn of the century Flagstaff had turned from a town with Wild West leanings into a settled Victorian community dependent on natural resources. Nowadays, although the railroad continues to be a lively presence, lumber and livestock have declined, replaced by jobs linked mainly to federal, state, and local governments, or higher education and tourism.

Start with a visit to the **Flagstaff Visitor Center** (open Mon–Sat 7am–6pm; tel: 800-842 7293), located in the old 1926 railroad depot on Route 66. From here, stroll across the street and visit the funky diners, bars, and newer breweries and boutiques in what was once called New Town. Continue north on San Francisco Street for a walking tour of downtown's many refurbished brick buildings.

On the corner of San Francisco and Aspen streets is the 1887 **Babbitt Building**, still owned by a descendant of the Babbitt brothers who came here to ranch in 1886 and opened so many businesses in Flagstaff that it was said even the sheep said "Baa-bbitt." Just west, where Aspen and Leroux streets meet, is the 1900 **Weatherford Hotel**, now a youth hostel and which once hosted travelers like Theodore Roosevelt, William Randolph Hearst and writer Zane Grey, who wrote *Call of the Canyon* while staying here.

Flagstaff is unusually rich in cultural institutions for such a small city. One of the most famous is **Lowell Observatory** (open daily 9am–5pm in summer, noon–5pm in winter; tel: 520-774 2096; admission fee) atop Mars Hill, easily reached on foot or by car just west of downtown. There is some evening telescope viewing; call for hours. The observatory was founded in 1894 by Percival Lowell, an astronomer who used his family fortune to search for signs of intel-

BELOW: golden eagle ready to fly from its nest.

ligent life on Mars. His work also led him to predict the existence of the planet Pluto, although it was not actually located until after his death, in 1930.

More recently, the observatory hit the headlines when the late astronomer and geologist Eugene Shoemaker and his wife Caroline were the first to identify the Shoemaker-Levy comet. Shoemaker made his home in Flagstaff, attracted by the fellowship of fellow scientists in the area, including those at the U.S. Geological Survey here.

Just south of downtown is **Northern Arizona University**, the center of Flagstaff learning with a student population of 15,000. Founded in 1899 as the Normal School, the university still turns out many of the state's teachers and is also known for its anthropology and forestry schools. Cultural events abound here, many of which are held at Ardrey Auditorium, home to the Flagstaff Symphony. The university also hosts a busy series of public lectures by visiting authors, scientists, and others.

Next to the campus is **Riordan State Historic Park** (open daily 8am–5pm summer, 11am–5pm in winter; tel: 520-779 4395; admission fee), which preserves the elegant 1904 log-and-stone home of Flagstaff's most successful lumbermen, Timothy and Michael Riordan. Designed by Charles Whittlesey, also the architect for El Tovar Hotel at the Grand Canyon, the home is open daily for hourly tours and is well worth a visit. It sits just off Milton Road, now a busy commercial artery but once called Mill Town, a separate community for millworkers in the area. Another terrific place to learn about local lore is the **Arizona Historical Society Pioneer Historical Museum** (open Monday–Saturday 9am–5pm; tel: 520-774 6272; admission fee), a few miles north of downtown on Highway 180. Built as the community hospital in 1908 and now the home of

Map on page 311

Nearly 7,000 feet (2,130 meters) in elevation and with a population of 50,000, Flagstaff is the largest city on Interstate 40 between Los Angeles and Albuquerque.

BELOW: cliff dwellings at Montezuma Castle National Monument.

the Arizona Historical Society, it houses artifacts dug up from Old Town (now known as Plaza Vieja and located on Coconino Avenue, west of downtown), as well as pioneer Ben Doney's cabin.

When the arbiters of urban refugee chic decide that a small Western town is the newest place for harmonically converging one's oneness... Barrios become Espresso Land. Real estate becomes religion. Cowboys sing the blues.

– BRUCE SELCRAIG
THE NEW YORK TIMES

South of Flagstaff

For a further look at late-period Sinagua ruins head south from Flagstaff on Interstate 17 for about 50 miles (80 km) to the retirement haven of Verde Valley to view the dramatic remains of a 12th-century cliff pueblo at **Montezuma Castle National Monument** ❷ (open daily 8am–7pm in summer, to 5pm in winter; tel: 520-567 3322; admission fee), so named by early explorers who thought it the work of Aztecs, not northerners moving into areas vacated by earlier farmers of the Hohokam culture. For an early Hohokam pithouse, visit **Montezuma Well**, 11 miles (18 km) north.

These ruins are one of the main reasons to visit **Sedona** ❷, a former fruit-growing center that has become the overhyped New Age Santa Fe of Arizona, with high prices and overpriced art as common as millionaire mansions and four-wheel-drive tours to power-vortex meditation sites. More down to earth, Sedona is where the Cowboy Artists of America was founded, and the arts are still vital here, with many world-class artists and musicians resident or visiting.

There's no denying the area's great beauty and pleasant climate, though, and no visitor to northern Arizona should miss the breathtaking scenic drive down Oak Creek Canyon on Highway 89A, which drops from 7,000 feet (2,100 meters) to 5,000 feet (1,500 meters) in a series of dramatic, shady switchbacks backed by sheer cliff walls. Continue west about 15 miles (24 km) to the attractive little town of **Cottonwood** and turn off to visit **Tuzigoot National Monument** ❷ (open

BELOW: reds and greens of Sedona.

daily 8am–7pm in summer, to 5pm in winter; tel: 520-634 5564; admission fee), a large pueblo in a clearly defensive setting above the river and built around the same time as Montezuma Castle. More Sinagua ruins can be seen in the valley of Sedona to the north, where cliff sites such as Palatki are hidden among the glorious redrock canyons surrounding Sedona and Oak Creek.

Hill-top dwellings of the Victorian era can be seen at the old copper-mining town of **Jerome** ㉙, off Highway 89A, where fading "painted lady" homes clinging to the slopes of Cleopatra Hill high on 7,743-foot (2,360-meter) Mingus Mountain have been rescued and fixed up by artists. To learn about copper mining and the wealth it brought Arizona, visit **Jerome State Historical Park** (open daily 8am–5pm; tel: 520-634 5381; admission fee), located in the 1916 home of "Rawhide Jimmy" Douglas, a local mine owner. It's a great place to find unusual artwork and kick back with views nearly to infinity.

Much more sedate is **Prescott** ㉚, about 75 miles (120 km) southwest of Flagstaff and now one of the fastest growing communities in Arizona. Prescott became Arizona's first territorial capital in 1864 and remained the state's seat of government until the capital moved to Phoenix. Tree-shaded streets, solid Victorian buildings, a stately courthouse, and several historic hotels grace the town center, which also attracts local cowboys to the saloon bars along Gurley Street on a Saturday night and to the world's oldest rodeo, held each July.

Prescott offers a window on Arizona history through its superb **Sharlot Hall Museum** (open Monday–Saturday 10am–5pm, Sunday 1–5pm; tel: 520-445 3122; admission fee), housed in the Old Governor's Mansion and other buildings and named for pioneer Prescott rancher, writer, and former territorial historian Sharlot Hall.

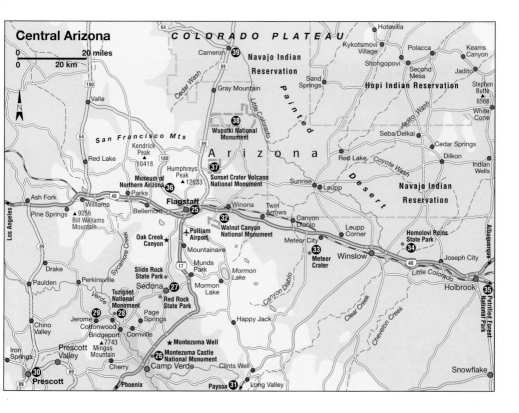

Central Arizona's most spellbinding drive begins east of Camp Verde, along the 200-mile-long (320-km) **Mogollon Rim**, the great volcanic scarp that towers over the Verde Valley. Take Highway 260 east then pick up Forest Road 300, a 45-mile-long (70-km) gravel road that twists and turns along the limestone cliff edge and offers lakes, picnic areas, trailheads and campgrounds. At the junction with Highway 87, drop south through the quaint little western backwaters of Strawberry and Pine to **Payson ③**, at an elevation of 5,000 ft (1,500 meters) and known for its guest ranches, rodeo and long association with Zane Grey, who built a cabin nearby and set many of his novels in this rugged Tonto country.

The **Rim Country Museum** (open Wednesday–Sunday noon–4pm; tel: 520-474 3483; admission fee) has exhibits about Grey and the area, as does the **Zane Grey Museum** and **Counseller Art Gallery** (open Monday–Sunday 11am–4pm; tel: 520-474 6243; free), run by Western artist Mel Counseller, who was the caretaker for the Grey Cabin for 11 years.

East of Flagstaff

In the 13th century, cultural pressures and a long drought led the Sinagua to move to **Walnut Canyon National Monument ②** (open daily 8am–4pm; tel: 520-526 3367; admission fee), a few miles east of Flagstaff and off Interstate 40. The people once living here built snug cliff homes in sheltered alcoves above a stream, farmed mesa-top fields and constructed what appear to be forts, perhaps as a defense against interlopers.

Meteor Crater ③ (open daily 6am-6pm in summer, 8am–5pm in winter; tel: 520-289 2362; admission fee), east of Flagstaff, was formed approximately 50,000 years ago by an iron meteor 100 feet (30 meters) in diameter and weigh-

Walnut Canyon is rugged and 400 feet (122 meters) deep. Its 300 small dwellings, dating to AD 1100, are well-preserved because of a sheltered location in the limestone cliffs.

BELOW: Meteor Crater is nearly a mile wide.

ing 60,000 tons. Hitting the earth at 45,000 miles an hour (72,000 kph), it left a crater 4,000 feet wide (1,200 meters) and 570 feet (173 meters) deep. Nearly 85 percent of the meteor melted on impact. The remainder was spread far and wide as grain-size particles now called Canyon Diablo meteorites.

Before leaving the area, stop at **Homolovi Ruins State Park** ❸❹ (open daily 8am–5pm; tel: 520-289 4106; admission fee), near Winslow and which preserves more than 300 partly excavated Indian ruins and a number of petroglyphs that show a blend of Mogollon and Ancestral Pueblo influences. These ruins are considered ancestral sites by the Hopi, whose mesa-top homes lie just to the north.

Scenic drives and outdoor activities abound in the densely forested White Mountains, but since more than 1.6 million acres (650,000 hectares) of the area belong to the White Mountain Apache Tribe, you'll need to get permits (tel: 520-338 1230) for fishing, hunting and camping when on reservation land. For solitude, head to **Greer** or **Alpine**, where travelers can rent a log cabin for a romantic weekend getaway or walk for miles in the forest.

Head back through the primarily Mormon communities of Show Low and Snowflake and turn east on Highway 180 to access the southern section of **Petrified Forest National Park** ❸❺ (open daily 7.30am–5pm; tel: 520-524 6228; admission fee). Some 200 million years ago this was the province of dinosaurs wandering amid equatorial swamps populated by giant cycads and other large flora and fauna.

Trees falling into the swamp were quickly entombed by mud mixed with thick ash from highly active volcanoes in the region. Cut off from oxygen, the trees, woody cells were replaced by crystalline structures of many hues – today's

Map on page 311

BELOW: petrified wood fragment at Petrified Forest National Park.

Map on page 311

Wupatki Pueblo was the largest of 2,500 sites occupied by Sinagua and Anasazi between 1100 and 1250. It stood three stories high with around 100 rooms.

Bᴇʟᴏᴡ: slickrock bike trail.
Rɪɢʜᴛ: Petrified Forest National Park.

petrified wood – which were then buried by encroaching streams, rivers and seas over millions of years. Later, Pueblo people living along the Rio Puerco found the "wood" eroding out of the crumbly Chinle Formation and used it to build structures like Agate House.

North of Flagstaff

The geological, natural and cultural history of the Colorado Plateau is beautifully presented through permanent and revolving exhibits at the outstanding **Museum of Northern Arizona** ㊱ (open daily 9am–5pm; tel: 520-774 5213; admission fee), a few miles farther north on Highway 180. This should be one's only Flagstaff stop if driving through town en route to Grand Canyon and the surrounding area.

A respected research and educational institution, the museum was founded by Harold Colton, a wealthy intellectual from the eastern U.S. who fell in love with the area's rich archaeology in the 1920s and stayed. Colton's wife, Mary, was drawn to the arts and crafts of the surrounding Indian reservations – principally the Navajo and Hopi to the northeast – and encouraged artisans to improve the quality of their offerings through juried shows at the museum. This tradition continues, with annual summer shows that include high-quality rugs, jewelry, pottery, sculpture and other crafts by the Navajo, Hopi, Zuni and Paiute, with items for sale in the museum store.

Two places with strong Sinagua connections are **Sunset Crater Volcano National Monument** ㊲ (open daily sunrise to sunset, visitor center 8am–5pm; tel: 520-526 0502; admission fee), to the northeast of Flagstaff on US 89, and **Wupatki National Monument** ㊳ (open sunrise to sunset daily, visitor center 8am–5pm; tel: 520-679 2365, admission fee), about 20 miles (30 km) northwest of Flagstaff, off Highway 89. **Sunset Crater Volcano**, a 1,000-foot (300-meter) cinder cone named by explorer John Wesley Powell, is part of the extensive San Francisco Volcanic Field, which includes the San Francisco Mountains and Kachina Peaks Wilderness. Eruptions in this active volcanic field formed the cone starting in 1065 and ending in the 1200s, witnessed by Sinagua farmers who fled but later returned to soil made fertile by the volcanic ash.

A loop drive passes huge lava flows that still look remarkably fresh, then continues on to Wupatki National Monument, with views to the Painted Desert and the Hopi mesas in the east, and the San Francisco Mountains to the west. The monument preserves a number of major pueblos, with the largest, Wupatki, showing strong signs of having been the northernmost great house on a vast trading route that took in Chaco Canyon to the east and Mesoamerica to the south.

A hundred years ago, a trading post grew up at the river crossing at **Cameron** ㊴. It is now open to visitors in the form of **Cameron National Historic Site** (open daily; tel: 520-679 2231), a good place to buy Indian arts and crafts, enjoy a meal of local fare in the tin-ceilinged dining room, or stay the night in a modern hotel. ❑

LAS VEGAS

Leave any ambivalence at home. This town demands a response to its completely over-the-top extravagance and assault on the mind and pocketbook. Still, it can be seductive and fun

Maps:
Area 270
City 321

Las Vegas

Phoenix

Reputedly Lady Luck's favorite piece of real estate, **Las Vegas** ⓴ is a neon valley of round-the-clock risk-taking and, increasingly, endless theme-park extravagance intended to make the town primarily a family, not a gambler's, destination. The ultimate urban extrovert, Las Vegas serves little purpose except to entertain and vacuum in immense amounts of cash, enough to fund most of the State of Nevada's operating budget from gambling taxes alone. At one time, the casino-hotels came with motherload names like the Nugget and Frontier. Then more extravagant places took on names suggesting venues, like Circus Circus. Then came the ancient icons like Luxor. But even that wasn't enough for Las Vegas, and the recent hotels reflect entire cities in both name and contrived ambience, like New York and Venice.

Las Vegas is improbably centered in a desert valley ringed by treeless mountains. The sky seems endless, especially to big-city eyes. Gaming and glitter in the middle of nowhere creates a fantasyland atmosphere.

Roots of Las Vegas

The earliest white people in the area were Anglo traders traveling from Santa Fe to California on the old Spanish Trail. They found Las Vegas to be an oasis of refreshing springs and grassy fields, a discovery reflected in the Spanish meaning of Las Vegas: The Meadows. Although explorers like Jedediah Smith and Capt. John C. Fremont noted this oasis in their travels, the area remained largely uninhabited until 1855, when Mormon leader Brigham Young sent a band of 30 Mormon men from Utah to Las Vegas to mine for lead in the mountains and, of course, to convert the Indians. They did not stay long, discouraged by their lack of success in converting the Indians and in smelting the ore they found here.

They could not have known it then, but the unsatisfactory lead was, in fact, silver.

When the fabled Comstock Lode, a rich vein of gold and silver, was discovered in 1849, Nevada came into its own. Towns sprang up all around. Nevada became a territory in 1861 and was rushed into statehood in 1864 – the Union needed the wealth of the Comstock Lode to win the Civil War.

In time, the area around the abandoned Mormon settlement became the property of a succession of ranchers, who provided a way station for California-bound travelers. One of these ranchers, Helen Stewart, remained a rancher – and a lone woman with several children – after her husband was mysteriously shot and killed. She ran the 1,800-acre (750-hectare) ranch, cooked meals for travelers and offered lodging for boarders until the coming of the railroad.

PRECEDING PAGES:
long view of
casinos and resorts
in Las Vegas.
LEFT: simplicity is
no virtue here.
BELOW: Fremont
Street, downtown.

Las Vegas is still in the profitable trade of gambling.

In 1902, Stewart sold her property to the forerunner of the Union Pacific Railroad, which had come to link the West with the East; Las Vegas was to be a division point depot. The town was born on May 15, 1905, when the railroad auctioned off some 1,200 lots to high-bidding speculators. In two days, all the lots were sold and a boom town of tents and shacks soon appeared on the scene.

Las Vegas stayed a small and sleepy railroad town until the 1930s, when the immense Boulder (Hoover) Dam project on the Colorado River brought in workers from all over the country. In 1931, gambling was legalized in Nevada to funnel revenue into the state. Liberal marriage and divorce laws were also enacted in 1931 and Las Vegas became an easy option for a quick Nevada divorce. In some counties, prostitution was, and still is, legalized.

The Las Vegas Strip

Las Vegas is an easy town to navigate. There's not a lot to it, actually: casinos and hotels along a few main corridors, and residential areas dissolving into the desert. Most of the gambling activity is concentrated in two main areas: the famed **Las Vegas Strip** Ⓐ and the downtown area on **Fremont Street**, about 3 miles (5 km) north of the Strip area. The Strip (properly known as Las Vegas Boulevard South) begins at Sahara Avenue and runs south as far as the airport. Most of the newer mega-hotels are in this southern part of the Strip.

The Strip is a special effect made reality. Where else would you find a Roman palace and a circus-topped casino – both of the "old school" of Vegas casino-hotel – and the "new school" of Venetian canals and Eiffel Tower sharing the same stretch of highway? In fact, most of the newer Strip hotels are self-contained attractions, increasingly shifting the emphasis from gambling to shopping

BELOW: Fremont Street Light Experience.

and amusement. And in the past few years, there's been a determined effort to change, or at least broaden, the city's appeal. Now that gambling is legal in Atlantic City and in many other states, including Indian reservations, the state of Nevada has been forced to rethink its prime attraction and main source of revenue. In the background are the high-rollers, in the foreground are families that spend, spend, spend.

The **Frontier Hotel** Ⓑ is one of the original glamour hotels and casinos in Las Vegas, still brilliantly illuminated inside and out but now overshadowed by the ostentatious mega-hotels of the late 1990s.

The newer buildings themselves are the stars of the show. At **New York, New York** Ⓒ, visitors can stroll in "Central Park," walk along the "Brooklyn Bridge," or ride a Coney Island-style roller coaster looping around the hotel towers. The 30-story pyramid at the glass-paneled **Luxor** has an atrium big enough to hold nine Boeing 747s. The 3,000-room **Bellagio** Ⓓ, opened in 1998 at a cost of $1.6 billion, is geared for the upscale consumer with shops that include Prada, Armani, and Tiffany and comes complete with an 8-acre artificial lake. In 1999, the cheaper-to-construct but equally large-scale **Venetian** opened nearby at a cost of just $1.5 billion, it too with upscale shops like Movado and Davidoff – accessible by gondola or on foot. Gilded ceilings with Renaissance frescoes hover over the hotel's insides.

At night, the magnificent and more traditional **Caesars Palace** ⓔ is theatrically bathed in blue-green light, with an arcaded automatic "people mover" and a geodesic-domed Omnimax Theater. **Treasure Island** stages a sea battle in its own lagoon. The MGM **Grand** has a casino bigger than a football field. The MGM stands on what is known as the **Golden Corner** – Las Vegas Boulevard South at Flamingo. Other Golden Corner occupants are the Flamingo Hilton and the Barbary Coast. The list – and the statistics – about the Strip's hotels can go on and on, and do go on and on.

The **Liberace Museum** ⓕ (open daily 10am–5pm; tel: 702-798 5595; admission fee) of course, honors the showman who could match the Strip's electric glow. Located just over 2 miles (3 km) east of the Strip, the museum offers memorabilia of Liberace's career – the planet's largest rhinestone, samples from his ample wardrobe, pianos and custom automobiles.

Downtown and Fremont Street

Just a mile north of the Strip – and where Downtown is said officially to begin – is the **Stratosphere Tower** ⓖ (open daily, 10am–1am; tel: 702-380 7777; admission fee). Soaring to 1,825 feet (556 meters), it is the tallest structure in the West. In 30 seconds elevators whisk visitors to a revolving restaurant, observation decks and thrilling rides. Visitors with romantic inclinations and little fear of heights can get married near the top.

Unlike the Strip, which had miles of empty desert on which to build sprawling resort hotels, the downtown gambling area was always limited to just a few blocks of **Fremont Street** ⓗ in the commercial center. The refurbishment of a pedestrian mall called the **Fremont Street Experience** gave the area a whole

No, this is not a good town for psychedelic drugs. Reality itself is too twisted.
— HUNTER S. THOMPSON
FEAR AND LOATHING IN LAS VEGAS

BELOW:
Stratosphere Tower.

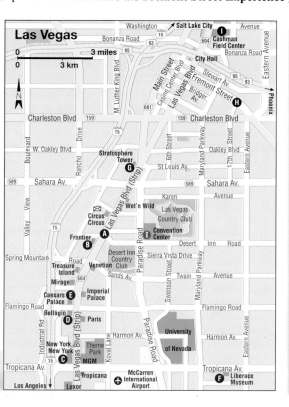

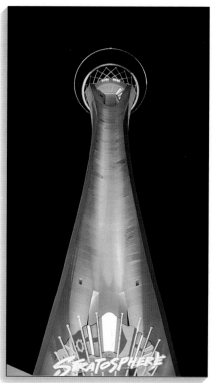

new lease of life. Years ago, the downtown area was known to one and all as Glitter Gulch. The merchants ran a contest to find a more sophisticated name for the district and "Casino Center" was the winner. Nonetheless, the old names are still in everyday use – Downtown, Glitter Gulch or simply Fremont Street.

The oldest and newest in promotional advertising is very much in evidence with the Fremont Street Experience. Visitors stroll along a five-block, casino-lined mall, attracting huge crowds every hour to enjoy a computer-generated high-tech light and sound show projected onto a screen. (It takes 45 hours to manually design and input the 6-minute show into the computers.) The lattice-work unveils a spectacular moving picture show in which cartoon characters and animals dance to music, buffalo stampede, and jet fighters scream overhead. No fewer than two million light bulbs are used in the display.

Downtown is also home of the **Four Corners**, the intersection of Fremont and Casino Center Boulevard. The lights of the Golden Nugget (whose computer-ized marquee spells out messages and flashes pictures), Four Queens and Fre-mont hotels combine to make this the most brilliantly illuminated intersection in the world, or so it's claimed. The downtown area also has its own mini-con-vention facility, the **Cashman Field Center** ❶.

As a rule, it costs less to gamble downtown than on the Strip. Stakes are lower and it is still possible to find inexpensive craps tables. Some people think downtown dealers are friendlier and more tolerant, too. Downtown casinos are said to have "loose" slots – slot machines that have been adjusted to pay out up to 90 percent of the money deposited in them. The volume of slot enthusiasts is so high that frequent payoffs are good promotions for the casinos.

BELOW: marriages are a gamble in Las Vegas, too.
RIGHT: rollercoaster at New York, New York hotel.

Outside of Vegas

Two more north-to-south crossings of central Arizona are possible along the state's boundaries. In the east, US 666 stays in little-populated high country where forestry is the leading industry. In the west, State 95 parallels the **Colorado River** from Davis Dam to Parker, then heads straight south to Yuma. "River" no longer seems an honest word for the succession of reservoirs and wide sluices that this stretch of the Col-orado has become, lined with resorts and trailer parks, converged upon during the summer by thousands of weekend revelers from Phoenix and Los Angeles.

Its most famous attraction is the **London Bridge**, the famous bridge bought and shipped over from Eng-land by the developer of **Lake Havasu City** ❹ to call attention to his desert, non-Elizabethan real estate. That the Colorado River has not just been tamed but Thamed may seem a last absurdity, but those who go to laugh at the bridge may be surprised.

Hoover Dam ❷ (open daily for tours; tel: 702-293 8421; admission fee), one of the biggest projects of its time, stands 726 feet (221 meters) high, damming the Colorado River into **Lake Mead**, part of the **Lake Mead National Recreation Area**. High plateaus and canyons define this desert; the lake itself is the largest – by volume – artificial reservoir, 110 miles (176 km) long, with over 500 miles (800 km) of shoreline and is 500 feet (150 meters) deep in places. ❑

INSIGHT GUIDES

TRAVEL TIPS

New
Insight Maps

Maps in Insight Guides are tailored to complement the text. But when you're on the road you sometimes need the big picture that only a large-scale map can provide. This new range of durable Insight Fleximaps has been designed to meet just that need.

Detailed, clear cartography
makes the comprehensive route and city maps easy to follow, highlights all the major tourist sites and provides valuable motoring information plus a full index.

Informative and easy to use
with additional text and photographs covering a destination's top 10 essential sites, plus useful addresses, facts about the destination and handy tips on getting around.

Laminated finish
allows you to mark your route on the map using a non-permanent marker pen, and wipe it off. It makes the maps more durable and easier to fold than traditional maps.

The first titles
cover many popular destinations. They include Algarve, Amsterdam, Bangkok, California, Cyprus, Dominican Republic, Florence, Hong Kong, Ireland, London, Mallorca, Paris, Prague, Rome, San Francisco, Sydney, Thailand, Tuscany, USA Southwest, Venice, and Vienna.

INSIGHT GUIDES
The world's largest collection of visual travel guides

CONTENTS

Getting Acquainted

The continental US is divided into four time zones. From east to west, later to earlier, they are Eastern, Central, Mountain and Pacific, each separated by one hour. The Southwest is on Mountain Standard Time (MST), except for Nevada, which follows Pacific Standard Time. Mountain Standard Time is seven hours behind Greenwich Mean Time, and Pacific Standard Time eight hours behind.

In spring, Colorado, Utah, Texas and New Mexico move the clock ahead one hour for Daylight Savings Time. In fall, the clock is moved back. Arizona does not observe Daylight Savings Time, but the Navajo Nation does. Thus, during spring and summer, Arizona is one hour behind the Navajo Nation, much of which is also in Arizona. Yes, confusing, a result of politics, mostly. Mexico does not observe Daylight Savings Time.

Climate

The Southwest spans half a dozen climate and life zones, but by and large you will find sunny skies, low humidity and limited precipitation. Climate varies widely with elevation. Climbing 1,000 feet (300 meters) is equivalent to traveling 300 miles (500 km) northwards. In temperature, traveling from the lowest to the highest points of Arizona is like traveling from Mexico to the north of Hudson Bay in Canada.

Arizona

Arizona gets 80 percent of available sunshine annually. Annual rainfall averages 12.5 inches (30 cm). Wind velocity for most cities is under 8 mph (13 kph). Northern regions average around 73 percent sunshine; southern areas average around 90 percent.

Average temperatures in **Phoenix** reach 100°F (38°C) in summer and fall to 30°F (−1°C) in winter. Phoenix gets about 7 inches (18 cm) of rain per year. In **Flagstaff**, 145 miles (230 km) to the north, temperatures range from 75 to 80°F (24 to 27°C) in summer and fall to around 15°F (−10°C) in winter. Annual precipitation in Flagstaff averages 84 inches (210 cm), most of it falling in July, August and December.

At its hottest, the south rim of the **Grand Canyon** reaches 90°F (32°C) rising to 100°F (38°C) or more at the bottom of the gorge. Flash thunderstorms are common. Generally, the weather is more comfortable in the spring and fall. Always bring sweaters when visiting the Canyon.

Nevada

In **Las Vegas**, from June through September, daytime temperatures rarely register below 100°F (38°C). Spring and fall seasons are short, with temperatures around 75°F (24°C).

Daytime winter temperatures are generally 50–70°F (10–20°C) with January and February nights near freezing point.

New Mexico

Every part of New Mexico gets at least 70 percent sunshine year-round, with July and August thunderstorms providing most of the precipitation.

From December to March, snowfalls vary from 2 inches (5 cm) in the lower **Rio Grande Valley** to 300 inches (750 cm) or more in the north-central mountains. **Albuquerque** registers highs just over 90°F (32°C) in summer; winter lows are below 30°F (−1°C) in January. Only 59 miles (95 km) to the north, but at a higher elevation, **Santa Fe** reports July highs above 90°F (32°C) and January lows below 20°F (−7°C).

Utah

Southern Utah has sunny days, cool nights and little precipitation. Occasional summer days warm up past 100°F (38°C), which makes hiking inadvisable during the day. **Arches National Park** is the warmest spot in Utah, with consistent summer temperatures of 110–115°F (43–46°C). **Bryce Canyon** is much higher and therefore much cooler, with July and August temperatures of 70–90°F (21–32°C) falling to around a brisk 45°F (7°C) overnight. Thunderstorms, usually brief, occur in all the parks. Visitors can count on warm to hot days and should prepare for much cooler nights requiring heavier clothing.

Public Holidays

On public holidays, post offices, banks, most government offices and a large number of shops and restaurants are closed. Public transport usually runs less frequently.

New Year's Day: January 1
Martin Luther King, Jr.'s Birthday: January 15
Presidents Day: The third Monday in February
Good Friday: March/April – date varies

Easter Sunday: March/April – date varies
El Cinco de Mayo: May 5
Memorial Day: Last Monday in May
Independence Day: July 4
Pioneer Day: July 24 (Utah)
Labor Day: First Monday in September
Columbus Day: Second Monday in October
Veterans Day: November 11
Thanksgiving Day: Fourth Thursday in November
Christmas Day: December 25

Planning the Trip

Clothing

Weather can be unpredictable in any season, so be prepared for just about anything. Dress in layers that can be peeled off or put on as conditions dictate. Rain gear is always a good idea. A high-factor sunblock, wide-brimmed hat and sunglasses are advisable too, even if the day starts out cloudy. The sun can be merciless, especially in deserts or prairies where there is little shade.

If you plan on doing a lot of walking or hiking, it's worth investing in a sturdy pair of hiking shoes or boots. Consider buying them a half or full size larger than usual and be sure to break them in properly before arriving. A thin, inner polypropylene sock and a thick, outer sock will help keep your feet dry and comfortable. If blisters or sore spots develop, quickly cover them with moleskin, available at just about any pharmacy or camping supply store.

With few exceptions, western dress is informal. A pair of jeans or slacks, a polo or button-down shirt, and boots or shoes are appropriate at all but the fanciest places and events.

Electricity

Standard electricity in North America is 110-115 volts, 60 cycles A.C. An adapter is necessary for most appliances from overseas, with the exception of Japan.

Maps

Accurate maps are indispensable in the Southwest, especially when leaving primary roads. Highway

Film

All consumer formats of photographic films are available in most grocery stores, pharmacies and convenience stores. If you need professional-quality photographic equipment or film (especially transparency or black-and-white films), consult the local telephone directory for the nearest camera shop. If you don't have a camera, consider the relatively inexpensive disposable cameras available at many supermarkets, pharmacies and convenience stores.

maps can be found at bookstores, convenience stores and gas stations. Free maps may be available by mail from state or regional tourism bureaus. Free city, state and regional maps as well as up-to-date road conditions and other valuable services are also available to members of the Automobile Association of America. If you are driving any distance, the service is well worth the membership fee.

Maps of national parks, forests and other natural areas are usually offered by the managing governmental agency. Good topographical maps of national parks are available from **Trails Illustrated**, PO Box 3610, Evergreen, CO 80439, tel: (303) 670-3457 or toll-free 800-962-1643; these maps are often in bookstores. Extremely detailed topographical maps are available from the **US Geological Survey**, PO Box 25286, Denver Federal Center, Denver, CO 80225, tel: (303) 236-7477. Like maps from Trails Illustrated, USGS maps are often available in higher end bookstores and also in outdoor shops.

Entry Regulations

PASSPORTS & VISAS

A passport, visitor's visa and evidence of intent to leave the US after your visit are required for entry into the US by most foreign nationals. Visitors from the United King-

dom and several other countries staying less than 90 days may not need a visa if entering as tourists. All other nationals must obtain a visa from a US consulate or embassy. An international vaccination certificate may be required depending on your country of origin.

Canadians entering from the Western Hemisphere, Mexicans with border passes and British residents of Bermuda and Canada do not normally need a visa or passport, but it's best to confirm visa requirements before leaving home.

Once in the US, foreigners may visit Canada or Mexico for up to 30 days and re-enter the US without a new visa. For additional information, contact a US consulate or embassy or the US State Department, tel: (202) 663-1225.

Extensions of Stay

Visas are usually granted for six months. If you wish to remain in the country longer than six months, you must apply for an extension of stay at the **US Immigration and Naturalization Service**, 2401 E St, Washington, DC 20520, tel: 202-514-4330.

CUSTOMS

All people entering the country must go through US Customs, a time-consuming process. To speed things up, be prepared to open your luggage for inspection and keep the following restrictions in mind.
• If you are bringing in more than $10,000 you must declare it.
• Anything for personal use may be brought in duty- and tax-free.
• Adults are allowed to bring in one liter of alcohol for personal use.
• You can bring in gifts worth less than $400 duty- and tax-free. Anything over the $400 limit is subject to duty charges and taxes.
• Agricultural products, meat and animals are subject to complex restrictions, especially if entering in California. Leave these items at home if at all possible.

For more details contact a US consulate or write the Department of

Agriculture, or US Customs, 1301 Constitution Avenue NW, Washington, DC 20520, tel: (202) 514-4330.

Health

PRECAUTIONS

Insurance: It's vital to have insurance when traveling. Unless you go to a free clinic, which are few and far between, especially in the Southwest, you may have to prove you can pay for your treatment. Know what your policy covers and have proof of the policy with you at all times.

Sunburn: A beautiful day of rafting can result in sunburn, so protect yourself with a sunscreen and sunglasses. The elderly and the ill, small children and people with fair skin should be especially careful. Excessive pain or redness and blistering or numb skin mean you need professional medical attention. Minor sunburn can be soothed by taking a cold bath.

Dehydration: Drink plenty of water in the American Southwest and, if outdoors, try to carry liter bottles of water and something to eat. Don't wait to get thirsty – start drinking extra liquids as soon as you get up. Also avoid the sun at its hottest: 2–4pm.

Cacti: To avoid being stung, stay on the trail and wear long pants and sturdy boots. Some people may have allergies to the prickly varieties of these beautiful desert plants.

Hypothermia: This occurs when the core body temperature falls below 95°F (35°C). At altitude, combinations of alcohol, cold, and thin air can produce hypothermia. Watch for drowsiness, disorientation and sometimes increased urination. If possible get to a hospital, otherwise blankets and extra clothing should be piled on for warmth. Don't use hot water or electric heaters and don't rub the skin. The elderly should be especially careful in extremely cold weather.

Drinking water: All water from natural sources must be purified before drinking. *Giardia* is found throughout the West, even in crystal-clear water, and it can cause severe cramps and diarrhea. The most popular purification methods are tablets or filters (both available from camping supply stores) or by boiling water for at least 15 minutes. Drink only bottled water in Mexico, and avoid ice cubes.

Frostbite: Symptoms for frostbite, which occurs when living tissue freezes, include numbness, pain, blistering and whitening of the skin. The most immediate remedy is to put frostbitten skin against warm skin. Simply holding your hands for several minutes over another person's frostbitten cheeks or nose, for example, may suffice. Otherwise, immerse frostbitten skin in warm (not hot!) water. Refreezing will cause even more damage, so get the victim into a warm environment as quickly as possible. If one person is frostbitten, others may be too.

Altitude sickness: The air thins as you go higher. Unless properly acclimatized, you may feel uncharacteristically winded. If you experience nausea, headache, vomiting, extreme fatigue, light-headedness or shortness of breath, you may be suffering from altitude sickness. Although the symptoms may be mild at first, they can develop into a serious illness. Head lower down and try to acclimatize gradually. Although much of the Southwest is desert, it is also at rather high elevations.

INSECTS & ANIMALS

Snakes: There are rattlesnakes and coral snakes in the Southwest, but not in great numbers.

Only around 3 percent of people bitten by a rattlesnake die, and these are mainly small children. Walk in the open, proceed with caution in rocks, make noise in grass, do not step close to dark places or overgrown areas where snakes might lurk, shake out bedding or clothing that has been lying on the ground, and wear sturdy hiking boots. Snakes often lie on roads at night because of the residual heat radiating from the pavement, so use a flashlight if walking on a desert highway after dark. Don't poke under rocks or let your children pick things up in the desert.

Snakebite kits are good psychological protection but there is controversy over how effective they really are. If bitten, apply a tourniquet lightly above the bite toward the heart. Try to identify the species and go immediately to a doctor.

Gila monsters: The only poisonous Southwestern lizards, Gila monsters are big and menacing but easily recognized and rarely encountered.

Insects: Bees are abundant, which should concern only those allergic to the sting. The kissing bug is an unusual looking black bug with an unpleasant bite. There are stinging fire ants and some varieties of wasp. These bugs are neither friendly nor normally dangerous.

However, black widow spiders and scorpions can be a problem if encountered. Scorpions are nocturnal, so use flashlights if you walk barefoot in the desert at night. Scorpions also hide in recesses of old buildings and wood piles. They crawl into things, so shake out clothes and bedding and check stores in the morning.

Abandoned Mines

Exercise caution around old buildings and abandoned mines. Structures may be unstable and the ground may be littered with broken glass, nails and other debris. Mine shafts are particularly dangerous. Never enter a mine shaft or cave unless accompanied by a park ranger or other professional.

Money Matters

CURRENCY

The basic unit of American currency, the dollar ($1), is equal to 100 cents. There are four coins, each worth less than a dollar: a penny or 1 cent (1¢), a nickel or 5 cents (5¢), a dime or 10 cents (10¢) and a quarter or 25 cents (25¢).

More colour
for the world.

HDCplus. New perspectives in colour photography.

Probably the <u>most</u> <u>important</u> TRAVEL TIP you will ever receive

Before you travel abroad, make sure that you and your family are protected from diseases that can cause serious health problems.

For instance, you can pick up *hepatitis A* which infects 10 million people worldwide every year (it's not just a disease of poorer countries) simply through consuming contaminated food or water!

What's more, in many countries if you have an accident needing medical treatment, or even dental treatment, you could also be at risk of infection from *hepatitis B* which is 100 times more infectious than AIDS, and can lead to liver cancer.

The good news is, you can be protected by vaccination against these and other serious diseases, such as *typhoid, meningitis* and *yellow fever*.

Travel safely! Check with your doctor at least 8 weeks before you go, to discover whether or not you need protection.

Consult your doctor before you go... not when you return!

SB
SmithKline Beecham
VACCINES

Produced as a service to public health

There are several denominations of paper money: $1, $5, $10, $20, $50, $100 and, rarely, $2. Each bill is the same color, size and shape; be sure to check the dollar amount on the face of the bill.

It is advisable to arrive with at least $100 in cash (in small bills) to pay for ground transportation and other incidentals.

TRAVELERS' CHECKS

Foreign visitors are advised to take US dollar travelers' checks since exchanging foreign currency – whether as cash or checks – can be problematic. A growing number of banks offer exchange facilities, but this practice is not universal.

Most shops, restaurants and other establishments accept travelers' checks in US dollars and will give change in cash. Alternatively, checks can be converted into cash at the bank.

CREDIT CARDS

These are very much part of daily life in the US. They can be used to pay for pretty much anything, and it is also common for car rental firms and hotels to take an imprint of your card as a deposit. Rental companies may oblige you to pay a large deposit in cash if you do not have a card.

You can also use your credit card to withdraw cash from ATMs (Automatic Teller Machines). Before you leave home, make sure you know your PIN and find out which ATM system will accept your card. The most widely accepted cards are Visa, American Express, Master-Card, Diners Club, Japanese Credit Bureau and Discovery.

Money may be sent or received by wire at any **Western Union** office (tel: 800-325-6000) or **American Express Money Gram** office (tel: 800-543-4080).

Insurance

Most visitors to the US will have no health problems during their stay. Even so, you should never leave home without travel insurance to cover both yourself and your belongings. Your own insurance company or travel agent can advise you on policies, but shop around since rates vary. Make sure you are covered for accidental death, emergency medical care, trip cancelation and baggage or document loss.

Getting There

BY AIR

If driving to the Southwest from elsewhere in the country is impractical because of distance, the next best way to get there is to fly to a nearby city. The major hubs in the Southwest are:
Arizona: Phoenix Sky Harbor International, Tucson International.
Colorado: Denver International, Colorado Springs Airport.
Nevada: McCarran International (Las Vegas).
New Mexico: Albuquerque International.
Texas: El Paso International.
Utah: Salt Lake City International.

BY TRAIN

Amtrak offers more than 500 destinations across the US. The trains are comfortable and reliable, with lounges, restaurants, snack bars and, in some cases, movies and live entertainment. Most routes offer sleeper cars with private cabins in addition to regular seating.

Amtrak's **Southwest Chief** runs from Chicago to Los Angeles. Stops include Albuquerque and Gallup, New Mexico; Winslow, Flagstaff (Amtrak Thruway bus service to Grand Canyon) and Kingman, Arizona.

The **Sunset Limited** runs from Miami to Los Angeles. Stops on this route include El Paso, Texas; Deming, New Mexico; and Tucson and Phoenix, Arizona.

The **Desert Wind** runs from Chicago to Los Angeles. Stops on this route include Denver, Colorado; Salt Lake City, Utah; and Las Vegas, Nevada.

Ask about two- or three-stopover discounts, senior citizens' and children's discounts, and Amtrak's package tours. International travelers can buy a USA Railpass, good for 15 to 30 days of unlimited travel on Amtrak throughout the United States.

Amtrak, tel: 800-872-7245 for detailed scheduling.

Airlines and Airports

National Airlines		Regional Airlines	
Alaska	800-426-0333	Air Nevada Airlines	
America West	800-235-9292		800-634-6377
American	800-433-7300	Las Vegas Airlines	
Continental	800-525-0280		800-634-6851
Delta	800-221-1212	Reno Air	800-736-6247
Northwest	800-225-2525	Scenic	800-634-6801
TWA	800-221-2000	Skywest	800-453-9417
United	800-241-6522	Southwest	800-435-9792
US Air	800-428-4322		

The following airport numbers are for general information only, not for airline reservations or schedules:
Sky Harbor Int'l Airport (Phoenix): tel: (602) 273 3300
Tucson Int'l Airport: tel: (520) 573-8100
Albuquerque Int'l Airport: tel: (505) 842-4366
Santa Fe Municipal Airport: tel: (505) 473-7243

BY BUS

One of the least expensive ways to travel in America is by interstate bus. The largest national bus company is **Greyhound**, tel: 800-231-2222. The company routinely offers discounts such as go-anywhere fares . An Ameripass offers unlimited travel for 7, 15, 30 and 60 days, depending upon the fare paid. Call the nearest Greyhound office for information . However, Greyhound generally does not service remote areas. A rental car or other transport will be necessary from the major hubs.

BY CAR

Driving is by far the most flexible and convenient way to travel in the Southwest, especially for outside the major cities. Major roads are well-maintained, although back-country roads may be unpaved. If you plan on driving into remote areas or in heavy snow, mud or severe weather, it's a good idea to use a four-wheel-drive vehicle with high chassis clearance.

Maps & Information

Your greatest asset as a driver is a good road map. They can be obtained from state tourism offices, filling stations, supermarkets and convenience stores. Although roads are maintained even in remote areas, it is advisable to listen to local radio stations and to check with highway officials or police officers for the latest information on weather and road conditions, especially in winter or if planning on leaving paved roads.

Weather Hazards

Flash floods may occur during the rainy season, from early summer to fall. Stay out of arroyos, washes and drainage areas. Driving conditions vary dramatically depending on elevation. During fall, winter and early spring, your car should be equipped with snow tires or chains, a small collapsible shovel, and an ice scraper. Also, be

Hitchhiking

Hitchhiking is illegal in many places and ill-advised everywhere. It's an inefficient and dangerous method of travel. Don't do it!

prepared for the extra time required to drive along winding, narrow mountain roads.

Driving in Remote Areas

If you plan to drive in desert areas, carry extra water – at least 1 gallon (4 litres) per person per day. Service stations can be few and far between in remote areas. Not every town will have one, and many close early. It's always better to have more fuel than you think you will need.

A word of caution: If your car breaks down on a back road, do not attempt to strike out on foot, even with water. A car is easier to spot than a person and gives shelter from the elements. Sit tight and wait to be found.

Vehicle Rental

CAR RENTALS

National car rental agencies are located at all airports, and in cities and large towns. In most places, you must be at least 21 years old (25 at some locations) to rent a car and you must have a valid driver's license and at least one major credit card. Drivers under 25 may

AAA

If you intend to do a lot of driving, consider joining the American Automobile Association (AAA). Fees are cheap and the services many: emergency road service, maps, insurance, travelers' checks, bail bond protection and other services. The AAA has reciprocity agreements with many foreign automobile associations.

AAA, 4100 E. Arkansas Drive, Denver CO 80222, tel: (800) 222-4357.

have to pay an extra fee, as will additional drivers. Foreign drivers must have an international driver's license. Be sure that you are properly insured for both collision and personal liability. Insurance won't be included in the base rental fee. Additional cost varies depending on the car and the type of coverage, but it is usually $10–20 per day. You may already be covered by your own auto insurance or credit-card company, so check with them first.

Cheapest rates are usually in Arizona and Las Vegas. Most rentals in the Southwest, especially if by the week, offer unlimited mileage. If not, you may be charged an extra 10–25¢ or more per mile over a given mileage. Rental fees vary depending on the time of year, location, how far in advance you book your rental, and if you travel on weekdays or weekends. Inquire about discounts or benefits for which you may be eligible, including corporate, credit-card or frequent-flyer programs.

Alamo	800-327-9633
Avis	800-331-1212
Budget	800-527-0700
Dollar	800-800-4000
Enterprise	800-325-8007
Hertz	800-654-3131
National	800-227-7368
Thrifty	800-367-2277

RV RENTALS

No special license is necessary to operate a motor home (or recreational vehicle – RV for short), but they aren't cheap. When you add up the cost of rental fees, insurance, gas and campsites, renting a car and staying in motels or camping may be less expensive.

Keep in mind, too, that RVs are large and slow and may be difficult to handle on narrow mountain roads. If parking space is tight, driving an RV may be extremely inconvenient. Access to some roads may be limited. For additional information about RV rentals, call the **Recreational Vehicle Rental Association**, tel: 800-336-0355.

Practical Tips

Newspapers

Every city and town has a local newspaper. For national and international news, along with local and regional activities and events, check the following metropolitan daily papers. Also available in most cities are *The New York Times, Los Angeles Times,* and *The Wall Street Journal.* Forget about finding overseas newspapers, except in a few hotels and bookstores.

Albuquerque Journal
7777 Jefferson NE, Albuquerque NM 87109
Tel: (505) 823-4400.

Arizona Republic
120 E. Van Buren, Phoenix, AZ
Tel: (602) 257-8300.

Las Vegas Sun
800 S. Valley View, Las Vegas NV 89107
Tel: (702) 385-3111.

Las Vegas Review-Journal
1111 W. Bonanza Road, Las Vegas NV 89107
Tel: (702) 383-0211.

New Mexican
202 E. Marcy, Santa Fe, NM 87501
Tel: (505) 983-3303.

Phoenix Gazette
120 E. Van Buren, Phoenix, AZ
Tel: (602) 257-8300.

Salt Lake Tribune
143 S. Main Street, Salt Lake City UT 84111
Tel: (801) 237-2045.

Tucson Citizen
4850 S. Park Avenue, Tucson AZ 85714
Tel: (520) 573-4400.

Postal Services

Even the most remote towns are served by the US Postal Service. Smaller post offices tend to be limited to business hours (Monday–Friday 9am–5pm), although central, big-city branches may have extended weekday and weekend hours.

Stamps are sold at all post offices. They are also sold at some convenience stores, filling stations, hotels and transportation terminals, usually from vending machines.

For reasonably quick delivery at a modest price, ask for priority mail.

For overnight deliveries, try US **Express Mail** or one of several domestic and international courier services:
Fedex, tel: 800-238-5355;
DHL, tel: 800-345-2727;
United Parcel Service, tel: 800-272-4877.

Poste Restante

Visitors can receive mail at post offices if it is addressed to them, care of "General Delivery", followed by the city name and (very important) the zip code. You must pick up this mail in person within a week or two of its arrival and will be asked to show some form of valid personal identification.

Telephone, Telegram, Telex and Fax

Public telephones are located at many highway rest areas, service stations, convenience stores, bars, motels and restaurants.

To call from **one area to another,** dial 1 before the three-digit area code, then the local seven-digit number. If you want to pay for the call with coins, a recorded voice will tell you how many to insert. Unless

Business Hours

Standard business hours for offices are Monday–Friday 9am–5pm. Many banks open a little earlier, usually 8.30am . A few open on Saturday morning. Post offices are usually open Monday–Friday 8am–5pm and Saturday 8am–noon. Most stores and shopping centers are open weekends and evenings.

you have a credit card with the telephone company, your only other option is to call your party "collect" (reversing the charges). Rates vary for long-distance calls. Take advantage of lower long-distance rates on weekends and after 5pm on weekdays.

For **local calls** from pay telephones which accept coins, insert a coin and dial the seven-digit local telephone number. There is no time limit for local calls.

Many businesses have **toll-free** (no charge) telephone numbers; these are always prefaced with (800) rather than an area code. Note that if you dial a toll-free number from abroad, you will be charged the normal international rate for the call.

The quickest way to get information is to dial 0 for the operator. Directory Assistance calls from pay telephones are free. However, to be connected to some of them you must first insert a coin, but as soon as you are connected with the operator it will be returned to you. To get the **information operator** dial 411, but to get an information operator in another city, dial 1-(area code of the city)-555-1212.

Dialling Abroad

To dial abroad (Canada follows the US system), first dial the international access code 011, then the country code. If using a US phone credit card, dial the company's access number below, then 01, then the country code.
Sprint, tel: 10333.
AT&T, tel: 10288.

Country codes:

Australia	61
Austria	43
Belgium	32
Brazil	55
Denmark	45
France	33
Germany	49
Greece	30
Hong Kong	852
Israel	972
Italy	39
Japan	81

Korea	82
Netherlands	31
New Zealand	64
Norway	47
Singapore	65
South Africa	27
Spain	34
Sweden	46
Switzerland	41
United Kingdom	44

Western Union (tel: 800-325-6000) can arrange telegram, mailgram and telex transmissions. Check the local phone directory or call information for local offices.

Fax machines are available at most hotels and even some motels. Printers, copy shops, stationers and office-supply shops may also have them, as well as some convenience stores.

Weights & Measures

Despite efforts to convert to metric, the US still uses the Imperial System of weights and measures.

1 inch	=	2.54 cm
1 foot	=	30.48 cm
1 yard	=	0.9144 meter
1 mile	=	1.609 km
1 pint	=	0.473 liter
1 quart	=	0.946 liter
1 ounce	=	28.4 grams
1 pound	=	0.453 kg
1 acre	=	0.405 hectare
1 sq mile	=	259 hectares
1 centimeter	=	0.394 inch
1 meter	=	39.37 inches
1 kilometer	=	0.621 mile
1 liter	=	1.057 quarts
1 gram	=	0.035 ounce
1 kilogram	=	2.205 pounds
1 hectare	=	2.471 acres
1 sq km	=	0.386 sq. mile

Useful Addresses

STATE TOURISM OFFICES

Arizona

Arizona Office of Tourism
2702 N. Third Street
Suite 4015
Phoenix 85004
Tel: (602) 230-7733 or toll free
800-842-8257.
www.arizonaguide.com

Flagstaff Convention and Visitors Bureau
211 W. Aspen Avenue
Flagstaff 86001
Tel: (520) 779-7611.
Grand Canyon Chamber of Commerce
PO Box 3007, Grand Canyon 86023
Tel: (520) 638-2901.
www.thecanyon.com/chamber
Navajo Nation Tourism Office
PO Box 663, Window Rock 86515
Tel: (520) 871-6436.
Phoenix Convention and Visitors Bureau
400 E. Van Buren #600
Phoenix 85004
Tel: (602) 254-6500.
Prescott Chamber of Commerce
117 W. Goodwin Street
Prescott 86302
Tel: (520) 445-2000.
Scottsdale Chamber of Commerce
7343 Scottsdale Mall
Scottsdale 85251
Tel: (602) 945-8481.
Tombstone Office of Tourism
PO Box 917, Tombstone 85638
Tel: (520) 457-3929 or toll free
800-457-3423.
Tucson Convention & Visitors Bureau
130 S. Scott Avenue
Tucson 85701
Tel: (520) 624-1817 or toll free
800-638-8350.

Colorado
Colorado Tourism Authority
1625 Broadway
Suite 1700
Denver 80202
Tel: toll-free 800-265-6723.

Tipping

Service workers in restaurants and hotels depend on tips for a significant portion of their income. With few exceptions, tipping is left to your discretion and gratuities are not automatically added to the bill. In most cases, 15–20 percent is typical for tipping waiters, taxi drivers, bartenders, barbers and hairdressers. Porters and bellmen usually get $1 per bag.

Durango Chamber Resort Association
111 S. Camino del Rio
Durango 81301
Tel: (970) 247-0312.

Nevada
Nevada Tourism
Capital Complex, Carson City 89710
Tel: (702) 687-4322 or toll free
800-237-0774.
Las Vegas Chamber of Commerce,
711 E. Desert Inn Road
Las Vegas 89104
Tel: (702) 735-1616.
Las Vegas Convention and Visitors Authority
Convention Center, 3150 Paradise
Road, Las Vegas 89109
Tel: (702) 892-0711 or toll free
800-332-5333.

New Mexico
New Mexico Dept. of Tourism,
Lamy Building
491 Old Santa Fe Trail
Santa Fe 87503
Tel: (505) 827-7400 or toll 800-545-2040.
Alamogordo Chamber of Commerce
PO Box 518, Alamogordo 88311
Tel: (505) 437-6120.
Albuquerque Convention and Visitors Bureau
PO Box 26866, Albuquerque 87125
Tel: (505) 842-9918 or toll free
800-284-2282. www.abqcvb.org
Fort Sumner Chamber of Commerce
PO Box 28, Fort Sumner 88119
Tel: (505) 355-7705.
Gallup Convention and Visitors Bureau
PO Drawer Q, Gallup 87305
Tel: (505) 863-3841.
Old West Country
1103 N. Hudson, Silver City 88061
Tel: (505) 538-0061 or toll free
800-548-9378.
Santa Fe Convention & Visitors Bureau
PO Box 909, Santa Fe 87501
Tel: (505) 984-6760.
www.santafe.org
Taos County Chamber of Commerce
PO Drawer I, Taos 87571
Tel: (505) 758-3873 or toll free
800-732-8267.

Insight Guides portray destinations in depth, providing the complete picture and the top photography

Insight Pocket Guides focus on the best choices for places to see and things to do and include large fold-out maps

Insight Compact Guides' portability makes them the perfect books to carry with you for on-the-spot reference

Three types of guide for all types of travel

INSIGHT GUIDES Different people need different kinds of information. Some want *background information* to help them prepare for the trip. Others seek *personal recommendations* from someone who knows the destination well. And others look for *compactly presented data* for on-the-spot reference. With three carefully designed series, Insight Guides offer readers the perfect choice. Insight Guides will turn your visit into an experience.

The world's largest collection of visual travel guides

When you're
bitten by the travel bug,
make sure you're protected.

Check into a British Airways Travel Clinic.

British Airways Travel Clinics provide travellers with:
- A complete vaccination service and essential travel health-care items
- Up-dated travel health information and advice

Call **01276 685040** for details of your nearest Travel Clinic.

BRITISH AIRWAYS
TRAVEL CLINICS

Foreign Embassies in the United States

Australia: 1601 Massachusetts Ave NW, Washington, DC 20036, tel: 202-797-3000.
Belgium: 3330 Garfield St NW, Washington, DC 20008, tel: 202-333-6900.
Canada: 501 Pennsylvania Ave NW, Washington, DC 20001, tel: 202-682-1740.
Denmark: 3200 Whitehaven St NW, Washington, DC 20008, tel: 202-234-4300.
France: 4101 Reservoir Road NW, Washington, DC 20007, tel: 202-944-6000.
Germany: 4645 Reservoir Road NW, Washington, DC 20007, tel: 202-298-4000.
Great Britain: 3100 Massachusetts Ave NW, Washington, DC 20008, tel: 202-462-1340.
Greece: 2221 Massachusetts Ave NW, Washington, DC 20008, tel: 202-667-3168
India: 2536 Massachusetts Ave NW, Washington, DC 20008, tel: 202-939-7000.
Israel: 3514 International Drive NW, Washington, DC 20008, tel: 202-364-5500.
Italy: 1601 Fuller St NW, Washington, DC 20009,

tel: 202-328-5500.
Japan: 2520 Massachusetts Ave NW, Washington, DC 20008, tel: 202-939-6700.
Mexico: 1911 Pennsylvania Ave NW, Washington, DC 20006, tel: 202-728-1600.
Netherlands: 4200 Wisconsin Ave NW, Washington, DC 20016, tel: 202-244-5300.
New Zealand: 37 Observatory Circle NW, Washington, DC 20008, tel: 202-328-4800.
Norway: 2720 34th Street NW, Washington, DC 20008, tel: 202-333-6000.
Portugal: 2125 Kalorama Road NW, Washington, DC 20008, tel: 202-328-8610.
Singapore: 3501 International Place NW, Washington, DC 20008, tel: 202-537-3100.
South Korea: 2600 Virginia Ave NW, Washington, DC 20037, tel: 202-939-5600.
Spain: 2375 Pennsylvania Ave NW, Washington, DC 20037, tel: 202-452-0100.
Taiwan: 4201 Wisconsin Ave NW, Washington, DC 20016, tel: 202-895-1800.

Utah Office
324 S. State Street
Salt Lake City
UT 84145
Tel: (801) 539-4001.
National Forest Service
Southwest Regional Office
517 Gold Ave. SW, Albuquerque
NM 87102
Tel: (505) 842-3292.
National Park Service
Southwest Region, PO Box 728
Santa Fe, NM 87504-0728
Tel: (505) 988-6016
www.nps.gov/
New Mexico State Park and Recreation Division
408 Galisteo Street
Santa Fe, NM 87504
Tel: (505) 827-7465.
Utah Division of Parks and Recreation
1636 W. North Temple
Suite 116
Salt Lake City, UT 84116
Tel: (801) 538-7221.

Security & Crime

Emergency (police/fire): **911**

A few common-sense precautions will help keep you safe while traveling in the Southwest. For starters, know where you are and where you're going. Whether traveling on foot or by car, bring a map and plan your route in advance. Ask for directions. Most people are happy to help.

Don't carry large sums of cash or wear flashy or expensive jewelry. Lock unattended cars and keep your belongings in the trunk. If possible, travel with a companion, especially after dark.

If involved in a traffic accident, remain at the scene. It is illegal to leave the scene of an accident. Find a nearby telephone or ask a passing motorist to call the police, and then wait for emergency vehicles to arrive.

Driving under the influence of alcohol carries stiff penalities, including fines and jail. Wearing seatbelts is required in all states. Children under four must be in a child's safety seat.

Texas
Texas Tourism
PO Box 12728, Austin, TX 78711
Tel: (512) 478-0098 or toll free 800-888-8839.
El Paso Convention and Visitors Bureau
1 Civic Center Plaza, El Paso TX 79940
Tel: (915) 534-0658.

Utah
Utah Travel Council
Council Hall, Capitol Hill
Salt Lake City 84114
Tel: (801) 538-1030 or toll free 800-200-1160.
Canyonlands
117 S. Main, Monticello 84535
Tel: (801) 587-3235.
Color Country
906 N. 1400 West

St George 84771
Tel: (801) 628-4171 or toll free 800-233-8824.

NATIONAL PARKS & WILDERNESS AREAS

Arizona State Parks Office
1300 W. Washington, Phoenix
AZ 85007
Tel: (602) 542-4174.
Bureau of Land Management:
Arizona Office
3707 North Seventh St., Phoenix
AZ 85011
Tel: (602) 650-0528.
New Mexico Office
1474 Rodeo Road
Santa Fe
NM 87502
Tel: (505) 438-7400.

Where to Stay

Hotels are listed in alphabetical order by state.

ARIZONA

Arizona Biltmore
24th Street and Missouri Avenue
Phoenix, AZ 85016
Tel: (602) 955-6600 or toll free
800-950-0086
Fax: (602) 381-7600
An elegant grand hotel designed by
Frank Lloyd Wright and in
landscaped grounds. Amenities: air
conditioning, television, pools,
fitness room, golf courses, biking,
restaurants, bars, shops, parking.
$$$$

Arizona Inn
2200 E. Elm St, Tucson, AZ
Tel: (520) 325-1541
Fax: (520) 325-1541
Fourteen acres of guest houses
with patios and fireplaces.
Understated, elegant lodging only
five minutes from University. **$$$**

Best Western Grand Canyon Squire Inn
Highway 64, Grand Canyon
AZ 86023
Tel: (520) 638-2681
Comfortable, modern hotel located
just outside Grand Canyon
National Park. Amenities: air
conditioning, television, pool,
tennis, restaurant, bar, parking.
$$–$$$

Bisbee Grand Hotel
61 Main Street, Bisbee, AZ 85603
Tel: (520) 432-5900
An elegantly restored Victorian
building with period decor in a
historic southern Arizona mining
town. Amenities: parking, saloon,
billiard room, free breakfast; no in-

room telephones or televisions. **$$**

Bright Angel Lodge
W. Rim Drive, Grand Canyon
AZ 86023
Tel: (520) 638-2631
An old rustic lodge and bungalows
with simple accommodation set in
Grand Canyon National Park.
Amenities: television, restaurant,
parking, bar. **$$**

Copper Queen Hotel
11 Howell Avenue, Bisbee
AZ 85603
Tel: (520) 432-2216
A turn-of-the century Victorian
landmark built during the heyday of
the Copper Queen Mine; guests
have included John Wayne and
Teddy Roosevelt. Amenities:
parking, television, restaurant,
saloon, pool. **$$**

Desert Rose
3424 E. Van Buren Street
Phoenix, AZ 8500
Tel: (602) 275-4421
A modest but comfortable small
hotel a short drive from downtown.
Amenities: air conditioning,
television, pool, restaurant, parking.
$

El Tovar Hotel
Grand Canyon National Park
Lodges, PO Box 699
Grand Canyon, AZ 86023
Tel: (520) 638-2401 or (303) 297-
2757
A rustic lodge built in 1905 on the
edge of the South Rim. Amenities:
air conditioning, television, parking,
restaurant, bar, gift shop, some
rooms with balcony. **$$$$**

Grand Canyon Lodge
Bright Angel Point, AZ 86052
Tel: (520) 638-2611
Basic motel accommodations and
cabins on the North Rim of the
Grand Canyon; open seasonally.
Amenities: air conditioning,
restaurant, bar, parking. **$$**

Hotel Congress
311 E. Congress, Tucson AZ
Tel: (520) 622-8848 or (800) 722-
8848.
John Dillinger and his gang stayed
here. Why shouldn't you?
Idiosyncratic and inexpensive. All
rooms have radios, restored original
furniture, steam heat and windows
that open. **$**

Innsuites Hotel, Tucson Randolph Park
102 N. Alvernon Way, Tucson
AZ 85711
Tel: (520) 795-0330
Spanish-style hotel with
comfortable rooms and attractive
setting. Amenities: air conditioning,
television, pool, in-room refrigerator
and microwave, some rooms with
kitchenette. **$$**

Lodge on the Desert
306 N. Alvernon, Tucson AZ
Tel:(520) 325-3366 or (800) 456-
5634
In-town resort that has been
restored to its original casual
charm. Most rooms have red tiled
patios and fireplaces. Its
restaurant, Cielos, is recognized as
one of the best in Tucson. **$$–$$$**

Loews Ventana Canyon Resort
7000 N. Resort Drive
Tucson, AZ 85750
Tel: (520) 299-2020
Luxurious hotel in the desert
outside the city. Amenities: air
conditioning, television, pools,
tennis, golf courses, fitness room,
restaurants, bar, shops, parking.
$$$$

Navajo Nation Inn
Highway 264, Window Rock
AZ 86515
Tel: (520) 871-4108
Simple, comfortable motel located
in the capital of the Navajo Nation.
Amenities: air conditioning,
television, restaurant, parking. **$$**

Ritz Carlton Phoenix
2401 E. Camelback Road
Phoenix, AZ 85016
Tel: (602) 468-0700 or toll free
800-241-3333
Fax: (602) 468-9883
Luxurious grand hotel with plush
furnishings. Amenities: air
conditioning, television, pool,

fitness room, tennis, restaurants, bar, parking. **$$$–$$$$**

Royal Palms Hotel and Casitas
5200 E. Camelback Road
Phoenix 85018
Tel: (602) 840-3610
Fax: (602) 840-6927
A classic renovated in the 1990s and considered to be rather romantic, especially the 14 casitas. **$$$$**

Scottsdale Princess
7575 E. Princess Drive
Scottsdale 85255
Tel: (602) 585-4848
Fax: (602) 585-0091
Of Moorish and Spanish ambience, this deluxe resort comes with everything, including romanticism. **$$$$**

Thunderbird Lodge
PO Box 548, Chinle, AZ 86503
Tel: (520) 674-5841
Simple but comfortable accommodations at Canyon de Chelly National Monument in the Navajo Nation. Amenities: air conditioning, television, cafeteria, Jeep tours, parking. **$$**

Wahweap Lodge and Marina
100 Lakeshore Drive
Page, AZ 86040
Tel: (520) 645-2433
Modern, comfortable hotel on Lake Powell. Amenities: air conditioning, television, pools, boating, restaurants, bar, fitness room, parking. **$$–$$$**

COLORADO

General Palmer Hotel
567 Main Avenue
Durango, CO 81301
Tel: (970) 247-4747 or toll free
800-523-3358
A gracious, midsized Victorian house fully restored with period furnishings. Amenities: air conditioning, television, parking, library, restaurant, bar, one room with Jacuzzi. **$$–$$$**

Strater Hotel
699 Main Avenue
Durango, CO 81301
Tel: (970) 247-4431 or toll free
800-247-4431
A fine Victorian mansion built in

1887 with authentic period furnishings and an Old West saloon. Amenities: air conditioning, television, parking, restaurant, saloon. **$$–$$$**

Tamarron Resort
40292 Highway 550 North
Durango, CO 81301
Tel: (970) 259-2000 or toll free
800-678-1000
A plush full-service resort in San Juan National Forest. Amenities: air conditioning, television, pool, fitness room, tennis, golf, horseback riding, restaurants, bars. **$$$–$$$$**

NEVADA

Caesars Palace
3570 Las Vegas Blvd South
Las Vegas, NV 89109
Tel: (702) 731-7110 or toll free
800-634-6001
A glitzy pleasure palace in Roman theme; a monument to Vegas style. Amenities: air conditioning, television, pools, tennis, fitness club, restaurants, bars, nightclub, Omnimax theater, casino, entertainment, shops, parking. **$$$–$$$$**

Center Strip Inn
3688 Las Vegas Blvd South
Las Vegas, NV 89109
Tel: (702) 739-6066 or telephone toll free 800-777-7737
Comfortable motel on the Strip. Amenities: air conditioning, television, pool, free breakfast, parking. **$$–$$$**

Circus Circus
2880 Las Vegas Blvd South
Las Vegas, NV 89109
Tel: (702) 734-0410 or toll free
800-634-3450
This comfortable hotel takes the circus theme to extremes; high-wire artists perform above the casino floor. Amenities: air conditioning, television, pools, restaurants, bars, casino, shops, parking. **$–$$**

MGM Grand Hotel
3799 Las Vegas Blvd South
Las Vegas, NV 89109
Tel: (702) 891-1111 or toll free
800-929-1111
The world's largest hotel is Las

Vegas at its most extravagant; worth visiting for the spectacle alone. Amenities: air conditioning, television, pool, tennis, fitness club, restaurants, bars, casino, entertainment, sports arena, 33-acre theme park, shopping mall, parking. **$$$–$$$$**

NEW MEXICO

Albuquerque Hilton
1901 University Blvd NE,
Albuquerque, NM 87102
Tel: (505) 884-2500
Big, spacious hotel with many amenities and downtown location. Amenities: air conditioning, television, pools, tennis courts, restaurants, bar, fitness room, tennis courts, parking. **$$$–$$$$**

Bishop's Lodge
P.O. Box 2367, Santa Fe 87504
Tel: (505) 983-6377
Fax: (505) 989-8739
Established nearly a century ago, this venerable establishment is expanding but retaining its distinguished classic-retreat foundations. **$$$–$$$$**

Doubletree
201 Marquette Avenue NW
Albuquerque, NM 87102
Tel: (505) 247-3344. Comfortable, contemporary downtown hotel popular with business people. Amenities: air conditioning, television, restaurant, bar, workout room, pool, parking. **$$$–$$$$**

Eldorado Hotel
309 W. San Francisco Street
Santa Fe, NM 87501
Tel: (505) 988-4455 or toll free
800-955-4455
Luxurious contemporary hotel with lovely Southwestern design. Amenities: air conditioning, television, pool, workout room, restaurants, bars, shops, parking. **$$$–$$$$**

Hotel Loretto
211 Old Santa Fe Trail
Santa Fe 87501
Tel: (505) 988-5531
Fax: (505) 984-7988
Built in 1975 to look like Taos Pueblo, this classic has been renovated and updated. Rooms are

simple, small but pleasant.
$$$–$$$$.

Hyatt Regency
330 Tijeras SW
Albuquerque, NM 87102
Tel: (505) 842-1234
Elegant and contemporary
downtown hotel. Amenities: air
conditioning, television, pool,
fitness room, restaurant, bar, gift
shop, parking. **$$–$$$**

Inn of the Anasazi
113 Washington Avenue
Santa Fe, NM 87501
Tel: (505) 988-3030 or toll free
800-688-8100
New, luxurious hotel near the Plaza
with Pueblo-style decor. Air
conditioning, television, restaurant,
fireplaces, parking. **$$$$**

Inn of the Mountain Gods
PO Box 269 Mescalero, NM 88340
Tel: (505) 257-5141 or toll free
800-545-9011
Owned by the Mescalero Apache
tribe, this resort hotel is located on
a lake in the Sacramento
Mountains and offers a variety of
recreational activities. Amenities:
air conditioning, television, golf
course, tennis courts, pool, fishing,
boating. **$$–$$$**

La Fonda
100 E. San Francisco Street
Santa Fe, NM 87501
Tel: (505) 982-5511 or toll free
800-523-5002
Historic Pueblo Revival-style hotel
on the Plaza rebuilt in 1919.
Amenities: air conditioning,
television, parking, pool, restaurant,
bars, nightclub, some rooms with
fireplaces, shops. **$$$–$$$$**

La Posada de Albuquerque
125 2nd Street NW
Albuquerque, NM 87102
Tel: (505) 242-9090 or toll free
800-621-7231
Comfortable old hotel with nice
architectural touches from the
1930s. Amenities: air conditioning,
television, restaurant, bar, parking.
$$

La Posada de Santa Fe
330 E. Palace Avenue
Santa Fe, NM 87501
Tel: (505) 986-0000 or telephone
toll free 800-727-5276
Comfortable older hotel in a lovely

Spanish colonial design. Near the
Plaza. Amenities: air conditioning,
television, pool, restaurant, bar,
some rooms with fireplace, parking.
$$–$$$$

St Francis
210 Don Gaspar Avenue
Santa Fe, NM 87501
Tel: (505) 983-5700 or toll free
800-666-5700
Charming older hotel built in the
1920s and now fully restored with
period decor. Amenities: air
conditioning, television, restaurant,
bar, parking. **$$–$$$**

UTAH

Apache Motel
166 S. 4th Street, Moab, UT 84532
Tel: (801) 259-5727
Basic motel accommodation.
Amenities: air conditioning,
television, pool, parking. **$–$$**

Bryce Canyon Lodge
TW Recreational Services
PO Box 400, Cedar City, UT 84720
Tel: (801) 586-7686
Built in 1923 by the Utah Pacific
Railroad and on the Register of
Historic Places. Set in the heart of
Bryce Canyon National Park.
Amenities: some rooms with air
conditioning, television, parking,
pool, horseback riding, restaurant.
$$$

Capitol Reef Inn
360 W. Main Street
Torrey, UT 84775
Tel: (801) 425-3271
Small seasonal hotel with simple
accommodation. Amenities: air
conditioning, television, parking,
restaurant. **$**

Goulding's Monument Valley Lodge
PO Box 1, Monument Valley
UT 84536
Tel: (801) 727-3231
Simple accommodation in
Monument Valley. Amenities: air
conditioning, television, restaurant,
pool, Indian shop, parking. **$$–$$$**

The Lodge at Brianhead
314 Hunter Ridge Drive
Brianhead, UT 84719
Tel: (801) 677-3222
Comfy hotel in Dixie National Forest
near Cedar Breaks National

Monument. Amenities: air
conditioning, television, parking,
pool, fitness room, restaurant.
$–$$

Recapture Lodge
Highway 191, Bluff, UT 84512
Tel: (801) 672-2281
Rustic accommodations about 45
minutes from Monument Valley.
Amenities: television, air
conditioning, slide shows and
interpretive talks, tours of
Monument Valley by reservation,
some rooms with kitchenettes,
pool, playground, parking. **$–$$**

Zion Lodge
TW Recreational Services
Cedar City, UT 84720
Tel: (303) 297-2757
Rustic but comfortable facilities in
the glorious scenery of Zion
National Park. Amenities: air
conditioning, parking, restaurant,
horseback riding, bus tours. **$$**

Chain Hotels & Motels

Chain hotels and motels are
reliable and convenient but tend to
lack unique character. You can
usually depend on a clean,
comfortable room for a reasonable
cost. In general, prices range from
$50 to $150 depending on location
and additional amenities such as a
pool, lobby or restaurant.

Moderate to Expensive

Best Western	800-528-1234
Hilton	800-HILTONS
Holiday Inn	800-HOLIDAY
Hyatt	800-228-9000
Sheraton	800-325-3535
La Quinta	800-531-5900
Marriott	800-228-9290
Radisson	800-333-3333
Ramada	800-2-RAMADA
Westin	800-228-3000

Budget

Comfort Inn	800-228-5150
Days Inn	800-325-2525
Econo Lodge	800-553-2666
Howard Johnsons	800-654-2000
Motel 6	800-466-8356
Quality Inn	800-228-5151
Red Lion Inn	800-733-5466
Super 8	800-800-8000
Travelodge	800-578-7878

Bed & Breakfast Inns

Bed-and-breakfasts tend to be more homey and personal than hotels. In many cases, you're a guest at the innkeeper's home. Some are historic homes or inns decorated with antiques, quilts, art and other period furnishings; others offer simple but comfortable accommodations. Before booking, ask whether rooms have telephones or televisions and whether bathrooms are private. Ask about breakfast, too. The meal is included in the price but may be anything from a few muffins to a multicourse feast. Guests may be served at a common table, a private table or in their rooms.

Arizona Association of Bed & Breakfast Inns
P.O. Box 7186, Phoenix, AZ 85011
Tel: 800-284-2589.
Bed and Breakfast of New Mexico
PO Box 2805, Santa Fe, NM 87504
Tel: (505) 982-3332.
Bed and Breakfast Inns of Utah
PO Box 3066, Park City, UT
Tel: (801) 645-8068
Bed & Breakfast Southwest
P.O. Box 51198, Phoenix AZ 85076
Tel: (602) 947-9704.

ARIZONA

Adobe Rose Inn
940 Rose Inn, Tucson AZ
Tel: (520) 318-4644
One-foot-thick pink adobe walls. Built in 1933. Vibrant southwestern style rooms. The host can meet special dietary requests with notice. **$$**
Betsy's Bed and Breakfast
1919 Rock Castle Drive
Prescott, AZ 86301
Tel: (520) 445-0123
Modern redwood house set on a hillside above Prescott. Amenities: private baths, breakfast, parking. **$–$$**
Cathedral Rock Lodge
61 Los Amigos Lane
Sedona, AZ 86336
Tel: (520) 282-7608
Large country home near

mountains. Amenities: private baths, some rooms with television, breakfast, parking. **$$–$$$**
Dierker House
423 W. Cherry, Flagstaff, AZ 86001
Tel: (520) 774-3249
Well-appointed old home in historic district. Amenities: private and shared baths, parking, breakfast. **$**
Elysian Grove Market
400 W. Simpson, Tucson AZ
Tel: (520) 628-1522
Adobe built in 1920s as corner market in Historic Barrio district. Four rooms furnished with folk art. Two rooms converted from old wine cellar. **$$**
Kennedy House
2075 Upper Red Rock Loop Road
Sedona, AZ 86336
Tel: (520) 282-1624
A comfortable, contemporary home near Sedona's Red Rock Crossing. Amenities: private baths, breakfast, parking, guided nature hikes. **$$**
Maricopa Manor
15 W. Pasadena Avenue, Phoenix
AZ 85013
Tel: (602) 274-6302
Spanish-style home built in the 1920s and furnished with antiques and art. Amenities: all rooms are suites with air conditioning, television and private bath; breakfast, pool, spa, gardens, parking. **$$–$$$**

Price Guide

Price categories for bed and breakfast are based on the average cost of a double room per night.
$ $50 or less
$$ $50–150
$$$ $150–150
$$$$ $150 or more

COLORADO

Country Sunshine Bed and Breakfast
35130 Highway 550 North,
Durango, CO 81301
Tel: (970) 247-2853 or toll free
800-383-2853
Comfortable ranch home on the Animas River 12 miles north of

Durango. Amenities: private baths, hot tub, breakfast, parking. **$$**
Logwood Bed and Breakfast
35060 Highway 550
Durango, CO 81301
Tel: (970) 259-4396
A comfortable, western-style log home set on 15 acres on the Animas River. Amenities: suite with fireplace and television, breakfast and deserts, fishing, hiking, parking. **$$**

New Mexico

Adobe Abode
202 Chapelle, Santa Fe
NM 87501
Tel: (505) 983-3133
Historic adobe home with eclectic decor three blocks from the Plaza. Amenities: television, private bath, some rooms with fires and private patios, breakfast, parking. **$$$**
La Posada de Chimayo
PO Box 463
Chimayo, NM 87522
Tel: (505) 351-4605
A traditional adobe with brick floors and viga ceilings near a charming Hispanic village. Amenities: private baths, breakfast, fireplaces, parking. **$$**
Mabel Dodge Luhan House
PO Box 3400, Taos, NM 87571
Tel: (505) 758-9456
This lovely bed and breakfast inn is the former home of Mabel Dodge Luhan, socialite and patron of the arts whose guests included D.H. Lawrence and Georgia O'Keeffe. Amenities: parking, breakfast, hot tub, fireplaces; no in-room televisions or telephones. **$$–$$$$**
Water Street Inn
427 W. Water Street
Santa Fe, NM 87501
Tel: (505) 984-1193
A comfortable, Southwestern-style inn within walking distance of the Plaza. Amenities: air conditioning, television, private baths, breakfast, fireplaces. **$$–$$$$**

UTAH

Bluff Bed and Breakfast
PO Box 158, Bluff, UT 84512
Tel: (801) 672-2220

Contemporary home set on 17 acres near the San Juan River in southern Utah's red-rock country. Amenities: private baths, breakfast, parking. No credit cards. **$$**

Seven Wives Inn
217 N. 100 West
St George, UT 84770
Tel: (801) 628-3737
A Comfortable inn located in town near the Brigham Young house and within driving distance of Zion and Bryce Canyon national parks. Amenities: air conditioning, television, private bath, breakfast, pool, parking. **$$–$$$**

O'Toole's Under the Eaves Guest House
980 Zion Park Blvd
Springdale, UT 84767
Tel: (801) 772-3457
Historic stone cottage near the entrance to Zion National Park with air conditioning, private and shared baths, breakfast, parking. **$$–$$$**

Dude Ranches

Dude ranches range from working cattle operations with basic accommodation to rustic resorts with swimming pools, tennis courts and other amenities. Most ranches offer horseback riding and lessons, guided pack trips, entertainment like rodeos, square dances and storytellers, and plenty of hearty food. For more information and an extensive list of dude ranches contact:

Dude Ranchers Association
PO Box 471, LaPorte, CO 80535
Tel: (970) 223-8440.

Price Guide

The price categories for dude ranches indicate weekly rates per person including lodging, meals and activities. Rates may vary depending on season and size of party. Some ranches offer daily rates and family/children's rates.

$$	$1,000–$1,500
$$$	$1,500–$2,500
$$$$	$2,500–$3,000
$$$$$	$3,000–$3,500
$$$$$$	$3,500 or more

ARIZONA

Grapevine Canyon Ranch
PO Box 302, Pearce, AZ 85625
Tel: (520) 826-3185 or toll free 800-245-9202
In southern Arizona's Dragoon Mountains, this is a working cattle ranch with guest cabins and *casitas*. Amenities: horseback riding and instruction, pool, hot tub, cookouts, fishing, entertainment. **$–$$**

Lazy K Bar Guest Ranch
8401 N. Scenic Drive
Tucson, AZ 85743
Tel: (520) 744-3050 or toll free 800-321-7018
Guests stay in cabins in the Tucson Mountains overlooking the Santa Cruz Valley. Amenities: horseback riding and instruction, pool, spa, tennis courts, volleyball, basketball and other activities, ranch store, entertainment. **$**

Tanque Verde Guest Ranch,
14301 E. Speedway Blvd
Tucson, AZ 85748
Tel: (520) 296-6275 or 800-234-3833
Casitas at this former stagecoach station situated at the base of the Rincon Mountains. Amenities: horseback riding and instruction, pools, tennis, cookouts, outdoor sports, entertainment. **$$$–$$$$$**

White Stallion Ranch
9251 W. Twin Peaks Road
Tucson, AZ 85743
Tel: (520) 297-0252 or toll free 800-782-5546
A 3,000-acre cattle ranch bordering Saguaro National Park in southern Arizona. Amenities: horseback riding, pool, tennis, hot tub, petting zoo, hayrides, cookouts. No credit cards. **$$–$$$$**

COLORADO

Colorado Trails Ranch
12161 County Road 240
Durango, CO 81301
Tel: (970) 247-5055 or toll free 800-323-3833
Cabins in the San Juan Mountains, southwest Colorado. Amenities: horseback riding and instruction, tennis, pool, shooting, water-skiing, river rafting, fishing, children's counselors. **$$$$–$$$$$**

Lake Mancos Ranch
42688 County Road
Mancos, CO 81328
Tel: (970) 533-7900
Cabins and ranch house at the base of the La Plata Mountains near Mesa Verde National Park with horseback riding and instruction, pool, hot tub, fishing, children's program, entertainment. **$$**

Wilderness Trails Ranch
1776 County Road 302
Durango, CO 81301
Tel: (970) 247-0722 or toll free 800-527-2624
Authentic log cabins surrounded by wilderness area in the Pine River Valley near Lake Vallecito, offering horseback riding and instruction, pack trips, pool, water-skiing, fishing, children's program, recreation room, guided trips, rafting, boating, entertainment. **$$**

Wit's End Guest Ranch and Resort
254 County Road 500
Bayfield, CO 81122
Tel: (970) 884-4113
Located in the Vallecito Valley northeast of Durango, the ranch offers beautifully appointed log cabins and a main lodge. Amenities: horseback riding and instruction, pool, tennis, hot tubs, fishing, biking, pack trips, entertainment, guided hikes, children's program. **$$$$$**

NEW MEXICO

The Lodge at Chama
PO Box 127
Chama, NM 87520
Tel: (505) 756-2133
A rustic but elegant lodge with private rooms located about 100 miles (160 km) north of Santa Fe. Amenities: guided horseback riding, fishing, hunting, shooting. **$$$$**

Los Pinos Ranch
Route 3, Box 8
Tererro, NM 87573
Tel: (505) 757-6213 or (winter) 505-757-6679
Rustic lodge and cabins on the Pecos River in the Sangre de Cristo Mountains with horseback riding, fishing, hiking. No credit cards. **$**

UTAH

Pack Creek Ranch
PO Box 1270
Moab, UT 84532
Tel: (801) 259-5505
A 300-acre ranch in the foothills of the La Sal Mountains near Arches and Canyonlands national parks. Amenities: horseback riding, pack trips, hiking, pool, fishing. (Riding extra.) **$**

Camping

Most tent and RV sites in national and state parks and in national forests are available on a first-come, first-served basis, although increasingly campground space in popular national parks are on a reservation basis. Arrive as early as possible to reserve a campsite. Campgrounds fill early during the busy summer season (spring, fall and winter in the desert parks). A limited number of campsites in the most popular parks may be reserved in advance. Contact the parks for information on availability. Fees are usually charged for campsites. Backcountry permits may be required for wilderness hiking and camping.

There are hundreds of private campgrounds, too, some with swimming pools, RV hookups, showers and other facilities. The largest network is:
Kampgrounds of America (KOA)
PO Box 30558
Billings, MT 59114
Tel: (406) 248-7444.

Where to Eat

What To Eat

Southwestern cuisine is as varied and interesting as the land itself. A single dish may include a savory mix of red and green chilies, yellow and blue cornmeal, a dark brown mound of beans with snowy sour cream, a pile of shredded lettuce, an improbably neon-green whip called *guacamole* with salty fried tortilla chips stuck in like banners, and a brightly colored sauce of red tomatoes, green chilies, coriander and white onions.

A couple of local customs to keep in mind: you may be asked by your waiter if you prefer red or green chilies (green ones tend to be a bit milder); and traditional New Mexican meals are usually served with *sopapillas*, a puffy fried dough eaten with honey.

In addition to the native dishes, large towns like Santa Fe, Albuquerque, Phoenix and Tucson offer everything from pasta parlors to sushi. Many of the most interesting restaurants have built their reputations on blending Southwestern flavors with a variety of international cuisines. Still, it's hard to go wrong with the traditional repertoire: *enchiladas*, *tacos*, *burritos*, *posole*, *guacamole* and lots of red-hot chilies.

Restaurant Listing

ARIZONA

Blue Burrito Grille
Biltmore Plaza, 3118 E
Camelback Road
Phoenix, AZ
Tel: (602) 955-9596
Mexican cuisine with a healthy bent.
$–$$

Cafe Express
Flagstaff, AZ
Tel: (520) 774-0541
Lively and popular with hip college crowd; good baked goods and vegetarian dishes. **$**

Cafe Terra Cotta
4310 N. Campbell Avenue
Tucson, AZ
Tel: (520) 577-8100
Imaginative Southwestern dishes with a nouvelle influence. **$–$$**

Cafe Terra Cotta
6166 N. Scottsdale Road
Scottsdale, AZ
Tel: (602) 948-8700
Low-key like the original in Tucson, with extensive menu peppered with Southwestern twists.

Christopher's
2398 E. Camelback Road
Phoenix, AZ
Tel: (602) 957-3214
Formal, intimate, contemporary French dining. Will impress your business associates, in-laws or date; the bistro is less expensive and somewhat less formal. **$$–$$$**

Dakota Cafe
6541 E. Tanque Verde Road
Tucson, AZ
Tel: (520) 298-7188
Popular cafe with broad menu and vegetarian dishes. **$**

Depot Cantina
300 S. Ash Avenue, Tempe, AZ
Tel: (602) 966-6677
A fun place in a renovated train station with tasty Mexican standards. **$**

Ed Debevic's Short Orders Deluxe
2102 E. Highland, Phoenix, AZ
Tel: (602) 956-2760
Old-fashioned bustling diner with the usual almost-like-mom's fare – burgers, fries, meat loaf, etc. **$**

El Minuto
354 S. Main Avenue, Tucson, AZ
Tel: (520) 882-4145
Spicy and filling Mexican food in a stripped-down *cantina* popular with locals. **$**

Janos
150 N. Main Avenue, Tucson, AZ
520-884-9426
Inventive French-Southwestern cuisine served in a lovely 19th-century adobe. **$$**

Jean Claude's Petit Cafe
7340 E
Shoeman Lane
Scottsdale, AZ
Tel: (602) 947-5288
Contemporary French bistro good
for a romantic night out. **$–$$**

Rox Sand
2594 E
Camelback Road
Phoenix, AZ
Tel: (602) 381-0444
A hip, fashionable restaurant
offering imaginative combinations
of international cuisines. **$$**

The Stockyards
5001 E
Washington Street
Phoenix, AZ
Tel: (602) 273-7378
Steakhouse with 19th-century decor
and Old West specialties like Rocky
Mountain Oysters (the bits you
remove to make a bull into a steer)
and excellent steaks. **$–$$**

Shogun
12615 N. Tatum Blvd
Scottsdale, AZ
Tel: (602) 953-3264
A good choice for sushi
tempura and other Japanese
specialties when you tire of
Southwestern cooking. **$–$$**

Tomaso's
3225 E. Camelback Road
Phoenix, AZ
Tel: (602) 956-0836
Fine Italian food in a friendly,
comfortable setting. **$–$$**

Vincent on Camelback
3930 E. Camelback Road
Phoenix, AZ
Tel: (602) 224-0225
Elegant but not stuffy, this is

Price Guide

Price categories indicate the
approximate cost of dinner for
two excluding beverages, tax
and tip. The standard tip is 15
percent, more for exceptional
service or a large party. In some
cases, the gratuity may be
included in the bill.

$	less than $40
$$	$40–100
$$$	$100 or more

regarded by some as one of the
finest restaurants in the Southwest,
combining French and Mexican
tastes. **$$**

COLORADO

Henry's
Strater Hotel, 699 Main Avenue
Durango, CO 81301
Tel: (970) 247-4431 or toll free
800-247-4431
Hotel restaurant featuring steak
and seafood in a fine Victorian
building. **$–$$**

Palace Grill
1 Depot Place
Durango, CO
Tel: (970) 247-2018
Filling American dishes served in a
historic Victorian building. **$–$$**

NEW MEXICO

Anasazi Restaurant
113 Washington Avenue, Santa Fe
Tel: (505) 988-3236

A completely satisfying
Southwestern eating experience
with some American Indian accents.
$–$$

Apple Tree
123 Bent Street, Taos, NM
Tel: (505) 758-1900
Fine Southwestern and International
cuisine in a romantic setting. **$$**

Assets Grill Brewing Company
6910 Montgomery NE
Albuquerque, NM
Tel: (505) 889-6400
A mixture of ethnic cuisines with a
New Mexican twist in a lively
country setting; a great selection of
beers including a brew made at the
restaurant. **$**

Cafe Pasqual's
121 Don Gaspar Street
Santa Fe, NM
Tel: (505) 983-9340
Innovative
International/Southwestern cuisine
very popular with both residents
and tourists. **$$**

Conrad's
125 2nd Street NW
Albuquerque, NM 87102
Tel: (505) 242-9090
Hotel restaurant serving imaginative
Mexican fare in comfy modern
atmosphere. **$**

Coyote Cafe
132 W
Water Street
Santa Fe, NM
Tel: (505) 983-1615
American and New Mexican fare
served in an imaginatively
decorated site (a former bus depot);
extremely popular due in part to the
owner's cookbooks. **$$**

Geronimo
724 Canyon Road
Santa Fe
Tel: (505) 982-1500
In Santa Fe's art gallery district
Geronimo is in a 1756 adobe
building and has several small
dining rooms, assuring some
intimacy, Food is diverse
and delicious. **$$–$$$**

M & J Sanitary Tortilla Factory
403 2nd Street SW
Albuquerque, NM
Tel: (505) 242-4890
Authentic and filling Mexican dishes
in a casual diner-like setting. **$**

Drinking

Laws governing liquor sales vary
from state to state. The legal
drinking age is 21. In Arizona and
Nevada, state laws permit sale of
liquor by the bottle or glass in any
licensed establishment. In New
Mexico, bottled liquor is sold in
drug, grocery and liquor stores
and sold by the glass in bars and
other licensed establishments. In
Colorado, you can find bottled

liquor in liquor stores and most
drug stores, which also may sell
by the glass, with some
restrictions. Liquor sales in Utah
are made at state licensed stores.
All package stores (where liquor is
not consumed on the premises)
are closed on Sunday and
holidays. Beer is available at most
restaurants, grocery and drug
stores seven days a week.

Michael's Kitchen
305 Paseo del Pueblo Norte
Taos, NM
Tel: (505) 758-4178
Warm, homey place with a tasty selection of filling American and New Mexican standards. **$**

Monte Vista Fire Station
3201 Central Avenue NE
Albuquerque, NM
Tel: (505) 255-2424
Carefully prepared American cuisine in a restored firehouse. **$–$$**

Natural Cafe
1494 Cerrillos Road
Santa Fe, NM
Tel: (505) 983-1411
Healthy and vegetarian menu served in a cozy, arty setting. **$**

Pink Adobe
406 Old Santa Fe Trail
Santa Fe, NM
Tel: (505) 983-7712
A very popular restaurant in a lovely historic building featuring New Mexican and Continental dishes and a good wine list. **$–$$**

Rancho de Chimayo
Chimayo, NM
Tel: (505) 351-4444
An old-fashioned hacienda-style restaurant with traditional New Mexican fare, A favorite for travelers visiting the Santuario de Chimayo. **$**

Santacafe
231 Washington Avenue
Santa Fe, NM
Tel: (505) 984-1788
Understated elegance is the theme at this historic adobe featuring a wide-ranging menu with New Mexican flare. **$$**

66 Diner
1405 Central Avenue NE
Albuquerque, NM
Tel: (505) 247-1421
This is located on old Route 66 near the University of New Mexico, this spiffy diner is a walk down memory lane. **$**

Tomasita's
500 S. Guadalupe Street
Santa Fe, NM
Tel: (505) 983-5721
A spicy selection of New Mexican dishes at the former Santa Fe Railroad terminal; lively and informal, popular with both locals and tourists. **$**

Villa Fontana
Highway 522, Taos, NM
Tel: (505) 758-5800
Gourmet northern Italian cuisine at a lovely country restaurant. **$$**

Wild and Natural Cafe
812 Paseo del Pueblo Norte
Taos, NM
Tel: (505) 751-0480
A savory selection of vegetarian dishes, with Southwestern and Asian specialties. **$**

UTAH

Adriana's Restaurant
S100 West
Cedar City, UT
Tel: (801) 865-1234
Romantic old-English atmosphere with steaks, seafood and pasta. **$–$$**

Bit and Spur Saloon and Mexican Restaurant
1212 Zion Park Blvd
Springdale, UT
Tel: (801) 772-3498
Fine Mexican food in a casual atmosphere, near the entrance to Zion National Park. **$**

Capitol Reef Cafe
360 W. Main Street
Torrey, UT
Tel: (801) 425-3271
Friendly restaurant with fresh and natural foods, and plenty of vegetarian dishes. **$**

New Garden Cafe
138 S, Main
Hurricane, UT
Tel: (801) 635-9825
An informal eatery with tasty burgers, enchiladas, pizza and a few choices for vegetarians. **$**

Libby Lorraines
1035 S
Valley View Drive, St George, UT
Tel: (801) 673-7190
Casual Italian. **$**

Grand Old Ranch House
1266 N, Highway 191
Moab, UT
Tel: (801) 259-5753
A steakhouse with some seafood and German specialties; the building is listed on the National Register of Historic Places. **$**

Culture

Performing Arts

ARIZONA

Arizona Theater Company
403 E. 14th Street, Tucson, AZ 85701, tel: (520) 884-8210.

Ballet Arizona
3645 E. Indian School, Phoenix, AZ 85018, tel: (602) 381-0184.

Phoenix Symphony
3707 N. 7th Street, Phoenix, AZ 85014, tel: (602) 264-6363.

Scottsdale Center for the Arts
7380 E. 2nd Street, Scottsdale, AZ 8525, tel: (602) 994-2787.

Tucson Symphony
443 S. Stone Avenue, Tucson, AZ 85701, tel: (502) 792-9155.

NEW MEXICO

Albuquerque Civic Light Opera Association
4201 Ellison NE, Albuquerque, NM 87109, tel: (505) 345-6577.

New Mexico Symphony Orchestra
3301 Menaul Blvd, Albuquerque, NM 87107, tel: (505) 881-9590.

Santa Fe Symphony Orchestra
200 W. Marcy, Santa Fe, NM 87501, tel: (505) 983-3530.

Santa Fe Opera
PO Box 2408, Santa Fe, NM 87504, tel: (505) 986-5900.

Native American Cultures

Cultural sensitivity is vital in American Indian Country. Because some Indian people may feel uncomfortable or ambivalent about the presence of outsiders, it is very important to be on your best behavior. Below are a few "dos" and "don'ts" to keep in mind.

• Don't use racist terms. Referring to an Indian as chief, redskin, squaw, buck, Pocahontas, Hiawatha or other off-color terms is highly offensive.

• Abide by all rules and regulations while on Indian land and at Indian events. These may include prohibitions on photography, sketching, taking notes, video and audio recording. In some cases a photography fee may be required. If you wish to take an individual's picture, you must ask permission first (a gratuity may be requested).

• Respect all restricted areas. These are usually posted, but ask permission before hiking into wilderness or archaeological areas, driving on back roads, wandering around villages, and entering ceremonial structures.

• Try to be unobtrusive. Remember that you are a guest at Indian communities and events. Be polite and accommodating. In general, it is better to be too formal than too casual.

• Don't ask intrusive questions or interrupt during Indian ceremonies or dances. Even if an Indian event is not explicitly religious (such as a powwow), it may have a spiritual component. Show the same respect at Indian ceremonies that you would at any other religious service. At all events, try to maintain a low profile. Do not talk loudly, push to the front of a crowd, block anyone's view, or sit in chairs that do not belong to you.

• Keep in mind that many Indian people have a looser sense of time than non-Indians. You may hear jokes about "Indian time." Prepare for long delays before ceremonies.

Arizona

Ak Chin Indian Community, Route 2, Box 27, Maricopa, AZ 85239, tel: (520) 568-2227.
Cocopah Tribe, PO Bin G, Somerton, AZ 85250, tel: (602) 627-2102.
Colorado River Indian Tribes, Route 1, Box 23B, Parker, AZ 85344, tel: (520) 669-9211.
Gila River Pima-Maricopa Indian Community, PO Box 97, Sacaton,

AZ 85247, tel: (520) 562-3311.
Havasupai Tribe, PO Box 10, Supai, AZ 86435, tel: (520) 448-2961.
Hopi Tribe, PO Box 123, Kykotsmovi, AZ 86039, tel: (520) 734-2445.
Hualapai Tribe, PO Box 179, Peach Springs, AZ 86434, tel: (520) 769-2216.
Kaibab Band of Paiute Indians, Tribal Affairs Building, HC 65, Box 2, Fredonia, AZ 86022, tel: (520) 643-7245.
Navajo Nation, PO Box 308, Window Rock, AZ 86515, tel: (520) 871-6352.
Pascua Yaqui Tribe, 7474 S. Camino de Oeste, Tucson, AZ 85746, tel: (520) 883-5000.
Quechan Tribe, PO Box 11352, Yuma, AZ 85364, tel: (619) 572-0213.
Salt River Pima-Maricopa Indian Community, Route 1, Box 216, Scottsdale, AZ 85256, Tel: (602) 941-7277.
San Carlos Apache Tribe, PO Box 0, San Carlos, AZ 85550, tel: (520) 475-2361.
Tohono O'odham Nation, PO Box 837, Sells, AZ 85634, tel: (520) 383-2221.
Tonto Apache Tribe, Tonto Reservation No. 30, Payson, AZ 85541, tel: (520) 474-5000.
White Mountain Apache Tribe, PO Box 700, White River, AZ 85941, tel: (520) 338-4346.
Yavapai-Apache Tribe, PO Box 1188, Camp Verde, AZ 86322, tel: (520) 567-3649.

Colorado
Southern Ute Tribe, PO Box 737, Ignacio, CO 81137, tel: (970) 563-4525.
Ute Mountain Ute Tribe, Towaoc, CO 81334, tel: (970) 565-3751.

Nevada
Las Vegas Paiute Tribe, 1 Paiute Drive, Las Vegas, NV 89106, tel: (702) 386-3926.

New Mexico
Acoma Pueblo, PO Box 309, Acomita, NM 87034, tel: (505) 552-6604.
Cochiti Pueblo, Po Box 70, Cochiti,

NM 87041, tel: (505) 465-2244.
Isleta Pueblo, PO Box 317, Isleta, NM 87022, tel: (505) 869-3111.
Jemez Pueblo, PO Box 100, Jemez, NM 87024, tel: (505) 834-7359.
Jicarilla Apache Tribe, PO Box 507, Dulce, NM 87528, tel: (505) 759-3242.
Laguna Pueblo, PO Box 194, Laguna Pueblo, NM, tel: (505) 552-6654.
Mescalero Apache Tribe, PO Box 176, Mescalero, NM 88340, tel: (505) 671-4495.
Nambe Pueblo, PO Box 117, Santa Fe, NM 87501, tel: (505) 455-2036.
Picuris Pueblo, PO Box 127, Penasco, NM 87553, tel: (505) 587-2519.
Pojoaque Pueblo, Route 11, Box 71, Santa Fe, NM 87501, tel: (505) 455-2278.
Sandia Pueblo, PO Box 6008, Bernalillo, NM 87004, tel: (505) 867-3317.
San Ildefonso Pueblo, PO Box 315-A, Santa Fe, NM 87501, tel: (505) 455-2273.
San Juan Pueblo, PO Box 1099, San Juan, NM 87566, tel: (505) 852-4400.
Santa Ana Pueblo, Star Route Box 37, Bernalillo, NM 87532, tel: (505) 867-3301.
Santa Clara Pueblo, PO Box 580, Espanola, NM 87532, tel: (505) 753-7326.
Santo Domingo Pueblo, PO Box 99, Santo Domingo, NM 87052, tel: (505) 465-2214.
Taos Pueblo, PO Box 1846, Taos, NM 87571, tel: (505) 758-8626.
Tesuque Pueblo, Route 11, Box 1, Santa Fe, NM 87501, tel: (505) 983-2667.
Zia Pueblo, General Delivery, San Ysidro, NM 87053, tel: (505) 867-3304.
Zuni Pueblo, PO Box 339, Zuni, NM 87327, tel: (505) 782-4481.

Utah
Paiute Indian Tribe of Utah, 600 North 100 East, Cedar City, UT 84720, tel: (801) 586-1112.
Ute Tribe, PO Box 190, Fort Duchesne, UT 84026, tel: (801) 722-5141.

Calendar of Events

January
Arizona National Livestock Show, 1826 W. McDowell Road, Phoenix, AZ 85007. Tel: (602) 258-8568.

Parada del Sol and Rodeo, Scottsdale Chamber of Commerce, 7343 Scottsdale Mall, Scottsdale, AZ 85251. Tel: (602) 945-8481.

Phoenix Open Golf Tournament, Scottsdale Chamber of Commerce, 7343 Scottsdale Mall, Scottsdale, AZ 85251. Tel: (602) 945-8481.

San Ildefonso Feast Day, San Ildefonso Pueblo, PO Box 315-A, Santa Fe, NM 87501 Tel: (505) 455-2273.

Snowdown in Durango and Purgatory, Durango Chamber Resort Association, 111 S. Camino del Rio, Durango, CO 81301 Tel: (970) 247-0312.

Southwestern Livestock Show and Rodeo, PO Box 10239, El Paso, TX 79993. Tel: (915) 532-1401.

Turtle Dance, Taos Pueblo, PO Box 1846, Taos, NM 87571 Tel: (505) 758-8626.

February
Las Vegas International Marathon, Las Vegas Convention and Visitors Authority, Convention Center, 3150 Paradise Road, Las Vegas, NV 89109. Tel: (702) 892-0711 or toll free 800-332-5333.

Los Comanches Dance, Taos Pueblo, PO Box 1846, Taos, NM 87571. Tel: (505) 758-8626.

O'odham Tash Indian Celebration, Tohono O'odham Nation, PO Box 837, Sells, AZ 85634 Tel: (520) 383-2221.

Tucson Rodeo – La Fiesta de los Vaqueros, Tucson Convention & Visitors Bureau, 130 S. Scott Avenue, Tucson, AZ 85701 Tel: (520) 624-1817.

March
Heard Museum Indian Fair and Market, 22 E. Monte Vista Road, Phoenix, AZ 85004 Tel: (602) 252-8848.

San Jose Feast Day, Laguna Pueblo, PO Box 194, Laguna Pueblo, NM Tel: (505) 552-6654.

April
Albuquerque Founder's Day, Albuquerque Convention and Visitors Bureau, PO Box 26866, Albuquerque, NM 87125 Tel: (505) 243-3696 or toll free 800-284-2282.

Gathering of Nations Powwow, Albuquerque Convention and Visitors Bureau, PO Box 26866, Albuquerque, NM 87125 Tel: (505) 243-3696 or toll free 800-284-2282.

Institute of American Indian Arts Powwow, 1369 Cerillos Road, Santa Fe, NM 87501 Tel: (505) 988-6463.

San Xavier Pageant and Fiesta, Tucson Convention & Visitors Bureau, 130 S. Scott Avenue, Tucson, AZ 85701 Tel: (520) 624-1817.

May
Buckskinner Rendezvous, Arizona Office of Tourism, 1100 W. Washington Street, Phoenix, AZ 85007. Tel: (602) 542-8687 or toll free 800-842-8257.

Cinco de Mayo Celebration, Albuquerque Convention and Visitors Bureau, PO Box 26866, Albuquerque, NM 87125 Tel: (505) 243-3696 or toll free 800-284-2282.

Fiesta de Santa Fe Baile de Mayo, Santa Fe Convention & Visitors Bureau, PO Box 909, Santa Fe, NM 87501. Tel: (505) 984-6760.

Iron Horse Bicycle Classic, Durango Chamber Resort Association, 111 S. Camino del Rio, Durango, CO 81301 Tel: (970) 247-0312.

Santa Cruz Feast Day, Taos Pueblo, PO Box 1846, Taos, NM 87571 Tel: (505) 758-8626.

June
Durango Pro. Rodeo Series, Durango Chamber Resort Association, 111 S. Camino del Rio, Durango, CO 81301 Tel: (970) 247-0312.

St George Arts Festival, Color Country, 906 N. 1400 West, St George, UT 84771. Tel: (801) 628-4171 or toll free 800-233-8824.

Fort Union Trading Post Rendezvous, Fort Union Trading Post National Historic Site, RR 3, Box 71, Williston, ND 58801 Tel: (701) 572-9083.

Old Fort Days, Fort Sumner State Monument, PO Box 356, Fort Sumner, NM 88119 Tel: (505) 355-2573.

Old Miners Day, Chloride, Arizona Office of Tourism, 1100 W. Washington Street, Phoenix, AZ 85007. Tel: (602) 542-8687 or toll free 800-842-8257.

San Antonio Feast Day–Comanche Dance, San Ildefonso Pueblo, PO Box 315-A, Santa Fe, NM 87501 Tel: (505) 455-2273.

San Felipe Fiesta, Albuquerque Convention and Visitors Bureau, PO Box 26866, Albuquerque, NM 87125. Tel: (505) 243-3696 or toll-free 800-284-2282.

San Juan Feast Day, Taos Pueblo, PO Box 1846, Taos, NM 87571 Tel: (505) 758-8626.

Santa Fe Trail Rendezvous, Raton Chamber of Commerce, PO Box 1211, Raton, NM 87740 Tel: (505) 445-3689.

Territorial Days, Prescott Chamber of Commerce, 117 W. Goodwin Street, Prescott, AZ 86302 Tel: (520) 445-2000.

July
Dixie Folkfest, Color Country, 906 N. 1400 West, St George, UT 84771. Tel: (801) 628-4171 or toll free 800-233-8824.

Durango Cowgirl Classic, Durango Chamber Resort Association, 111 S. Camino del Rio, Durango, CO 81301. Tel: (970) 247-0312.

El Paso Festival, El Paso Arts Alliance, 333 E. Missouri Street, El Paso, TX 79901 Tel: (915) 533-1700.

Frontier Days and World's Oldest Rodeo, Prescott Chamber of Commerce, 117 W. Goodwin Street, Prescott, AZ 86302 Tel: (520) 445-2000.

Mescalero Festival, Mescalero Apache Tribe, PO Box 176, Mescalero, NM 88340 Tel: (505) 671-4495.

Soldiering on the Santa Fe Trail, Fort Union National Monument, PO

Box 127, Watrous, NM 87753
Tel: (505) 425-8025.
Spanish Market, Spanish Colonial
Arts Society, PO Box 1611,
Santa Fe, NM 87504
Tel: (505) 983-4038.
Taos Fiesta, Taos County Chamber
of Commerce, PO Drawer I, Taos,
NM 87571
Tel: (505) 758-3873 or toll free
800-732-8267.
Taos Pueblo Powwow, PO Box
1846, Taos, NM 87571
Tel: (505) 758-8626.
Utah Shakespearean Festival,
Southern Utah University, Cedar
City, UT. Tel: (801) 586-7878.

August
Fiesta de San Agustin, Tucson
Convention & Visitors Bureau, 130
S. Scott Avenue, Tucson, AZ 85701
Tel: (520) 624-1817.
Flagstaff Festival in the Pines,
Flagstaff Convention and Visitors
Bureau, 211 W. Aspen Avenue,
Flagstaff, AZ 86001
Tel: (520) 779-7611.
Indian Market, Santa Fe
Convention & Visitor Bureau, PO
Box 909, Santa Fe, NM 87501
Tel: (505) 984-6760.
Old Lincoln Days, New Mexico
Tourism, Lamy Building, 491 Old
Santa Fe Trail, Santa Fe, NM 87503
Tel: toll-free 800-545-2040.
**Palace Mountain Man Rendezvous
and Buffalo Roast**, Museum of New
Mexico, Palace of the Governors,
105 W. Palace Avenue, Santa Fe,
NM 87501
Tel: (505) 827-6483.
Santa Clara Feast Day, Santa Clara
Pueblo, PO Box 580, Espanola, NM
87532. Tel: (505) 753-7326.

September
Fiesta de Santa Fe, Santa Fe
Convention & Visitor Bureau, PO
Box 909, Santa Fe, NM 87501
Tel: (505) 984-6760.
Ghost Dancer All-Indian Rodeo,
Durango Chamber Resort
Association, 111 S. Camino del Rio,
Durango, CO 81301
Tel: (970) 247-0312.
Navajo Nation Fair, Navajo Nation
Tourism Office, PO Box 663,
Window Rock, AZ 86515

Tel: (520) 871-6436.
New Mexico State Fair and Rodeo,
New Mexico Tourism, Lamy Building,
491 Old Santa Fe Trail, Santa Fe,
NM 87503
Tel: toll free 800-545-2040.
Old Taos Trade Fair, Taos County
Chamber of Commerce, PO Drawer I,
Taos, NM 87571
Tel: (505) 758-3873 or toll free
800-732-8267.
San Esteban Feast Day, Acoma
Pueblo, PO Box 309, Acomita, NM
87034. Tel: (505) 552-6604.
San Geronimo Feast Day, Taos
Pueblo, PO Box 1846, Taos, NM
87571. Tel: (505) 758-8626.
Southern Utah Folklife Festival,
Zion National Park, Springdale, UT
84767-1099. Tel: (801) 772-3256.

October
**Albuquerque International Balloon
Fiesta**, Albuquerque Convention
and Visitors Bureau, PO Box
26866, Albuquerque, NM 87125
Tel: (505) 243-3696 or toll free
800-284-2282.
Apache Days, Globe, San Carlos
Apache Tribe, PO Box 0, San
Carlos, AZ 85550
Tel: (520) 475-2361.
Arizona State Fair, Phoenix & Valley
of the Sun Convention and Visitor
Bureau, 400 E. Van Buren #600,
Phoenix, AZ 85004
Tel: (602) 254-6500.
Helldorado Days, Tombstone Office
of Tourism, PO Box 917,
Tombstone, AZ 85638
Tel: (520) 457-3929 or toll free
800-457-3423.
La Fiesta de los Chiles, Tucson
Convention & Visitors Bureau, 130
S. Scott Avenue, Tucson, AZ 85701
Tel: (520) 624-1817.
**Las Vegas Invitational Golf
Tournament**, Las Vegas Convention
and Visitors Authority, Convention
Center, 3150 Paradise Road, Las
Vegas, NV 89109
Tel: (702) 892-0711 or toll free
800-332-5333.
Northern Navajo Fair, Shiprock,
Navajo Nation Tourism Office, PO
Box 663, Window Rock, AZ 86515
Tel: (520) 871-6436.
Old West Rodeo, Durango Chamber
Resort Association, 111 S. Camino

del Rio, Durango, CO 81301
Tel: (970) 247-0312.
**Tucson Heritage Experience
Festival**, Tucson Convention &
Visitors Bureau, 130 S. Scott
Avenue, Tucson, AZ 85701
Tel: (520) 624-1817 or toll free
800-638-8350.
Utah State Chili Competition, Color
Country, 906 N. 1400 West, St
George, UT 84771. Tel: 801-628-
4171 or toll free 800-233-8824.

November
Celebrity Golf Tournament
Color Country, 906 N. 1400 West,
St George, UT 84771.
Tel: (801) 628-4171 or toll free
800-233-8824.
Indian National Finals Rodeo, New
Mexico Tourism, Lamy Building, 491
Old Santa Fe Trail, Santa Fe, NM
87503. Tel: toll free 800-545-2040.
Thunderbird Balloon Classic,
Phoenix & Valley of the Sun
Convention and Visitor Bureau,
400 E. Van Buren #600, Phoenix,
AZ 85004. Tel: (602) 254-6500.

December
Indian Market, Phoenix & Valley of
the Sun Convention and Visitor
Bureau, 400 E. Van Buren #600,
Phoenix, AZ 85004
Tel: (602) 254-6500.
National Finals Rodeo, Las Vegas
Convention and Visitors Authority,
Convention Center, 3150 Paradise
Road, Las Vegas, NV 89109
Tel: (702) 892-0711 or toll free
800-332-5333.
Red Rock Balloon Rally, Gallup
Convention and Visitors Bureau,
PO Drawer Q, Gallup, NM 87305
Tel: (505) 863-3841.
Sun Carnival, El Paso Convention
and Visitors Bureau, 1 Civic Center
Plaza, El Paso, TX 79940
Tel: (915) 534-0658.
Winter Spanish Market, Santa Fe
Convention & Visitors Bureau,
PO Box 909, Santa Fe, NM 87501
Tel: (505) 984-6760.
Ye Merry Olde Christmas Faire,
Albuquerque Convention and
Visitors Bureau, PO Box 26866,
Albuquerque, NM 87125
Tel: (505) 243-3696 or toll free
800-284-2282.

The Great Outdoors

ARIZONA

Alamo Lake State Park
PO Box 38, Wenden, AZ 85356
Tel: (520) 669-2088.
Apache National Forest
PO Box 640, Springerville, AZ
85938
Tel: (520) 333-4301.
Canyon de Chelly National Monument
PO Box 588, Chinle, AZ 86503
Tel: (520) 674-5436.
Casa Grande National Monument
1100 Ruins Drive, Coolidge
AZ 85228
Tel: (602) 723-3172.
Chiricahua National Monument
Dos Cabezas Route, Box 6500
Willcox, AZ 85643
Tel: (520) 824-3560.
Coronado National Forest
Federal Building, 300 W. Congress
Tucson, AZ 85701
Tel: (520) 670-5798.
Coronado National Memorial
4101 E. Montezuma Canyon Road
Hereford, AZ 85615
Tel: (520) 366-5515.
Dead Horse Ranch State Park
675 Deadhorse Ranch Road
Cottonwood, AZ 86326
Tel: (520) 634-5283.
Fort Bowie National Historic Site
PO Box 158, Bowie, AZ 85605
Tel: (520) 847-2500.
Fort Verde State Historic Park
PO Box 397, Camp Verde
AZ 86322. Tel: (520) 567-3275.
Glen Canyon National Recreation Area. PO Box 1507, Page
AZ 86040. Tel: (520) 608-6404.
Grand Canyon National Park
PO Box 129, Grand Canyon
AZ 86023. Tel: (520) 638-7888.

Hubbell Trading Post National Historic Site
PO Box 150, Ganado, AZ 86505
Tel: (520) 755-3475.
Jerome State Historic Park
PO Box D, Jerome, AZ 86331
Tel: (520) 634-5381.
Lake Havasu State Park
1801 Highway 95, Lake Havasu
AZ 86406. Tel: (520) 855-7851.
Lost Dutchman State Park
Apache Junction, AZ
Tel: (520) 982-4485.
Montezuma Castle National Monument, PO Box 219
Camp Verde, AZ 86322
Tel: (520) 567-3322.
Monument Valley Navajo Tribal Park, Box 93, Monument Valley
UT 84536. Tel: (801) 727-3287.
Navajo National Monument
HC 71, Box 3, Tonalea, AZ 86044-9704. Tel: (520) 672-2366.
Organ Pipe Cactus National Monument, Route 1, Box 100, Ajo
AZ 85321. Tel: (520) 387-6849.
Patagonia Lake State Park
PO Box 274, Patagonia, AZ 85624
Tel: (520) 287-6965.
Petrified Forest National Park
PO Box 2217, Petrified Forest,
AZ 86028. Tel: (520) 524-6228.
Picacho Peak State Park
PO Box 275, Picacho, AZ 85241
Tel: (602) 466-3183.
Pipe Spring National Monument
HC 65, Box 5, Fredonia, AZ 86022

Access Grand Canyon Village and the South Rim Visitor Center are about 85 miles (137 km) from Flagstaff, Arizona, via Highway 180/64. Although only 10 miles (16 km) across the canyon, the North Rim is about 215 miles (346 km) by road from Grand Canyon Village. Take Route 64 east to Cameron, Highway 89/Alt. 89 north to Jacob Lake, then Route 67 south to the North Rim. Visitors can also arrive by air at the Grand Canyon National Park Airport, just outside the park in Tusayan, or by rail from Williams, Arizona, on the Grand Canyon Railway.

If you plan to visit several parks on your vacation, or to return within 12 months, it's worth considering buying a **Golden Eagle Passport**. For $50 this gives unlimited free admission to all the national parks, monuments, recreation areas, etc that charge an entrance fee. It is valid for a year and admits the passholder and family (or all the passengers in your car).
Apply in person at any park which charges an entrance fee, or by mail to:
Golden Eagle Passport, National Park Service, 1100 Ohio Drive SW, Room 138, Washington, DC 20242.

Tel: (520) 643-7105.
Prescott National Forest
344 S. Cortez, Prescott, AZ 86302
Tel: (520) 771-4700.
Riordan State Historic Park
1300 S. Riordan Ranch Street,
Flagstaff, AZ 86001
Tel: (520) 779-4395.
Saguaro National Park
3693 S. Old Spanish Trail, Tucson,
AZ 85730. Tel: (520) 733-5153.
San Xavier del Bac Mission
1950 W. San Xavier, Tucson
AZ 85706. Tel: (520) 294-2624.

Seasons & Hours The South Rim is open year-round; the visitor center is open daily 8am–5pm. (Note: Arizona does not observe Daylight Savings Time.) The North Rim is open May–October.
Entrance Fee Yes.
Handicapped Access South Rim Visitor Center and some shuttle buses. Contact park for free Accessibility Guide.
Activities Scenic drive, backpacking, wildlife-watching, river trips, mule packing, fishing.
Note Grand Canyon is heavily visited most of the year, so apply well in advance for permits, accommodations, and car parking.

Saguaro National Park

Access The Rincon Mountain District visitor center is on South Old Spanish Trail, about 2 miles (3 km) east of Tucson. The Tucson Mountain District information center is on Kinney Road, to the west of Tucson.
Seasons & Hours Both park districts are open daily from sunrise to sunset. The visitor centers are open daily 8am–5pm; closed Christmas.
Entrance Fee Yes, in Rincon Mountain District.
Handicapped Access Visitor centers, picnic areas and trails.
Activities Scenic drive, backpacking, hiking, wildlife-watching, interpretive programs.

Sunset Crater National Monument, Route 3, Box 149, Flagstaff AZ 86004. Tel: (520) 556-7042.
Tombstone Courthouse State Historic Park, 219 Toughnut Street, Tombstone, AZ 85638
Tel: (520) 457-3311.
Tonto National Monument
HC 02, Box 4602, Roosevelt
AZ 85545
Tel: (520) 467-2241.
Tumacacori National Historical Park, PO Box 67, Tumacacori
AZ 85640. Tel: (520) 398-2341.
Tuzigoot National Monument
PO Box 68, Clarkdale, AZ 86324
Tel: (520) 634-5564.
Yuma Territorial Prison State Historic Park, PO Box 10792, Yuma, AZ 85366. Tel: (520) 783-4771.
Walnut Canyon National Monument, Walnut Canyon Road, Flagstaff, AZ 86004-9705
Tel: (520) 526-3367.
Wupatki National Monument
HC 33, Box 444A, Flagstaff, AZ 86004
Tel: (520) 556-7040.

COLORADO

Great Sand Dunes National Monument, 11500 Highway 150, Mosca, CO 81146
Tel: (719) 378-2312.

Hovenweep National Monument
McElmo Route, Cortez, CO 81321
Tel: (970) 529-4465.
Mesa Verde National Park
PO Box 8, Mesa Verde National Park, CO 81330
Tel: (970) 529-4465.

NEVADA

Great Basin National Park
Baker, NV 89311-9702
Tel: (775) 234-7331.
Lake Mead National Recreation Area, 601 Nevada Highway, Boulder City, NV 89005-2426
Tel: (702) 293-8907.

NEW MEXICO

Aztec Ruins National Monument
PO Box 640, Aztec, NM 87410
Tel: (505) 334-6174.
Bandelier National Monument
HCR 1, Box 1, Suite 15
Los Alamos, NM 87544-9701
Tel: (505) 672-3861.
Capulin Volcano National Monument, PO Box 40, Capulin, NM 88414. Tel: (505) 278-2201.
Carlsbad Caverns National Park
3225 National Parks Highway
Carlsbad, NM 88220
Tel: (505) 785-2232.
Carson National Forest, Forest Service Building, Taos, NM 87571
Tel: (505) 758-6200.
Cathedral of St Francis of Assisi
131 Cathedral Plaza, Santa Fe
NM 87501. Tel: (505) 982-5619.

Chaco Culture

Access The park is about 65 miles (107 km) north of Thoreau in northwest New Mexico via Routes 371 and 57. The last 21 miles (34 km) are unpaved road and may be impassable in bad weather. From the north, the park is about 70 miles (113 km) from Bloomfield via Routes 44 and 57. The last 16 miles (26 km) are unpaved and may be impassable in bad weather.
Seasons & Hours The park is open daily year-round. The sites and trails are open sunrise–sunset. The visitor center is open 8am–5pm, extended summer hours; closed Christmas and New Year's Day.
Entrance Fee Yes.
Handicapped Access Two campsites and some trails, with assistance.
Activities Camping, hiking, guided and self-guided tours, interpretive programs.

Carlsbad Caverns

Access The park entrance is 23 miles (37 km) southwest of Carlsbad, NM, and 150 miles (240 km) east of El Paso, TX, via Highway 180/62.
Seasons & Hours The park is open daily year-round, except Christmas. The visitor center is open daily 8am–5.30pm, 8am–7pm in summer.
Entrance Fee Cave entrance.
Handicapped Access Visitor center, large section of Big Room cavern tour, a nature trail and picnic sites.
Activities Cave tours, camping, hiking, wildlife-watching, interpretive programs. Experienced cavers may arrange exploration of backcountry caves by contacting the Cave Resource Office, tel: 505-785-2232.

Chaco Culture National Historical Park, PO Box 220, Nageezi
NM 87037. Tel: (505) 786-7014.
Cibola National Forest
10308 Candelaria NE
Albuquerque, NM 87112
Tel: (505) 761-4650.
Coronado State Monument and Park, PO Box 95, Bernalillo
NM 87004. Tel: (505) 867-5351.
Cristo Rey Church, 1120 Canyon Road, Santa Fe, NM 87501
Tel: (505) 983-8528.
El Malpais National Monument
PO Box 939, Grants, NM 87020
Tel: (505) 285-4641.

El Morro National Monument
Route 2, Box 43, Ramah, NM
87321. Tel: (505) 783-4226.
Fort Selden State Monument, c/o
New Mexico State Parks, 2040 S.
Pacheco, Santa Fe, NM 87501
Tel: (505) 827-7173.
Fort Sumner State Monument
PO Box 356, Fort Sumner
NM 88119
Tel: (505) 355-2573.
Fort Union National Monument
PO Box 127, Watrous, NM 87753
Tel: (505) 425-8025.
**Gila Cliff Dwellings National
Monument**, Route 11, Box 100,
Silver City, NM 88061
Tel: (505) 536-9461.
Gila National Forest
3005 E. Camino del Bosque
Silver City, NM 88061
Tel: (505) 388-8201.
Jemez State Monument, Route 4,
Jemez, NM. Tel: (505) 829-3530.
Kit Carson Memorial State Park
c/o New Mexico State Parks, 2040
S. Pacheco, Santa Fe, NM 87501
Tel: (505) 827-7173.
Lincoln National Forest, Federal
Building, Alamogordo, NM 88310
Tel: (505) 434-7200.
**Lincoln State Monument and
National Landmark**
PO Box 36, Lincoln, NM 88388
Tel: (505) 653-4372.
Loretto Chapel, 211 Old Santa Fe
Trail, Santa Fe, NM 87501
Tel: (505) 984-7971.
Pancho Villa State Park
c/o New Mexico State Parks, 2040
S. Pacheco, Santa Fe, NM 87501
Tel: (505) 827-7173.
Pecos National Historical Park
PO Box 418, Pecos, NM 87552
Tel: (505) 757-6414.
Petroglyph National Monument
PO Box 1293, Albuquerque,
NM 87103. Tel: (505) 768-3316.
Puye Cliff Dwellings, Santa Clara
Pueblo, PO Box 580, Espanola
NM 87532. Tel: (505) 753-7326.
**Salinas Pueblo Missions National
Monument**, PO Box 496,
Mountainair, NM 87036
Tel: (505) 847-2585.
San Francisco de Asis Church
PO Box 72, Rancho de Taos
NM 87557
Tel: (505) 758-2754.

San Miguel Mission, 401 Old Santa
Fe Trail, Santa Fe, NM
Tel: (505) 983-3974.
Santa Fe National Forest
1220 St Francis Drive, Santa Fe
NM 87501
Tel: (505) 438-7800.
Santuario de Chimayo
PO Box 235, Chimayo, NM 87522
Tel: (505) 351-4889.
Santuario de Guadalupe
100 Guadalupe, Santa Fe, NM
Tel: (505) 988-2027.
White Sands National Monument
PO Box 1086
Holloman Air Force Base
NM 88330
Tel: (505) 479-6124.

TEXAS

Big Bend National Park
PO Box 129, Big Bend National
Park, TX 79834-0129
Tel: (915) 477-2251.
**Guadalupe Mountains National
Park**, HC 60, Box 400, Salt Flat, TX
79847-9400. Tel: (915) 828-3251.

UTAH

Anasazi Indian Village State Park
PO Box 1329, Boulder
UT 84716-1329
Tel: (801) 335-7308.
Arches National Park
PO Box 907, Moab, UT 84532
Tel: (801) 259-8161.
Bryce Canyon National Park
Bryce Canyon, PO Box 170001,
UT 84717
Tel: (801) 834-5322.

Canyonlands

Access The Island in the Sky
District is 32 miles (52 km) from
Moab via Highway 313 and Route
313. The Needles District is 80
miles (129 km) from Moab via
Highway 313 and Route 211.
Seasons & Hours The park is
open daily year-round. Vistor
centers are open 8am–4.30pm,
extended hours in spring and fall;
closed Christmas.

Entrance Fee Applies from March
to October.
Handicapped Access Visitor
centers, some campsites and
some overlooks.
Activities Scenic drive, four-wheel
driving, camping, hiking, biking,
float trips, river-running,
backpacking, horseback riding,
rock-climbing, wildlife-watching,
interpretive programs.

Bryce Canyon

Access The park is 80 miles
(129 km) east of Cedar City via
Routes 14, 89 and 12, and 26
miles (42 km) southeast of
Panguitch via Routes 89 and 12.
Seasons & Hours The park is
open daily year-round. The visitor
center is open 8am–4.30pm,
extended hours in summer;
closed Thanksgiving, Christmas
and New Year's Day.
Entrance Fee Yes.
Handicapped Access Visitor
center, some campsites and a
section of Sunset–Sunrise Point
Trail.
Activities Scenic drive, camping,
hiking, backpacking, horseback
riding, wildlife-watching,
interpretive programs.

Canyonlands National Park
2282 SW Resource Blvd, Moab,
UT 84532. Tel: (801) 259-7164.
Capitol Reef National Park
HC 70 Box 15, Torrey, UT 84775
Tel: (801) 425-3791.
Cedar Breaks National Monument
82 N. 100 East, Cedar City, UT
84720. Tel: (801) 586-9451.
Coral Pink Sand Dunes State Park
PO Box 95, Kanab, UT 84741.
Tel: (801) 874-2408.
Dead Horse Point State Park
PO Box 609, Moab, UT 84532.
Tel: (801) 259-6511.
Edge of the Cedars State Park
660 W. 400 North, Blanding, UT
84511. Tel: (801) 678-2238.
**Glen Canyon National Recreation
Area**, PO Box 1507, Page, AZ

86040. Tel: (520) 608-6404.
Grand Staircase
Escalante National Monument, PO
Box 225, Escalante, UT 84726
Tel: (801) 826-4291.
Iron Mission State Park
585 N. Main, Cedar City, UT 84720
Tel: (801) 586-9290.
**Natural Bridges National
Monument**, Box 1, Lake Powell, UT
84533. Tel: (801) 692-1234.
**Timpanogos Cave National
Monument**, RR 3, Box 200,
American Fork, UT 84003-9803.
Tel: (801) 756-5238.
Zion National Park, Springdale, UT
84767-1099. Tel: (801) 772-3256.

Historic Railroads

Cumbres & Toltec Scenic Railroad
PO Box 789, Chama, NM 87520
Tel: (505) 756-2151. Daily late May
to mid October.
**Durango & Silverton Narrow Gauge
Railroad**, 479 Main Avenue,
Durango, CO 81301. Tel: (970)
247-2733. Daily year-round.
Grand Canyon Railway
123 N. San Francisco Street, Suite
210, Flagstaff, AZ 86001
Tel: (520) 773-1976. Daily year-
round.

Zion National Park

Access The Zion Canyon Visitor
Center is 46 miles (74 km) east
of St George via I-15 and Route 9.
The Kolob Canyons Visitor Center
is 18 miles (29 km) south of
Cedar City via Exit 40 from I-15.
Seasons & Hours The park is
open daily year-round. Both
visitor centers are open
8am–7pm in summer, 8am–5pm
rest of the year.
Entrance Fee Yes.
Handicapped Access Visitor
centers, Zion Lodge, three trails,
Riverside Walk (with assistance)
and some campsites at the
South Campground.
Activities Scenic drive, camping,
hiking, biking, backpacking,
backroad driving, horseback
riding, rock climbing, wildlife-
watching, interpretive programs.

Outdoor Activities

Outfitters & Horseback Riding

Adrift Adventures
378 N. Main Street, Moab, UT
Tel: (801) 259-8594.
Float trips on the Colorado and
Green rivers and Jeep tours of
Canyonlands National Park.
ara Lake Powell
Wahweap Lodge, Page, AZ 86040
Tel: (520) 645-2433.
Motorboat and houseboat rentals
on Lake Powell.
Arizona River Runners
PO Box 47788
Phoenix, AZ 85068
Tel: (602) 867-4866.
Float trips on the Colorado River
through the Grand Canyon.
Canyonlands Field Institute
PO Box 68
Moab, UT 84532
Tel: (801) 259-7750.
Guided nature-trips into
Canyonlands and Arches national
parks and surrounding wilderness
areas.
Canyon Trail Rides
PO Box 128
Tropic, UT 84736
Tel: (801) 679-8665.
Trail rides in the national parks and
red-rock country of southern Utah
and northern Arizona.
Four Corners Rafting
PO Box 1032
Buena Vista, CO 81211
Tel: (719) 395-4137 or toll free
800-332-7238.
Raft trips on the Arkansas,
Gunnison and Dolores rivers.
**Goulding's Lodge Monument Valley
Tours**
Highway 163, Goulding
UT 84536
Tel: (801) 727-3231.

Tours of Monument Valley by four-
wheel-drive.
Kokopelli River Adventures
541 W. Cordova Street
Santa Fe, NM
Tel: (505) 983-3734. Float trips on
the Rio Grande and Rio Chama.
**Monument Valley Navajo Tribal
Park**
Box 93, Monument Valley, UT 84536
Tel: (801) 727-3287.
Inquire about horseback riding tours
at visitor center.
Pack Creek Ranch
PO Box 1270
Moab, UT 84532
Tel: (801) 259-5505.
Pack trips around La Sal
Mountains.
Wilderness Adventures
PO Box 63282
Phoenix, AZ 85082
Tel: (602) 220-1414.
Rock/mountain climbing instruction
and other outdoor skills.

Hunting & Fishing

Hunting and fishing licenses are
needed at nearly all times and
places and are generally available
at local marinas, bait shops,
sporting-goods shops and trading
posts. Regulations change, so
contact state authorities for up-to-
date information.
Arizona Game and Fish Department
2222 W. Greenway Road
Phoenix, AZ 85023
Tel: (602) 942-3000.
Colorado Division of Wildlife
6060 N. Broadway, Denver
CO 80216
Tel: (303) 297-1192.
**New Mexico Department of Fish
and Game**
PO Box 25112
Santa Fe
NM 87504
Tel: (505) 827-7911.
Utah Division of Wildlife Resources
1095 W. Motor Avenue
Salt Lake City, UT 84116
Tel: (801) 538-4700.

Hiking

Avoid solitary hiking. The best
situation is to hike with at least two

other partners. If one person is injured, one member of the party can seek help while the other two remain behind. If you must hike alone, be sure to tell someone your intended route and time of return. Back-country hiking may require a permit. Ask a ranger before setting out.

Use common sense on the trail. Don't attempt routes that are too strenuous for your level of fitness. Concentrate on what you're doing and where you're going. Even well-trodden and well-marked trails can be dangerous. Be careful near cliffs, rocky slopes, ravines, rivers and other hazards. Don't attempt anything you're not comfortable with, or anything that's beyond your level of skill.

Environmental Ethics

The old saw is good advice: "Take nothing but pictures, leave nothing but footprints." The goal of low-impact/no-impact back-packing is to leave the area in the same condition as you found it, if not better. If you're camping in the back-country, don't break branches, level the ground or alter the landscape in any way. Make fires in designated places only. Otherwise, use a portable stove. When nature calls, dig a hole 6 inches (15 cm) deep and at least 100 feet (30 m) from water, campsites and trails. Take away all trash, including toilet paper.

Wildlife

Never approach wild animals. Don't try to feed or touch them, not even the "cute" ones like chipmunks, squirrels and prairie dogs (they may carry diseases). Some animals, such as bison, may seem placid and slow-moving but will charge if irritated. People who have tried to creep up on bison in order to get a better photograph have been seriously injured by the animals. If you want close-ups, buy a telephoto lens.

Further Reading

Nonfiction

The Arizona Rangers, by Bill O'Neal. Austin, TX: Eakin Press, 1986.

Art of the Golden West, by Alan Axelrod. New York, Abbeville Press, 1990.

Best of the West: An Anthology of Classic Writing from the American West, edited by Tony Hillerman. New York, Harper Collins, 1991.

Beyond the Hundredth Meridian, by Wallace Stegner. New York: Penguin, 1953.

Billy the Kid: A Short and Violent Life, by Robert M. Utley. Lincoln: University of Nebraska Press, 1989.

Bless Me, Ultima, by Rodolfo Anaya. Warner Books, 1972. An eloquent *entrada* into Hispanic culture.

Book of the Hopi, by Frank Waters. New York: Penguin, 1963.

Book of the Navajo, by Raymond Locke. Los Angeles: Mankind Publishing, 1976.

Buckaroo, edited by Hal Cannon and Thomas West. New York, Callaway, 1993.

Dancing Gods, by Erna Ferguson. Albuquerque: University of New Mexico, 1931.

The Desert, by John C. Van Dyke. Scribner, 1901, reprinted by Peregrine Smith Books, 1980. The first book to appraise the desert eloquently and appreciatively.

Desert Notes: Reflections in the Eye of a Raven, by Barry Holstun Lopez. New York: Avon, 1981.

Desert Solitaire: A Season in the Wilderness, by Edward Abbey. New York: McGraw-Hill, 1968. Essays on a season in the southern Utah wilderness. The best book ever written about the Southwest deserts.

The Desert Year, by Joseph W. Krutch. Tucson: University of Arizona, 1990.

Earthtones: A Nevada Album, by Ann Ronald and Stephen Trimble. Reno: University of Nevada Press, 1995.

The Exploration of the Colorado River and its Canyons, by John Wesley Powell. New York: Penguin, 1987.

500 Nations, by Alvin Josephy. New York, Knopf, 1994.

Fighting Men of the Indian Wars, by Bill O'Neal. Stillwater, OK, Barbed Wire Press, 1991.

Geronimo: The Man, His Time, His Place, by Angie Debo. Norman: University of Oklahoma, 1976.

Ghost Towns of the American West, by Bill O'Neal. Lincolnwood, IL, Publications International, 1995.

Grand Canyon: An Anthology, by Bruce Babbitt. Flagstaff: Northland Press, 1978.

Grand Canyon: A Traveler's Guide, by Jeremy Schmidt. Jackson Hole: Free Wheeling Travel Guides, 1991.

Grand Canyon National Park: A Natural History Guide, by Jeremy Schmidt. Boston: Houghton Mifflin Company, 1993.

Grand Canyon: Today and All Its Yesterdays, by Joseph Wood Krutch. Tucson: University of Arizona, 1989.

The Guide to National Parks of the Southwest, by Nicky Leach. Tucson: Southwest Parks & Monuments Association, 1992.

In the House of Stone and Light: A Human History of the Grand Canyon, by Donald J. Hughes. Grand Canyon: Grand Canyon Natural History Association, 1978.

Indian Villages of the Southwest, by Buddy Mays. San Francisco: Chronicle Books, 1985.

The Man Who Walked Through Time, by Colin Fletcher. New York: Random House, 1989.

Masked Gods, by Frank Waters. Athens: Swallow Press, 1950.

Native America, by Christine Mather, photographs by Jack Parsons. New York: Clarkson Potter, 1991.

The People: Indians of the American Southwest, by Stephen Trimble. Santa Fe: School of American Research Press, 1993.

Santa Fe Style, by Christine

Mather, photographs by Jack
Parsons. Rizzoli, 1986.
***True West: Arts, Traditions, and
Celebrations**,* by Christine Mather,
photographs by Jack Parsons. New
York, Clarkson Potter, 1992.
***The West: A Treasury of Art and
Literature**,* edited by T.H. Watkins
and Joan Watkins. New York, Hugh
Lauter Levin Associates, 1994.

Fiction & Poetry

***Almanac of the Dead**,* by Leslie
Marmon Silko. New York: Simon &
Schuster, 1991.
***Anything for Billy**,* by Larry
McMurtry. New York: Simon &
Schuster, 1988.
***Ceremony**,* by Leslie Marmon Silko.
New York: Viking, 1977.
***The Dance Hall of the Dead**,* by
Tony Hillerman. New York: Harper &
Row, 1973.
***The Dark Wind**,* by Tony Hillerman.
New York: Harper & Row, 1982.
***Death Comes for the Archbishop**,*
by Willa Cather. New York: Knopf,
1927.
***Milagro Beanfield War**,* by John
Nichols. New York: Holt, Rinehart,
Winston, 1974.
***Riders of the Purple Sage**,* by Zane
Grey. New York: Penguin, 1990.
***Skinwalkers**,* by Tony Hillerman.
New York: Harper & Row, 1987.

Movies/Videos

***Bugsy**,* 1991. Warren Beatty
portrays mobster Ben "Bugsy"
Seigel, founder of the Flamingo
Hotel, the first big-time casino in
Las Vegas.
***Casino**,* 1995. A Martin Scorsese
film about the Las Vegas
underworld with Robert De Niro,
Sharon Stone and Joe Pesce.
***The Dark Wind**,* 1991. This
adaptation of a Tony Hillerman
mystery takes place on the Navajo
and Hopi reservations.
***Gunfight at the OK Corral**,* 1957, and

High Chaparral (television series).
Just two of the many Westerns filmed
at the Old Tucson Studios.
***Geronimo**,* 1994. Yet another telling
of Geronimo's story, much of it shot
in southern Utah.
***Honeymoon in Vegas**,* 1992. Las
Vegas provides the backdrop for
this off-the-wall comedy.
***Milagro Beanfield War**,* 1988. John
Nichols' novel is thoughtfully
adapted to the screen by director
Robert Redford. An interesting look
at the people and land of Hispanic
northern New Mexico.
***My Darling Clemetine**,* 1946. John
Ford's version of the infamous
gunfight at the O.K. Corral with
Henry Fonda as Wyatt Earp and
Victor Mature as Doc Holliday.
***Stagecoach**,* 1939, and *Fort
Apache*, 1948. The stunning
landscape of Monument Valley is
featured in countless Westerns,
most notably in John Ford's
classics.
***Wyatt Earp**,* 1995. Kevin Costner
takes a shot at the classic gunfighter with rather lackluster results.

Other Insight Guides

Nearly 200 companion titles to this
volume cover every continent. More
than 40 of the titles are devoted to
the US and include:

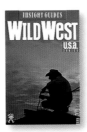

Insight Guide: Wild West explores
the history, culture, romance and
actual sites of the American West.
It's the perfect read, whether on
the trail or in an armchair.

Insight Guide: Native America
provides both absorbing text about
the Native American culture and a
detailed guide to Indian
reservations, historic sites,
festivals and ceremonies, from the
Southwest to the East Coast.

***Insight Guide: US National Parks
West**,* written by park rangers and
other experts, ranges from Texas to
North Dakota, from California to
Colorado, and then on to the
national parks of Alaska and Hawaii.
It includes top nature photography.

Insight Guide: The Rockies takes
the reader through Colorado,
Wyoming, Montana and Utah while
exploring the beauty of the national
parks and the rich culture and
history of the area and the people.

ART & PHOTO CREDITS

Picture Spreads

INSIGHT GUIDE
american SOUTHWEST

Cartographic Editor **Zoë Goodwin**
Production **Stuart A Everitt**
Design Consultants
Carlotta Junger, Graham Mitchener
Picture Research **Hilary Genin**

Index

*Numbers in italics refer to
photographs*